PULBOROUGH FOOTBALL CLUB

1st Edition

Published in 2015 by

Woodfield Publishing Ltd
Bognor Regis PO21 5EL England
www.woodfieldpublishing.co.uk

ISBN 978- 1-84683-163-8

Printed and bound in England

Typesetting & page design: Nic Pastorius
Cover design: Klaus Berger

Pulborough FC by Mick Hatchard [final] r1

Pulborough Football Club

A history of 'The Robins' 1898-2010

MICK HATCHARD

Woodfield
woodfieldpublishing.co.uk

Woodfield Publishing Ltd
Bognor Regis ~ West Sussex ~ England ~ PO21 5EL
tel 01243 821234 ~ **e/m** info@woodfieldpublishing.co.uk

Interesting and informative books on a variety of subjects

For full details of all our published titles, visit our website at
www.woodfieldpublishing.co.uk

Dedicated to
Trish, Allison, Tim, Little Mick and Claire
for their help and encouragement
... and never forgetting Martin

Pulborough FC Reunion 2015
From left , Peter Harrison, Mick Hatchard and John Rayner.
Peter and John are the oldest surviving Pulborough FC players,
they both played for the club in the 1940s & 50s.

Contents

The Ladies

OVER THE YEARS many ladies have contributed to PFC in a variety of ways. Whether as Vice-President, Club Secretary, serving in the Supporters' Club or on the Committee, washing the team's kit, making the tea and serving food after matches, I'm sure everyone will agree with my saying how much their efforts were and are greatly valued. On behalf of the Club I would like to thank the following ladies:

Miss G. Warner, Miss Lowther, Mrs Marsh-Horrocks, Mrs I. A. Puttick, Mrs L. Greenfield, Mrs Spain, Mrs V. Chapman, Mrs Forty, Lady Barttelot, Mrs B. Leadbeatter, Mrs S. Leadbeatter, Mrs Burchell, Mrs Pope, Mrs J. Hookey, Mrs V. Cordingley, Mrs L. Rhoder, Mrs S. Goodchild, Miss C. Richards, Mrs S. Cox, Mrs V. Roberts, Mrs E. Murphy, Miss C. Richey, Miss C Munnery, Miss P. Rhoder, Mrs M. Boulton, Mrs. S Jupp, Miss S. Howes, Miss R. Jupp, Miss C. Wadey, Mrs E. Jupp, Mrs P. Browning, Mrs J. Philpot, Miss Cox and Miss J. Blunden.

I apologise for any omissions. **MH**

Our Sponsors

PFC IS GRATEFUL to all those who have been kind enough to sponsor us over the years. **Harwood's Garage**, **Coombelands Racing Stables** and **J.M. Wadey** have been particularly generous. We also thank **The Rose & Crown**, **Cranleigh Car Clinic**, **Pulborough Sports & Social Club**, **North West Airlines** and **R.D.A. Jilton**. My apologies for any omissions. **MH**

Family Members

A NUMBER OF FAMILIES have multiple links with Pulborough FC, including husbands and wives, fathers, sons, grandsons, brothers, sisters and daughters.

Adsett, Len, Chris; **Allfrey**, William, Graham; **Anderson**, Barry, Ian; **Bailey**, John, Jason, Wally, Malcolm; **Barnett**, Arthur, Charles (Percy); **Blunden**, Trevor, Graham, Liam; **Brockhurst**, A & N; **Browning**, Mick, Pat, Steve; **Bryant**, Jim, Richard, Jimmy; **Burletson**, George, John; **Buss**, Terry, Steve; **Carter**, George, Tony, Colin; **Chapman**, Peter, Valerie, Matt; **Clark**, Gerry, Keith, Gavin; **Corden**, Tom, Vic; **Cordingly**, Mark, Vanessa; **Cousins**, Frank, Trevor; **Cox**, Cliff, Sue, Steve; **Davy**, Jeff & Russell, **Eager**, S & F; **Greenfield**, John, Lionel (Toby), Lillian; **Habgood**, Francis (Charlie), John, Dave; **Hall**, Chris, Matt; **Harrison**, Peter, John; **Harwood**, Tom, Wally; **Hatchard**, Mick, Terry, Tim; **Heasman**, Derek, Brian, Robin, Vic; **Hill**, Graham (Charlie), Roger; **Hookey**, Len, Jenny; **Jones**, Roger, Trefor; **Jupp**, Bert, Elsie, John, Sheila, Rebecca, Malcolm, Janice, Roger, Craig, Shaun, Rupert, Ted; **Leadbeatter**, Ernie (Fred), Tony, Babs, Michael (Jimmy), Sue, Melvin (Bill), Steve, Dave, Anthony, Simon, Jason; **Lewis**, Alan, Glen, Dean; **Madell**, Albert, John; **Merriot**, Steve, Colin (Bert); **Messenger**, David, Geoff; **Murphy**, Stan, Poore, Esme; **Pattenden**, Alan, Mick; **Pavey**, Charlie, Fred; **Payne**, Albert, Connie, Victor, Vic; **Phillips**, Russ, Chris, Stuart; **Philot**, Peter (Jeff), Jan; **Pope**, Les, Mrs Pope, Nigel; **Puttock**, William, Alan; **Ralph**, Mick, Nick, Martin; **Rhoder**, Jim, Lil, Frank, Dave, Mandy, Penny; **Roberts**, Peter, Dennis, Terry, Roberts; **Rowland**, Dave, Andrew; **Scott**, Dave, Paul; **Scutt**, Ken, Stan, Phillip (Tibby), John, Gregg; **Smith**, Alan, David; **Spain**, Tony, Michael, Colin; **Spicer**, Mick, Graham, Nick; **Stentiford**, Derek, Steve; **Stewart**, Michael, John; **Streeter**, Danny, Richard; **Underwood**, Stuart, James; **Vincent**, Reg, Ron; **Wadey**, John, Liam, Clare; **Wardell**, Mark, Pete; **Wells**, Bern, Trevor; **Zalesny**, Nick, Robin.

There may be others; I apologise if I have missed anyone out. **MH**.

Acknowledgements

WITHOUT THE INPUT and assistance from many people I could not have written this book. To all those who gave information to me and there were many, thank you. Special thanks to Mr Ted Anderson, Mr Dennis Corden, Mrs Sheila Corden, Mr Tony Frogley, Mr Peter Harrison, Mrs Marguerite Harrison, Mr Len Hookey and Mr Alan Puttock.

I must give Mr Terry Reilly and Mr Andy Singleton a big vote of thanks for their assistance with some of the printing of photographs. To Mr Jeff Davey and Mr John Jupp and the Pulborough Football Club for allowing me access to the Club's archives and for offering help with the book, thank you.

To Coleen Pearce for background work, and to Martin Dale for stepping in at the last moment, because I was badly let down by the man who was going to do the book originally.

To the libraries of Burgess Hill, Chichester, Horsham, Littlehampton, Worthing and Pulborough, where I spent many hours going through the microfilm, also to the Chichester County Records Office and the Storrington Museum thank you; all the staff were very helpful, especially Sue at the Pulborough Library.

My gratitude to Mr Steve Bone and all the other Sports Editors for allowing me to print articles from their newspapers. I have scanned through the microfilm for the following newspapers: The Bognor Observer, The Mid Sussex Times, The West Sussex County Times, The West Sussex Gazette, The Chichester Observer, The Midhurst and Petworth Observer, The Worthing Herald, The Worthing Observer, The Evening Argus and The Sussex Daily News.

For any errors or omissions, I apologise.

Mick Hatchard, April 2015

Author's Preface

WHEN I RETIRED, in February 2008, I did not envisage writing a book about the history of Pulborough Football Club. About a year after retiring I started having some health problems, which meant that I could not pursue the things that I had been enjoying until then. Along with two friends, I had enjoyed long walks in the countryside and working in the garden, but even this I now found difficult.

In early 2010 I realised that I needed something to occupy my mind, so I thought of the idea of researching the history of The Robins. I must admit that had I foreseen how frustrating and time-consuming this project was going to be, I'm not sure I would have undertaken the task, but once I had started I was determined to do my best to complete it.

I was given access to the Club's archives, which was very helpful, but unfortunately several of the books were absent and there were pages missing from some of the remaining books.

I endeavoured to find the results of every match that was played by the Club. To obtain this information meant many hours going through microfilm records at local libraries and newspapers. Unfortunately, it was not possible to find every single result or every goal scorer – I suppose that sometimes the club secretary did not send in the results, or was late sending them in, so they were not printed. In some of the games that were recorded, the information was incomplete or incorrect (for example, sometimes the goal scorers did not tally up with the scores).

I have included two smaller chapters which the reader may find interesting; one about Codmore Hill Football Club and another about the junior side, which I helped set up for the young lads of the village.

When scanning through the microfilm I also found some reports about Pulborough and its inhabitants, which may be of interest; I have included a few of them (see page 210).

I also managed to track down some ex-players, or their relatives, so I could give the reader some idea of their backgrounds and their playing abilities. I hope the pen pictures will be of interest.

It was not possible to cover every year in detail or to mention every player, so I have tried to concentrate on the years when the Club had some success.

I hope this book will be of interest, not just to the footballers who played for the Club, but also for the supporters and other members of the local community.

Mick Hatchard, April 2015

Some views of Pulborough: *from top* 'Swan Bridge' (the old road bridge over the River Arun);
St Mary's Church; Stopham bridge.

The Village of Pulborough

WITHOUT GOING INTO too much detail, I would like to give a little information about the village of Pulborough. *Poleberg*, as it was called by the Saxons, is mentioned in the Domesday Book of 1086. The village, surrounded by the South Downs, lies in the beautiful county of West Sussex.

In around 43AD the Romans invaded and a large and important settlement was based in our Parish. A road was constructed to connect Chichester (*Noviomagus*) with London (*Londinium*) and runs South to North. At Swan Corner is the crossroads which connects the A29 to the A283, which runs from East to West. There was a large villa at Borough Farm and a fort stood at Park Mound as protection for the river.

The River Arun (*Trisantona Flumen*) is the second fastest flowing river in the country and has always been important to the village. Barges would transport their cargo from the coast and there were quays along the river bank at Pulborough. Over the years improvements were made so that the barges could convey their cargo on what is now the Wey & Arun Canal up to London. The River Arun has always been popular with anglers, who travel many miles to fish the waters.

With the coming of the railway, opening in 1859, trade was taken away from the waterways, as transport was more convenient and quicker by rail. Situated adjacent to the railway line was a livestock market. Opened in 1866, it was held on Mondays. It closed in the 1970s.

Lower Street is thought to be the longest street in Sussex; it runs from East to West. A century ago the population was just under 2,000, with very good amenities. There were over thirty shops, catering for all you required; there were bakers, butchers, clothing and footwear shops, a pharmacy, a barber's, a jeweller's, a gunsmith, a cycle shop, a grocer's, a harness maker and saddler, an ironmonger's and hardware store, a fruit and vegetable shop and two sub Post Offices. You did not have to leave the village for anything you required. At one time there were eight hotels and inns in the village and all had histories worth reading about.

There are many old and interesting buildings in the Parish. The Church dates from the thirteenth century; Old Place Manor was built around 1450 with its lake and watermill; New Place Manor is thought to be mentioned in the Domesday Book and there are many other places within the Parish which are interesting.

Employment was never a problem. During the 1900s Harwood Engineering, later to become Spiro Gills, would employ around two hundred locals. Mr W. Allfrey employed many people in his building firm. Mr Cordery also had a number of people working for him. He owned an ironmonger's yard and also a shop. There were several brickworks in the Parish and the hotels and inns always needed staff. Sport was played and was an important part of village life: bowls, cricket, football, tennis and even a ladies' hockey team.

Today's Village

Over the last century or so the village has undergone many changes. Some have been good, others not so good. The population is now about 5,000 and with more development planned this will mean more housing and more people. I don't think the infrastructure is in place to warrant this. I understand there are drainage problems in the village. The medical centre has been very good for the community, but can it cope with the extra people? The local School is under pressure, having to erect more classrooms.

We now have fewer shops than we used to; there was a far greater variety of them when I was growing up. On the social side of things, what has happened to all our hotels and inns? We now have just one hotel and one pub in the village. Sadly, the days when you had a choice of places to enjoy a drink and socialize with your neighbours have gone. The village has grown but unfortunately the amenities have not grown with it.

Pulborough has always been a country village and the vast majority of local people want to keep it that way. We do not want a concrete jungle. We like the open spaces. One of the joys of living here is that we can walk through the copses and meadows and appreciate the peace and quiet of the countryside. I can only hope that the people in charge do not ruin our village.

Some Football Firsts

O F ALL THE many different sports played in this country, soccer or, as most people call it, football, is the most popular. Millions of people watch it every week, be it at village or professional level, and thousands of people play the game each week.

It is thought that the game originated in China as far back as the 4th century BC and that the Romans brought it to this country; it was called 'Harpastum'. The game has been played in Great Britain for over 800 years.

The Sheffield Club is the oldest in England, formed in 1857, but is not to be confused with the other Sheffield Clubs, United and Wednesday. Formed in 1862, Notts County are the oldest Club still playing in the Football League. The Football Association was formed in 1863 and in 1888 the Football League was started. Original members were Accrington Stanley, Aston Villa, Blackburn Rovers, Bolton Wanderers, Burnley, Derby County, Everton, Notts County, Preston North End, Stoke, West Bromwich Albion and Wolverhampton Wanderers. Preston North End were the first champions, in 1889. They also won the F.A. Cup to do the double. The first official international game between England and Scotland was played on 30th November 1872, resulting in a nil-nil draw.

- In 1873 the Scottish Football Association was formed.

- In 1876 the Welsh Football Association was formed.

- In 1880 the Irish Football Association was formed.

- In 1885 professionalism was recognized.

- In 1893 the Football Association Amateur Cup was formed.

- In 1904 F.I.F.A. was started.

The first southern side to win the League was Arsenal in 1930/31. Small Heath were the first winners of Division Two, in the 1892/93 season. The first southern team to win Division Two were Bristol City, in the 1905/06 season. The Arsenal were the first London side to win the First Division title, in the 1930/31 season. The first F.A. Cup Final was in 1871/72, when Wanderers beat the Royal Engineers by one goal to nil; the game was played at the Oval. The first Cup Final played at Wembley was in 1923, when Bolton Wanderers beat West Ham United 2-0 before a crowd of 126,047.

In 1956 Manchester United was the first English team to enter the European Cup and in 1968 they were the first English team to win the trophy; Celtic were the first British Club to win, in 1967. Uruguay were the winners of the first World Cup, held in 1930. England are the only British side to have lifted the World Cup after beating West Germany at Wembley in 1966.

Herbert Chapman was the most famous manager in the 1920s and 1930s. He guided Huddersfield Town to a hat-trick of titles during the 1920s. He then took The Arsenal to repeat this feat in the 1930s. In 1905 when Alf Common was transferred from Sunderland to Middlesbrough he became the first £1,000 player. In 1928 the first £10,000 player to be transferred was David Jack, when he moved from Bolton Wanderers to The Arsenal.

Dixie Dean of Everton scored 60 goals in 39 matches in a season in 1928. Joe Payne scored 10 goals for Luton against Bristol Rovers in 1936 in Division Three South. J. Ross of Preston North End scored 7 times against Stoke City in 1888; Ted Drake of The Arsenal repeated the feat in 1935 against Aston Villa. In 1935 R. Bell scored 9 goals for Tranmere against Oldham in Division Three North.

Pulborough pick up all four points
Pulborough 2, Portfield 0

FADING PULBOROUGH JUST MANAGE IT
Emsworth 2, Pulborough 3

Pulborough certain of promotion – and may be the champions
Rudgwick 0, Pulborough 1

PULBOROUGH RALLY KEEPS THEM TOP
Wick 3, Pulborough 5

PULBOROUGH DEFENCE IN GREAT FORM
Pulborough 5, Ferring 1

Billingshurst make it easy for Pulborough in their local derby
Billingshurst 0, Pulborough 4
Billingshurst made it easy for Pulborough

LEWIS HAT-TRICK IN PULBOROUGH VICTORY
Pulborough 7, West Tarring 3

Local Leagues

BEFORE I GO into the history of Pulborough Football Club 'The Robins', I would like to give some information about the different Leagues that we played in.

Horsham & District Football Association

The H&DFA was formed in 1895 and the League started in 1901. The winners of the first Division 1 Shield were Horsham YMCA, who also won the next two. Carfax United won the next three. A Second Division was formed in 1913/14, Crawley Athletic II being the first champions. Division Three started in 1922/23, Handcross finishing first. Henfield won a hat-trick of titles in Division One in the mid-Twenties. The first **Senior Charity Cup** winners were Bishopric Wanderers in 1908/09. Faygate United in 1927/28 were the first winners of the **Intermediate Charity Cup**. The first **Junior Charity Cup** was won by YMCA in 1913/14. The Horsham & District League merged with the West Sussex League in 1970/71.

The West Sussex Football League

When Ford is mentioned, most people will think of the prison, but it was there, on 5th March 1896 at the Arundel Arms Inn, that a meeting was held at which it was proposed that a League was formed, to be called the West Sussex League. On 25th June 1896 it was put forward that two Divisions, one senior and one junior, should be formed. The Senior League of ten teams were Arundel, Bognor, Chichester, Horsham, Petworth, Shoreham Swifts, Steyning, Worthing Athletic, Southwick and the 35th Regimental District. The Junior League of ten teams were Bognor, Crawley, Littlehampton, Littlehampton Swifts, St Andrews of Worthing, Southwick, Wick, Worthing, Worthing II, 35th Regimental District and St Phillips of Arundel. Southwick were the first winners of the Senior League in 1896/97. The first Junior champions were Worthing Reserves. The Senior Division continued until 1920, when the **Sussex County League** was formed. Bognor Town won the Senior League of the West Sussex League from 1920 to 1925. RAF Tangmere won four consecutive titles from 1926 to 1930. The **West Sussex Benevolent Cup**, later changed to the **Malcolm Simmonds Cup**, was first won by Westbourne in 1935/36. From 1955 to 1959 it was won by Selsey. North Holmwood won four in a row from 1983/84 to 1986/87.

Sussex County League Division Two

In the 1952/53 season the County League formed a Second Division for the first time. After winning the West Sussex League three years in a row, Pulborough were invited to be a founder member of this new Division. Other members were Hastings Rangers, Hastings & St Leonard's, Turners Hill, Goldstone, Seaford, Moulsecombe Rovers, Cuckfield, Uckfield, Wigmore Athletic, Three Bridges, Hove White Rovers, Rye United and Sidley United.

There were other local Leagues:
Midhurst & District League, the first champions in 1909/10 were Tillington.
Littlehampton & District League, Storrington were the first winners in 1929/30.
Bognor & District League, the first winners were RAF Tangmere in 1925/26.
Chichester & District League, champions in 1946/47 were Portfield.
Rudgwick & District League was formed around 1920.

Early 'action' photographs, of a game played on the Recreation Ground on 14th April 1911 between Pulborough and Petworth, who won 6-3. (Photos by kind permission of Angela Brookfield).

The Early Years 1898-1914

THE CLUB HAS no records at all until 1922, so it was not easy getting information before this time. Going through old newspapers, I managed to find some reports and results.

It's possible that Pulborough Football Club ('The Robins') was founded before 1898, but that is the earliest date that I found.

In September 1898 we beat our local rivals Storrington by 1-0. I believe we only played friendly matches for the next few years.

On 20th October 1906 we played Worthing Reserves in the Sussex Junior Cup, but I don't think we played in a League until 1907/08 when we played in the West Sussex Junior League. (I think you were able to play County Cup games even if you were not in a league.)

In the 1907/08 season the Club entered the West Sussex Junior League. It was a tough start for The Robins; despite a good result in their first game against Horsham Reserves, a draw, they lost the next eleven to finish up bottom, with just one point.

1908/09 saw an improvement, with six wins and two draws. In the Sussex Junior Cup they beat Arundel Reserves and claimed the scalp of Horsham Reserves in the next round, before losing to 35th Regiment in the 3rd round.

In the same year they reached the final of the Wisborough Green & District Cup, losing 0-2 to Petworth. The side continued to improve and had a reasonable season in 1909/10.

1910/11 was to be a very poor year; they lost by 30 goals to nil against Arundel, the worst defeat in the Club's history.

Early Players

PHILLIP DAVID SCUTT (TIBBY) was born in Pulborough on 2nd February 1885 and died 8th November 1956. He lived in Lower Street before moving to Stane Street Close. He did his apprenticeship in 1901 as a painter and decorator. He played as a forward.

TOM CORDON was the son of Mr Louis Corden, the local Pharmacist. He was born in 1887 in Pulborough and died in 1968. Apart from playing football he was a popular member of the local community as well as being a local councillor who did a lot for the village.

FRED KNIGHT was born in 1887 and died in 1942 at the age of just 55. He was a member of the family who owned the Golden Boot Shop in Lower Street and worked in the shop. Fred normally played at half back for Pulborough FC.

SIDNEY STILLWELL lived at Swan Corner. He worked for Mercedes Benz (he also drove one).

GEORGE KNIGHT 1883-1948 played as a half back. He went on to become the landlord of The Oddfellows and the Rose & Crown.

1906 – Pulborough v Horsham II (at cricket)
J. Boxall, J. Stoner, F. Wright, D. Nash, L. Eames,
E. Greenfield, H. Sandiland, W. Knight, W. Boxall,
J. Shepherd, N. Woods.

11.10.1907 – Sussex Junior Cup
J. Boxall (goal)
L. Jennings, F. Cower (full backs)
S. Cordon, H. Sandilands, Upperton (half backs)
J. Stoner, S. Stillwell, J. Barnes,
H. Jennings, H. Ward (forwards)
Result: Worthing Reserves 6-1 Pulborough

Team Sheet – 2.11.1907
1 J. Boxall
2 S. Corden 3 F. Ward
4 R. Holden, 5 H. Soffe, 6 R. Sandiland
7 P. Scutt, 8 J. Stoner, 9 P. R. Randell,
10 J. Barnes, 11 G. Knight.
Result Pulborough 1-1 Worthing Reserves (J. Stoner)

29.10.1909
After a scramble at Amberley, which at times resembled water polo, the whistle blew with Pulborough one goal up. The players left the field and several of the visitors were clothed and ready to cycle back to Pulborough when they were told that the referee wished to go back, as he had made a mistake in the time, although some spectators said the right time was played. The game may have to be replayed.

Exact date unknown but thought to be early 1900s. Notice P.R. on shirts 'Pulborough Robins'. Only player known Mr Phillip Scutt (Tibby), second from left in bottom row.

Results 1898 – 1911

FRIENDLY MATCHES 1898/1906

15.09.1898 [H] **Storrington** (W 1-0)

Jan-1899 [H] **Ashington & Washington** (L 1-3)

20.01.1900 [H] [A] **Bryces Eleven** (L 0-5)

13.09.1902 [H] **Petworth** (L 2-14)

04.10.1902 [A] **Carfax United** (L 0-10)

28.02.1904 [A] **Carfax United** (L 2-4)

10.09.1904 [H] **Petworth** (L 1-9)

01.10.1904 [H] **Shelley United** (L0-6)

02.09.1905 [A] **Petworth** (L 2-4)

14-10-1905 [A] **Storrington** (score not known)

04.11.1905 [A] **Ashington** (W 6-0)

03.02.1906 [A] **Midhurst** (W 11-1)

22.09.1906 [H] **Petworth** (L 1-5)

20.10.1906 SJC[A] **Worthing Reserves** (L 1-6)

03.11.1906 [H] **Wick** (L 0-11)

24.11.1906 [H] **Petworth** (L 4-8)

WSJL 1907/8

28.09.1907 [A] **Horsham Reserves** (D 2-2)

05.10.1907 [H] **Petworth** (L 1-5)

12.10.1907 [A] **Arundel** (L 0-4)

19.10.1907 SJC1 [A] **Worthing Reserves** (L 1-6) Upperton 1*

26.10.1907 [H] **Amberley** (L 1-2)

02.11.1907 SJC1 *replay* [H] **Worthing Res** (D 1-1) J. Stoner 1

06.11.1907 SJC1 *replay 2* [A] **Worthing Res** (L 1-9)

16.11.1907 [H] **Worthing Reserves** (L 1-10)

30.11.1907 [A] **Amberley** (L 4-5)

22.02.1908 [H] **Wick** (L 0-3)

29.02.1908 [A] **Petworth** (L 1-3)

07.03.1908 [A] **Worthing Reserves** (L 0-4)

21.03.1908 [H] **Arundel** (L 1-5)

04.04.1908 [A] **Wick** (L 2-6)

18.04.1908 [H] **Horsham Reserves** (L 1-2)

* Worthing played an unregistered player

P12 | W0 |D1 | L11 |GF14 |GA51 | 1pt | Bottom

WSJL 1908/9

26.09.1908 [H] **Amberley** (L 1-2)

03.10.1908 [A] **Petworth** (L 1-4)

10.10.1908 [H] **35th Regiment District** (D 3-3)

17.10.1908 [H] **Petworth** (W 2-1)

24.10.1908 [A] **Warnham** (L1-6)

07.11.1908 SJC-1 [H] **Arundel** (W 4-0)

14.11.1908 [H] **Warnham** (W 4-0)

21.11.1908 [H] **Littlehampton Reserves** (W 5-1)

28.11.1909 SJC-2 [H] **Horsham Re** (W 1-0) A. Soffe 1

05.12.1908 [H] **Portslade** (W 5-1)

12.12.1908 [A] **Worthing Reserves** (L 2-3)

19.12.1908 SJC-3[A] **35th Regiment District** (L 3-5)

09.01.1909 [A] **Amberley** (L 2-3)

23.01.1909 [H] **Wick** (L 1-3)

13.02.1909 [A] **Wick** (L 0-8)

20.02.1909 [A] **Littlehampton Reserves** (D 2-2)

27.02.1909 [H] **Arundel** (L 0-2)

20.03.1909 [A] **35th Regiment District** (scratched)

27.03.1909 [A] **Portslade** (W 1-0)

10.04.1909 [A] **Arundel** (L 0-1)

24.04.1909 [H] **Worthing Reserves** (W 3-1)

07.04.1909 WG&DL Cup Final v Petworth (L2-0)

P18 | W6 |D2 | L9 | GF33 | GA41 | 14pts

WSJL 1909/10

16.10.1909 [H] **Littlehampton** (W 4-1)

23.10.1909 [A] **Steyning** (L 1-5)

06.11.1909 SJC [A] **Horsham Trinity** (L1-5)

20.11.1909 [A] **Arundel** (L 1-6)

27.11.1909 [A] **Amberley** (L 0-3)

18.12.1909 [H] **Steyning** (L 1-2)

22.01.1910 [A] **Littlehampton** (L 0-1)

02.02.1910 [H] **35th Regiment District** (L 1-4)

05.02.1910 [H] **Bognor II** (W 5-1)

12.02.1910 [A] **Warnham** (W 4-2)

26.02.1910 [H] **Warnham** (W 5-0)

12.03.1910 [H] **Amberley** (W 1-0)

26.03.1910 [A] **Bognor II** (W 4-0)

02.04.1910 [A] **Worthing II** (L 0-3)

08.04.1910 [H] **Wick** (W 8-0)

16.04.1910 [H] **Worthing II** (L1-2)

P18 | W7 | D1 | L10 | GF39 | GA36 | 15pts | 7th

WSJL WEST 1910/11

24.09.1910 [H] **Littlehampton Reserves** (W 4-1) Barnes 2, Knight 1, Porter 1

15.10.1910 [A] **Petworth** (L 0-7)

22.10.1910 [A] **Wick Reserves** (L 1-7)

29.10.1910 [A] **Arundel** (L 0-30)

03.12.1910 [A] **35th Regiment District** (L 0-2)

10.12.1910 [H] **Bognor** (L 1-4)

17.12.1910 [A] **Littlehampton Reserves** (D 1-1)

24.12.1910 [A] **Chichester Reserves** (L 2-8)

14.01.1911 [H] **Petworth** (L 3-6)

28.01.1911 [A] **Bognor** (L 1-7) Ward 1

11.02.1911 [H] **35th Regiment District** (L 2-5)

18.02.1911 [H] **Wick Reserves** (L2-3) Ward 2

04.03.1911 [H] **Arundel** (L 2-11)

25.03.1911 [H] **Chichester Reserves** (W 2-0)

P16 | W2 | D1 | L13 | GF24 | GA97 | 5pts | 8th

FRIENDLY AND SJC GAMES 1911/14

01.12.1911 [A] **Horsham Trinity** (L 1-8)

02.11.1912 [H] **Horsham Railway** (W 5-3)

03.01.1914 [A] **Petworth** (L 3-4)

SJC 10.01.1914 [A] **Petworth** (L 0-4)

07.02.1914 [A] **Midhurst** (L 1-4)

ABBREVIATIONS

WSJL = West Sussex Junior League

SJC = Sussex Junior Cup

WG&DL = Wisborough Green & District League

07.11.1909
Pulborough v Horsham Trinity

This tie was played on the Horsham Ground in delightful weather, before a fair attendance of spectators. The kick off had been advertised for 2-30, but in the absence of the referee there was a good deal of hanging about.

Eventually the teams agreed to the game being started with Mr G. Mitchell in charge. The kick off took place at eight minutes to three. Trinity playing downhill but with the sun right in their eyes. Ide was the first keeper called upon repelling an overhead kick and also a low return. Corden conceded a corner, but it proved barren and the visitors took up the attack, A. Agate clearing to the stand. In the next assault the Pulborough outside right was offside.

At two minutes to three the appointed referee came onto the ground and a minute later Soffe got through and with a clear course, took it easy and, going almost up to the keeper, sent the ball into the corner of the net, one to nil.

Restarting with Mr Kenward in charge, Soffe passed out to Ward who was pulled up by W. B. Agate. Ide cleared from a centre by Cook, then the Pulborough left attacked strongly, but were pulled up. Trinity turned the tables and Snelling dashed down and put in a good centre, the ball hitting the upright and rebounding into play. Then Pulborough forced a corner and all but scored. Just afterwards White missed a good chance by shooting wide and Ward kicked over.

Eighteen minutes from the start Trinity got on terms, Buckton scoring a soft goal following a fierce attack. One all. Just after the restart Buckton shot from some distance back and in clearing Ide

came to the ground with the ball, but there was no one up. Redford and Snelling put in good work, but without result. A. Agate nicely pulled up the Pulborough outside right and W. B. Agate was also in evidence. Pulborough at this period attached strongly and the home forwards neglected to drop back. Lawrence gathered and threw out and Mills pulled up the opposing forwards. Barttelot received from the centre and spoilt a good chance by a little more than a pass to the keeper, who received the ball just outside the post.

A little later Barttelot worked through to within a nice range and shot wide. Twice the Trinity forwards got forward, but in the melee could not do anything but score. The second onslaught produced a corner and there was another melee in front of goal as a result of Snelling's accurate centre. Eventually, when lying on the ground, Ide cleared round the side posts. Presently amid shouts of "corner" the ball was kept in and Redford passed to Snelling, who with a prettily judged shot, found the further corner of the net. Two to one. This was after thirty-eight minutes play.

On resuming A. Agate pulled up the right wing men in clinking style. However Smith and Barttelot came again and the ball was accurately dropped in from almost the corner, Lawrence fisted out and the next attack fizzled out behind the goal.

Several times the visitors came within an ace of scoring. Trinity got a barren corner and the whistle blew for the interval. Trinity 2 goals Pulborough one goal.

On restarting the Horshamites forced a corner but Cook placed behind. Lawrence cleared well from wither wing and White nearly skimmed the bar with a long shot. Trinity all but scored, Stillwell nipping in at the finish. W. B. Agate miskicked, but followed his man and averted disaster. Ward put in a long shot at the other end, but Lawrence caught and cleared. A lot of

attacking round Ide's quarters ensued. One particularly good centre by Snelling gave the other forwards an opportunity, but for a time through combining prettily they could not shoot. Snelling nicely dropped a corner and Cook with a good opening, shot behind. The same players a little later forced a corner. It was nicely put in and Snelling scored. Three to one.

Retaining all the play, Trinity were continually dangerous. Ide ran out and cleared well and at the other end Lawrence fisted away a shot by Cook. Pulborough got a corner, but it was drawn blank. Then the old condition of affairs was resumed, Ide in negotiating a fine shot by Snelling, beat the ball down with both hands, as Knight happened to be nearest he netted the ball at once. Four to one.

Pulborough made several attacks, trying hard to reduce the lead, Barttelot had a fourth chance, but shot wide. About five minutes from the finish Trinity gained a corner and from Snelling's cross Redford headed into the net. Trinity 5 – Pulborough 1.

For the winners Lawrence was uncertain in goal in the early stages, but did well later on. Alfred Agate was the mainstay of the defence, his long kicks often proving most opportune. Thompsett was the best in the half line. Snelling, Redford and Buckton were the best forwards. For the visitors Ide kept well in goal, only making one slip. The backs worked hard and the halves acquitted themselves well.

Soffe, Barttelot and White were the best forwards.

Pulborough: L. Ide, T. Corden, S. Stillwell, F. Knight, G. Knight, C. Harrison, F. Smith, C. Barttelot, A. Soffe, E. White, W. Ward.

Trinity: A. Lawrence, A.T. Agate, W.B. Agate, E. Parker, F. Thompsett, W. Mills, E. Cook, H. Knight, A. Buckton, C. Redford, A. Snelling.

During this period, the Club was thought to have played its home games at Sopers Meadow, I have no idea about changing facilities there. When playing away over short distances some players would cycle, on longer trips it was thought they would travel in the back of a lorry, or take the train and walk to the ground from the station.

27.11.1909

Through the referee's mistake on the 29th October the game was replayed, the result was reversed with Amberley winning 3-0. Amberley put on a much heavier and bigger side. Their rushing tactics paid off, the smaller Pulborough side, lightweights, occasionally got out of the way. Mr Stone the referee kept the players in hand. He was the best man on the field.

12.03.1910

Pulborough were the better side, Amberley played their usual bustling game, many Pulborough lads left the field bearing marks. Result Pulborough won 1-0.

An early example of 'action photography' featuring players from Storrington Wednesday and Pulborough teams in a friendly match on 4th October 1905. The final score is not known.

**Pulborough FC, 1926/27 season winners of the Pulborough Benevolent Cup
after beating Bury & West Burton 6-1 in the final on 16th April 1927**
Back row 5th from left is Captain Neston Diggle; the goalkeeper in the white jumper is F. Green, then W.
Harwood, R. Heasman and R. Baker. *Front row from left* E. Jupp, J. Johnson, R. West, W. Bevan.

The 1929/30 Season Pulborough Benevolent Cup being presented to the
Pulborough Captain, Ronald West, by Lady Gladys Barttelot (Mrs Neston Diggle).

The Inter-War Years 1920-1939

BEFORE I GO onto the playing and running of the club, I think it right to mention our Vice Presidents. Most people, players especially, only think about the playing side of the game, but without the support and donations of the vice-presidents, the club would not exist. We at Pulborough were very lucky, from the 1920s right into the 1960s, to have had many vice-presidents, who enabled the club to keep playing. It is not possible to list all of them, but I have listed some of them; they range from ordinary working people to the more affluent members of the parish.

- Mr W. Adames, a local farmer
- Mr W.J. Allfrey, a local builder
- Dr. Archdeacon, a local G.P.
- Sir Walter Balfour Barttelot & Lady Gladys Barttelot of Stopham House
- Mr B. Benger, a local garage owner
- Mr W. Bevan a local Schoolteacher
- Mr Blackmore, a local headmaster
- Mr Boxall, a local auctioneer
- Commander Bragg
- Dr. Cope, a local GP
- Mr L.N. Corden, a local pharmacist
- Mr A.C. Cordery, a local ironmonger
- Mr H.E. Cosens, a local garage owner
- LT Commander H.E. Dennis of Holme Manor
- Captain Neston Diggle, RN
- S. Durkin esq
- Mr Farmer, manager of Barclays Bank
- Dr Foot, a local GP
- Captain Forsythe
- Rev Frost, a local clergyman
- Mr H. Gilbert, a local ironmonger
- Captain A. Head
- Lt Colonel Helme
- Captain J.S. Henderson
- Henty & Constable Ltd
- Commodore Hilliard of Bramfold House
- Mr L. Jarvis, a local grocer
- Mr H.E. Jennings, owner of the Swan Hotel
- Mr W.F. Jennings
- Mr E. Kent, a local dentist
- Mr P. Kitchen, owner of the Station Hotel and local garage owner
- Mr F. Killick, a local baker
- Mr G. Knight of the Oddfellows Arms and the Rose and Crown
- Colonel Leader
- Mr R. Leeson, of the Five Bells Inn
- Miss Lowther
- Rev Lynne
- Sir Dunscombe Mann
- Mrs Marsh Horrocks
- Mr H.J. Moger
- Colonel McNeile
- Mr E.C. Neighbour, manager of NatWest Bank
- Mr G.R. Newbury
- Mr J.S. Oliver, a local grocer
- Commander Olgilvy
- Mr Orford, a local harness maker
- The Hon. C. Pearson of Parham
- Mr Picton, a local grocer
- Mr W.C. Pilcher
- Mr W. Pope
- Mr W. Puttock
- Mr Rathbone
- Lt Colonel Ravenscroft JP
- Mr N.W. Rydon
- Mr W. Shaft
- Mr N. Short
- Mr A. Stillwell, a local baker
- Mrs Templar
- Mrs Thorpe
- Newland Tompkins Esq, a local auctioneer
- J.B. Tribe
- Miss Warner
- Mrs Warner
- Dr. Whyte Venables, a local G.P.
- Major Wilberforce
- Lord Winterton, a local M.P.

11-09-1920 – *West Sussex Junior League – Bognor Reserves 3 Pulborough 3*

Bognorians made the acquaintance of Pulborough footballers for the first time on Saturday and the Reserves found them a rare handful as a Junior League team. In fact, on the afternoon's play, the visitors showed to the best advantage. They were not only heavier, but could kick better and more readily and appeared to have more stamina. The result of the game was 3-3, but 4-3 in favour of Pulborough could not have been found fault with in comparing the work of the two teams.

The old ground at Nyewood Lane is once more the home of football and on Saturday it was hard work in the warm sun, the weather being such that games of cricket, tennis and croquet were in full swing on adjacent grounds.

Bognor scored first, from a penalty taken by Fowler, after a previous successful essay by Sharp, which was nullified by some technical infringement by a player. Pulborough later equalised with a fine shot by F Johnson and assured the lead through Carden. Subsequently, Welfare forced a corner and, following another corner, Richardson nicely passed to Lucas in front of goal and he drew level for the homesters. Welfare again did good work and shot across to Gilbert, who secured Bognor's third goal.

The play was very scrappy and disjointed, Bognor especially showing want of judgement and cohesion, but it was late in the second half before Harper equalised for Pulborough. A little later Fowler, who was maimed in the war, met with a couple of hard knocks and had to be assisted off the field.

Of the homesters, bachelor (although miskicking now and again), Welfare and Lucas were the most resourceful. The visiting backs and halves were the best of the respective divisions. The homesters need more practice; they have some promising youngsters in the front line.

Bognor: Edney, Sharp, Bachelor, Stamford, J Hyde, E Jones, J Richards, C Gilbert, W Welfare, C Lucas, W Fowler.

Pulborough: Millersh, Brockhurst, Johnson, Vincent, Hampshire, S Wadey, T Jupp, Corden, C Johnson, A Standing, B Harper.

With the First World War at an end, it was time to get back to some kind of normality. The nation was trying to get back on its feet and its people were recovering from the horrors of war. Sport was one way of taking people's minds off their everyday worries. Pulborough was no different to any other city, town or village. Football and cricket were starting to be played, which gave the male population, in particular, something to look forward to, whether playing or as a spectator. The ladies also played stoolball and hockey. 'The Robins' resumed at the start of the 1920/21 season.

Pulborough FC has an accounts book from this time, which makes very interesting reading. Unfortunately there is no other information, such as teams and results. Not every item has been recorded, but it gives some idea of how the Club was run. In the 1920/21 season, senior players subscriptions were 5/- and juniors 2/6, the average fee for a referee was 7/- a match. Some interesting items included: l bladder and 2 laces 2/6, lemons 3d, 1 ball 19/6. Even in the 1920s and 30s, running a football club was expensive; transport and equipment did not come cheap. On more than one occasion the President, Captain Neston Diggle RN, donated money to allow the club to keep playing.

The club's headquarters were at the Five Bells Inn, in London Road; the landlord in 1920 was a Mr Thomas Berryman. Apart from holding their meetings there, the pub was used for all the players to change before the game and to wash and change after the game.

The club played its home matches on Soper's Meadow, a piece of land situated just off the A29, where Stane Street Close now stands. The land was owned by the Brooker family and the club paid £4-1-0 to rent the field for the season. Mr B. Cockerell was appointed Groundsman and paid £3 per annum.

Mr B. Johnson was appointed Gateman and also paid £3 a year. This was an important job, because even in those days the club had many supporters. The pitch was cordoned off during the 1920s and 1930s, which quite surprised me.

In 1931 the land was owned by Mr W. Adames and the ground rent was £8 for the season. Mr Robert Leeson took over the Five Bells Inn from 1929 to 1940 but The Robins' headquarters remained there.

The club didn't have a team in 1932/33 or in 1933/34.

Transport for away games during the 1920s was provided by Mr Kitchen, who ran the Station Hotel and also owned a local garage. He had a 14-seater vehicle and also ran a taxi service. Mr H.E. Cosens also used his cars to transport the players. Mr Atfield was used by the club in the 1930s to transport the team to matches. Very few people had their own cars in those days and when playing sides such as Amberley, Storrington or West Chiltington, some of the players would ride their bicycles to matches. This cannot have been much fun if it was pouring with rain, or freezing cold and you had to cycle home after losing!

In 1920 the club restarted and entered the West Sussex Junior League. Clubs we played that year were: Arundel A, Bognor A, Broadwater, Felpham, Lavant, Littlehampton A, Midhurst, North Bersted, Shippams United, Singleton and West Dean, Selsey, Walberton and Wick. Our first game was against Bognor A at Nyewood Lane. The game was drawn, but we were unlucky not to come away with a win. Our first season back was a very satisfactory one.

29-11-1921 – Pulborough 6 Lavant 1

Lavant were heavily defeated on Saturday. Opening the scoring through Vincent, the homesters attacked strongly in the first half and at the interval led by 3-0, centre forward Weller getting two. Lavant gave a better account of themselves on resumption and Horn scored. 'The Robins' became very aggressive in the later stages and further goals were added by Whickens the outside left and Jupp and Vincent.

10-12-1921 – Storrington 2 Pulborough 2

Vigorous methods are essential to success in football, but it has been represented to us that there ought to be some modification of the tactics used by the Pulborough team on Saturday. The Storrington players were paid a visit from the neighbouring township to fulfil a fixture in the West Sussex Junior League and an impartial observer of the contest compares it as an encounter between bulls and lambs. This comparison would seem to be borne out by the fact that no fewer than three of the Storrington players were laid out in the course of the game. It is suggested that the referee exhibited to much leniency, but it is obvious some check should be exercised in such cases where scientific play is opposed by sheer physical strength. Despite the obvious disadvantages from which they laboured, in this respect Storrington contrived to effect a draw, the score was 2-2.

The 1921/22 season seemed to be a very good one. I could not find a final league table but I did come across two match reports (see above).

Members of the Pulborough Ladies Hockey Team circa 1917 (by kind permission of Trevor Cousins).

10-01-1925 Pulborough 11 Midhurst 0

The local football eleven certainly showed their superiority over Midhurst on Saturday, when that team visited Sopers to fulfil a League fixture. Though the result was a win for Pulborough by the large score of 11 goals to nil, the possibility is that it might have been more had the visiting goalkeeper not brought off some good saves, whilst for a large part of the game the local players were only able to muster nine players through unfortunate accidents that occurred to Habbin and Cosens. As circumstances show it was extremely one sided, the goals being shared by Habbin 1, Bevan 3, J. Johnson 5, E. Johnson 1, Cosens 1 and a very interesting match was brought to a conclusion with the score mentioned above.

Team. A. Pink, R. Kenward, E. Johnson, W. Harwood, W. Hampshire, H. Taylor, D. Kirby, J. Johnson, W. Bevan, H. Cosens, R. Habbin.

14-02-1925 – Pulborough 21 Wick 0

It would hardly be right to describe the encounter between the 'Robins' and Wick seconds as a football match at Sopers on Saturday, for when the whistle blew for time, it was found that Pulborough had won by the overwhelming score of 21-0. The game opened in fine weather and within two minutes West who was making his first appearance in the senior eleven scored a goal. It was a farce practically all through the game, as the visitors were very weakly represented and a hailstorm did not add to the comfort of any of the players. The score stood at 12-0 at halftime, after the commencement of the second half Wick were weakened by the loss of one of their players through injury and when the score at 15-0 three of the visiting players left the field, when the Final whistle blew the score was 21-0.

The scorers were Habbin, West, Wadey, J. Johnson, Cosens, Harwood, Hampshire, E. Johnson, Kenward. Team. A. Pink, R. Kenward, E. Johnson, W. Harwood, W. Hampshire, H. Taylor, J. Johnson, R. West, R. Habbin, W. Wadey, H. Cosens.

Match Report 21-3-1925

Pulborough came through their Benevolent Cup Semi-Final on Saturday by defeating Wisborough Green by 3 goals to 0 at Sopers. The home team won the toss, giving the visitors the advantage of the wind. Each end was visited in turn, with Pulborough having a little more of the advantages, though it was found that the wind did not help matters very much and hard work on the visitors side kept them from scoring. When the whistle went for half time no goals had been scored. Pulborough took advantage of the wind in the second half and after about 15 minutes, Harwood opened the scoring by rushing the ball into the net. Good work on the right led to West scoring the second goal, lifting the ball high into the net. The visitor's goal had some narrow shaves and had it not been for the good goalkeeping, there would have been a larger score. From a corner on the left wing Wadey added the third. Just before the end, Wisborough Green's outside left was compelled to leave the field, owing to an injury, but this made no material difference and the whistle went with the score 3-0.

Team: N. Brockhurst, R. Kenward, E. Johnson, H. Baker, W. Hampshire, A. Pink. J. Johnson, R. West, W. Harwood, W. Wadey, R. Habbin.

The 1922/23 season proved to be a good one for the club, who finished joint top of the league, level with Horsham Trinity, with goal difference not counting in those days. As both teams had equal points, a play off game was held on Arundel's ground in Mill Road. Unfortunately, the team did not play to their usual standard and lost by 4 goals to nil, so Horsham Trinity were promoted.

Over the next three seasons 1923/24, 1924/25 and 1925/26, the side finished in second place. Being so close on four occasions must have been very frustrating for the players and their supporters.

During the early 1920s the team seemed to change quite a bit, the mainstays of the side were: Billy Bevan, Norman Brockhurst, Billy Hampshire, Wally Harwood, Eddie Johnson, Jessie Johnson and Reg Vincent, who transferred from Littlehampton to play for us.

In 1925/26 PFC entered the English Amateur Cup for the first time in their history. After beating Broadwater in the first round, they were drawn to play against Hastings, who were a senior club and at the time top of their league. After a fine performance, PFC eventually lost by four goals to one after leading by one goal to nil at half-time.

During the 1925/26 season PFC entered a side into the Littlehampton and District Benevolent Cup, which they eventually won. In the first round they beat the Littlehampton British Legion side by 9 goals to nil, with Reg Vincent scoring 4 goals. They then played Wick at home and the game was a draw; the replay at Wick was also a draw. The third game was played on Arundel's ground and 'The Robins' won by 2 goals to 1 before a very big crowd. It was a bad tempered match, with three players being sent off. The final was played at Wick, Arundel being the opposition. Leading by 3 goals to one at half time, 'The Robins' ended up by winning the match by 3 goals to two. The team just had time to receive the cup and their medals before dashing back to Pulborough to play in the final of the Pulborough Benevolent Cup.

It's amazing to think that the team had to play five games in seven days. On the Saturday they played Wick, on Wednesday they played in the replay, and, as games were both drawn, another match was played on Friday evening. Having won this match, they had to play the final on Saturday afternoon and then on Saturday evening they had to play in the final of the Pulborough Benevolent Cup!

Having played three games in two days it was not surprising that they lost the second if the finals by 10 goals to 1. They would normally have beaten Fittleworth, but could not even make a game of it, being worn out before the match even started. The money taken that evening was £10-18-9. To reach three cup finals and finish second in the League in the same season was a great achievement.

3-10-1925 – Sussex Junior Cup – Chichester B 2 Pulborough 2

The most interesting match in the Chichester District on Saturday was the Cup tie between Chichester and Pulborough, which took place in Priory Park before a large attendance. Fast, exciting and even play characterised the game, which was fought in a true Cup tie spirit and a draw was undoubtedly a representative result. The Pulborough team. Picton, T. Johnson, Kenward, Cousins, Hampshire, Pink, C. Johnson, West, Brain, Wadey and Brockhurst. Both keepers were kept fairly busy in the first half throughout which the city team was predominant. Norris opened their account with a fine shot and a few minutes later Adams added another goal with a smart cross shot. The teams crossed over with Chichester leading 2-0. However, the visitors had the better in the second half and gave the home defence a warm time, never the less, the Lillywhites made some breakaways and in one of these, Picton the visitors goalkeeper (who, incidentally gave a fine display throughout) was called upon by Tallick and effected a great save. After continued pressure, Wadey reduced the 'Cicestrians' lead and in a keen play that followed, West managed to bring the scores level. Both teams tried doggedly to gain the supremacy but at the Final whistle, the score remained unchanged.

10-10-1925 – English Amateur Cup Pulborough 2 Broadwater 1

Ill fortune still dogs Broadwater in the matter of putting a fully representative team in the field. The side which did so well at Chichester was an experimental one, but after their excellent work it was hoped that they might remain together as a winning side. They all turned out against Horsham. Had Broadwater's full side been out there would have been a different tale to tell, as it was Pulborough although fully extending the visitors for the greater part of the game may consider themselves lucky to have been returned victors, for in the closing stages of the game there was no holding the fierce attacks of the Broadwater forwards and but for a wonderful display by S. Picton their young goalkeeper the decision would have been reversed. The game although well contested was by no means a pleasant one, as there was too much wrangling among players.

The Sussex Junior Cup Final 8-4-1926
Ringmer 3 Pulborough 2

Nearly a thousand spectators were present at the sports field Littlehampton on Saturday when Pulborough opposed Ringmer in the Sussex Junior Cup. Both teams came with good support, the red and white of Pulborough being very evident. Ringmer played a clever and pretty game, which gave them a distinct advantage over the Robins, who by adopting a kick-and-rush tactic frittered away many promising chances. Ringmer elected to defend the western goal, a free kick for a foul on Hampshire resulted in nothing tangible, but within five minutes Ringmer took the lead. The goal was the outcome of a free kick for an infringement by a Pulborough player, and Ellis put the ball well into the goalmouth for Hodgins to score. Wadey took advantage of a blunder by Gurr but failed in his eagerness. Two successive off-sides marred the progress of the Ringmer men, but eventually Bedman severely tested Elliott who saved the shot. Hampshire was seen to advantage and presented Vincent with a good chance but the centre forward was deprived of possession through hesitancy. Smith of Ringmer was making headway when offside was given against him. J. Johnson took the free kick and Divall obtained possession, the winger dashed along the line and placed a centre from which Hodgkins scored, Ringmer two up at half time.

The second half opened in rather a sensational manner for Pulborough, who had displayed inferior football took up the offensive, and there was great enthusiasm among their supporters when West went through and scored. Following this success the Robins showed marked improvement as a team, but their forwards failed dismally in front of goal. Pulborough were frequently dangerous but the Ringmer defence were taking no chances packing their goal. West narrowly missed with a good shot, and then Wadey had possession and was unmarked a goal looked certain, but he skied it over the bar. Vincent from five yards shot wide with only the keeper to beat. Pulborough netted but the whistle had gone for an infringement and hopes were again shattered. As a result of hands against Ringmer during another raid a penalty was given, E. Johnson took this, but Parris saved well. Then, from a free kick, Divall got away and after outrunning Johnson he finished a brilliant effort with a fine shot, Elliott was well beaten. Pulborough went on with renewed vigour and energy and were eventually rewarded, for following a general rush to the Ringmer goal Wadey extracted the ball from a crowd of players and netted. They kept plugging away until the end. Ringmer 3 Pulborough 2.

Pulborough: J. Elliott, R. Kenward, E. Johnson, W. Bevan, W. Hampshire, A. R. Pink, J. Johnson, R. West, R. Vincent, W. Wadey, N. Brockhurst.

The 1925/26 season saw PFC form a Second XI for the first time in its history. They were entered into the Horsham and District League, in Division Three. The teams they played that season were: East End Ramblers, Horsham YMCA, Staplefield, Warninglid, Warnham, West Chiltington, Dial Post Reserves, Lower Beeding, Slaugham and Handcross Reserves. They did well in their first season, finishing as runners-up winning 12 games, drawing 2 and losing 4. Outstanding players that year were: L. Jarvis, D. Kirby, J. Beacher, H. Johnson and R. Heasman.

In 1926/27, after being promoted to Division Two, they struggled. They only won 3 games and finished bottom of the table.

The 1927/28 season saw the Second XI leave the Horsham and District League and join the West Sussex Junior League. Their first game was against Littlehampton at home; they won by 4 goals to 3, the goal scorers were Carter 2 and Jarvis 2. The team that day was A. Brain, R. Heasman, H. Maher, W. Woods, C. Cooper, L. Stringer, N. Beaton, G. Carter, L. Woodland and W. Johnson. After a bright start the team started to struggle, they could not always put out a full side. In November they suffered at the hands of Petworth, losing by 16 goals to nil. It was not to be a good season for the Second Eleven.

The 1928/29 season saw the Second XI apply to join the Horsham and District League again, but before the season even started they had to withdraw through a lack players.

The 1926/27 season was to be another good one for the first team. After missing out on promotion for several years, they finally finished in first place, losing only one league game

9-10-1926 Pulborough v Horsham in the English Amateur Cup

Pulborough, a team which has been, for five consecutive seasons, runners-up in the West Sussex Junior League, were matched against Horsham on Saturday, on the latter's ground, in the first round of the English Amateur Cup. The short spell of rain in the morning had improved the ground, and the high wind, blowing from the direction of Denne Park, had a cold "nip" in it that infused into the players just that energy which is necessarily a feature of the winter game. The boisterous wind was evidently to the liking of the Pulborough men, whose bustling tactics threw Horsham, at times, off their form, and consequently both the home and visiting supporters were disappointed by such ragged play.

Pulborough won the toss and kicked with the sun and wind in their favour. In the first few minutes there was a miskick by H. Charman and Kirby bore down on the home goal, Kenwood, however, shot just over. Horsham attacked from the goal kick, Corbett failing to get his head to a nice forward pass from Burrage, who capably deputised at centre-half for Antill. Carter led the forwards while Boxall partnered the elusive Channon. Both players were somewhat uncomfortable in their new positions. Freddy Grant, as active as ever on the right wing, swung in a nice centre, resulting in a melee being dispersed in front of the visitors' goal. "Nutty" ineffectually at tempted to clear and Kirby got possession and parted to Kenward, who nearly found the target with a high corner shot.

On the other side of the field, J. Johnson hit the rigging from close range. Burrage worked effectively in clearing the ball to Channon and he centred to Carter. Horsham continued to be the aggressors. Grant centred nicely for Carter to forge through and shoot along the gr ass to the keeper. Picton threw the ball out and Channon, coming up at the double, shot the return over the bar. Grant centred again into the goal-mouth, Picton saving from Burrage at the expense of a corner. The ball sailed over splendidly from the spot, and the captain narrowly missed with a beauty past the post.

The tables were soon turned, Etheridge caught and cleared and A. Charman sent Kirby spinning when the latter was making tracks Jupp winged his way down the line and eluded Charman, Etheridge was tested and caught and cleared. The two Charmans found it very difficult to clear in the face of the wind, and more than once the home defence was harassed by the bustling play and sharp shooting of the riverside men. Boxall passed right across the field and Corbett robbed a back of the ball and shot just over the bar. Horsham's long desired and expected lead came after thirty-five minutes play. Boxall sent a long forward pass to Channon, who for a wonder was unmarked and sprinted for goal, near that objective, with four or five desperate defenders fast closing upon him, he shot through a maze of legs into the far corner of the net. The remainder of the first half was comparatively uneventful. There was some excitement almost on half-time when Grant placed the ball between on-rushing Carter and Picton, both missed, and Channon with an empty goal sent outside. Half-time score Horsham 1 Pulborough 0.

The second half was quieter than the first. Many of the spectator s thought that Horsham would rapidly increase their lead when helped by the sun and wind, but this they could not do until quite late in the half. Boxall made headway and passed out to Channon, who centred without effect. Another attack was initiated by Boxall, bringing Picton to his knees with a fine shot. The keeper cleared a short distance, Carter back-heeled to Channon who eluded three men and obtained a corner. The visitors then took a hand in the game, R. West trying to clinch matters with a long shot which Etheridge muffed but cleared. Henry Charman, when well up the field, failed to clear by heading, giving Johnson a clear run for goal.

"Nutty" came across to intercept him but failed to stop the shot. Etheridge, however, was in waiting and punched clear. At the other end Carter carried the ball through by forceful tactics, but Corbett shot wide. After some ten minutes of unproductive play, Channon forced a corner that proved barren. Charman gave Grant a splendid pass, he centred, and another corner was obtained by Channon. Shortly afterwards, "Nutty" skimmed the bar with a much applauded shot. Grant wriggled through the defence and was brought heavily to the ground. H. Charman missed the ball, and away went West with Clare and Charman after him. Before he could be overhauled, Etheridge rushed out and cleared. Horsham continued to press. Carter relieved a back and passed to Corbett, who scored with a splendid rising shot, which Picton just touched. Later on Grant passed back to Harry Etheridge, and the latter hit the underside of the bar, with Corbet t nearly scoring from the rebound. Corbett and Channon were next in the picture, Carter rushed for the ball, Harwood and the keeper missed and the centre-forward scored when almost on the line. Result Horsham 3 Pulborough 0.

Pulborough: S. Picton, W. Harwood, E. Johnson. W. Bevan, W. Hampshire, A. Pink. J. Johnson, R. West, R. Kenwood, D. Kirby, E. Jupp.

Horsham: A. Etheridge, A. Charman, H. Charman. H. Etheridge, G. Burrage, A. Clare. F. Grant, D. Corbett, M. Carter, F. Boxall, H.V. Channon.

04-01-1927 – Sussex Junior Cup
Sussex Old Boys 1 Pulborough 4

Pulborough were undoubtedly the better side in their Sussex Junior Cup game with Sussex Old Boys at the Manor Field on Saturday. But the result was by no means a fair indication of the play. The home team played well and Pulborough were not allowed to settle. Both defences were sound and the Sussex keeper J. Poulter had a fine game. Once it was true, he apparently let the ball into the net without troubling about it. But several of his saves gained applause from the crowd. It was in the forward line that Pulborough were most prominent, Vincent was a sharp shooting centre forward and deserved his hat-trick. Both sides missed chances in front of goal. In the first half there was little to chose between the teams, the ball being kept in midfield a good deal, but the balance seemed in the favour of Pulborough. At the start of the second half the Old Boys attacked strongly, but the Pulborough defence withstood for the Sussex Old Boys.

Pulborough team. S. Picton, R. Kenward, W. Harwood, T. Jupp, W. Hampshire, Ron Vincent, J. Johnson, R. West, Reg Vincent, W. Wadey, D. Kirby.

all season. They had another good run in the Sussex Junior Cup, losing out to Tarring after a replay in the quarter final. They were again unlucky in drawing to play a senior club in the first round of the English Amateur Cup. Having played against Hastings the previous year, they were now to play Horsham at their Queen Street ground. The team put in a fine performance, finally losing by 3 goals to nil against a higher ranked club. There were some outstanding achievements that season: in October the team beat Littlehampton by 20 goals to nil, with Reg Vincent scoring 9 of them; the return match at Littlehampton saw the team win by 3 goals to 2, with only 8 players. Ron West was to play for Sussex against Surrey in November, an honour for himself and the club.

The 1927/28 season saw the team playing in the West Sussex Senior League for the first time. Sides they played against that year were: Littlehampton Reserves, RAF Tangmere, Chichester A, North Bersted, Horsham A, Westgate Brewery, Crawley, Broadwater Athletic, Petworth, Horsham Trinity, Midhurst, Arundel, Bognor A and Wick.

Considering they were now playing a higher standard of football, the team did very well. In past years the side did very well in the Cup competitions, but they went out in the first round of the English Amateur Cup and also in the Sussex Intermediate Cup. They did give East Grinstead a very good game in the Amateur Cup, before losing by 3 goals to 4. In the League the team had some good results, notably against Westgate Brewery, who they defeated by 7 goals to 2 away from home and by 6 goals to nil at home, with Wally Harwood scoring a hat-trick. They also beat Bognor away from home by 5 goals to nil, Jessie Johnson getting a hat-trick. Their only poor result was against Crawley when they lost by 6 goals to 1 at Soper's Meadow.

By 1928/29 the team had established itself in the West Sussex Senior League. The first game of the season was an away match against Arundel, which resulted in a win by 3 goals to 1; Gange 2 and Corden 1 being our scorers. The team that day was: S. Picton, R. Vincent, W. Crockford, F. Green, V. Corden, E. Jupp, L. Jarvis, R. Gange, J. Johnson, L. Woodland and R. Heasman.

An unusual thing happened when the side played at Midhurst on 22nd September 1928. After fifteen minutes play the referee stopped the game and called the two teams together to inspect their boots. After doing so, he then sent off Hampshire and Newman (two Pulborough players) and the Midhurst goalkeeper for having brads sticking out of their boots. Pulborough had to play on with only 9 men and Midhurst were reduced to playing with 10 men. 'The Robins' lost the game by 6 goals to 1.

On 4th October 1928 the side were again unlucky to be drawn against a senior club in the English Amateur Cup. The side had to travel all the way to Lewes and lost the game by 10 goals to 2. They had the additional misfortune of losing their goalkeeper, who dislocated a finger and had to play on the field. The last game of the season saw the team travel to Horsham to play their reserve team. Despite only having ten men, they came away with a great result, winning by 1 goal to 0.

The side finished in 7th place, another good season for the club.

The Annual General Meeting was held at the Five Bells Inn on 15th July 1929. It was to be a very interesting AGM. Captain Neston Diggle was unanimously re-elected as President of the Club. Mr A. Brockhurst was re-elected as the Chairman, the following were elected to form a committee, Mr H. Jennings, Mr A. Brain, Mr H. Cosens, Mr A. Vincent and Mr E. Jupp. Mr H.R. Baker was elected as secretary and Mr L. Woodland was assistant secretary. Mr H. Taylor was re-elected treasurer, Mr V. Corden was re-elected as captain and Mr R. West was to be vice-captain, Mr A. Hampshire was re-elected as groundsman, the Club's linesman was to be Mr A. Brain, the club's League representative was Mr A. Vincent. Subscriptions for playing members was to remain at 5/-, each player to pay 6p for away matches, season tickets were to remain at 5/- for the season. Conveyance of the team was Mr Kitchen and also by Mr H. Cosens when required. The statement of accounts was presented, showing a provisional balance of £4-10-11, in view of the fact that a further sum of £5-19-4 was due to Mr Kitchen for conveyance of players, the final statement showed a deficit of £1-8-5, the season could have been over before it had even started. Our President, Captain Diggle came to the rescue and very generously agreed to pay off the debt, so the club could start the season with a clean sheet. It was agreed to write to Captain Diggle to to thank him for his generosity and keen interest in the club's welfare.

It was to be another satisfactory season for PFC, the side finished in 9th place. The cup competitions were not so successful, we were knocked out by Hove in the English Amateur Cup and lost to Worthing A in the Sussex Intermediate Cup.

On 28-09-1929 PFC held a trial match in which the teams selected were:

First XI: S. Picton, E. Heasman, W. Woods, W. Standing, V. Corden, L. Jarvis, R. Crowther, R. West, J. Johnson, F. Cousins, R. Goodsell.

Second XI: J. Elliott, H. Cosens, A. Brain, J. Clarke, N. Osborne, T. Bevan, R. Clarke, F. Mattews, W. Leigh, E. Cooper, J. Merrydeus.

The team's first win of the season did not come until 09-11-1929, when they travelled to play Littlehampton, where a fine win was recorded, Ron West scoring 4 goals and the team winning by 7 goals to 1.

On 1st February 1930 PFC were at home to Durrington and won by 6 goals to 1. The 22nd March 1930 brought a good win when the team beat Bognor by 6 goals to 4 at Bognor, Wally Harwood getting a hat-trick.

The only interesting topic that came up at the 1930/31 AGM was about allowing ladies to be admitted to watch home matches for half price (3d) and this was agreed, so the ladies were able to watch all league and cup home games for 3d per game or 2/6 for the season.

The first game of the season was against Chichester away, which resulted in a big defeat by 10 goals to nil. Two more heavy defeats were suffered later in the season: PFC were beaten by the

RAF Tangmere by 7 goals to 1 and by Horsham A by 7 goals to nil. They were unlucky again in the English Amateur Cup. They were drawn to play away and lost to Littlehampton First IX by 4 goals to 2 but they put up a fine performance against a higher ranked team. Although not one of their best seasons, they maintained their position in the senior League.

The Annual General Meeting of the Club was held at The Five Bells on July 8th 1931. Captain Diggle was re-elected as president and thanked for his help during the last seasons. The vice presidents were elected en-bloc.

The committee elected for the new season was: Mr A. Brockhurst, Mr V. Corden, Mr H. Jennings, Mr H. Cosens, Mr T. Harwood, Mr G. Scutt, Mr M. Hoole was to be treasurer and Mr H. R. Baker was the club secretary. Mr V. Corden, last season's captain, notified that he was retiring from playing, because of knee problems. Mr E. Heasman was elected captain and Mr J. Johnson vice-captain. Subscriptions were to be the same as last years, 5/- for seniors and 2/6 for under eighteens plus 6d to away matches as part fare. Owing to some difficulty about the ground, it was proposed that this matter be left to the honorary secretary to see Mr Adames with a view to getting Sopers again. Mr A. Hampshire was to be groundsman for the season and Mr T. Harwood to be gateman, a job which he had carried out admirably last season.

A statement of accounts was next placed before the meeting. The honorary secretary pointed out that a big decrease was sustained in gate money and subscriptions were down to the extent of £7. Entertainments also suffered in this respect, but the honorary secretary was able to show a balance carried forward of £18-3-9, against the balance of £16-1-6, the previous year. Gate money was agreed to remain as last season: ladies 6d, Boys 3d for League matches. Season tickets 5/- and 2/6 for ladies to be issued for all home League games. The meeting closed with a hearty vote of thanks to Mr Brockhurst for presiding and for his help during the season on the ground.

At a committee meeting held on 25th August, the secretary reported that he had obtained permission for the use of Sopers again this season, but stipulated we might be put to the inconvenience of a roadway across the ground. This was accepted by the committee. The secretary reported a problem with the transport of the team for away matches. Mr Kitchen, who had supplied transport in previous years, informed the club that his lorry was out of commission. Mr Atfield had offered his 14-seater when available, it was left to honorary secretary to fix up the best possible transport, either by train, bus or Mr Atfield, if neither available to co-opt Mr Cosens' three cars.

The first game of the season was away to Bognor A, the match being lost 5 goals to 2. The team that day was: W. Woods, H. Johnson, E. Heasman, T. Bevan, G. Sissons, E. Wood, J. Johnson, R. West, D. Adamson, W. Harwood, R. Goodsell. It was to be a very poor season for the club. On two occasions games had to be cancelled because we were unable to raise a side and on another occasion we had to play with only nine men. The team suffered some heavy losses, the worst result being against Angmering, an embarrassing 11-0 defeat. There was, once again, to be no luck in the cup competitions; the team went out in the first round of the English Amateur Cup to Bognor's first IX and in the Sussex Intermediate Cup they lost to Broadwater.

PFC did not have a side in seasons 1932/33 and 1933/34. I was unable to establish exactly why this was. In my opinion there are two possible reasons (although this is just guesswork on my part; I have no proof). My first thought is that we were short of players; in the previous season two matches had to be cancelled because we could not field a team and on another occasion we were only able to put nine players on the field. The other reason was that we had no ground to play on. It was stated at the 1931/32 AGM that there was a possibility of a roadway being put through the ground at Sopers Meadow. In 1932 Mr Adames was the owner of Sopers Meadow. In 1935 the club was paying rent for the hire of another piece of land which Mr A. Brockhurst of New Place Manor owned. I believe this land is now the village recreation ground. In 1939 when Pulborough Parish Council bought this land from Mr A.H. Bowerman, to be used for the sports Clubs of the village, it was pointed out that Pulborough Football Club were already playing on part of it.

A committee meeting was held on 28th September 1934, present were Chairman, Captain Clark, Mr Bartlett, Mr Vincent, Mr T. Harwood, Mr Adamson, Mr West and Mr Corden. They decided to enter a side in the Horsham and District League Division 1. At the next meeting Mr Baker, Mr Elliott and Mr Jupp, were added to the committee. Mr Adamson was to be captain and Mr W. Harwood was named as vice-captain. It was not a great season; the side only won 4 games.

A general meeting was held at The Five Bells on Friday March 1st 1935 at 8:15pm to discuss the project of reconstructing the club. Captain Clark took the chair on the motion of Captain Diggle. It was put to the meeting whether the club should be restarted and the result was unanimously in favour. About 20 persons present signified their willingness to become playing members. Selection of officers then took place. Captain Diggle was proposed as President and stated his willingness to assume that office, which was received with applause. Various names were proposed for the post of secretary, but none of the persons proposed would accept the office. Mr H. Vincent Finally volunteered to act as secretary and his offer was unanimously accepted with applause. By unanimous agreement, other offices were filled as follows: Treasurer Mr Bartlett, Captain Mr West, Vice- Captain Mr Adamson. Committee: Captain Clark (Chairman) Mr T. Harwood, Mr V. Corden, Mr. P. Scutt, Mr E. Jupp and Mr H. Vincent.

This was taken from Pulborough Football Club's minute book 1929/35. The Club was clearly in danger of folding but luckily for all concerned this did not happen.

A committee meeting was held at The Five Bells on 13th September 1935, present were Captain Clark, W. Bartlett, R. Heasman, T. Harwood, W. Harwood, R. E. Jupp, E. Jupp, D. Adamson, H. Vincent and A.D. Hughes. It was decided that an approach be made to members of the defunct Fittleworth Club with a view to signing them for Pulborough FC. The Club should try to enter the Rudgwick Charity Cup and also the Littlehampton Benevolent Cup. The secretary was then instructed to write to Mr Brockhurst to order that the field be cut and rolled. Season tickets were to be fixed at 3/-. Eight new red shirts were to be ordered from Pictons Stores and 2 new footballs from Mr Orford. The painting of the goalposts and the construction of a lavatory were discussed. The conveyance of the team was given to Mr A.H. Sayers. The Pulborough Benevolent Cup was considered and the secretary was instructed to write to the following teams: West Chiltington, Marley Sports, Wisborough Green, Billingshurst, Storrington, Bury, Rudgwick, Sutton & Bignor and Codmore Hill, to ask if they were willing to enter.

The team continued to play in the Horsham and District League until 10th February 1940, when they were due to play Slinfold. The match was scratched; PFC could only raise 8 players, because the others had been called for military service. The team selected for that game was: Pellett, Muggeridge, P. Barnett, Lewery, Unsted, Greening, Hughes, Williams, Cosham, Greenfield, A. Barnett.

From 1935 to 1940 the team were not very successful, but in the 1937/38 season they did reach the semi-final of the Horsham and District League Junior Charity Cup, losing to Loxwood after a replay. The following season 1938/39, they reached the semi-final of the Intermediate Cup, losing out to Sussex Bricks. In the team that restarted in 1934/35 there were only 3 players from the late 1920s and early 30s; the team had to be rebuilt.

I managed to find one or two interesting bits and pieces when going through the records:

- At a meeting on 17th September 1935 it was agreed that Mr Bartlett should write to the *West Sussex Gazette* contradicting notice in said paper to the effect that Pulborough Football Club had ceased functioning. At the same meeting it was agreed that the use of the ground be extended to Pulborough School.

- At the AGM on 23rd July 1937 a discussion took place as to whether black or white socks were to be worn by the team; they decided on white.

- At a meeting on 25th October 1937 it was reported that Mr N. Vincent had left the field of play without informing anyone and for no apparent reason in the match against West Chiltington. Neither the referee nor the captain knew that the player had left the field and when he was informed the captain decided to play on with ten men. The incident was discussed and the result was that Mr N. Vincent be informed by letter that the club had no future need of his services as a result of his unsporting behaviour.

- At a committee meeting on 7th March 1938 it was reported that damage had been done to the hut on the football ground. Mr Bundy, headmaster of Pulborough School, was asked to speak to the pupils, as the damage was thought to have been caused by his schoolboys.

- At the AGM held on 26th July 1938 the secretary read a letter he had received from Captain Diggle RN stating that he would be unable to continue as President of the Club, as he was leaving the district. This news was received with great regret by all and was a huge loss to the club and the village. Captain Diggle had done a lot of good work and had been very generous to all the sports clubs and the village in general.

To sum up the years 1920-1940... I already knew that PFC had its headquarters at The Five Bells Inn and that its home games were played at Sopers Meadow. However, I did not know that you had to pay to watch the team, that you could purchase season tickets, or that the ground was cordoned off, which was a surprise. Neither did I realise that Codmore Hill had its own football club or where they played (see later chapter for details). And I wonder how many people knew that Mare Hill and Stopham had cricket teams or that Pulborough had a ladies hockey team?

The highlights for Pulborough FC were gaining promotion to the Senior League, getting to the final of the Sussex Junior Cup and playing in the English Amateur Cup.

The disappointment was the club having to stop playing for two years. Fortunately, the break was only temporary and the club restarted – and is still going strong to this day.

Players of the 1920s & 30s

Mr T. BEVAN was a teacher at St Mary's School; he left to take up another teaching post in London in 1932. He played bowls, cricket and football for local clubs.

Mr W. BEVAN (BILLY), a popular figure in the village, was assistant headmaster at St Mary's School. He was later appointed headmaster at Easebourne School, near Midhurst. During the First World War he served in the Royal Flying Corps. Billy was captain of the side in the 1920s, a forward and a very good player. He also played for and was secretary of the local Cricket Club and was in the choir at St Mary's Church.

ALFRED BRAIN (ALF) ran the Red Lion pub in Lower Street from 1924 to 1934. His brother was Jimmy Brain, the famous Arsenal player, who played in the 1927 FA Cup Final at Wembley. Jimmy would come down to Pulborough to watch Alf play when he was not playing himself. Afterwards they would go back to the Red Lion, where they were joined by the locals who knew he was coming. Alf was a good player in his own right and usually played as a winger. After he gave up playing, he served on the committee.

NORMAN BROCKHURST, a police officer, was the brother of Albert, who was our chairman for several years. Norman played in a number of different positions for the team.

JAMES BRYANT (JIM) was born on 12th May 1919 in South Grounds, Stopham. He attended Pulborough Primary School, leaving when fourteen years of age. His first job was working for Mr Anderson, a local builder, as a painter and decorator. Jim was a reservist and was one of the first to be called up in the Second World War. He served with 4th Battalion Royal Sussex Regiment and worked his way up to become Company Sergeant Major. He was among the thousands of our troops stranded at Dunkirk in 1940. As a boy he had learnt to swim in the river Arun and was a very strong swimmer. Stripping down to his underpants, he swam out and was picked up by a battleship, but this was blown up and he had to swim for his life. He was then picked up by a London paddle steamer and brought back to England. After spending the next six months in Yorkshire, he was sent to North Africa and with his regiment he fought in the campaign in the Middle East, including the battle of El Alamein. After being demobbed he went back to work for Mr Anderson before becoming a self-employed painter and decorator. Jim passed away on 19th November 1989. His sons Richard and Jimmy played for PFC in later years.

VICTOR CORDEN (VIC) see Presidents.

Mr H.E. COSENS (TIM) was born in Hunston in 1898. In around 1910 he went to live in Canada. He returned several years later, enlisted in the army and fought in the First World War. He was captured by the Russian Army but managed to escape. I don't know when he came to live in Pulborough but he signed on for PFC in 1924. Tim was a keen sportsman; as well as playing football he was a very good bowls player and was chairman of the Cricket Club. He was a local garage owner and ran a taxi service and a lorry business. Tim was a popular man in the village.

FRANK COUSINS (1900-1980) was born in Havant, Hampshire, one of thirteen children, nine of whom were boys. He came to live in Pulborough in the late 1920s. He served in the army during the war years. On leaving the Forces he worked for the Parham Estate, then went to work for W.P. Tracey in Station Road, as a lorry driver. After a serious operation Frank was unable to return to manual work, and worked at Spiro Gills as a progress chaser until he retired. He was a very good footballer and in his younger days had a trial for Portsmouth. In the 1950s he arranged friendly matches for the young boys of the village. He also played cricket for the local team. Frank loved his fishing and spent many hours fishing the river Arun, sometimes from the riverbank but also from his boat. He was married to Winifred, who wrote a book about her experiences of life in the village of Pulborough. His son Trevor played for PFC in the 1950s and 1960s.

RICHARD CROWTHER (1909-1944) lived in Carpenters Hill Pulborough. A very intelligent young man, he was educated at Harrow and Cambridge University. He joined the RAF and became a Flying Officer, was mentioned in dispatches and was highly thought. Sadly, he was killed in action in 1944. Richard only played for one season for PFC in 1929/30.

REG GOODSELL (TAPPER) see Chairmen.

EDWIN JUPP was born in Worthing 4th November 1870. The family moved to West Chiltington and then lived in London Road Pulborough. He worked for the Parham Estate as a gardener. He was a committee member for PFC. He passed away 24th February 1942.

Mr R.E. JUPP (RUPERT) (27th Nov 1899 – 24th Feb 1942) was the son of Edwin and lived in London Road with the family. Rupert worked as a plumber. He was a very good player, a winger and really fast.

EDWARD JOHNSON (EDDIE) lived in London Road Pulborough. He was an excellent player who sometimes played up front but was mostly a defensive player. In 1926 Eddie played for Sussex against Middlesex.

JESSIE JOHNSON, the brother of Eddie, was another talented player. He was a forward, a good goal scorer and very quick. Jessie played for the West Sussex League side.

STANLEY PICTON (STAN) was born in Petworth in 1907. His parents owned Pictons stores in Lower Street Pulborough. When he left the local St Mary's School he went to work as a delivery boy for his parents. Stan later moved to Horsham, where he got married. He then started work for Scrase and Company, which sold fizzy drinks and went on to run the company. When he retired he went to live in the West Country and died there in 1994. He was a superb goalkeeper, the finest of his era. Stan played for Worthing at one time and was also selected to play for Sussex.

KENNETH SCUTT (KEN) was born in Thakeham 7th April 1910, the son of Mr George Scutt and the family came to live in Lower Street in Pulborough. Ken was a sales representative, working for the Hollis Tobacco Company. He died in Lewes in 1987.

STANLEY SCUTT (STAN) was born in Bromley in 1914. Moving to Pulborough, he lived in Sopers Cottages. Stan attended Midhurst Grammar School and on leaving worked as a librarian in Chichester Library. In 1940 he joined the Royal Air Force Volunteer Reserve. He later became a Flight Lieutenant (pilot) in No.57 Squadron, RAF Bomber Command based at East Kirby. Stan and his Lancaster crew were dispatched to drop mines off the German port of Swinemunde on 17th August 1944 but their aircraft was shot down over the Baltic. Stan is buried in Poznan Old Garrison Cemetery (coll.grave5.c.1-10).

GEORGE SCUTT was born in Shipley in 1866, moved to Sussex and lived in Lower Street, Pulborough. He was the owner of Scutt Agricultural Engineers in Station Road. George died in 1953.

ALAN HUGHES, a Welshman, was a teacher at St Mary's School in Rectory Lane. When Rydon County Secondary School opened he went there as the PE teacher and was my teacher when I went there in 1954. Alan first played for PFC in 1934, was a forward, a skilful player and a good goal scorer.

TREFOR WILLIAMS (CHIPPY) was another Welshman, who taught at St Mary's School and then went on to Rydon County Secondary School. Trefor was the woodwork teacher and was my housemaster when I started there in 1954. He made his debut for PFC in 1936 and was captain in the 1939/40 season. He returned after the war and started playing again in 1946; he retired in 1948. In his early years he was an inside forward, then played at fullback. He was a very fine player who could have played at a higher level.

FREDERIC PENNICOTE (FRED) lived in Watersfield. He was a goalkeeper, having joined 'The Robins' in 1936. Fred was a prisoner of war during the Second World War.

ROBIN HEASMAN lived in Mare Hill. He joined PFC as a junior in the early 1920s. He lived in Stopham Road. He joined PFC as a junior in 1925 and soon established himself in the side, he was a big man and played in the defence. He was a very good player. Vic was captain of the team in the 1936/37 season.

JOHN BURNINGHAM lived in Stopham Road and worked for Newland Tompkins auctioneers. He played for PFC from 1932 to 1936.

BERT HAWKINS joined PFC in 1935. He was a car mechanic and lived in Lower Street.

FREDERIC MATTHEWS (FRED) lived in Mare Hill, was a farm worker and joined PFC in 1929.

RONALD WEST (RON) lived in Lower Street and was a post office clerk in the Pulborough branch.

He made his debut for 'The Robins' in 1924. Ron was one of the stars of the side, played in the forward line and was good in every aspect of the game. In 1926 he played for Sussex Junior against Surrey, in 1929 he was put forward to play in a junior county trial match and in 1932 he was put forward to play for the West Sussex League side. Ron was a huge Portsmouth fan, his ashes were scattered on Fratton Park.

HARRY WHITNEY first played for PFC in 1931. He was a goalkeeper but on occasion played as a forward. Harry was a self-employed bricklayer and lived in Broomers Hill.

JOHN SOPP, a police officer, lived opposite Stane Street Close in a bungalow. He joined PFC in 1931.

LEONARD JARVIS (LEN) first played for PFC in 1921. He played in the forward line and was a good goal-scorer. Len had a grocer's shop next to the old Chequers Hotel in Church Place.

WILLIAM WADEY (BILL) was a lorry driver and lived in London Road. Bill was a very fine player who joined PFC in 1936.

LEONARD BURCHELL (LEN) after leaving the Navy became a Civil Servant before taking over a confectionery shop at the bottom of Station Hill. He first played for PFC in 1925.

REGINALD VINCENT (REG) came to The Robins in 1922 after playing for Littlehampton FC. He was a regular in the side and another very fine player.

WALLACE HARWOOD (WALLY) – see Presidents.

FRANK ELLIOTT (JIM) (16 Oct 1896 – 11 Jan 1971) was a plumber and lived in Sopers Cottages. He joined PFC in 1925.

PATRICK LEWERY (PAT) joined PFC in 1934. Pat lived in Station Road and was the manager of Harwood's Garage in Petworth.

EDWARD LANGHAM (TED) lived in Sopers Cottages, was a clerk and worked for British Rail. He started playing for PFC in 1936.

WILLIAM WOODS (BILL) (1904-1984) on leaving school worked for the local baker, Mr Stillwell. He was then living in Potts Lane. Bill later moved to live in Lower Street and became a bus driver. He made his debut for The Robins in 1922.

JACK SOAL lived in Watersfield and worked as a warehouseman for Mr Cordery in Lower Street Pulborough. He joined PFC in 1936.

Mr H. BAKER (BOB) He lived in London Road and worked at Harwood's Garage. He played for PFC in 1921 and later he became a committee member.

Mr R. KENWARD joined PFC in 1922.

Mr J. BEACHER first played for PFC in 1924.

Mr A.R. PINK joined PFC in 1923.

Mr D. KIRBY made his debut in 1923.

Mr W. STANDING made his debut in 1923.

Mr A. SULLY first played in 1922.

Mr A. WAITE made his debut in 1928.

Mr F. GREEN signed for PFC in 1928.

Mr L. WOODLAND joined PFC in 1928.

Mr K. GANGE played for us in 1929.

Mr W. LEESON made his debut in 1930.

Mr H.G. LEESON also made his debut in 1930.

COLIN BRAGG first played for us in 1928.

Mr W. WHITE made his debut in 1928.

Mr R. HABBIN joined PFC in 1924.

Mr W. CRAFT played his first game in 1922.

Mr W. HAMPSHIRE (Billy) was a very good player and made his debut in 1921.

Mr R. PINK joined PFC in 1923.

Mr B. HARPER joined PFC in 1923.

Mr T. JOHNSON made his debut in 1923.

Mr H. TAYLOR played his first game for PFC in 1921.

Mr H. JOHNSON joined PFC in 1924.

Mr P. SMITH played his first game in 1923.

Mr C. JENNINGS joined PFC in 1924.

Mr F. NEWMAN joined PFC in 1927.

There were many others who occasionally played for The Robins during this era – the above is just a selection of those who played regularly.

First 11 results 1920 – 1940

WSJL 1920/21

[A] **Bognor A** (D 3-3)

[A] **Littlehampton A** (L 0-2)

[A] **Midhurst** (L 0-7)

[A] **Shippams United** (L 1-3) Harper 1

[H] **Broadwater** (L 2-9) Harper 1 Jupp 1

[A] **Arundel A** (L 0-4)

[H] **North Bersted** (W 4-0) Chitwing, Hampshire, Morris, Wadey

[A] **Selsey** (L 0-2)

[H] **Wick** (L 0-1)

[H] **Midhurst** (L 4-6) Simpson 2, Jupp, Vincent

[A] **Broadwater** (L 2-5)

[H] **Shippams United** (D 2-2) Burt, Harper

[A] **Felpham** (D 2-2)

[H] **Lavant** (W 1-0)

[H] **Walberton** (D 2-2)

[A] **Singleton & West Dean** (L 0-3)

[H] **Singleton & West Dean** (D 1-1)

[H] **Littlehampton A** (D 2-2) Jarvis 2

[H] **Felpham** (D 2-2)

[A] **Lavant** (W 4-1)

[A] **Walberton** (W 2-0)

[H] **Arundel A** (W 2-0)

[H] **Bognor A** (L 1-3)

P26 | W6 | D6 | L14 | GF34 | GA64 | 18pts

WSJL 1921/22

[H] **Bognor A** (D 2-2)

[H] **Lavant** (W 6-1) Vincent 2, Weller 2, Jupp, Wickens

[H] **Storrington** (W 6-3)

[A] **Wick** (W 4-1)

[H] **Littlehampton A** (W 6-0) Craft 2, Elliott, Jupp, Reg Vincent, Roy Vincent

[H] **Littlehampton Railway** (W 2-0)

SJC [A] **Arundel** (L 2-9)

[A] **Storrington** (D 2-2)

[A] **Littlehampton A** (W 2-0)

[H] **Arundel A** (W 5-1)

[H] **Singleton & West Dean** (D 1-1)

[A] **Bognor A** (D 1-1)

[A] **Lavant** (W 6-0)

[A] **Littlehampton Railway** (W 5-0)

[H] **Wick** (W 2-0)

WSJL 1922/23

9-9-1922 [A] **Bognor A** (W 2-1) Craft, Jupp

23-9-1922 [A] **Singleton** (W 3-1)

14-10-1922 **North Bersted** (W 3-0)

21-10-1922 SJC [A] **Littlehampton** (D 3-3) Bevan, Brain, 1 OG

28-10-1922 SJC [H] **Littlehampton** (W 5-3) AET

4-11-1922 SJC [A] **Durrington** (L 0-1)

18-11-1922 [A] **Storrington** (W 2-0)

25-11-1922 [A] **Horsham Trinity** (L 0-2)

9-12-1922 [H] **Fernhurst** (D 1-1) Elliott 1

26-12-1922 [H] **Storrington** (W 2-1)

6-1-1923 [H] **Midhurst** (W 4-0)

10-2-1923 [H] **Horsham Trinity** (D 2-2) *To be replayed*

17-2-1923 [A] **Sidlesham** (W 2-1)

3-3-1923 [A] **Fernhurst** (L 0-1)

10-3-1923 [H] **Bognor A** (D 1-1)

17-3-1923 [A] **Midhurst** (W 3-1)

24-3-1923 [H] **Singleton** (D 1-1)

7-4-1923 [H] **Sidlesham** (D 0-0)

25-4-1923 [H] **Horsham Trinity** (W 2-0) Replayed Game

P16 | W10 | D4 | L2 | 24pts | Joint 1st

Play-off against **Horsham Trinity** for promotion (L 0-4)

WSJL 1923/24

8-9-1923 [A] **Westgate Brewery** (L 2-3)

15-9-1923 [A] **Bognor A** (L 0-4)

22-9-1923 [H] **Fernhurst** (W 4-0) Baker, Bevan 2, Hampshire

29-9-1923 [A] **Midhurst A** (L 1-2) Cousins

1-10-1923 [A] **Nomads** (W 1-0) Bevan

20-10-1923 SJC [H] **Worthing Old Grammarians** (W 6-2) Bevan 4, Hampshire, E. Johnson

27-10-1923 [A] **Arundel** (W 3-2)

4-11-1923 SJC [H] **Amberley & Hougthon** (W 4-0)

11-11-1923 [H] **Wick A** (D 3-3) Bevan, Craft, J. Johnson

18-11-1923 **Littlehampton A** (W 4-0) Bevan, Brain, Hampshire, J. Johnson

25-11-1923 SJC [H] **Littlehampton A** (L 3-4) Baker, J. Johnson, Sully

8. 12.1923 [A] **Midhurst A** (D 2-2)

15. 12.1923 [H] **Amberley & Houghton** (W 2-1)

12-1-1924 [H] **Littlehampton A**

19-1-1924 [H] **Bognor A** (D 2-2)

2-2-1924 [A] **Amberley** (W 2-1) Bevan, Kirby

9-2-1924 [A] **Wick A** (W 5-0)

8-3-1924 [H] **Nomads** (W 5-0)

15-3-1924 [A] **Fernhurst**

22-3-1924 [H] **Westgate Brewery** (W 2-1)

12-4-1924 [H] **Arundel A**

P18 | W10 | D4 | L4 | GF46 | GA24 | 24pts | 2nd

WSJL 1924/25

13-9-1924 [A] **Lancing** (W 3-2)

17-9-1924 [H] **Littlehampton A** (W 8-2) J. Johnson 6, Harwood, Habbin

4-10-1924 [A] **Wick A** (W 4-2)

11-10-1924 SJC [A] **Broadwater** (D 0-0)

18-10-1924 SJC [H] **Broadwater** (D 0-0)

25-10-1924 SJC [A] **Broadwater** (L 1-2)

15-11-1924 [A] **Midhurst** (W 5-3)

22-11-1924 [A] **Littlehampton** (W 4-1)

13-12-1924 [A] **Amberley**

10-1-1925 [H] **Midhurst** (W 11-0) J. Johnson 5, Bevan 3, Habbin, E. Johnson, Cosens

24-1-1925 [A] **North Bersted** (L 1-3) Bevan

7-2-1925 [A] **Amberley** (D 1-1) Harwood

14-2-1925 [H] **Wick A** (W 21-0) Cosens, Habbin, Hampshire, Harwood, E. Johnson, J. Johnson, Kenward, Wadey, West

21-2-1925 [A] **Arundel A** (D 4-4) Bevan 2, Brockhurst, Wadey

28-2-1925 [H] **Arundel A** (W 6-1) Bevan, Habbin, Harwood, J. Johnson, Wadey, West

14-3-1925 [A] **Bognor A** (W 2-0) Wadey 2

28-3-1925 [A] **North Bersted** (W 4-1) Wadey 2, Bevan, Harwood

4-4-1925 [H] **Lancing**

18-4-1925 [H] **Bognor A** (L 0-1)

P16 | W12 | D2 | L2 | GF83 | GA22 | 26pts | 2nd

WSJL 1925/26

12-9-1925 [A] **Bognor A** (L 0-1)

26-9-1925 [A] **Littlehampton A** (W 7-1)

3-10-1925 SJC [A] **Chichester A** (D 2-2) Wadey, West

10-10-1925 EAC [H] **Broadwater** (W 2-1) J. Johnson, West

17-10-1925 SJC [H] **Chichester A** (W 5-2) Brockhurst, Hampshire, J. Johnson, Vincent, Wadey

24-10-1925 EAC [H] **Hastings** (L 1-4) West 1

31-10-1925 [H] **Amberley & Houghton** (W 9-0) Vincent 3, Wadey 3, West 2, Kenward

7-11-1925 SJC [A] **Graylingwell** (D 3-3)

14-11-1925 [H] **North Bersted** (W 6-3) Vincent 2, Wadey 2, Bevan, West

21-11-1925 SJC [H] **Graylingwell** (W 4-3)

28-11-1925 SJC [H] **Bognor A** (W 4-3) Brockhurst, Vincent, Wadey

2-1-1926 [A] **Wick A** (W 5-1) W. Bevan 4, Wadey

9-1-1926 SJC [A] **RAF** (W 4-1) J. Johnson, Vincent, Wadey, West

23-1-1926 [A] **Arundel A** (W 8-0) West 3, Bevan, Brockhurst, Hampshire, Vincent, Wadey

13-2-1926 SJC [H] **Tarring** (W 5-1) Wadey 2, West 2, Vincent

20-2-1926 [H] **Arundel A** (W 3-2) Wadey 2, Vincent

27-2-1926 [H] **Wick A** (W 9-0)

13-3-1926 SJC Semi-Final [at Littlehampton] vs **St Marks Old Boys** (W 2-1) AET Vincent, West

20-3-1926 [H] **Bognor A** (W 5-1)

27-3-1926 [H] **Littlehampton** (who scratched)

3-4-1926 [A] **North Bersted** (L 2-4) J. Johnson, Vincent

10-4-1926 SJC FINAL [at Littlehampton] vs **Ringer (L** 2-3) Wadey, West

24-4-1926 [A] **Amberley & Houghton** (W 7-4) Kirby 2, Vincent 2, West 2, Bevan

P12 | W10 | D0 | L2 | GF61 | GA17 | 2nd

WSJL 1926/27

18-9-1926 [A] **Broadwater Juniors** (D 2-2) Bevan 2

2-10-1926 [H] **RAF Tangmere** (D 2-2) Kenward, Kirby

1-10-1926 EAC [A] **Horsham 1st** (L 0-3)

23-10-1926 [H] **Littlehampton A** (W 20-0) Vincent 9

30-10-1926 [A] **Wick A** (W 1-0) West

6-11-1926 SJC [A] **Bury & West Burton** (W 6-0)

20-11-1926 [A] **Bury & West Burton** (W 7-0) Mather 2, Vincent 2, Beacher, Hampshire, Harwood

27-11-1926 SJC [A] **Graylingwell** (D 3-3) J. Johnson, Kirby, Vincent

4-12-1926 SJC [H] **Graylingwell** (W 4-3) AET Vincent 2, Kenward, Wadey

11-12-1926 [H] **Amberley** (W 5-0)

1-1-1927 [H] **Wick A** (W 7-2)

15-1-1927 SJC [A] **Sussex Old Boys** (W 4-1) Vincent 3, Wadey

22-1-1927 [H] **Bury & West Burton** (W 9-2) Vincent 5, West 2, J. Johnson, Maher

29-1-1927 [A] **Amberley** (D 2-2) Kirby 2

12-2-1927 SJC [H] **Tarring** (D 2-2) Kirby, Vincent

19-2-1927 SJC [A] **Tarring** (L 3-4)

19-3-1927 [H] **Broadwater Juniors** (L 2-3) Kirby, Wadey

9-4-1927 [A] **RAF** (W 4-1) Vincent 2, J. Johnson, Kirby

13-4-1927 [A] **Littlehampton A** (W 3-2)

P12 | W8 | D3 | L1 | GF64 | GA16 | 17pts | Finished 1st

WSSL 1927/28

10-9-1927 [H] **Littlehampton** (D 3-3) Vincent

17-9-1927 [A] **RAF** (L 1 -2) Vincent

1-10- 1927 [H] **Chichester** (W 4-2) Vincent 2, West, Woodland

8-10-1927 EAC [H] **East Grinstead** (L 3-4)

15-10-1927 [A] **North Bersted** (W 3-2) Vincent, West, Woodland

29-10-1927 [H] **Horsham A** (L 1-2) West 1

5-11-1927 SIC [A] **Wick** (L 1-3) Corden 1

12-11-1927 [A] **Westgate Brewery** (W 7-2) Harwood 2, West 2, Woodland 2, Hickish

19-11-1927 [A] **Crawley** (L 2-5) Bevan, Jupp

26-11-1927 [A] **Broadwater** (L 1 -2) Harwood

3-12-1927 [H] **Horsham Trinity** (W 1 -0) Bevan

10-12-1927 [H] **Midhurst** (W 2-1)

7-1-1928 [H] **Westgate Brewery** (W 6-0) Harwood 3, Bevan, Hampshire, Kirby

21-1-1928 [H] **Crawley** (L 1-6) Kirby

28-1-1928 [A] **Horsham A** (D 2-2) [H] Johnson 2

4-2-1928 [H] **Littlehampton** (L 1-2) [H] Johnson

11-2-1928 [A] **Horsham Trinity** (W 3-1)

25-2-1928 [H] **Arundel** (L 1-3)

3-3-1928 [A] **Wick A** (W 2-1)

10-3-1928 [H] **Broadwater** (D1-1) Abandoned at half-time; snow

17-3-1928 [H] **Bognor** (L 1-2)

24-3-1928 [H] **Wick** (L 2-5)

31-3-1928 [H] **North Bersted** (W 4-3) Jarvis, J. Johnson, Jupp, Woodland

7-4-1928 [A] **Arundel** (W 5-2)

14-4-1928 [A] **Chichester** (L 1-3)

21-4-1928 [A] **Bognor** (W 5-0) J. Johnson 3, Jupp, Price

28-4-1928 [H] **Midhurst** (W 6-2)

3-5-1928 [H] **RAF Tangmere** (L 0-3)

P26 | W12 | D3 | L11 | GF66 | GA57 | 27pts | 6th

WSSL 1928/29

8-9-1928 [A] **Arundel** (W 3-1) Gange 2, Corden

15-9-1928 [H] **Bognor A** (W 5-2) J. Johnson 2, Gange, Green, Heasman

22-9-1928 [A] **Midhurst** (L 1-6) Gange

29-9-1928 [H] **RAF** (L 0-3)

4-10-1928 EAC [A] **Lewes 1st** (L 2-10) Kirby, Woodland

13-10-1928 [H] **Westgate Brewery** (W 3-2)

20-10-1928 [H] **Arundel** (W 3-0) Crockford, Kirby, Standen

27-10-1928 SIC [A] **Broadwater** (L 1-5) Corden

3-11-1928 [H] **Petworth** (D 1-1) Crockford

17-11-1928 [A] **Broadwater** (L 1-4)

24-11-1928 [H] **Crawley** (W 3-2) J. Johnson, Vincent, Woodland

31-11-1928 [H] **Horsham A** (D 2-2) Corden, Newman

5-1-1929 [A] **Littlehampton A** (W 3-0) J. Johnson 3

19-1-1929 [A] **Crawley** (L 2-4) Gange, J. Johnson

26. 1.1929 [H] **Littlehampton A** (W 4-2) Woodland 2, Hampshire, Rufus

2-2-1929 [H] **North Bersted** (W 7-1) J. Johnson 3, West 3, Rufus

9-2-1929 [H] **Chichester A** (W 2-0) Crockford, Rufus

23-2-1929 [H] **Broadwater** (W 2-1) Woodland 2

9-3-1929 [A] **RAF** (L 2-4) Crockford, Rufus

16-3-1929 [A] **Chichester A** (L 0-2)

23-3-1929 [A] **Midhurst** (W 5-2) Crockford 2, Woodland 2, Gange

27-3-1929 [A] **Horsham A** (W 1-0) Gange

P26 | W12 | D2 | L12 | GF56 | GA51 | 26pts | 7th

WSSL 1929/30

21-9-1929 [A] **Durrington** (D 2-2)

5-10-1929 [A] **Chichester A** (W 3-1)

12-10-1929 **EAC** [H] **Hove** (L 2-6) J. Johnson 2

26-10-1929 [H] **Wick** (L 1-2) J. Johnson

2-11-1929 **SIC** [H] **Worthing A** (L 1-5) F. Cousins

9-11-1929 [A] **Littlehampton A** (W 7-1) West 4, Cairns, J. Johnson, Woodland

16-11-1929 [H] **Arundel** *they scratched – 2pts*

23-11-1929 [A] **RAF** *cancelled*

7-12-1929 [H] **Petworth** (L 2-3) Goodsell, West

21-12-1929 [H] **Crawley**

28-12-1929 [H] **Broadwater** (W 2-1)

4-1-1930 [A] **Arundel** (W 2-1) Goodsell, Heasman

11-1-1930 [A] **Petworth** *lost 2pts*

18-1-1930 [H] **Horsham A** (D 2-2) Corden, West

25-1-1930 [A] **Midhurst** (L 1-10)

1-2-1930 [H] **Durrington** (W 6-1) Harwood 2, West 2, Heasman, Rowland

8-2-1930 [H] **RAF** (L 1-6) Harwood

15-2-1930 [H] **Midhurst** (L 2-3) Corden, West

22-2-1930 [H] **Bognor A** (L 3-4)

1-3-1930 [A] **Crawley** (L 0-1)

8-3-1930 [H] **Littlehampton A**

15-3-1930 [A] **Broadwater** (W 2-1) Crowther, Harwood

22-3-1930 [A] **Bognor A** (W 6-4) Harwood 3, J. Johnson 2, Goodsell

29-3-1930 [A] **Wick**

12-4-1930 [H] **Chichester A** (W 2-1) Woodland 2

19-4-1930 [A] **RAF**

30-4-1930 [A] **Horsham A** (W 2-1) E. Johnson 2

P24 | W10 | D4 | L10 | GF55 | GA58 | 24pts | 9th

WSSL 1930/31

13-9-1930 [A] **Chichester** A (L 0-10)

20-9-1930 [H] **Littlehampton**

4-10-1930 [H] **North Bersted** (L 0-1)

11-10-1930 **EAC** [H] **Littlehampton** (L 2-4) Harwood, H. Johnson

18-10-1930 [H] **Bognor A**

25-10-1930 [A] **RAF**

1-11-1930 [H] **Horsham A** (L 1-4) J. Johnson

8-11-1930 [A] **Durrington** (W 2-0) Harwood 2

22-11-1930 [A] **Crawley** (L 1-3) Harwood

13-12-1930 [A] **Midhurst** (L 0-2)

20-12-1930 [H] **Petworth**

3-1-1931 [A] **Petworth** (L 1-3) OG 1

10-1-1931 [H] **Midhurst** (W 2-1) E. Johnson 2

24-1-1931 [H] **Wick** (W 3-0) Corden, Harwood, 1 OG

31-1-1931 **SIC** [A] **RAF** (L 1-4) West

7-2-1931 [H] **Chichester A** (L 1-3)

14-2-1931 [A] **Wick**

28-2-1931 [H] **RAF** (L 1-7)

7-3-1931 [A] **North Bersted**

14-3-1931 [A] **Littlehampton** (L 0-2)

21-3-1931 [H] **Durrington**

11-4-1931 [H] **Crawley** (W 6-1)

18-4-1931 [A] **Horsham** (L 0-7)

25-4-1931 [A] **Bognor A** *cancelled*

Played 22 *(not all results available)*

WSSL 1931/32

19-9-1931 [A] **Bognor A** (L 2-5) Adamson 2

26-9-1931 [A] **Chichester A** (L 1-6) H Johnson

3-10-1931 [H] **Chichester A**

10-10-1931 **EAC** [A] **Bognor** (L 1-5) Adamson 1

17-10-1931 [H] **Durrington** (W 6-2)

24-10-1931 **SIC** [A] **Broadwater** (L 1-4)

31-10-1931 [A] **North Bersted**

7-11-1931 [H] **RAF**

14-11-1931 [A] **Wick** (L 2-7)

21-11-1931 [H] **Crawley** (W 4-1)

28-11-1931 [H] **Midhurst** (W 5-3)

5-12-1931 [H] **Midhurst**

12-12-1931 [H] **Easebourne** (L 1-3)

19-12-1931 [A] **Petworth** (L 2-5)

2-1-1932 [H] **Littlehampton** (L 2-4)

9-1-1932 [H] **Petworth** *we scratched; lost 2pts*

16-1-1932 [A] **Easebourne** (L 1-6)

23-1-1932 [H] **Horsham A** (L 2-6) Goodsell, J Johnson

6-2-1932 [H] **Angmering** (L 0-2)

27-2-1932 [H] **Wick**

5-3-1932 [A] **Littlehampton** (L 0-2)

19-3-1932 [H] **North Bersted**

26-3-1932 [A] **Angmering** (L 0-11)

2-4-1932 [A] **Durrington** (L 0-4)

9-4-1932 [A] **RAF** *we scratched; lost 2pts*

16-4-1932 [H] **Bognor A**

20-4-1932 [A] **Crawley**

30-4-1932 [A] **Horsham A** (L 0-3)

Played 26

HDL DIV1 1934/35

29-9-1934 [A] **Horsham YMCA** (L 1-2)

6-10-1934 [H] **Partridge Green** (L 1-4)

13-10-1934 **HDLSCC** [H] **Billingshurst** (L 0-2)

27-10-1934 [H] **East End Ramblers** (L 0-2)

3-11-1934 [H] **Horsham Labour** (W 2-1)

17-11-1934 [A] **Horsham Trinity** (D 2-2)

8-12-1934 [A] **Dial Post** (W 4-2)

22-12-1934 [H] **Roffey Institute**

12-1-1935 [A] **Billingshurst** (L 0-1)

26-1-1935 [H] **Dial Post** (W 4-3)

2-2-1935 [H] **Roffey Institute** (L 0-7)

16-2-1935 [H] **Horsham YMCA** (L 0-2)

9-3-1935 [A] **Partridge Green** (D 1-1)

16-3-1935 [A] **East End Ramblers** (L 1-5)

23-3-1935 [H] **Horsham Trinity** (D 2-2)

30-3-1935 [A] **Horsham Labour** (L 2-4)

6-4-1935 [A] **Territorials** (L 0-2)

13-4-1935 [H] **Territorials** (L 1-2)

22-4-1935 [H] **Billingshurst**

Played | 18 | W4 | D3 | L11 | GF27 | GA51 | 9pts | 8th

HDL D1 1935/36

21-9-1935 [A] **Ockley** (L 2-4) Harwood, Hughes

28-9-1935 [H] **Territorials** (W 3-0) Duncton, Goodsell, Hughes

12-10-1935 [H] **East End Ramblers** (L 1-6) Hughes

19-10-1935 [A] **Horsham Trinity** (L 2-4) R E Jupp 2

26-10-1935 [A] **Broadbridge Heath** (L 3-5)

2-11-1935 [A] **East End Ramblers** (L 0-6)

9-11-1935 [A] **Partridge Green** (L 2-3) Hughes, Lewery

16-11-1935 **HDLSCC** [A] **Roffey Institute** (D 0-0)

23-11-1935 **HDLSCC** [H] [Lost Replay]

7-12-1935 [H] **Roffey Institute** (L 0-2)

14-12-1935 [H] **Billingshurst** (W 2-0)

4-1-1936 [A] **Horsham YMCA**

18-1-1936 [A] **Billingshurst**

25-1-1936 [A] **Roffey Institute**

1-2-1936 [H] **Horsham Trinity** (W 3-1)

8-2-1936 [H] **Partridge Green** (L 1-2)

7-3-1936 [H] **Broadbridge Heath** (L 1-6)

14-3-1936 [A] **Territorials**

21-3-1936 [H] **Horsham YMCA** (L 2-9)

11-4-1936 [H] **Ockley** (L 0-4)

P18 | W6 | D0 | L12 | GF34 | GA60 | 12pts | 7th

HDL DIV 3B 1936/37

17-10-1936 [H] **Slinfold** (L 0-1)

31-10-1936 [A] **Ashurst** (L 0-6)

7-11-1936 [A] **Codmore Hill** (L 1-6)

1.4-11-1936 [H] **Rudgwick** (L 0-4)

5-12-1936 [H] **Broadbridge Heath** (D 2-2)

12-12-1936 [A] **Plaistow Juniors** (L 2-5)

2-1-1937 [A] **Ockley Res** (L 1-2)

9-1-1937 [A] **Loxwood** (L 0-3)

23-1-1937 [H] **Balls Cross** (L 0-6)

30-1-1937 [H] **Codmore Hill** (L 0-7)

6-2-1937 [A] **Slinfold** (D 1-1)

13-2-1937 [A] **Balls Cross** (D 5-5)

20-2-1937 [H] **Loxwood** (L 2-3)

27-2-1937 [H] **Plaistow Juniors** (W 2-1)

6-3-1937 [H] **Ashurst** (W 3-1)

13-3-1937 [A] **Rudgwick** (L 0-7)

27-3-1937 [H] **Ockley Res** [H] (W 3-1)

10-4-1937 [A] **Broadbridge Heath** (L 3-6)

P18 | W3 | D3 | L12 | GF25 | GA67 | 9pts | 10th

HDL DIV 3B 1937/38

25-9-1937 [A] **Plaistow Juniors Res** (L 4-5)

2-10-1937 [H] **Five Oaks** (W 4-1)

16-10-1937 [A] **Broadbridge Heath Res** (W 4-0)

30-10-1937 [H] **Balls Cross** (W 5-4)

13-11-1937 [H] **Plaistow Juniors Res** (W 7-2)

27-11-1937 HDLJCC [H] Henfield Athletic Res (W 5-2)

4-12-1937 [A] **Loxwood** (L 1-6)

11-12-1937 HDLJCC [H] **Balls Cross** (W 2-1)

8-1-1938 [A] **Slinfold** (D 2-2)

22-1-1938 [A] **Balls Cross** (L 1-4)

29-1-1938 [H] **4th Royal Sussex Regt** (D 3-3)

19-2-1938 [H] **Loxwood** (L 0-3)

5-3-1938 [H] **Broadbridge Heath Res** (W 5-2)

12-3-1938 [A] **Five Oaks** (W 7-1)

19-3-1938 [A] **Council United** (L 3-4)

26-3-1938 HDLJCC Semi-Final [at West Chiltington]v **Loxwood** (D 1-1)

2-4-1938 HDLJCC Replay [at Barns Green] v **Loxwood** (L0-3)

10-4-1938 [H] **Slinfold** (D 3-3)

15-4-1938 [A] **4th Royal Sussex Regt** (L 1-2)

24-4-1938 [H] **Council United** (W 2-1)

P16 | W7 | D3 | L6 | GF52 | GA43 | 17pts | 5th

HDL D21938-1939

17-9-1938 [H] **Nuthurst** (D 2-2)

24-9-1938 [A] **Balls Cross** (W 6-1)

8-10-1938 [H] **4th Royal Sussex Regt** (L 2-5)

15-10-1938 HDLICC [A] **Balls Cross** (W 6-2)

22-10-1938 [A] **Lower Beeding** (W 8-2)

24-10-1938 [H] **West Chiltington** (W 7-2)

19-11-1938 [H] **Codmore Hill** (L 0-1)

26-11-1938 HDLICC [H] **Slinfold** (W 3-2)

3-12-1938 [H] **Sussex Bricks** (W 3-1)

17-12-1938 [A] **Warnham** (D 1-1)

7-1-1939 [A] **Codmore Hill** (W 2-1)

14-1-1939 [H] **Loxwood** (W 3-0)

4-2-1939 [A] **Nuthurst** (L 4-6)

11-2-1929 [A] **West Chiltington** (L 1-3)

18-2-1939 [A] **Loxwood** (D 2-2)

25-2-1939 [H] **Lower Beeding** (W 8-0)

4-3-1939 [A] **Staplefield** (W 7-1)

11-3-1939 [H] **4th Royal Sussex Regt** (L 1-3)

18-3-1939 [H] **Balls Cross**. Who Scratched

25-3-1939 HDLICC Semi-Final [at Horsham] v **Sussex Bricks** (L1-5)

1-4-1939 [A] **Slinfold** (L 1-8)

8-4-1939 [A] **Sussex Bricks** (D 4-4)

15-4-1939 [H] **Slinfold** (L 2-6)

22-4-1939 [H] **Staplefield** (W 8-0)

29-4-1939 [H] **Warnham** (W 8-0)

P22 | W11 | D4 | L7 | GF80 | GA49 | 26pts

HDL D2 1939/40

18-11-1939 [H] **Slinfold** (D 3-3)

25-11-1939 [A] **West Chiltington** (W 3-0)

2-12-1939 [A] **Five Oaks** (W 3-1)

9-12-1939 [A] **Royal Sussex Regt** (W 6-0)

16-12-1939 [H] **Royal Sussex Regt** (W 5-4)

30-12-1939 [A] **Slinfold** (Scratched)

6-1-1940 [H] **West Chiltington** (L 1-4)

13-1-1940 [H] **Five Oaks** (W 2-0)

P7 | W5| D1 | L1 | GF23 | GA12

Pulborough FC Team – Season 1947/48
Percy Barnett, Ted Watkinson, Ernie Leadbeatter, Laurie Larby, Bern Rowland, John Rayner, Mr Feakes.
Charlie Booker, Sid Greenfield, Tony Frogley, Peter Harrison, George Purnell, Dennis Roberts.

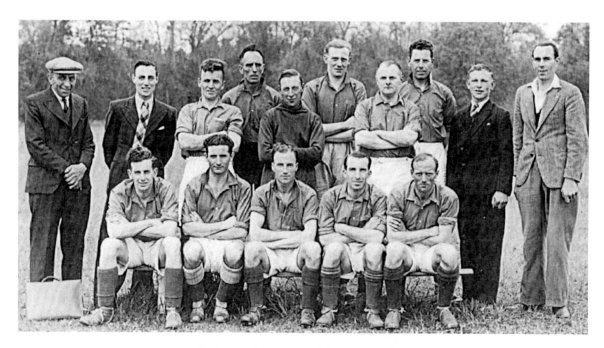

Pulborough FC Team – Season 1948/49
(Back row) Mr Feakes, Ron Cooper, Percy Barnett, Ernie Leadbeatter, Laurie Larby, Dennis Bagley,
Bill Williams, Ted Hilton, Richard Padwick, Stan Poore.
(Front) Peter Harrison, George Purnell, Dennis Roberts, Sid Greenfield, Peter Roberts.

The Golden Years 1946-1959

LIKE THOUSANDS OF other clubs, we restarted in 1946, after the Second World War. PFC held it's AGM on 7th August 1946, at the Five Bells Inn. The election of officers was as follows: Chairman, Mr R. Goodsell; Secretary, Mr S. Greenfield; Treasurer, Mr L. Tracy; the Committee was Mr W. Bartlett, Mr J. Elliott, Mr S. Ayling, Mr F. Beacher and Mr L. Edwards. The Linesman for the season Mr F. Beacher, the Groundsman Mr S. Ayling. The Captain elected was Mr P. Lewery and the Vice-Captain Mr R. Greening. The Secretary explained the position of the club regarding the Pulborough Sports Association and it was decided that the club's assets be handed over to them. Subscriptions to be 7/6 and those under 18 to be 5/-, with a standard fee of 1/- per match. Transport to be arranged by the Secretary. PFC was to be entered into the Horsham and District League Division 1 and also the Sussex Junior Cup.

The first League match of the season was away to Roffey, which was a 6-6 draw. The team that day was: R. Cooper, E. Hilton, P. Barnett, R. Padwick, P. Lewery, R. Greening, N. Johnson, G. Purnell, P. Roberts, D. Roberts, D. Bagley. Other players that came into the side that season were Dilloway, Greenfield, C. Pavey, Poore and Rolfe. It was a satisfactory start, the team finished 7th.

The 1947/48 season saw the start of what was to become the most successful period in the Club's history. At the AGM the only changes made from the previous season were that Mr S. Greenfield was made both Secretary and Treasurer and the Committee was now S. Ayling, F. Beacher, W. Burchell, H. Cooper, V. Feakes, A. Knight, J. Knight, F. Pavey and E. Roberts. The new Captain was Peter Roberts and the Vice-Captain George Purnell. It was suggested that a member of the club should receive the visiting team on arrival. Mr Ambridge of The Five Bells was thanked for his kindness in availing his room for changing and meetings. Mr Rolfe commented on the sportsmanlike manner in which Peter Roberts had refused the opportunity of playing for Horsham in preference to staying with Pulborough. Mr N. Woods was unhappy at paying his subscription, but only playing one game.

With more people finishing their time in the forces, the side that went on to be so successful was starting to take shape. The season was to be a very good one for the side, with the team finishing in 14th place. After scanning through the newspapers, mainly the *West Sussex County Times* because we were playing in the Horsham and District League, I could find very little in the way of match reports. Although match results were recorded in the Club's archives, no one thought to record the goal scorers, which was unfortunate, as the team were prolific scorers. That season saw the team score 102 goals and concede only 38. Heavy defeats were inflicted on several teams: HTE Lintott were beaten by 17 goals to 1; against Horsham YMCA the score was 13 goals to 2; a 7-1 win and a 9-2 win against Plaistow and Partridge Green were other highlights.

The 1948/49 season was the first time the side looked as though it could become something special. Off the field the club was in a healthy position financially, so it was decided that as well as proving shirts, the club would also buy shorts. Before this, players had to buy their own shorts and socks. Getting back to on-field activities, a practice match was held on 27th September, when the Reds played the Whites, the Whites winning by 6 goals to 5.

The Red team lined as follows:
LARBY
ROWLAND   RAYNER
PURNELL   WATKINSON   LEADBEATTER
CLARK J   PAVEY C   COLLINS   STENTIFORD   COOPER

The White team was:
POORE
BARNETT   CLARK F
PADWICK   BAGLEY   GLOVER
HARRISON   BOOKER   FROGLEY   GREENFIELD   ROBERTS D

G. JOHNSON played in place of COLLINS, A. SPAIN in place of ROBERTS. Peter Roberts had decided to play for Horsham, after refusing to play for them the previous season. This was a huge loss to the club but the committee wished him the best of luck. He was to become a regular player in the first team there. Younger readers may find the formation of the teams a bit strange, but that was how most teams played before the 1960s. Teams played with 2 full backs, 3 half backs and 5 forwards. [In my opinion, this led to more exciting matches; things today seem to be overcomplicated, with sides adopting so many different formations.] After the practice match, the team selected for the next match – against Plaistow in the 1st round of the Sussex Junior Cup – was Larby, Rowland, Rayner, Purnell, Watkinson, Leadbeatter, Harrison, Booker, Frogley, Greenfield and D. Roberts. The only change to the side was that Poore came into the side towards the end of the season.

At the end of the season the team finished in second place, having lost just one game, against Sussex Bricks, the champions (the only game they lost was against PFC). Pulborough scored 122 goals but conceded only 25. Beating Partridge Green 15-1 and Kirdford 13-1, were the two biggest results, but other sides were beaten by scores of 7 or 8. Attacking football was the order of the times. The team also reached the final of the Horsham and District Senior Charity Cup, where, at the Queen Street ground, they played Sussex Bricks. Another report shows a match played at the end of the season, between a Horsham and District League XI and the Horsham 1st XI. 'The Robins' had four players in the League side: Bern, Rowland, Peter Harrison, Tony Frogley and Dennis Roberts. Playing for the Horsham XI was Peter Roberts, the brother of Dennis.

The second XI were not entered into a league that year, but they did play some friendly matches. On 3rd January 1949 they played a match against Storrington reserves; a 0-0 draw. The team that day was Poore, Jennings, Padfield, Padwick, Glover, Marden, Stentiford, Woods, J. Clark, Pavey and Spain.

A committee meeting was held on 21st July 1949, at the Five Bells. The Secretary reported that he had attended the General Meeting of the West Sussex Senior League and that the club had been admitted to compete in that league for the 1949/50 season. He also stated that he had been instructed by the League Committee to report to his committee that the changing facilities for visiting clubs and referee must be of the highest standard possible, whereon the Secretary reported that Mr Nighy of the Arun Hotel had offered the club better changing facilities than those which existed at the Five Bells Inn. After discussion it was decided that H. Cooper and V. Feakes and the Secretary should interview Mr Ambridge to see if he could improve conditions for visiting teams at the Five Bells. The Secretary was instructed to enter the 2nd XI in the Horsham and District League and the Horsham Senior Cup.

Changes were to be made both on the field and also in the running of the Club at the Club's AGM on 8th August 1949, held at the Five Bells Inn. Elected as Club President was Mr W.J. Harwood, the Chairman was to be Mr W. Bailey, Captain of the first XI was S. Greenfield and Vice-Captain was B. Rowland. Selection of Captain and Vice-Captain for the second XI would be decided after a trial match and the committee would decide. Supporters were to be charged 2/6 to travel on the coach to away matches. The next paragraph was taken from the Club's archives:

"The Secretary stated that he had been told by the committee of the West Sussex League, that the changing and washing facilities for visiting teams must be of a good standard and that Mr H. Cooper, Mr V. Feakes and himself had been instructed by the committee to approach Mr Ambridge of the Five Bells Inn, to see if he could do anything to improve the standard of facilities at the Inn for the coming season, but he had to say that Mr Ambridge was very sorry he could not improve on what had been done in previous seasons. The Secretary then stated that the Club had been offered use of better facilities at the Arun Hotel by Mr Nighy. It was then put to votes and carried that the headquarters of the Club be transferred to the Arun Hotel and that the Secretary write a letter of thanks to Mr Ambridge for his kindness for allowing use of room for changing and meetings."

Pulborough FC 1949/50 – West Sussex League Division 1 Champions
Back row from left Peter Roberts, Peter Harrison, Ted Watkinson, John Rayner,
Laurie Larby, George Purnell, George Carter, Percy Barnett.
Front row Bernard Rowland, Sid Greenfield, Ken Handley, Tony Frogley, Dennis Roberts, Jack Henley.

Pulborough FC 1949/50: *back row from left* Wally Bailey (chairman), Tony Frogley, Laurie Larby, Ted Watkinson, John Rayner, Peter Roberts, John Overnell, George Carter, Percy Barnett. *Front row* Peter Harrison, Ken Handley, Sid Greenfield, Bern Rowland, Dennis Roberts.

This was a big decision, as the Five Bells had been our headquarters since 1898 when the club was formed. There were no changing facilities on the recreation ground, the Pulborough players would come to the ground, having changed into their kit at home; the opposition would go to the club's headquarters, get changed and then walk to the ground, returning to the Five Bells Inn after the game to wash and change. In this day and age it is hard to imagine that sides had no changing facilities on the ground and that players would have to change in one of the local inns or hotels and then walk through the streets with their boots on to get to the ground.

When the first XI joined the West Sussex League, there was just one Division and it was intermediate standard. The first game of the season saw the team travel to play Bognor Regis Reserves and win by 3 goals to 1, a good start in this new venture. The side that played that day was: L. Larby, B. Rowland, J. Rayner, G. Purnell, E. Watkinson, S. Greenfield, P. Harrison, K. Handley, T. Frogley, D. Roberts, P. Roberts, after playing for Horsham, Peter Roberts had returned to play for 'The Robins'.

During our three years in the West Sussex League from 1949/50 to 1951/52, I was able to find reports of most of the games the first XI played but finding reports of second team games was not so easy, there seemed to be very few.

Moving away from the playing side, at a committee meeting on 11th April 1950 a letter was read out from the Pulborough Boys Club, saying that a meeting was being held at Harwood's Garage with the proposal of a building being constructed on the Playing Field to meet the needs of the various sporting and social organisations of the village. The club was asked to nominate two representatives. It was decided that Mr B. Rowland and the Secretary would attend the meeting on behalf of PFC.

From the late 1940s and into the 1950s, the club's transport for away matches was provided by Mr Sayers from Fittleworth. His coaches were not the most modern of vehicles but they did reach their destinations. This brings me to a couple of stories which made me chuckle... It was said that when the coach reached the bottom of Bury Hill, as many people as possible would go as far forward as they could, so that the weight was at the front, just in case the coach did not make it up the hill. They did not fancy getting off and pushing! The other story was that when it rained, the young lads who went to support the team would take it in turns to sit up next to the driver and work the windscreen wipers manually, as they did not always work. The lads thought this was great fun, but it made their arms ache! Coming home was alright, it was downhill, but not so interesting.

Back to the football and the 1949/50 season. A good result against Bognor in our first game was a confidence booster, as it was not known how the side was going to fare in the higher standard of football. For the first time since the 1928/29 season the club were going to run a second XI. They were in the same position as the first XI. It was unfortunate that they were to compete in the Horsham & District League Division 1. With a new side and with some players not having played much football and not at that level, it would have been better had they been put in a lower division. Their first league match was against Billingshurst on 24th September 1949 and resulted in a 9-0 defeat. The team that day was: Bjorkov, Smith, Blackman, Padwick, Penfold, Leadbeatter, Pavey, Spain, Carter, Greenfield and Poore. Cooper played in place of Carter.

The season was to be very tough for the second XI, who won only 3 games with 1 draw and they conceded 125 goals, while scoring only 24. The first XI settled down quickly and any doubts about their ability to compete at that level were dispelled very early on. They won their first 2 games, lost the next 2, then bounced back to beat Chichester A by 9 goals to 1.

Pulborough FC 1950/51 – at Petworth
Back row from left Percy Barnett, Bernard Wells, John Rayner, Tony Frogley, Laurie Larby, Peter Roberts, Ted Watkinson, Ellis Roberts (chairman).
Front row Bern Rowland, Peter Harrison, Dennis Roberts, Sid Greenfield, Ken Handley.

Pulborough FC 1950/51 – West Sussex League Division 1 Champions and Benevolent Cup Winners
Back row from left Ellis Roberts, Percy Barnett, Tony Frogley, John Rayner, Bernard Wells, John Overnell, Jack Veverines, Ted Watkinson, George Purnell.
Front row Peter Harrison, Sid Greenfield, Laurie Larby, Dennis Roberts, Peter Roberts.

17-3-1951 West Sussex League Benevolent Cup Semi-Final Portfield 0 Pulborough 2

Pulborough gave one of their best performances of the season to reach the Final of the West Sussex League Benevolent Cup, to be played in April, when they travelled to Portfield on Saturday and beat the League leaders 2-0. Portfield, incidentally, are the only team who have beaten Pulborough in a league encounter this season. The game was fought at a terrific pace, with no quarter asked or given. At the interval neither team could claim the edge, and it was anybody's game. After the resumption the same pace was set, and Pulborough lasted out just that little bit better. D. Roberts and B. Wells scored.

PFC team: Larby, Rowland, Rayner, Handley, Watkinson, Greenfield, Harrison, Frogley, Wells, D. Roberts, P. Roberts.

Match Report 21-4-1951 – West Sussex League Benevolent Cup Final, played at Bognor – Pulborough 3 Petworth 2

Playing for more than half the match with only ten men, Pulborough were undoubtedly worthy winners of the West Sussex League Benevolent Cup. The loss of right back Rowland with a knee injury resulted in the remaining players exerting tremendous efforts, and they were a great deal faster and more aggressive than their opponents. Within ten minutes both teams had scored, Pulborough through Harrison and Petworth through centre forward Stillwell, one of the most dangerous men on the field, thus the score remained till half time.

The Robins made many valiant attempts to take the lead, but it was not until well into the second half that Tony Frogley put them ahead. This was a remarkably neat goal, Peter Harrison's corner kick swung out, the inside right Frogley, hanging back from the goal mouth scrum, and he headed it directly and very smartly past keeper Heather. On a dry ground, and with a fair amount of wind, the ball was often out of control, but the dash of both sides was impressive. Bern Wells took the score to 3-1 to Pulborough, and with that commanding lead the team eased off and concentrated more on defence.

Despite this Petworth raised the hopes of their supporters with a good goal from R. Taylor. The rally was to no avail however, and the match ended with a fair result of a win for Pulborough. The cup was presented by Mr. Authur James, Chairman of the Bognor Regis Urban District Council, whose opinion was a most enjoyable game, with Pulborough just the better side.

Pulborough:
LARBY
ROWLAND–RAYNER
HANDLEY–WATKINSON–GREENFIELD
HARRISON–FROGLEY–WELLS–D. ROBERTS–P. ROBERTS

Petworth:
HEATHER
SADDLER–BEST
CROOK–BROWN–HOOK
J. TAYLOR–SCAMMEL–STILLWELL–SOPP–R. TAYLOR

Pulborough made sure of winning the League by beating Felpham 4-2 and Westbourne 2-1. Mr. M. W. Simmonds presented it and also the Benevolent Cup. The Pulborough team and over 200 supporters staged a victory march through the village.

Scenes from the celebratory dinner after winning the West Sussex League Division 1 Champions trophy and Benevolent Cup 1951/2

This is a different occasion and a different cup, not sure which one or who is in the photo.

Other impressive wins were against Midhurst 7-0, Littlehampton A 8-1 and another 8-1 against Midhurst. They had a very satisfying result when they beat Petworth 5-1 after losing to them in league and cup earlier in the season.

During the season only 14 players were used, they were: Larbey, Rowland, Rayner, Purnell, Watkinson, Greenfield, Harrison, Handley, Frogley, Roberts D, Roberts P, Carter, Ovenell. As champions, in the last game of the season they played against The Rest of the West Sussex League XI at Arundel and lost by 3-1. They also had a very good run in the West Sussex League Benevolent Cup, before losing in the semi-final to Portfield by the odd goal.

The AGM for the 1950/51 season was held at the Arun Hotel on 12th June 1950. The only real points of interest concerned players' subscriptions and the second XI. It was decided that subscriptions would be reduced from 7/6 to 3/6 and that each player to pay 1/- for each game. After much discussion it was found to be impossible to raise a second XI, so they were to be withdrawn from the Horsham & District League.

If the team thought the 1949/50 season was good, the 1950/51 season was even better. The only change to the squad was that B. Wells was added to it. The team made another great start, but as I have included reports from many of the games, there is no need to say anything about them here. However, a couple of things that occurred during the season deserve a mention. Peter Roberts was selected for the West Sussex League XI and Bern Wells scoring 9 goals in one match was special. The one downside of a successful year was the injury to Bern Rowland in the final of the West Sussex League Benevolent Cup; sadly, he never recovered fully from his injury and was not able to play first team football again.

The Arun Hotel was again the venue for the AGM held on 22nd June 1951. The secretary reported that the first XI had won the West Sussex League Championship and the West

Pulborough FC 1951/52 – West Sussex League Division 1 Champions and Intermediate Cup Winners
back row from left Trainer (unknown) Peter Harrison, Wally Harwood, Tony Frogley, Jack Veverines, Bob Heather, Ted Watkinson, John Overnell, John Rayner, Percy Barnett, Ellis Roberts.
Front row from left Ken Handley, Bernard Wells, Sid Greenfield, Dennis Roberts, Peter Roberts.

Pulborough Football Club ~ 53

31-11-1951 vs Felpham

Pulborough were another team who came near to having to share the points. They met Felpham and it was only in the last 20 minutes that they were able to make any headway, they won by 3-1. They were as near being rattled as they have ever been, and after the game a Pulborough player confessed it was the team's hardest match for a couple of seasons. Felpham's ground was in terrible condition and both teams found that wing passes would suddenly stop half way in a pool of water. As a result, close football was played, and for most of the match it looked as if the home team was going to get the better of it. Skipper Goodrum opened the score, and at half-time the score was 1-0 to Felpham. Pulborough equalised early in the second half and then fortunes swayed for the next half hour. Goals might come to either side at any minute and finally they did, to Pulborough. A quick goal putting them in the lead was followed by another to consolidate their position and Felpham could do nothing about it in the time remaining. Scorers for Pulborough were P. Roberts 2 and B. Wells 1.

Sussex League Benevolent Cup and reached the semi-final of the Sussex Intermediate Cup. The Treasurer reported a balance of £39-19-10, due to a most generous gift of £65 from the Pulborough Football Supporters Club. After much discussion it was proposed and carried that the annual subscription of the players was discontinued and that instead each player pay 1/- for every game that he played in. The fare for supporters travelling on the club's coach was to be 2/6. The formation of a second XI was discussed and it was decided that if Mr T. Cousins could produce a list of names for the Secretary, he was instructed to call a meeting to see what could be done about getting them into a league:

Committee meeting held on 26th July 1951. The Chairman read a list of names given to him by Mr T. Cousins, who were willing to play for the second XI and they were entered into the Horsham & District League Division 2. Mr R. Elliott was elected as Captain and Mr D. Heasman was elected as Vice-Captain. The Secretary stated that he had received a cheque for £8 from the Thakeham Tiles Sports Club, which had now disbanded and had shared out their assets to the Storrington, West Chiltington and Pulborough Football Clubs. It was decided that the visiting teams should still use the headquarters, The Arun Hotel, for changing, until facilities could be arranged at the pavilion on the ground.

This was the first season that I was able to get the results and the goal scorers for both sides. The first XI kicked off their League programme with a home match against Lavant on 8th September 1951, which resulted in a 7-1 victory. The team that day was: Heather, Veverines, Rayner, Purnell, Watkinson, Ovenell, Harrison, Greenfield, Wells, Roberts D, Roberts P.

The second XI played their first game 18th September 1951 away to Twineham and lost 3-5. The team was: Clark, Rowland, Sullivan, Parrish, Elliott R, Aves, Cousins, Stentiford, Scutt, Cooper, Heasman.

The first XI went on a fantastic run, unbeaten for 16 games, before losing to a very strong Arundel A side. Once again there is no point in going through all the games here, as there are reports on many of the matches included. As you read through the games you realise just how good the team was. They scored an amazing number of goals and the defence was very sound, with only 32 goals conceded that season.

Having spoken to some of the men who played during that era, they told me why they thought the team was so good. The team spirit was excellent and the players got on well both on and off the pitch. They said that everyone in the side was two-footed, especially the forwards, which is very unusual. There are many professional players who do not have the skill to do this. In the three seasons that the side was in the West Sussex League they were completely dominant, winning the Championship every year against sides that were meant to be superior to them. The standard of football was very high, far better than anything I have seen from a Pulborough side for many years. The team enjoyed tremendous support, often there would be hundreds of people watching. Their best result of the season was probably against Horsham Reserves in the semi-final of the Sussex Intermediate Cup. Nobody outside Pulborough gave us a chance, the Horsham team were one of the best in the county, with several of their players having played at senior level, so beating them by 4 goals to 2 was a great achievement. PFC played Hollington in the final, but they were no match for 'The Robins', who won 5-0.

The second XI unfortunately continued to struggle, but it was to their credit that they stayed together and it gave younger players a chance to come into the side, some of whom would go on to play for the first XI in the coming years. At a committee meeting 8th October 1951, Mr K. Handley stated that he was willing to play for the second XI and coach them on the field of play. The offer was accepted and he went on to be of great assistance to the team, especially the younger players. The side changed quite considerably during the season from the side that started, only 4 original players being in the side that finished the season. The side that played in the last game of the season was: Scutt, Lewis, Greenfield, Parrish, Purnell, Puttock, Elliott, Maybee, Handley, Carter, Heasman, but everyone who played for the Seconds gave something to the team.

An interesting committee meeting was held on 25th February 1952. The Secretary gave a report on the meeting he had attended at Brighton on 16th February 1952 concerning the club's application to the 2nd Division of the Sussex County League for season 1952/53. He stated that only one division was being formed and that the club had to verify their application by March 1st. This he was

23-2-1952
Intermediate Cup Semi-Final
Pulborough 4 Horsham Res 2

Pulborough took another step towards achieving a long standing ambition at Littlehampton Sports Ground on Saturday when they beat Horsham Reserves 4-2 in the semi-final of the Sussex Intermediate Cup. The other semi-finalists were Hollington, who beat Uckfield on Saturday, which gives the West Sussex team a better chance than ever of winning the cup this season.

Horsham and Pulborough have met on several occasions in friendly encounters and this was the first time Pulborough finished on the winning end. It seemed that Horsham had expected a much easier game in view of their previous victories, the most recent of which they scored on Boxing Day.

After an even 15 minutes Pulborough scored first, but it did not take their opponents long to equalize and the game remained even until just before the interval when Pulborough scored their second goal. Horsham were again on level terms ten minutes after the restart, but by that time they were tiring rapidly and the West Sussex League team netted two further goals to put the result beyond doubt. Pulborough's scorers were Peter Roberts, Peter Harrison, A. Frogley and D. Roberts.

Pulborough Intermediate Cup Final
Pulborough 5 Hollington United 0

Pulborough, who reached the final with a 41-7 goal average, were on top throughout this Sussex Intermediate Cup final at Horsham on Easter Monday morning. They used their speedy wingers well, repeatedly turning defence into attack with a long clearance and a quick rush downfield. Hollington could find no answer to these tactics.

Wells opened up the scoring after eight minutes with a shot into the corner of the net after beating the Hollington keeper to the ball. Five minutes before half-time, Harrison added a second with a 15-yard drive.

A few minutes after the restart, Wells robbed a defender in the penalty area and scored the third, and after 34 minutes Handley's hard shot was fumbled by the Hollington goalkeeper and allowed to pass into the net. One minute from time Harrison added the fifth, following a cross from the left.

Pulborough R Heather, J Veverines, J Rayner, S Greenfield, E Watkinson, J Cornell, R Harrison, K Handley, B Wells, D Roberts, P Roberts.

Hollington A Read, H Hollamby, E Saxby, G Lee, E Robins, K Neatby, E Pepper, R Wallace, A Breeds, D Boots, H Mewitt.

30-4-1952 vs Rustington

Pulborough had to play all out against a strong Rustington side before winning 5-3 on Wednesday. The score was 2-2 at half time, and 3-3 until the last 20 minutes, when Pulborough's great strength in attack forced 2 goals. Goals were scored by K. Handley 2 S. Greenfield 1 P. Roberts 1 B. Wells 1.

instructed to do. I have included this next piece simply because it was unusual for someone to be sent off in those days:

Committee meeting 10-03-1952 : After hearing a report from all members who were at Petworth on 08.03.1952 and who saw the incident which resulted in the referee Mr Atfield sending R. Heather, the Pulborough goalkeeper off the field in the second half. It was decided that the Secretary should call a Committee meeting, which he thought advisable after he had received the referee's report on the incident. He was also instructed to get a report from the goalkeeper R. Heather and also that he and J. Veverines and J. Rayner should also be requested to attend to give their version of the incident. This was to be done to give the Club some guidance as to how to report to the S.C.F.A. in their report.

It was always going to be a difficult season, how were the team going to adapt to a much higher standard of football? Could some of the older players raise their game to an even level or had they reached their peak? Was everyone able to take time away from work to make long journeys, when the coach had to leave Pulborough by midday? These questions would be answered in the coming months.

In the first game of the season, the following team was selected to play Hastings Rangers away, on Saturday 20th September 1952, K.O. 3-15pm: R. Heather, S. Brown, J. Rayner, G. Purnell, E. Watkinson, J. Ovenell, P. Harrison, A. Spain, B. Wells, D. Roberts, P. Roberts. R. Maybee was selected as reserve to travel. It had been proposed by P. Barnett, seconded by J. Elliott that for long distance away games, a reserve be elected to travel with the team. The result was a defeat by 4 goals to 1, our first goal in the County League being scored by B. Wells.

3-5-1952
Pulborough 11 Rustington 0
WONDERFUL RECORD

The game between Pulborough and Rustington attracted the largest crowd ever to watch a match on the ground, but play was disappointing. Rustington tried hard but they never had even a slight hope of putting the Pulborough football machine out of gear. Pulborough scored 6 in the first half and 5 in the second and might have added a dozen more. Goals came from B. Wells (6), D. Roberts (3), K. Handley & P. Harrison.

Before passing on from Pulborough's triumphs it is worth pausing to examine their wonderful record. This season they have taken part in a total of 35 games of all kinds, winning 28, drawing 3, losing 4 and scoring 202 goals with only 44 against. Outside-left P. Roberts set up an individual record by having scored 69 goals. Centre-forward B. Wells follows with 59 and outside-right P. Harrison has 38 to his credit. In the three years Pulborough have been in the league the figures make even more interesting reading and are league games only. Played 70 Won 53 Drawn 7 Lost 10, Goals for 326, Goals against 113.

Our first home match was against Hastings and St. Leonard's on 4th October 1952, which was won by 7 goals to 3, scorers D. Roberts 2, P. Roberts 2, P. Harrison 1, A. Smith 1, A. Spain 1. During the season the team suffered three heavy defeats: against Goldstone 2-12, Wigmore Athletic 0-10 and Sidley United 1-7. The rest of the season they more than held their own and had some very good results; there were notable wins against Moulsecoomb Rovers 5-1, Cuckfield 5-2 (a hat-trick for G. Wills), Three Bridges 7-3 and Hove White Rovers 9-4 (with P. Roberts scoring 4). In their first season in senior football the side should be very happy with the way they had performed. Their record was P22 W7 D5 L10 GF64, GA80 19pts, finishing 9th in the league.

A couple of incidents occurred during the County League years made me smile...

The stranded player

I heard two versions of this incident, one from a teammate and the other from the player's wife.

The teammate recalled that the team had played away at either Rye or Hastings and, on the return journey, the coach had stopped in Lewes for fish and chips. Thinking that everybody was on the coach, they drove off, but two or three miles down the road someone realised that player X was missing. The driver was informed, but refused to turn back, so the coach continued on to Pulborough, leaving the player stranded in Lewes.

According to his wife, player X was not selected for the game, but travelled on the coach and was dropped off in Lewes so that he could go and buy a new pair of shoes. She did not know whose fault it was that her husband was not picked up on the return journey. Did the driver forget, or was player X not at the designated pick-up point?

Whichever version is correct, the player was left stranded in Lewes.

He had arranged to meet his wife in the Five Bells Inn when he returned and on her arrival at the pub at the appointed hour in the evening she spied two of the team players sitting having a drink and asked where her husband was. Rather sheepishly, they informed her that he was stranded in Lewes. She stayed on and, just before closing time, in walked her husband, who was not in the best of moods. Lewes is not the easiest place to get back to Pulborough from and he had needed to use the train, bus and Shanks's Pony to complete his return journey.

The assaulted linesman

The other incident was a rather unsavoury one and an embarrassment for the Club. Although it did not occur in the County League, it happened during that period. At a committee meeting on 5th January 1953, the Secretary read a letter from the SCFA, asking for a report about the alleged striking of a Petworth linesman by a Pulborough supporter after a West Sussex League match, played at Petworth between the two teams, had finished.

At a subsequent committee meeting on 12th January 1953, the Secretary read a letter from the SCFA which said that the Club had been fined 10 shillings (50p) for the striking of the Petworth linesman by a Pulborough supporter on 27th January 1953.

It made me smile because I could not believe that anyone would be stupid enough to do that! It only takes one idiot to give your Club a bad reputation.

Pulborough FC 1ˢᵗ XI before a Sussex Senior Cup match at Bexhill on Saturday, 6ᵗʰ November, 1954
back row left to right Percy Barnett, John Rayner, Tony Spain, Charlie Smith,
Bill Holman, Jack Veverines, Peter Chapman, Charlie Parsons.
Front row left to right Peter Harrison, Terry Funnell, Tony Frogley, Pat Ginnaw, Peter Roberts.

Pulborough FC 1955/56 *back row from left* Stan Poore (chairman), Peter Harrison, Malcolm Sargent,
Graham Loomes, Graham Mason, Peter Chapman, Nick Goodyer, Percy Barnett (linesman)
Front row from left Ron Maybee, Ken Handley, Tony Spain, Alan Puttock, Tony Leadbeatter.

Pulborough FC 1956/57 *back row from left* Stan Poore (chairman), John Rayner, Peter Chapman, Ron Maybee, George Burleston, George Carter, Alan Puttock, Percy Barnett. *Front row from left* Peter Harrison, Ken Handley, Tony Spain, Tony Leadbeatter, Mike Anscombe.

Pulborough FC at Petworth 1958 *Back row from left* Derek Spain, Ken Handley, Ron Maybee, Tom Bishop, George Burleston, John Rayner, Don Massey, Toby Greenfield.
Front row from left Peter Harrison, Tony Leadbeatter, Tony Spain, Mike Anscombe, Peter Chapman.

The following season 1953/54 was not much different from the previous one, with some heavy defeats but also some very good wins. Match results were hard to find, the only one I managed to get was a home game, when we played Three Bridges. The team had started to change, some of the 'old guard' were coming to the end of their careers and a few of the younger lads were being given the opportunity to play in the first XI. If finding the results was hard, it was not possible to get our goal scorers, apart from a couple of matches. At the end of the season the table was very similar to the previous year. P20 W7 D3 L10 GF52 GA77 17pts finishing 8th in the league.

Sadly the 1954/55 season was to be the end of our time in the County League. The club was struggling to put out their best XI and at times found it hard to get eleven players to away games. Although their league results were poor, they had some very good games in the cup competitions. In the FA Amateur Cup they were drawn to play against Arundel, who were in the County League Division 1, with nobody expecting anything but an easy win for Arundel, 'The Robins' beat them by 3 goals to 2. Scorers for Pulborough were T. Funnell 1, P. Harrison 1 and P. Roberts 1.

On 23rd October 1954 they played at home to Hastings Rangers in the Sussex Senior Cup and won 4-7. On 1st January 1955, in the Sussex County Invitation Cup, they beat Goldstone 6-1. Unfortunately, PFC were unable to continue in the competitions because we had to withdraw from the league. On March 16th 1955 it was disclosed that Pulborough had applied to leave the County League Division 2. In April it was approved and our record was removed.

Apart from having a hard time on the field, it was thought that the decision to leave the County League was a financial one. To run coaches to such places as Hastings and Rye was very costly and the club was finding it difficult to cope financially. Our venture into the higher echelon of Sussex Senior Football had come to an end. For a small village club like Pulborough to reach the level of playing senior football was a great achievement. Had the County League Division 2 been formed a few years earlier, the team would have been in their prime and I think they would have been more successful. The club had received great support from the villagers, hundreds of whom had come to watch their heroes play in their red shirts. Up to March 26th 1955 they had played 14 matches, won 1, drawn 2 and lost 11.

F. A. AMATEUR CUP
Saturday October 2nd 1954
BRIGHTON OLD GRAMMARIANS - v - PULBOROUGH.

BRIGHTON OLD GRAMMARIANS

D. Rover
(1)
G. Pelling   B. Nettleton
(2)   (3)
E. Guiton   D. Talbot   E. Shipp
(4)   (5)   (6)
M. Morris   B. Nunn   J. Galway   M. Dove   D. Marchant
(7)   (8)   (9)   (10)   (11)

REFEREE: A.G.Howard   (Horsham)
LINESMEN: J. Foster (Littlehampton)
          L. Howell (Midhurst).

P. Chapman   P. Roberts   T. Funnell   A.Frogley   P.Harrison
(11)   (10)   (9)   (8)   (7)
        P. Ginnaw   W. Holman   A. Spain
          (6)   (5)   (4)
            J. Rayner   J. Veverines.
              (3)   (2)
                  C. Smith
                    (1)

PULBOROUGH

We extend a very hearty welcome to Pulborough this afternoon and hope that their first visit to Brighton for many years will prove to be a very happy one.

Our visitors were members of the West Sussex Senior League until they joined the County League Division II, two years ago and a fortnight ago they unexpectedly knocked Arundel out of the F.A. Amateur Cup with a most creditable 3-2 victory.

We are expecting an exciting struggle today and if the game assumes the character of our match with Whitehawk, spectators will see a fine, sporting tussle.

N.B.:   At Greyhound Stadium next Saturday Oct. 9th County League Match between Brighton Old Grammarians and East Grinstead.

Players from 1946-1959

Laurie Larby was born in West Chiltington in 1920. He went to the local School, leaving in 1934 at the age of fourteen. He moved to Pulborough and started to work at the West Sussex Golf Club on the ground staff. During the war years he was in the Royal Navy and served on HMS *Ceres*. Laurie returned to the West Sussex Golf Club on leaving the Navy and became a green-keeper. On leaving the village, where he lived in Lower Street, he took up a post as Head Greenkeeper at Hambleton and then at Walton-on-Thames. He was a very fine golfer himself. Laurie first played for the Club in 1939. After the War he returned and started playing again in 1947. He made 131 appearances for 'The Robins'. For a goalkeeper he must have been one of the shortest to have played the game; he was only about five feet tall. Despite his lack of height, he was a very good keeper, a good shot stopper and brave. In the 1948/49 season he won a cup-winner's medal in the Horsham & District Senior Cup. In 1950/51 he won a winner's medal for the West Sussex League Benevolent Cup, the same year a medal for the side winning the West Sussex League. Laurie passed away in 1986.

Robert Heather (Bob) (28th Feb 1922 – 5th May 1991) was born in Sutton and went to School there; on leaving he went to work on the land at fourteen years of age. Bob, I believe, spent many years working for the Tupper family at Bignor. He was not called up, as he was a land worker; I was told this meant you did not have to enlist. He had two elder brothers who were in the Forces. Bob played for Petworth before joining us. He played against us in 1950/51 in the Final of the West Sussex League Benevolent Cup, which Pulborough won. The following season he signed for us. In the 1951/52 season the side won the Sussex Intermediate and also won the West Sussex League for the second time. Bob played in every game that season. He also played several times in County League Division Two. He played 44 games for the Club. He was well built and around six foot tall. He was very good in the air and a good all-round goalkeeper. He passed away in 1991 and is buried at Sutton.

Charlie Smith (Smudger) was born Loxwood in 1926. The son of the landlord of the Onslow Arms in Loxwood, he attended the local School before going to work for his father in the pub. He joined the RAF and was a rear gunner in Halifax and Wellington bomber aircraft. After the conflict he returned to work for his father. Charlie was a very good all-round sportsman, a good cricketer and an excellent darts player. Charlie transferred to us from Littlehampton FC, playing his first game on 8th November 1952 in the Sussex Senior Cup. He played 53 times for the Club and scored one goal when he played on the field. He was not that tall for a goalkeeper, but I was told he was one of the best keepers the Club ever had, very good at every aspect of goalkeeping. He was a bit of a character; he was part of the 'card school' going to away matches on the coach and used to keep a bottle of whisky in the back of the net. Sadly, he died from cancer at the age of 42. He is buried at Loxwood.

John Rayner was born in North Heath, on the outskirts of Pulborough, in 1927. He used to walk from there to attend St Mary's School in Pulborough. When he was about twelve years of age, he left to go to agricultural college in Hampshire. In 1945 he was called up for National Service; John did his two years as a Marine Commando. He then went back to agriculture. He spent a year at Wansey Farm in North Heath before going to work for Broomers Hill Farm in Shipley. John is still there, working part time. He made his debut for us on 6th September 1948 and was first choice as full back until he retired in 1958. He played 197 games for 'The Robins' and scored two goals. John was about six feet tall, blond and always played with a smile on his face. He was good in the air and a solid defender; very few wingers got the better of him. He won a Horsham & District Senior Charity Cup Winner's medal in 1948/49. He won three medals when the team won the West Sussex League three years in a row, 1949/50, 1950/51 and 1951/52. In 1951/52 he won a winner's medal for winning the Sussex Intermediate Cup. In the 1952/53 season the Club was in the Sussex County League Division Two; John played in every game. In the 1954/55 season he played for the West Sussex League side. John also played cricket and was a very good bar billiards player. He lives in Shipley.

Bernard Rowland (Bern) I was informed that he was born in Roffey. He later moved to live in Watersfield. Bern worked as an insurance agent for the Liverpool Victoria Company. He used to ride his motorcycle around the local villages to collect their premiums. He joined the Club at the start of the 1948/49 season. Bern was the First Team right back until 21st April 1951, when in the Final of the West Sussex League Benevolent Cup he sustained a bad injury after thirty-five minutes and was never able to play on the field again. Bern left the Club in 1952 but went on to play as a goalkeeper for his home village of Watersfield for the next ten years. He played 91 games and scored one goal for us; he was probably the finest right back in the Club's history. In the Horsham & District League he won a winner's medal in the Senior Charity Cup; he also represented the League side. In 1950-51 he won a winner's medal in the West Sussex League Benevolent Cup. In the 1949-50 and 1950-51 seasons he won medals when the Club won the West Sussex League Division 1 Championship. He also played for Horsham.

Ken Handley (18th September 1922 – 19th May 1991) was born and brought up in Gosport in Hampshire. At the age of fifteen he joined the Royal Scots Greys, in the Band Service. He later served with the 14th/20th Royal Hussars and spent time in India and the Middle East. He became a Staff Sergeant in the Army Physical Training Corps. In 1946 he moved from Catterick Army Training Camp to Barns Farm Camp in Washington, Sussex. He served twelve years in the Army before settling down in Pulborough. While in the Army he played with Joe Mercer. Ken started work for Greenfields of Storrington as an Upholsterer and loose interior man; he went on to start up his own business.

He made his debut for the Club on 29th August 1948; he was an inside forward or half back. Ken made 174 appearances and scored 60 goals. Apart from his football ability, Ken was probably the fittest man in the side. He could run all game and was also very vocal, encouraging the team. In the 1949-50 season Ken was in the side that won the West Sussex League title; in 1950-51 season he was in the team that won the West Sussex League Benevolent Cup Final. The side also won the West Sussex League for the second time. At the start of the 1951/52 season the second team was re-formed and Ken very kindly offered to play for and coach the side, so he could help the young side mature and improve. The Club accepted his offer. He played his last game for the Club in 1960.

He played for Rudgwick and also Billingshurst, where he became coach. Ken played on into his fifties and one of his biggest joys was playing in the same team as his son. Ken is buried at Wiggonholt Churchyard.

Dennis Bagley was born in Birmingham in 1922. He joined the Royal Navy and during the War served on the Arctic Convoy expeditions. He moved to Storrington and worked at Spiro Gills, then Marley Tiles and for Hall & Company until he retired. Dennis made his debut for the Club in 1946; he made 44 appearances for the Club, usually at half back. A tall, well-built player, good in the air and a strong tackler. He now lives in Cheshire.

Ted Hilton was a policeman. He joined the Club in 1946 and played 37 games for us. A tall man, strong in the air, he played as a full back, in the old Horsham & District League.

Ted Watkinson first played for 'The Robins' in September 1948 and retired in April 1953. He lived in Gay Street, where he had a smallholding. Ted often wore a cravat and was known as a gentleman. A big man, he was a centre half, a rock at the heart of our defence. He was part of the side that won three West Sussex League titles, a West Sussex Intermediate Cup, a West Sussex League Benevolent Cup and a Horsham & District Senior Cup. He also played in the Sussex County League for us.

William Holman (Bill) is thought to have lived in Mare Hill. He worked for Citrus Nursery and also in the building trade. He played 36 games, scoring one goal. A centre half, he was a tough uncompromising player. He played in the Sussex County League. He also played cricket for Parham.

Charles Booker (Charlie) was born in Pulborough in 1926. He did his National Service in the Army. He worked as an odd job man. He started playing for us in 1948. He made 23 appearances in the old Horsham & District League. He was an inside forward and a good all-round player.

Frederick Leadbeatter 31st October 1910 – 19th May 2004 He was known in the Club as Ernie. He was born in Chichester. Fred was a reservist serving with the 2nd Battalion 'Buffs', the East Kent Regiment. During the Second World War he saw action in North Africa and Palestine. While in the Army he played a good standard of football. He played with Stan Cullis. In the 1930s Fred was playing for Chichester. Fred made his debut for the Club on 22nd November 1947 against Storrington. He won a winner's medal in the old Horsham & District League Senior Charity Cup. He played his last game for us in September 1949. As with many others, the War years took away his best days in football. Fred stood over six feet and was of athletic build. He was a half back, he had a good vision and could play great passes.

Charles P. Barnett (Percy) was born in Wisborough Green on 22nd September 1914. He went to School on Petworth and then St Mary's School in Pulborough. He was brought up by his grandmother. On leaving School he went to work for Allfrey's, a local firm, as a plumber. He did his two year's national Service in the Royal Engineers and was called up again in 1945 for a clean-up campaign and spent time in Belgium. On leaving the Forces he went to work at Spiro Gills until he retired. During the 1930s he played for Codmore Hill FC. Percy joined 'The Robins' in 1939/40. He started playing again in 1946, finishing his playing days at the end of 1949, but on odd occasions he would turn out for the Club if short of players. He played in the County League side for us at the age of 39. He made 52 appearances for the Club. he was a tough-tackling full back who gave his opponents a hard time. Percy became the Club Secretary in 1948 until 1958. In 1958 he was elected onto the Council of the Sussex County Football Association. He was also on the Selection Committee for the West Sussex League Intermediate Side. He was later made a Life Member of the West Sussex League. He was a good bar billiards player and an umpire for the local cricket team. Percy was a great servant to Club and County. He passed away in 2004.

George Purnell (28th March 1916 – 11th October 1979) was born in the East End of London. His father was an engineer and after leaving school he also took up this trade. When Spiro Gills opened a workshop in Petworth with machinery brought form London, George, who was a brilliant engineer, came down to live in Petworth and work at Spiro Gills; I have been told that he played a part in setting up this new venture. Later on Spiro Gills moved to Pulborough and George went to work there and lived in Pulborough for many years.

He made his debut for the Club in September 1946 and finished his playing days in 1954. He made 167 appearances and scored two goals. He was a half back and a good all-round player,

someone who never gave up. In 1948 he won a winner's medal in the Horsham & District Senior Cup. He was part of the side that won the West Sussex League in 1949-50 and 1950-51. He was Captain of the second team in 1951-52. He was a very good golfer and a well-liked man.

Sidney Greenfield (Sid) was born in Lower Street, Pulborough in 1907. He went to the local St Mary's School and then onto Midhurst Grammar School. I have been informed that he was in the Army, but I was not able to confirm this. Sid worked at the local Post Office as a counter clerk and later for Spiro Gills. He signed on for 'The Robins' in 1923 as a junior. He played for West Chiltington in the 1932/33 and 1933/34 seasons when Pulborough did not have a side. The Club re-formed in 1934/35 and Sid came back to play for us. He was also Club Secretary from 1937 to 1939/40. He took on the role of Secretary & Treasurer in 1947/48 and 1948/49. Sid was Captain of the First XI from 1948 to 1952. He won a Cup winner's medal in 1948/49 in the Horsham & District League Senior Cup. He won a hat-trick of medals when the Club won the West Sussex League in 1949/50, 1950/51 and 1951/52. He won winner's medals for the West Sussex League Benevolent Cup in 1950/51 and the Sussex Intermediate Cup in 1951/52.

At the age of 46 Sid played some games in the County League Division Two. He was a half back, a superb player among a very fine group of players. He stood out, the complete player and driving force of the team. He played for the West Sussex League side. In his spare time he was leader of the Boy's Club. I was lucky enough to meet him in 2000, when there was a reunion. He was a gentleman and a very modest man.

Jack Veverines was born in Brighton in 1919 and died in 1985 from a heart attack. He went to School in Brighton. He had a very tough upbringing in his early years, then joined the Navy at a young age. He became a Petty Officer on a destroyer and spent time in Norway, North Africa and New York. After nine years he bought himself out and joined the Police Force in Brighton. He was then posted to other forces, including Pulborough. Jack joined the Club at the start of the 1951/52 season. He made 38 appearances for us, before being posted on by the Police Force. He was a big man, a hard uncompromising defender; he gave forwards a hard time, the Club's regular right back that season. He was in the side that won the Sussex

Intermediate Cup and the West Sussex League in 1951/52. He also played for the West Sussex Police side. Jack returned to live in Pulborough and became a Council member.

John Overnell joined the Club towards the end of the 1949-50 season. He was in the team that won the Sussex Intermediate Cup in 1951-52 and also the West Sussex League title. He was made the Captain of the side in the 1952-53 season, when the Club joined the County League. He left the Club at the end of the season, having played 61 times and scoring one goal. John was a half back, a very good all-round player. He went on to play for West Chiltington. John made his living as a Schoolteacher.

Peter Harrison was born in London Road, Pulborough in 1925. His family moved to Storrington in 1929 and he went to the local Primary School. After passing his exams he went to Steyning Grammar School. While at Steyning he was allowed to play for Storrington Boys' team in the Pulborough Boys' Cup. He won medals in 1936, 1937 and 1939. The medals were hall-marked solid silver. On leaving School he started work for Mr W Harwood at his munitions factory behind Sopers Cottages. In 1943 he joined the Merchant Navy, coming out in 1945. In 1948 Peter returned to live in Pulborough and still lives here today. Peter spent the rest of his working life at Spiro Gills, first on the shop floor and then in the office.

He played his first game for 'The Robins' on 11th October 1947 against Horsham YMCA. He soon established himself in the first team and played on the right wing. Peter was probably the finest two-footed winger the Club has seen. He had the ability to beat his man on the outside and deliver crosses for his team mates to score. He could also come inside the full back and score with his left foot across the goalkeeper. He played 259 games for the Club, scoring 125 goals, a great feat for a winger. In the 1948/49 season he won a winner's medal in the Horsham & District Senior Charity Cup. He also represented the League side in 1949.

He won winner's medals in 1949/50, 1950/51 and 1951/52 when the team won the West Sussex League three times in a row. In 1950/51 the West Sussex League Benevolent Cup was won and in 1951/52 the Sussex Intermediate Cup. Peter was put forward to play for Sussex. He was a regular for the side when 'The Robins' entered the County League. He played his last game for

the Club in December 1959. He finished his playing days with Amberley. Peter was also a very useful cricketer. In his spare time he played in a band, on the piano. His children and grandchildren are all musical.

Tony Frogley was born in Watersfield in 1923. He went to St Mary's School in Pulborough. He volunteered to join to the RAF and was accepted, even though he was only seventeen. He spent time in the Middle East. Apart from a short period working for Spiro Gills, he spent the rest of his working life as a policeman. Tony played his first game for the Club in October 1936, at the age of thirteen, while still at School. He played alongside Mr Alan Highes and Mr Trefor (Bill) Williams, who were teachers at St Mary's School. In those days he played at outside right. In September 1948 he came back to play for the Club again, making 112 appearances and scoring 18 goals. He played for the Horsham & District League in the 1948/49 season and won a winner's medal in the Horsham & District Senior Cup. In the 1949/50, 1950/51 and 1951/52 seasons he was in the team that won the West Sussex League titles. Tony was in the teams that won the West Sussex League Benevolent Cup in 1950/51 and the Sussex Intermediate Cup in 1951/52. He was an inside forward or centre forward, not a great goal-scorer, but he was a hard and aggressive player who put defenders under pressure and a good team player. He also played for Bognor. Tony was a very fine cricketer; after playing for Pulborough against a Sussex XI he was asked by Patsy Hendren if he would like to join Sussex, but he turned down the offer. He was a fast bowler and on two occasions took 10 wickets for 12 runs. He played for Watersfield and Baskingstoke. Tony played football for the Police side. He now lives in North Bersted.

Bernard Wells (Bern) was born in Reading in 1921 and went to School there. He moved down to Sutton, near Pulborough, in the early 1940s. In 1939 he joined the RAF and was stationed in Bedford. He spent four years in India and the North-West Frontier. While in the RAF he won some medals playing for his squadron. After the War he came to live in Pulborough, residing in Stopham Road. Bern was a painter and decorator and worked for a while in the local builders, Allfrey's, before going as a self-employed man. Bern joined Pulborough in 1950 and played his first game against Billingshurst in a friendly on 6th September 1950. He quickly became a regular in the side. He sometimes played as an inside forward, but was mainly a centre forward. He was a prolific scorer for the side, a natural, always in the right position to finish off moves created by his team mates; he could also create chances for himself. In his first season, 1950/51, he netted 38 times, including scoring 9 goals in one match. When the Club entered the County League Division Two in 1952/53, he scored 22 goals, in a higher level of football. He scored 90 goals in 118 appearances, a great record. In 1950/51 and 1951/52 he was in the side that won the West Sussex League titles. He won winner's medals when the Club won the West Sussex League Benevolent Cup in 1950/51 and in 1951/52 they were winners of the Sussex Intermediate Cup. Bern played a few games for Petworth. He was a good all-round sportsman; he played cricket and tennis and became a good golfer. He passed away in 2012.

Dennis Roberts was born in Leatherhead in 1921. His godfather was Lord Beaverbrook. I could not find anything about his early life. Dennis enlisted in the Army and during the War years was in the 8th Army Tank Corps (the Desert Rats). He was captured and taken prisoner and interned in Italy. He managed to escape and returned to England; after a few months he returned to his unit. Dennis came to Sussex after the War and lived at Browns Hall in Stopham, before going to live at Pallingham Lock. Food was rationed after the War but Dennis made a living as a rabbit catcher.

Dennis joined the Club in 1946 and played his first game against West Chiltington on 14th September 1946. He was an inside forward, but he did play on the wing and sometimes at centre forward. He was a hard and aggressive player who liked to upset the opposition and could also have a moan at his own side on occasions. He scored 45 goals and made 246 appearances for the Club. In the 1948/49 season in the Horsham & District Senior Cup he got a winner's medal. In the same year he represented the League side. Dennis was in the side that won the West Sussex League three times in a row in 1949/50, 1950/51 and 1951/52. He also won winner's medals in the West Sussex League Benevolent Cup in 1950/51 and the Sussex Intermediate Cup. Dennis was a good bar billiards player and played for the Arun Hotel team. Sadly, he passed away in 1976, at the young age of 55.

Peter Roberts, brother of Dennis, was born in Sunningdale, Berkshire in 1920. I could find nothing about his early life. He was living in Berkshire when he was called up. He served in the 8th Army Tank Corps ('The Desert Rats') during the War years. He came to live in Stopham after the War, at Browns Hall, before moving to Pallingham Lock. Peter made his living as a rabbit catcher. He made his debut for 'The Robins' on 14th September 1946 against West Chiltington in a friendly. In the 1947/48 season he was Captain of the side. Peter won three winner's medals when the side won the West Sussex League in 1950/51, 1951/52 and 1952/53. In the 1950/51 season the side won the West Sussex League Benevolent Cup and the following season won the Sussex Intermediate Cup. Peter played for the West Sussex League side. In the 1948/49 season he played for Horsham FC. During the 1948/49 season he played for a Horsham side against the Horsham & District League side, playing against his brother, Dennis. Peter was a flying machine, probably the fastest player in the West Sussex League. He played wide left, but also played at centre forward. His record of scoring 136 goals in 246 games speaks for itself. When he was playing senior football at Horsham he was a regular in the side, scoring his share of goals. Even senior players found it hard to cope with his pace. He passed away in 1990.

George Carter (27th July 1923 – 14th April 1990) was born in Droxford, Hampshire and went to School in Soberton. After leaving School he worked at a golf course. George was a volunteer and joined the Royal Navy in 1941. He was on the HMS Collingwood, a land ship, before serving on HMS *Southern Prince*, HMS *Victory* and HMS *Zetland*, which were minelayers. He then went on to serve on a destroyer. He left the Royal Navy in 1948 and on leaving went to work at Spiro Gills, where he stayed until retiring. In 1948 he was living at Lower Jordans in Gay Street. George made his debut for the Club on 3rd September 1949 against Bury for the second team. His first team debut was against Petworth on 24th September 1949. He got a winner's medal in the 1949/50 season when the side won the West Sussex League title. He was tall and slim, very good in the air and in his early days he played as a forward. He later played at centre half and on the odd occasion as a goalkeeper. He scored 23 goals in 80 games for the Club.

Tony Spain was born on 20th March 1932 in Brighton. He moved to Pulborough when he was about three years old. He went to the local St

Mary's School, leaving when fourteen years old. On leaving School he did a four-year apprenticeship as a carpet layer, working for Greenfields in Storrington. From 1950 he did his two years' National Service in the RAF. He then went back to Greenfields for one year, before going to work at Spiro Gills for the rest of his working life. Tony made his debut for the Club against Bury on 3rd September 1949 in the Horsham & District League. He made his first-team debut against Midhurst in a friendly on 27th September 1952. He played in the Club's County League days and was a regular for many years. Up to 1960 he played 135 games, scoring three times. He went on to play many more games for the Club, but some of the records were lost, so I am not able to give his actual figures. Tony played his last game for 'The Robins' in October 1966. He played as an inside forward or half back, a very fine all-round player who could run all day. He played for the West Sussex League XI on more than one occasion. He was a good cricketer and a good athlete.

Alan Smith was born 15th December 1930 in Rackham. He went to School in Rackham and then Midhurst Grammar School. On leaving School he did two years' National Service in the Army, based in Shropshire. Alan was a fine athlete, loved running and ran in the British Army Cross-Country Championship with Chris Chataway. After National Service, Alan went to work in the office for Spiro Gills. He became sales manager and then a Director. He continued with his running and ran for the Worthing Harriers. He played his first game for the Club against Midhurst in a friendly on 27th September 1952. He played a lot of games in the County League Division Two and then in the West Sussex League. He left the Club in September 1960, having played 66 times for us and scoring 10 goals. He played in a number of positions: inside forward, half back, centre half and even left back; a very fit player and a good player in any position. Alan played for Arundel and also Amberley. He passed away in 2001.

Peter Chapman (14th September 1926 – 19th June 2003) was born in Worthing. He was brought up by his grandparents. From the age of eleven he was living with a family from Arundel. Peter went to School in Arundel, leaving when he was fourteen. He started work as a telegram boy for the Post Office; he then went to David Hilliard at the shipyard. In 1944 he was called up for War

Service, with the Royal Army Medical Corps. He was demobbed in 1948 but, unable to settle, went back and served another four years. In 1952 he went to work at Spiro Gills. He retired in 1963. Peter joined 'The Robins' in 1954 and retired from playing in 1972, at the age of 46. He was a versatile man, playing in many positions, from goalkeeper to outside left. Peter had a great left foot and preferred playing down the left side. He was a regular first team player for many years and was a good influence to the younger players when he went into the second eleven in his later years. After retiring he served on the Committee. Before he joined us, he played for Arundel. Peter was a fine cricketer and was captain at one time.

George Burletson 19th September 1927 – 23rd November 2006 was born in Hackney, London, which was where he went to School. He was evacuated during the War years. From 1946 to 1948 he was in the Paratroops Regiment. In 1949 George came to live in West Chiltington. He worked for a local firm, Carvers, before going to work for Spiro Gills. After playing for West Chiltington he joined us in the 1954/55 season, retiring in 1963. George was tall and slim; he played at centre half and was very good in the air. There were also times when he played in goal. He played a few games in the County League days.

Pat Ginnaw (26th February 1930 – 21st February 2004) was born in Tidworth in Hampshire. He went to School in Ireland and Arundel. Pat did his National Service as a rifleman driver in 1st Battalion Rifle Brigade. On leaving the Army he worked at the vinery in Poling and then went to work at Spiro Gills and then to Lec Refrigeration in Bognor. Pat then set himself up as a driving instructor, the Arundel School of Motoring. He joined the Club in 1954 when they were in the County League Division Two. He played 31 games and scored 14 goals. He was a half back or inside forward, a very fine player who had a touch of class. Pat played for Brighton Reserves at one time and also for Arundel and Littlehampton. Pat was a good all-round sportsman, a good cricketer and a very fine runner. He was also a qualified table tennis coach.

Graham Mason was born in Rustington, 26th September 1935. His School days were spent at St Mary's in Pulborough and then at Midhurst Grammar. On leaving School he went into banking. Graham did his two years' National Service in the Army. He then resumed his career in banking and rose to be a branch manager. He made his debut for the Club against Nuthurst on 3rd November 1951 in the Horsham & District League. His first team debut was against Midhurst on 5th April 1952. He played when the Club was in the County League Division Two. Graham's last game for the Club was against Stopham Reserves on 12th December 1970. Although not the quickest, he was a versatile player, who read the game very well and was a good passer. He played at full back, half back and finished up at centre half. He was a very fine cricketer for Pulborough. He now lives in Southwater.

Stanley Poore was born in Salisbury 25th March 1921. On moving to Sussex, he lived at Bignor, where he worked for the Tupper family. He did his two years' National Service in the Army and had spells in Europe and Korea. Stan then started work at Spiro Gills, where he worked for many years. He made his debut for the Club on 14th December 1946 against Evening Institute in the Horsham & District League. Stan usually played in goal, but could also play on the wing and in the 1948-49 season he played at outside left in the Horsham & District League Senior Cup Final, which was a drawn match, Sussex Bricks and Pulborough keeping the Cup for six months each. In the 1950-51 season he was skipper of the 2nd XI, but had to give this up as he was recalled to the Forces. He returned to play for the Club in the mid-1950s and was a good player for 'The Robins'. In 1957 he was elected as Chairman of the Club and served for two years; he was on the Committee until 1962. He was an umpire for the local Club. Stan was a very fine dancer and won competitions.

Graham Loomes was born 2nd July 1935 in Plymouth, where he went to School. On coming to live in Pulborough, he attended Rydon County Secondary in Thakeham. On leaving School he started to work as a plumber at Allfrey's. He then did his National Service in the Royal Navy. Graham then went back to work at Allfrey's, before moving on to Lovell's and then Lanceley's. In 1967 he emigrated to Australia. He is still there today and lives in Perth. He made his debut for the Club against Storrington on 31st January 1953, as an inside forward. He played his last game in January 1967. After appearing for two games on the field, he spent the rest of his career as a goalkeeper, Graham played the odd game in the Club's County League days and then in the West Sussex League and the Horsham & District

League, he became a regular. He was a brave keeper, not afraid to come for balls on the ground or in the air, made some good saves but sometimes made silly errors. A good Club man.

Geoff Wills was the son of the Landlord of The Bridge pub in Houghton. He made his debut on 1st November 1952 against Moulsecombe Rovers in the County League Division Two. He played 19 games for the Club, scoring 14 goals. Geoff was an inside forward or a centre forward. A tall man, he was a very good all-round player. He played for Arundel and also Amberley. He was an excellent cricketer and it was thought that he played for the Sussex Second Eleven. He now lives in Jersey, but retains a home in Arundel.

Derek Heasman was born in Watersfield 18th July 1933. He went to St Mary's School in Pulborough and then to Rydon County Secondary. He started work at Walter Wood's agriculture firm. Derek then did his National Service with the Army; he was with the REME. After his two years with them, he went back to work at Walter Wood's. After a short time he went to work at Spiro Gills, where he stayed until retiring. Derek made his debut for the Club on 6th September 1950 in a friendly against Billingshurst. He went on to make 117 appearances and scored 34 goals. He played his last game on 2nd September 1961. He played a few games when the Club was in the County League Division Two and then in the West Sussex League and the Horsham & District League. Derek had a good left foot and in his early days was usually at outside left or left half and sometimes at centre forward and scored his share of goals. He later moved to play at left back. He still lives in the village.

Trevor Cousins was born 29th September 1932 in Pulborough. He went to the local St Mary's School and then to Midhurst Grammar, before going on to Brighton Technical College. He started work at local firm W. Allfrey's as an apprentice surveyor. Trevor then did his two years' National Service in the RAF. He returned to work at Allfrey's, before going to Lovell's and then on to Waring's, where he became a Director of the company. Trevor built his own house in Gay Street, where he still lives. He played his first game for the Club on 1st April 1950 against Lintott's and made his First XI debut on 1st November 1952, against Moulsecoombe Rovers in the County League Division Two. He made his last appearance on 4th March 1961. Trevor was a forward; in his early years he was on the right wing and he then played at centre forward, where he scored his share of goals. He was also a very good cricketer.

Terry Funnell was born in Storrington 12th May 1937. He went to the local Storrington Primary School and then on to Rydon County Secondary School. On leaving School he started to work for his family's firm, Funnell's Furnishings. He stayed there until retiring. It was thought that he did his National Service, but I cannot confirm this. Terry joined 'The Robins' in 1954 when the Club was in the County League Division Two. He scored 22 goals and made 42 appearances. He was a fine all-round player. Terry also played for Storrington and Wigmore Athletic. He was also a very good cricketer. He now lives in Cyprus.

Alan Puttock was born in Hardham 3rd September 1935. He went to St Mary's School in Pulborough and then to Rydon County Secondary. On leaving there he started work in the plumbing department at Cordery's. He then went on to work at Spiro Gills for many years, starting off as an apprentice welder. He also worked for Marley Tiles and Tesla Engineering. Alan did his National Service in the Army with the Royal Artillery and was based in Shropshire. Alan made his debut for the Club against Kirdford on 29th September 1951 in the old Horsham & District League. He played two or three times in the County League Division Two. He gave up playing in 1968. Alan was a half back, a good all-round player. He was Captain of the Second XI in 1961-62. He still lives in the village and is a keen fisherman.

John Scutt was born 16th January 1931 in Pulborough and went to the local St. Mary's School. On leaving at fourteen he went to work for Padfield Dairies on the milk round. He did his National Service in the Army in the Royal Engineers, in Farnborough. After being demobbed he went to work at Spiro Gills and finished his working life at Corrall's. John made his debut for the Club on 18th September 1951 against Twineham in the Horsham & District League; he played at centre forward. His First XI debut as against Turners Hill on 25th October 1952 in the County League Division Two; he was now playing in goal. John was always very enthusiastic and played to enjoy himself, a very capable goalkeeper. He now lives in Storrington.

Ron Maybee 19th March 1928 – 27th November 2006. He was born in Billingshurst. Ron went to North Heath School and left when he was fourteen. He started work at a brickworks in Gay Street, before going on to a farm for Mr Ayres. After a few years, he became a self-employed builder and did this until he retired. Ron did not have to do his National Service, because he was a land worker. He made his first appearance for us against Slinfold on 1st October 1949 in the Horsham & District League. In the 1950/51 season, as we did not have a second eleven, Ron played for Billingshurst. He returned to play for us the next season. He made his First XI debut against Wigmore Athletic on 6th December 1952 in the County League Division Two. In his early days he played in the forward line, before ending up as a full back. He was Captain of the First XI at one time. Ron was stocky and strong; he scored his share of goals when playing up front and when he became a full back he made this position his own for several seasons; he was a very fine player. Ron played for the West Sussex League side. He was a good cricketer, turning out for the local team.

Jack Parrish was born in Sutton, Surrey, in 1926. He came to Sussex and went to School in Thakeham. On leaving School he went into horticulture. He then became manager of Mason's Nursery. On joining the Army he spent time serving in Egypt. His last employment was working for the Southern Water Board. He lived in a house called Oddstones. Part of his land was where Pulborough FC played; it was then called Sopers Meadow. Jack made his debut on 18th September 1951 against Twineham in the Horsham & District League. His First XI debut was against Turners Hill on 25th October 1952 in the County League Division Two. Jack was not the biggest, but he was a quick and skilful player, who played as an inside forward, or half back. Jack passed away in 2006. He scored 3 goals and played 59 times.

Eddie Blake was born 26th September 1937 in Rackham. He went to Amberley School and then to Rydon County Secondary in Thakeham. He started work for the Parham Estate as a stonemason. In 1955 he joined the Army and served for three years in the Royal Artillery. On leaving the Forces, he returned to the Parham Estate, where he spent the rest of his working life. Eddie was not with the Club for long; he only played 23 times, but he did play when the Club was in the County League Division Two. He was a bustling centre forward who put defenders under pressure, He played for Amberley, Arundel and Littlehampton. Eddie later became a referee, a very good one. He now lives in Storrington.

Fred Clarke (Nobby) (2nd September 1927 – 15th January 2010) was born in Chichester. Nobby went to School in Chichester and then went to North Heath and on to West Chiltington, before going on to Steyning Grammar School. On leaving there he started work at Harwood's Garage. He then went on to Gray & Rowsell and then to Watersfield Garage and on to Tripp Hill Garage. He finished up back at Harwood's, where he first started. He did his National Service in the Army. He joined the Club in the early 1950s, playing 39 times. Fred was a big man; he could play a full back or centre half, a good defender. He played a few times in the County League days. He played football for Watersfield and cricket for Petworth.

J. Ansell played in 13 occasions for the side in 1952/53, when the team were in the County League Division Two.

George Hampshire was a West Chiltington man, who went on to play senior football for Horsham and Worthing. He was a very talented player. George only played 4 games for us, towards the end of his career. He also played for his home Club, West Chiltington.

Albert Greenfield (John) was born 15th June 1929 in Pulborough. He went to the local St Mary's School. He left School when 14 years of age and worked as a messenger boy at the local Post Office. John did his National Service in the Army, with the RASA and spent time in Singapore. He returned to work as a postman in the village, before going to work for Spiro Gills as a welder for many years. John played 64 times for the Club, scoring 1 goal. He played a few times in the County League side. Over 6ft tall and slim, he could play at full back or centre half; he was a very good all-round player. He also played for West Chiltington, for one season. He lives in the Worthing area.

Don Macey was born in Nutbourne, on the outskirts of Pulborough, on 10th October 1937. He attended North Heath School, before going on to Midhurst Grammar School. Don went into the Civil Service on leaving Midhurst and into the Prison Service. Don did his National Service on the RAF. He then returned to work for the Prison Service, on the administration side. Owing to his work commitments he only played 33 games for the Club, scoring 30 goals, which was a great record. Don played on the wing, but was usually found playing at centre forward. Don was very quick, with a powerful shot and good in the air. He joined the Club as a fifteen-year-old and was put straight into the first team, but he found it tough for a young lad and went into the Second XI. In 2007, when I had a reunion, Don came all the way from Yorkshire, where he now lives, to attend. It was nice to see him after so many years.

5th September 1952:
The Pulborough F.C. supporters Club are holding a general meeting this evening in the Five Bells Inn Pulborough to discuss ways and means of raising money for the coming season. Mr J. Elliott will preside. The local football Club have won the League for 3 years running and are very proud of this record. They have now entered the County League, which will entail a lot of travelling and it is for this purpose the extra funds will be required.

More Match Reports from the 1950s

8-12-1951 vs Petworth

A wind which reached gale force with driving rain and ankle deep mud caused the referee to abandon the game between Petworth and Pulborough in the second half. Petworth were leading 2-0 at the time and the official's decision brought cries of protest from the home supporters. But the Petworth players had no real objection. They, like Pulborough, were on the verge of collapse. Just before the game was abandoned, the referee was knocked unconscious when a strong drive from a Pulborough player struck him in the back.

15-12-1951 vs Chichester

Pulborough came to Chichester with a hundred per cent record but had it dented by the City team who held them to a 1-1 draw, the first draw for either team this season. Pulborough are now the 'Aunt Sally' of the league and Chichester almost gained the distinction of being the first team to beat them this season. The home team had most of the play in the first half with every member giving of his best, Teamwork and team spirit gave them a temporary edge over Pulborough and midway through Dowling scored to put them ahead. Better shooting would have given the Chichester lads a more convincing lead but they missed several chances and were only one goal ahead at the interval. Pulborough missed an easy chance to equalise when their left winger broke through and had only the goalkeeper to beat from the penalty area but he shot wide. Then, 8 minutes before time, P. Roberts broke away and scored, beating the keeper as he came out. On level terms, the visitors improved tremendously and had Chichester extremely shaky in the last five minutes, but there was no further score.

22-12-1951 vs Storrington

When Pulborough played host to local rivals Storrington on Saturday it proved to be a non-event. Storrington posed no problems for the home team, Pulborough winning by 11-1. Goals for the home team came from P. Roberts 5 B. Wells 3 A. Frogley 1 P. Harrison 1 and D. Roberts 1.

5-1-1952 vs Chichester A

After holding Pulborough to a draw in Priory Park earlier in the season, Chichester A travelled for the return game with high hopes of doing even better. But they were sadly disillusioned, being beaten 6-1. Starting confidently, the City broke through the defence to score first – as so many other teams have done against Pulborough – centre-forward Millier banging home a well-placed pass from Easton on the right wing. But they were not given another chance to repeat the performance. Pulborough settled down to work and held a 2-1 lead when the teams changed round. They were complete masters in the second half; they added another 4 goals and it might have been double that figure but for sterling work by Norgate at centre half. Pulborough scorers. Harrison 2 Wells 2 Greenfield 1 P. Roberts 1.

19-1-1952 vs Petworth

When Pulborough beat Petworth they came right back to form with a bang. When last they met, Pulborough were losing 2-0 when the game was abandoned and Petworth supporters promise of a real beating next time did not materialise. Petworth's keeper Busby played a grand game and was in no way to blame for the shots which went past him. All ten were better than average. After 15 minutes Petworth let the first goal through and from then on they were completely outclassed. All the Pulborough forwards scored. Frogley 3, P. Roberts 3, Harrison 2, D. Roberts 1, Wells 1.

26-1-1952 vs Rye

Pulborough won their way to the Semi-Final of the Sussex Intermediate Cup for the second year in succession by beating Rye United. Last year they were eliminated by West Hove but are considered to stand a much better chance this time. Watched by some of the foremost officials of the County Football Association, Pulborough made a promising start and bombarded the Rye goal for most of the first half. They scored 3 goals in the first 20 minutes and two of their shots bounced back into play from the upright. Rye reduced the arrears when their left winger broke away, raced round the defence and gave the ball to the inside right, who scored. The United deserved another goal after the interval when they made frequent raids on the Pulborough goal, but they had no luck and the home side added a fourth. Pulborough scorers P. Roberts 2, Harrison 1, Wells 1.

2-2-1952 vs Littlehampton A

Littlehampton A played a brainy but somewhat dull game against Pulborough and had the distinction of holding their opponents to a 1-1 draw. For 15 minutes the game was like most other matches, with fortune swaying one way and then the other. Then Littlehampton scored a surprise goal and settled down in their own half for the rest of the game. From that point Pulborough had all the play but with backs, half-backs and even forwards packing the Littlehampton goal, they could not score. In the second half Littlehampton brought organised raids into the Pulborough half only twice, the remainder of play being centred round their goalmouth. 15 minutes from time, Pulborough equalised when Wells found space to shoot into the net to make the score even in an extremely one-sided game.

9-2-1952 vs Westbourne

Ever since they started chalking up victories over the teams in the top half of the table, Westbourne have been determined that they would not be overawed by Pulborough's reputation and would "have a crack", just as soon as the opportunity arose. They had the chance on Saturday when the teams were drawn to meet in the Cup and Westbourne won a hard game 4-3. It was one of the best games both teams had played this season and the football was well worthy of a cup-tie. Westbourne got away to a good start by pressing round the Pulborough goalmouth, but soon the cup holders forced them back and opened the score when B. Wells cracked in a sharp drive which was a goal all the way. By constant pressure Westbourne were on terms within five minutes, Macklin netting the equalizer

The same player scored another goal soon afterwards to give Westbourne a 2-1 lead at half-time. They resumed the attack with determination but Pulborough came back to the attack and P. Harrison equalized. Macklin completed his hat-trick to make the score 3-2 and Jefferies followed up quickly to make the gap even bigger before both teams went all out in a final struggle for supremacy. Pulborough's third goal

came from P. Roberts, with five minutes to go, but although they continued to play at top speed, they were unable to draw level.

16-2-1952 vs Littlehampton

Pulborough dominated the play against Littlehampton A to win 6-3, avenging their 1-1 draw of a few weeks ago. The game was fairly dull, with Littlehampton scoring first and falling back to defend their own goal in the hope of holding their lead. But Pulborough were not to be beaten in the same manner as the previous game and soon started scoring, to hold a 4-1 lead at the interval. Littlehampton were a little more adventurous after the interval and scored a couple of goals. Pulborough, who never seemed to be playing as hard as they could, kept comfortably ahead to win a game in which there were few highlights. P. Harrison 2, P. Roberts 2, D. Roberts 1 and B. Wells 1 were the Pulborough scorers.

1-3-1952 vs Bognor

Bognor have never lost a game on Pulborough's ground and with this thought behind them and against the Pulborough players, the 'Rocks' ran up a comfortable 3-0 win. Pulborough had a large percentage of the play and were definitely unlucky on several occasions. Their goalkeeper had little more than a dozen shots during the whole game but he could not be blamed for the defeat as the shots which went past him were well worthy of goals. Each side was awarded a penalty but, while Bognor made use of theirs, Pulborough failed to score. The visiting keeper, Paislow, played the game of his life.

15-3-1952 vs Lavant

Lavant were lucky to beat Pulborough 2-1 but they took every chance and, for that alone, they deserve credit. It was one of those games when Pulborough spent most of their time in the Lavant half and kicked the ball everywhere except between the posts, while Lavant had only a few opportunities but made the most of them. Pulborough scored mid-way through the first half, when P. Roberts cracked in the ball from the wing. Persistent attacking failed to change the score at the interval. In the second half J. Millier broke away and beat Heather to equalize and towards the end Gratwick scrambled the ball over the line after a melee in the Pulborough goalmouth. This is the second time that little Lavant in their first year in West Sussex League football have acted as giant killers. The first time was in the early rounds of the Benevolent Cup, when they knocked out Midhurst.

5-4-1952 vs Midhurst

The tit-bit of the day was undoubtedly the struggle between Midhurst and Pulborough. It promised to be a thriller, both sides-played football that left the crowd gasping but they missed many chances, probably due to nervousness. The goals, four of them, were crammed into 10 pulsating minutes during the first half. For 25 minutes the teams swept from end to end and then P. Roberts gave the champions the lead. This was quickly wiped out by a Sebright header and the Rother Valley boys took the lead with another header by their outside right. Within minutes the champions had replied, this time through Wells. In the second half it was the home side who had a slight advantage, although whenever the Pulborough team were attacking they looked the more dangerous. Pulborough were lucky on one occasion when a shot was punched out from under the bar. Many Midhurst supporters considered that the ball was over the line but the referee waved play on.

12-4-1952 vs Portfield

Pulborough were back in devastating form when they visited Portfield. They scored 6 of their goals in 30 minutes, a reward for an all-out effort which had the Portfield defence floundering from the start. Pulborough were complete masters in the first half, and thoroughly deserved their 6-0 interval lead. In the second half, however, Portfield regained their composure and the visitors were given a much more difficult time, although they managed to score the only goal of the half. Scorers were P. Roberts 3, B. Wells 1, K. Handley 1, P. Harrison 1.

19-4-1952 vs Graylingwell

Pulborough gave their goal average a boost and kept it safely better than Midhurst's, with a 7-0 win over Graylingwell. After a quiet start Pulborough got 4 quick goals in the first half, then there was a quiet spell before they got another 3 after the interval.

23-4-1952 vs Storrington

Pulborough travelled to their near neighbours Storrington on Wednesday evening and came away with comfortable 3-0 win. Scorers were S. Greenfield 1, P. Roberts 1, B. Wells 1.

26-4-1952 vs Felpham

Pulborough moved up to second place in the table with their 5-1 win over Felpham. Two of their goals came from penalties so their victory was not as devastating as might have been expected. Largely responsible for keeping the score down was Smith, the young Felpham goalkeeper, whose performance brought praise from even the visiting team and their spectators. Felpham played hard and their midfield work was good, but in finishing they were not in the same class as Pulborough, whose goals were scored by S. Greenfield 2, P. Harrison 1, P. Roberts 1, B. Wells 1.

28-4-1952 vs Westbourne

Pulborough's victory over Westbourne on Monday evening was as important as it was decisive. The biggest crowd ever to pack the Westbourne ground attended the game to see Pulborough right on top of their greatest form, crush Westbourne completely. They played so well that they even surprised their own spectators and officials. Goals were scored by P. Harrison 3, K. Handley 1, D. Roberts 1, P. Roberts 1, B. Wells 1.

26-2-1955 – Cuckfield 5 Pulborough 1

Cuckfield collected another couple of useful points on Saturday, when they overcame Pulborough at Cuckfield. The visitors could only muster 10 men and in the second half, the visiting right back temporally retired owing to a knee injury. Pulborough struggled pluckily, but were outclassed and out manoeuvred. Only a fine display in goal by G. Loomes prevented Cuckfield from recording double figures. The home side's goals were netted by Rumble 2 J. Towner 1 Swain and Burleston, who had the misfortune to deflect the ball through his own goal after he had hobbled on to the field. Swain shot wide from a penalty for hand ball and Pulborough's consolation goal was netted by T. Funnell their centre forward.

Results 1946 – 1955

HDL1 1946/47

21-9-1946 [A] **Roffey** (D 6-6)

5-10-1946 [H] **Ockley** (L 4-9)

12-10-1946 [A] **Henfield** (W 5-1)

19-10-1946 SJC [H] **Billingshurst** (W 5-4)

2-11-1946 [H] **Horsham Trinity** (L 2-3)

9-11-1946 SJC [H] **Fernhurst** (L 1-11)

16-11-1946 HDLSCC [H] **Evening Institute** (L 3-10) only ten men

30-11-1946 [A] **Sussex Bricks** (L 1-8)

7-12-1946 [H] **Council United** (L 3-5) only ten players

14-12-1946 [H] **Evening Institute** (W 6-5)

4-1-1947 [H] **Slinfold** (L 1-9)

18-1-1947 [H] **Horsham YMCA** (W 5-3)

15-3-1947 [H] **Sussex Bricks** (Abandoned at half time; snow)

22-3-1947 [A] **Partridge Green** (L 2-7)

29-3-1947 [A] **Slinfold** (W 7-5)

7-4-1947 [H] **Henfield** (W 2-1)

12-4-1947 [A] **Horsham Trinity** (W 4-1)

26-4-1947 [H] **Partridge Green** (L 1-4)

3-5-1947 [H] **Roffey** (D 2-2)

10-5-1947 [A] **Horsham YMCA** (D 3-3)

17-5-1947 [A] **Ockley** (W 4-3)

24-5-1947 [A] **Council United** (Match cancelled)

P20 | W7 | D3 | L10 | GF58 | GA76 17pts | 7th

HDL1 1947/48

20-9-1947 [H] **Ockley** (W 4-2)

27-9-1947 [A] **Partridge Green** (W 3-1)

4-10-1947 S JC [A] **Graffham** (W 6-3)

11-10-1947 [H] **Horsham YMCA** (L 0-1)

18-10-1947 SJC [H] **Nuthurst** (W 3-1)

25-10-1947 HDLSCC [H] **Henfield** (L 3-5)

1-11-1947 [H] **Slinfold** (W 4-0)

8-11-1947 S JC [H] **Sidlesham** (L 1-2)

29-11-1947 [A] **Plaistow** (W 5-2)

6-12-1947 [A] **Sussex Bricks** (L 1-4)

13-12-1947 [A] **Henfield** (L 2-4)

20-12-1947 [A] **Slinfold** (W 4-1)

3-1-1948 [H] **TE Lintott** (W 17-1)

17-1-1948 [A] **Roffey** (W 4-0)

24-1-1948 [A] **Horsham YMCA** (W 13-2)

14-2-1948 [H] **103 HAA Regt** (W 4-3)

28-2-1948 [H] **Sussex Bricks** (L 1-2)

6-3-1948 A [H] **TE Lintott** (W 8-3)

13-3-1948 [H] **Plaistow** (W 7-1)

27-3-1948 [H] **Henfield** (W 3-0)

3-4-1948 [A] **Ockley** (L 3-4)

10-4-1948 [H] **Partridge Green** (W 9-2)

17-4-1948 [A] **103 HAA Regt** (W 8-3)

24-4-1948 [H] **Roffey** (L 2-4)

P20 | W14 | D0 | L6 | GF102 | GA38 | 28pts | 4th

HDL1 1948/49

18-9-1948 [A] **Roffey** (W 2-0)

25-9-1948 SJC [A] **Broadbridge Heath** (W 11-1)

9-10-1948 SJC [A] **Plaistow** (W 4-0)

16-10-1948 HDLSCC [H] **Slinfold** (W 8-1)

23-10-1948 SJC [A] **Warnham** (W 2-1)

30-10-1948 [A] **Horsham YMCA** (W 5-0)

6-11-1948 [H] **Partridge Green** (W 15-1)

13-11-1948 SJC [H] **Rustington** (L 2-4)

20-11-1948 HDLSCC [H] **Horsham YMCA** (W 8-1)

27-11-1948 [H] **Kirdford** (W 13-1)

4-12-1948 [A] **Slinfold** (W 7-0)

11-12-1948 [A] **Ockley** (W 4-1)

18-12-1948 [H] **Billingshurst** (W 6-1)

1-1-1949 [A] **Plaistow** (W 6-0)

8-1-1949 [A] **Billingshurst** (W 8-1)

15-1-1949 [H] **Horsham YMCA** (W 5-2)

22-1-1949 [H] **Slinfold** (W 7-0)

29-1-1949 [A] **Sussex Bricks** (L 1-3)

5-2-1949 [H] **Lintotts** (D 1-1)

12-2-1949 [H] **Henfield** (W 7-0)

19-2-1949 [A] **Henfield** (D 1-1)

25-2-1949 [A] **Kirdford** (W 3-1)

5-3-1949 [A] **Lintotts** (D 2-2)

12-3-1949 [H] **Ockley** (W 6-4)

19-3-1949 [A] **Partridge Green** (W 8-4)

26-3-1949 [H] **Plaistow** (W 8-0)

9-4-1949 HDLSCC Semi-Final [venue unknown] v **Ockley** (W 2-5)

16-4-1949 [H] **Sussex Bricks** (W 1-0)

30-4-1949 [H] **Roffey** (W 6-2)

2-5-1949 HDLSCC Final [at Horsham] v **Sussex Bricks** (D 1-1 AET) T Frogley

The Cup was shared; Pulborough had it for 2nd 6 months

P22 | W18 | D1 | L1| GF122 | GA25 | 39pts | 2nd

WSL 1949/50

3-9-1949 [A] **Bognor A** (W 3-1) Frogley 3

10-9-1949 [H] **Westbourne** (W 3-2)

17-9-1949 [A] **Graylingwell** (L 1-4)

24-9-1949 [A] **Petworth** (L 0-4)

1-10-1949 [H] **Chichester A** (W 9-1)

8-10-1949 [A] **Rustington** (W 3-0)

15-10-1949 SIC [A] **Petworth** (L 3-5)

22-10-1949 [H] **Felpham** (W 4-3)

5-11-1949 WSLBC [H] **Felpham** (W 4-2)

12-11-1949 [H] **Midhurst** (W 7-0)

19-11-1949 [A] **Arundel A** (L 0-1)

26-11-1949 [A] **Chichester A** (W 4-2)

3-12-1949 [H] **Arundel A** (W 3-2)

10-12-1949 [A] **Littlehampton A** (W 8-1)

31-12-1949 [A] **Littlehampton A** (L 1-2)

14-1-1950 [H] **Portfield** (W 4-0)

21-1-1950 [A] **Midhurst** (W 8-1)

28-1-1950 [A] **Felpham** (W 4-3)

4-2-1950 [H] **Rustington** (W 9-0)

11-2-1950 **WSLBC** [A] **Rustington** (W 4-1)

25-2-1950 [H] **Petworth** (W 5-1)

4-3-1950 [H] **Graylingwell** (W 4-2)

11-3-1950 **WSLBC Semi-Final** [H] v **Portfield** (L 2-3) P Roberts 2

18-3-1950 [H] **Bognor A** (L 3-4)

25-3-1950 [A] **Portfield** (D 3-3)

1-4-1950 [A] **Westbourne** (W 4-2)

P22 | W16 | D1 | L5 | GF90 | GA39 | 33pts | Champions

WSL 1950/51

9-9-1950 [A] **Bognor A** (W 5-1) P Roberts 3, Harrison 1, Greenfield 1

16-9-1950 [H] **Chichester A** (W 6-3) D Roberts 2, Handley 1, Wells 1, P Roberts 1, Harrison 1

23-9-1950 [A] **Rustington** (W 4-2) Wells 2, Harrison, P Roberts

7-10-1950 **SIC** [A] **Skyways** (W 8-0) P Roberts 4, D Roberts 3, Handley 1

14-10-1950 [A] **Portfield** (L 3-7) D Roberts, Greenfield, Heasman

28-10-1950 **SIC** [H] **Abbey Rovers** (W 10-2) Handley 5, P Roberts 2, Harrison 1, D Roberts 1 Wells 1

4-11-1950 [A] **Graylingwell** (D 2-2) Harrison 2

18-11-1950 **SIC** [H] **Bognor A** (W 4-2) P Roberts 1, D Roberts 1, Wells 1, OG 1

25-11-1950 [A] **Littlehampton A** (W 6-3) P Roberts 2, Wells 2, Handley 1, Harrison 1

2-12-1950 [H] **Midhurst** (W 5-1) P Roberts 3, Handley 1, Wells 1

30-12-1950 [H] **Rustington** (W 8-2) D Roberts 3, Wells 2, Handley 1, Frogley 1, P Roberts 1

6-1-1951 [H] **Bognor A** (D 2-2) P Roberts 1, Wells 1

13-1-1951 [A] **Westbourne** (W 7-0) D Roberts 2, P Roberts 2, Wells 2, Handley 1

20-1-1951 **SIC** [H] **Westbourne** (W 4-2) Wells 2, Frogley, Handley

27-1-1951 [H] **Littlehampton A** (W 14-1) Wells 9, P Roberts 2, Frogley 1, Harrison 1, Greenfield 1

3-2-1951 [H] **Felpham** (W 6-3) P Roberts 2, Wells 2, Greenfield 1, Harrison 1

3-3-1951 **WSLBC** [A] **Felpham** (W 4-3) Wells 2, Harrison 1, P Roberts 1

10-3-1951 **SIC Semi-Final** [at Littlehampton] v **West Hove** (L 4-1) Frogley 1

17-3-1951 **WSLBC Semi-Final** v **Portfield** [A] (W 0-2) D Roberts 1, Wells 1

24-3-1951 [A] **Chichester A** (W 4-2) D Roberts, P Roberts, OG 2

7-4-1951 [A] **Petworth** (W 3-1) Harrison 2, P Roberts 1

14-4-1951 [H] **Arundel A** (W 10-2) Wells 4, Harrison 3, Hampshire 2, Greenfield 1

18-4-1951 [A] **Midhurst** (W 5-1) Harrison 3, P Roberts 2

21-4-1951 **WSLBC Final** [at Bognor] **Petworth** 2 Pulborough 3 Frogley 1, Harrison 1, Wells 1,

28-4-1951 [H] **Graylingwell** (W 9-0) Harrison 4, P Roberts 2, Wells 2, Frogley 1

2-5-1951 [A] **Arundel A** (D 0-0)

5-5-1951 [H] **Portfield** (L 2-5) Harrison 1, P Roberts 1

9-5-1951 [H] **Petworth** (W 4-2) Harrison 2, P Roberts 1, Wells 1

11-5-1951 [A] **Felpham** (W 4-2) D Roberts 1, P Roberts 1, Wells 1, OG 1

12-5-1951 [H] **Westbourne** (W 2-1) P Roberts 1, Wells 1

P22 | W17 | D3 | L2 | GF110 | GA42 | 37pts | Champions

WSL 1951/52

8-9-1951 [H] **Lavant** (W 7-1) Greenfield 3, P Roberts 2, Harrison 1, D Roberts 1

15-9-1951 [H] **Arundel** (W 3-0) P Roberts 2, Harrison 1

22-9-1951 [H] **Westbourne** (W 4-1) Wells 2, Harrison, P Roberts

29-9-1951 [A] **Bognor A** (W 5-1) Harrison 2, P Roberts 2, D Roberts

6-10-1951 [A] **Graylingwell** (W 6-0) P Roberts 3, Carter 1, Frogley 1, D Roberts 1

13-10-1951 **SIC** [A] **Three Bridges** (W 14-1) P Roberts 6, Wells 5, Harrison 3

20-10-1951 [H] **Midhurst** (W 5-2) Wells 3, Handley 1, D Roberts 1

27-10-1951 **SIC** [A] **Storrington** (W 11-2) Wells 6, Harrison 2, P Roberts 2, Frogley 1

3-11-1951 **WSLBC** [H] **Hove** (W 16-1) Harrison 6, P Roberts 6, Wells 4

17-11-1951 **SIC** [H] **Brighton Catholic** (W 8-1) P Roberts 4, Wells 3, Harrison 1

24-11-1951 [H] **Portfield** (W 3-1) P Roberts 2, Wells 1

31-11-1951 [A] **Felpham** (W 3-1) P Roberts 2, Wells 1

15-12-1951 [A] **Chichester A** (D 1-1) P Roberts 1

22-12-1951 [H] **Storrington** (W 11-1) P Roberts 5, Wells 3, Frogley 1, Harrison 1, D Roberts 1

5-1-1952 [H] **Chichester A** (W 6-1) Harrison 2, Wells 2, Greenfield 1, P Roberts 1

12-1-1952 [A] **Arundel A** (L 2-4) P Roberts 1, Wells 1

19-1-1952 [H] **Petworth** (W 10-0) Frogley 3, P Roberts 3, Harrison 2, D Roberts 1, Wells 1

26-1-1952 **SIC** [H] **Rye United** (W 4-1) P Roberts 2, Harrison 1, Wells 1

2-2-1952 [A] **Littlehampton A** (D 1-1) Wells 1

9-2-1952 **WSLBC** [A] **Westbourne** (L 3-4) Harrison 1, P Roberts 1, Wells 1

16-2-1952 [H] **Littlehampton A** (W 6-3) Harrison 2, P Roberts 2, Wells 1, D Roberts 1

23-2-1952 **SIC Semi-Final** [at Littlehampton] v **Horsham Res** (2-4) Frogley, Harrison, D Roberts, P Roberts

1-3-1952 [H] **Bognor A** (L 0-3)

8-3-1952 [A] **Petworth** (W 3-2) Harrison 1, P Roberts 1, Wells 1

15-3-1952 [A] **Lavant** (L 1-2) P Roberts 1

504-1952 [A] **Midhurst** (D 2-2) P Roberts 1, Wells 1

12-4-1952 [A] **Portfield** (W 7-0) P Roberts 3, Wells 2, Handley 1, Harrison 1

14-4-1952 **SIC Final** [at Queen Street, Horsham] v **Hollington** (W 5-0) Harrison 2, Wells 2, Handley 1

19-4-1952 [H] **Graylingwell** (W 7-0) Wells 4, P Roberts 2, D Roberts

23-4-1952 [A] **Storrington** (W 3-0) Greenfield, P Roberts, Wells

26-4-1952 [H] **Felpham** (W 5-1) Greenfield 2, Harrison 1, P Roberts 1, Wells 1

28-4-1952 [A] **Westbourne** (W 7-0) Harrison 3, Handley 1, D Roberts 1, P Roberts 1, Wells 1

30-4-1952 [A] **Rustington** (W 5-3) Handley 2, Greenfield 1, P Roberts 1, Wells 1

3-5-1952 [H] **Rustington** (W 11-0) Wells 6, P Roberts 3, Handley 1, Harrison 1

P26 | W20 | D3 | L3 | GF124 | GA31 | 43pts | Champions

ABBREVIATIONS

SCLD2 Sussex County League Division 2

FAAC Football Association Amateur Cup

SSC Sussex Senior Cup

SCIC Sussex County Invitation Cup

SUSSEX COUNTY LEAGUE DIV 2 1952/53

20-9-1952 [A] **Hastings Rangers** (L 1-4) B Wells 1

4-10-1952 [H] **Hastings & St Leonards** (W 7-3) D Roberts 2, P Roberts 2, P Harrison 1, A Smith 1, A Spain 1

11-10-1952 [A] **Goldstone** (L 2-12) A Smith 1, B Wells 1

18-10-1952 [H] **Seaford** (L 0-4)

1-11-1952 [A] **Moulsecoomb Rovers** (W 5-1) G Wills 2, A Smith 1, D Roberts 1, B Wells 1

8-11-1952 **SSC** [A] **Uckfield** (L 2-4) A Smith 2

15-11-1952 [A] **Cuckfield** (W 5-2) G Wills 3, A Smith, B Wells

22-11-1952 [H] **Wigmore Athletic** (L 1-3) B Wells 1

6-12-1952 [A] **Wigmore Athletic** (L 0-10)

20-12-1952 [H] **Three Bridges** (W 7-3) T Cousins 2, B Wells 2, P Harrison 1, D Roberts 1, P Roberts 1

10-1-1953 [H] **Hove White Rovers** (W 9-4) P Roberts 4, P Harrison 2, B Wells 2, G Wills 1

17-1-1953 [A] **Three Bridges** (L 3-5) A Smith 1, B Wells 1, G Wills 1

24-1-1953 [H] **Cuckfield** (W 4-1) G Wills 3, A Smith 1

31-1-1953 [A] **Hove White Rovers** (L 1-3) D Roberts 1

7-2-1953 [H] **Sidley United** (D 2-2) D Roberts 1, G Wills 1

14-2-1953 [H] **Hastings Rangers** (L 2-3) P Harrison 1, G Wills 1

21-2-1953 [H] **Rye United** (D 1-1) P Roberts 1

28-2-1953 [A] **Hastings & St Leonards** (L 1-2) B Wells 1

7-3-1953 [H] **Goldstone** (L 2-3) P Harrison 1 B Wells 1

14-3-1953 [A] **Seaford** (D 3-3) B Wells 3

4-4-1953 [H] **Moulsecoomb Rovers** (D 1-1) P Harrison 1

11-4-1953 [A] **Sidley United** (L 0-8)

17-4-1953 [A] **Rye United** (W 7-2)

P 22 | W7 | D4 | L 11 | GF64| GA80 | 18pts | 9th

SCL D2 1953/54

19-9-1953 [A] **Rye United** (L 2-7)

3-10-1953 [A] **Sidley United** (L 1-4)

17-10-1953 [A] **Hastings Rangers** (L 0-8)

31-10-1953 [H] **Three Bridges** (L 1-5) J Rayner 1

14-11-1953 [A] **Goldstone** (L 1-6)

21-11-1953 [H] **Goldstone** (D 3-3) T Funnell 2, P Harrison 1

28-11-1953 [A] **Cuckfield** (D 3-3) P Roberts 3

5-12-1953 [A] **Hove White Rovers** (L 2-6)

12-12-1953 [H] **Moulsecoomb Rovers** (L 2-6)

19-12-1953 [A] **Three Bridges** (W 3-0)

9-1-1954 [H] **Hove White Rovers** (L 2-4)

16-1-1954 [H] **Cuckfield** (W 4-3) P Roberts 3, P Harrison 1

6-2-1954 [H] **Hastings & St Leonard's** (W 8-3)

20-2-1954 [H] **Hastings Rangers** (W 4-2)

27-2-1954 [H] **Sidley United** (W 3-2)

6-3-1954 [A] **Seaford** (L 1-7)

20-3-1954 [H] **Rye United** (L 1-4)

3-4-1954 **SCIC** [H] **Three Bridges** (L 0-2)

10-4-1954 [H] **Moulsecoomb Rovers** (W 5-0)

24-4-1954 [H] **Seaford** (W 4-0)

P20 | W7 | D3 | L10 | GF52 | GA77 | 17pts | 8th

SCL D2 1954/55

4-9-1954 [H] **Moulsecoomb** (L 2-3)

11-9-1954 [A] **Rye United** (L 0-12

18-9-1954 **FAAC** [A] **Arundel** (W 3-2)

25-9-1954 [H] **Goldstone** (D 2-2)

2-10-1954 **FAAC** [A] **Brighton Old Grammarians** (L 2-6) P Harrison 1, P Roberts 1

9-10-1954 [A] **Seaford** (L 1-7)

16-10-1954 [A] **Hastings Rangers** (L 4-5)

23-10-1954 **SSC** [H] **Hastings Rangers** (W 4-1)

6-11-1954 **SSC** [A] **Bexhill Town** (L 1-3) T Funnell 1

13-11-1954 [A] **Chichester United** (L 1-9)

20-11-1954 [H] **APV** (Crawley) (W 5-0)

18-12-1954 [A] **Moulsecoomb** (L 0-7)

1-1-1955 **SCIC** [H] **Goldstone** (W 6-1) T Funnell 3, P Ginnaw 3

8-1-1955 [A] **Three Bridges** (L 1-8) P Ginnaw 1

22-1-1955 **SCIC** [A] **Chichester United** (L 2-4) T Funnell 1, P Ginnaw 1

29-1-1955 [H] **Chichester United** (D 0-0)

5-2-1955 [H] **Hastings & St Leonards** (L 1-2)

12-2-1955 [H] **Hastings Rangers** (L 1-10)

19-2-1955 [H] **Three Bridges** (L 1-7)

26-2-1955 [A] **Cuckfield** (L 1-5) T Funnell 1

On 16th March 1955 it is understood that Pulborough applied for withdrawal from the league and on 6th April they duly withdrew from the league and their record was removed

Pulborough FC 1960/61 *back row from left* R. Pyegate (linesman), Ron Maybee, Basil Davis, Graham Loomes, Len Hookey, Tony Spain, Nigel Pope. *Front row from left* Michael Brown, Jim Leadbeatter, Glen Lewis, Anthony Leadbeatter, Geoff Upjohn.

Pulborough FC – Early 1960s (exact date unknown) *back row from left* Dave Rowland, Terry Hatchard, Laurie Etheridge, Kenny Blackburn, Nigel Pope, Bill Leadbeatter, Toby Greenfield (chairman). *Front row* John Stewart, Glen Lewis, Terry Roberts, Mick Browning, Mick Hatchard.

The 1960s, 70s and 80s

THE FOLLOWING PAGES from the club archives show just how close Pulborough came to having no football club at all. The team adapted well to playing in a lower division and over the next few seasons there was steady improvement. The side finished in 11th place in 1960-61 and over the following four years they continued to improve. Defensively the side were conceding fewer goals, while they continued to score goals when going forward.

In 1964/65 the team finished in 3rd place, winning 17 games, losing 6 and drawing 3, GF81, GA52.

The 1965/66 season saw the West Sussex League form a Premier Division and Pulborough FC were to play in the 1st Division.

The 1966/67 season saw the team perform fairly well, but the players seemed to change a lot; we could never get a settled side for one reason or another. There were some good results and some disappointing ones, probably the best game of the season for PFC was beating Arundel Reserves by 8 goals to 3 in the Malcolm Simmons Cup.

There were fewer changes to the side in 1967/68 and the team had a very good season. But we were still conceding too many goals; this may have been because we were a very attack-minded team. The forwards certainly knew where the goal was; 96 goals were scored during the season. There were 12 different scorers, with G. Lewis scoring 49. The team finished in 4th place. There were great results against Portfield, Yapton, Slindon and in the Sussex Intermediate Cup against Tarring, when the team scored 7 goals and in the game, away to Slindon we won by 12 goals to nil, with Glen Lewis getting 7 of them, a great team performance.

Another good season came in 1968/69 when the side finished in 4th position, just missing out on promotion. There were some fine performances that season. We played Worthing Reserves in the Sussex Intermediate Cup at Woodside Road and I don't think anyone, apart from the team, thought we had a chance of winning. But, in heavy conditions, we played very well and the game went to extra time. There were some tired legs but we came away with a draw. The following week we had the replay, produced another good performance and beat them by 2 goals to 1.

In my opinion, possibly our best performance was against Littlehampton Town Reserves at home, in an evening game. They came with a very strong side, which included at least three first XI players. Two of their team were regular players for Sussex, one of whom was the captain. There were also several other players with County League experience. Knowing how good a side Littlehampton had brought, we were up for the game right from the start. Everyone played to their maximum and we thoroughly outplayed them, winning 4-1. During the second half, their skipper was getting pretty upset and I heard him say to his team, 'Come

Season 1967/68
back row l to r Terry Hatchard, Tony Leadbeatter, Mick Wallis, Jim Leadbeatter, Nigel Pope, Len Hookey.
Front row Mick Hatchard, Terry Roberts, Geoff Upjohn, Glen Lewis, Brian Huffer.

on! They are taking the piss!' The lads came off shattered with the effort we had put in, but it was worth it; we had beaten a very strong side.

By the end of the season we had scored 86 goals, with 10 different scorers.

At the Club's AGM on 3rd July 1969 an informal discussion took place with the members and secretary of the Pulborough Rugby Club with regard to their request to use of the pavilion and changing facilities of the football pitch. As this matter had been discussed at a Pulborough Parish Council meeting the evening before, at which our objections had been officially raised, nothing much could be done, except put forward our points of view. Our President Mr Corden informed the meeting that the decision of the council was that the Rugby Club could not use the pavilion, because the amenities could not accommodate over 50 players at once, but were welcome to the use of a pitch on the recreation ground.

The 1969/70 season did not get off to a good start. We had lost 2 important players; Brian Huffer was not available all season and Glen Lewis missed the first 9 games. We only picked up 4 points from our first 8 games. Considering the poor start, the side did well to finish in 6th place. The side did not score as many goals and the goals against tally was up on the previous year. But they had 3 good results in cup matches: they beat Angmering and Hunston in the Malcolm Simmonds Cup and Shoreham Boys Club Old Boys in the Sussex Intermediate Cup, but were then knocked out of both competitions by clubs from the Premier League. They lost narrowly, by the odd goal, to Midhurst and to Southwick Reserves after a replay. Once again, 10 players were on the score sheet.

15.4.1967 Petworth 4 Pulborough 3

Former Horsham FC player Den Stillwell scored Petworth's winner in the last minute of Saturday's West Sussex league match with Pulborough on Saturday.

But Pulborough took the lead when Upjohn on the left controlled the ball before beating the advancing keeper. The home team then settled down and Staker equalised.

From the corner and defender out-jumped the defence to put Petworth ahead. After the interval Petworth went further into the lead when Staker netted after a solo run.

Pulborough then bucked up their ideas and after M Hatchard had reduced the arrears, A Leadbeatter slipped the ball into the net off a defender to even matters. Just when it seemed certain to be a draw, Stillwell was given the winner on a plate.

Pulborough M Baker, T Hack Chard, G Mason, A Leadbeatter (captain), N Pope, B Davies, T Roberts, M Hack Chard, G Lewis, J Leadbeatter, G Upjohn.

Petworth B Adsett, B J Adsett, J Creswick, R Andrews, C Parker, B Tee, D Sopp, J Staker, D House, B Temple, D Stillwell.

15th April 1967
Petworth v Pulborough
PFC players (in stripes)
from left Glen Lewis,
Mick Hatchard, Mick Baker
(goalie), Basil Davis,
Graham Mason.

1960s
PFC players
(in white shorts)
from left
Terry Roberts, Graham
Hill,
Len Hookey (goalie),
Mick Hatchard

The Breakthrough

After just missing out on promotion on at least three occasions, the 1970/71 season was finally the year when everything fell into place. The first game of the season was a home match against Littlehampton Town Reserves, which resulted in a 3-2 win. The side that day was:

CARTER

POPE   BROWN

ROBERTS   LEADBEATTER A.   LEADBEATTER J.

WELLS   HATCHARD M.   FALLOWFIELD   LEWIS CLARK

We were still playing the formation that most sides played right up to the late 1960s. We drew with APV Athletic Reserves and in our next game we beat South Bersted 12-0. A couple of games later, we were getting changed, when Glen Lewis, who was the captain, spoke to me, as I was vice-captain, and explained that we had no-one to play in central defence; he suggested that one of us should play there. My reply was that if he played there it would take away our main threat up front, as he was our top goal scorer and had the ability to hold the ball up. I said that I had never played in defence before and because I was not the tallest and not that great in the air, I would play as a sweeper behind the defence. It seemed to work well. The formation was changed and we played with a back four, a midfield four, with two wide men and two strikers.

In the 2nd round of the Sussex Intermediate Cup we played host to Lavant, one of our main rivals in the league. We had lost to them in a league match earlier in the season, so we were out for revenge. The side played well and we beat them 3-1. We were drawn against Arundel

Pulborough FC 1969/70: *back row left to right* Terry Hatchard, Michael Brown, Colin Carter, Jim Leadbeatter, Mr Pope (committee), Tony Leadbeatter, Len Hookey, Toby Greenfield (chairman). *Front row left to right* Russ Phillips, Mick Hatchard, Glen Fallowfield, Terry Roberts, Geoff Upjohn.

The Pulborough FC side who beat Rudgwick 4-2 in the third round of the Sussex Intermediate Cup
back row from left Nigel Pope, Mick Hatchard, Colin Carter, Anthony Leadbeatter, Jim Leadbeatter, Michael Brown. *Front row from left* Gerald Clark, Terry Roberts, Brian Huffer, Glen Fallowfield and Glen Lewis.

Reserves, a Premier Division side, in the Malcolm Simmonds Cup and put up a good performance before losing by the odd goal of 3. In the 3rd round of the Sussex Intermediate Cup we beat our near neighbours Rudgwick 4-2. Our next match brought us back down to earth with a bump, we lost by six goals to nil against a very good Littlehampton side. Our next match, the 4th round of the Sussex Intermediate Cup, saw us drawn to play away to Storrington, who we had not played for several years. The match was an exciting one, with fortunes swaying one way and the other, but in the last minute of extra time Storrington grabbed the winner. There was nothing between the sides, in my opinion, and had we played on our ground I think we might have won.

In our next league match, against Graylingwell, the back four was changed; in came T. Hatchard on the right and N. Pope moved to the left. The side then went on an unbelievable run, we went 17 games unbeaten to the end of the season. We played 17 games, there were 14 wins and 3 draws, 64 goals were scored and only 12 conceded. The final match of the season was against Bognor Town Reserves at Nyewood Lane. It was going to be a tough match, they were a good side and wanted revenge, as we had beaten them 4-1 earlier in the season. We had already been promoted, but to go up as champions, we had to win this match. We were without Tony, who was injured, this was a big loss, losing a central defender in such a big game was not ideal, but we were confident that whoever came in would do a great job and so it turned out. There was a great atmosphere in the ground thanks to about 200 supporters who had made the trip to Bognor. Sitting in the changing room before the game, we could hear the noise they were making; it came over the tannoy system that the game would be cancelled if our supporters did not stop banging on the stands. They were still pretty noisy when the game got under way.

The first half was fairly even, we were not at our best, but never in any trouble. At half time, the talk was about whether we should attack right from the whistle or keep it tight for 15 minutes and then in the last 30 minutes go hard to get the winner. We did the latter, then went all out to score. With about 15 minutes to go we got what proved to be the winning goal. Although Bognor tried their best to equalise, they never really created any chances. Had we lost the game, Lavant would have been champions. Some of their players were at the game but, with about 10 minutes to go, they left; they knew we were not going to concede anything. Our supporters celebrated with us and we finally got back to the dressing room, very happy to be champions, but disappointed that we had not been presented with the cup – someone had made an error an not brought it! The team that day was:

CARTER

HATCHARD T.   HATCHARD M.   LEADBEATTER J.   POPE

WELLS   HUFFER   ROBERTS   CLARK

LEWIS   FALLOWFIELD

SUB: G. UPJOHN

Season 1970/71 – Champions of League Division 1 after the last game of the season, having beaten Bognor Town Reserves 1-0 to win the league. *Back row left to right* Tony Leadbeatter, Nigel Pope, Colin Carter, Mick Brown, Jim Leadbeatter, Geoff Upjohn, Mick Hatchard, Glen Lewis. *Front row left to right* Trevor Wells, Terry Hatchard, Terry Roberts, Gerry Clark, Glen Fallowfield, Brian Huffer.

Pulborough FC 1970/71: *back row left to right* Mick Hatchard, Colin Carter, Glen Lewis, Jim Leadbeatter, Nigel Pope, Brian Huffer, Toby Greenfield (chairman). *Front row left to right* Terry Hatchard, Trevor Wells, Glen Fallowfield, Gerry Clark, Terry Roberts, Geoff Upjohn.

Pulborough FC 1970 *back row from left* Toby Greenfield (chairman), Nigel Pope, Gerry Clark, Colin Carter, Glen Lewis, Jim Leadbeatter, Brian Huffer, Mick Brown. *Front row* Mick Hatchard, Trevor Wells, Terry Hatchard, Terry Roberts, Tony Leadbeatter.

Players from the 1960s / 70s

LEN HOOKEY born 12th March 1945 in Woking. He attended St. Mary's school in Pulborough, before going to The Weald in Billingshurst. He then went to work for Spiro Gills as an apprentice welder and went to Crawley College on day release. In 1972 he went to work on the oil rigs, offshore, in Aberdeen, he moved to live there in 1974. Len worked in Australia, West Africa and Ireland, in the oil industry. In 1996 he bought a croft in Keith, Scotland, he left there in 2004. He made his debut for the 2nd XI 19th September 1960, against Lec B Sports, his 1st XI debut 3rd February 1962, was against Boxgrove. He played in several positions, but he played in goal for most part. He was a very good keeper, brave, not afraid to dive at players' feet, or come for balls in the air. Len was a fine cricketer and played for the local team. He is back living in the village, which he has always regarded as his home.

DON MADGETT born in Wateringbury in Kent 6th December 1930. On moving to Storrington, he went to the local School and then went to Rydon in Thakeham. He worked at Spiro Gills, but left to do his National Service with the Royal Navy, he was also a Reservist for 5 years. He returned to his old vocation as a welder with Spiro Gills. Don then left and worked for Smith Cline Beacham, where he held a very good position, he travelled around Europe for the company. He had to take early retirement because of ill health. He started playing for us in the mid 1950s. He played in the forward line, he was a good all round player and was a regular in the first team. He played for Storrington. Don passed away in 2004.

MICK BAKER came to us from Storrington. He had his first team debut against Portfield Reserves 3rd September 1966 and scored a hat-trick. In his first season he was on the score sheet 24 times and in his second he netted 27 goals. During one match for the 2nd XI, he went off injured, but came back on, only to discover later, that he had played on with a broken leg. Mick played the odd game in goal, but it was as a forward he was at his best. He was not the quickest, but read the game well and took up good positions. He also played for Storrington and lives there.

GERALD PARKER (GERRY) born in Hampton 12th July 1942. He attended School there, on moving to Pulborough, he then went to Rydon School in Thakeham. Leaving there he worked for Hall & Co. At the age of 22 he moved to live in Australia. He then went to New Guinea and worked in the open cut mines, he returned to Australia, before coming back to this country in 1995. Gerry joined the Club during the 1957-1958 season, I believe he played his first game for the 2nd XI 29th March 1958 against North Holmwood, his first XI debut was at Angmering 12th April 1958. He usually played on the right wing and the couple of seasons he was with us he played well, he left for a while, but came back to play for us later on in 1962-1963. He played for West Chiltington and Gerry now lives there.

DAVE ROWLAND was born in Coolham 25th April 1936. He attended School in Nutbourne and then went to Rydon in Thakeham. He worked for a Lord and Lady in Nutbourne as their gardener. On leaving, the rest of his working life was with British Rail, he retired in 1994. He played his first match for the Club during the 1960-1961 season. I think work commitments stopped Dave from playing a lot of matches but when he did play he did not let the side down, he was a goalkeeper, who made the odd appearance on the field. Dave was a really good guy. He sadly passed away at a relatively early age.

PAUL GOODSELL was born in Petworth. He moved to Pulborough when he was 4. He went to the local St. Mary's School and he then went to Rydon in Thakeham. He worked in the drawing office at Spiro Gills for several years. I have no information as to where he worked after he left there. Paul emigrated to Australia and has lived in Perth for many years. He made his debut for the 2nd XI 13th September 1958 at Baynards, his first XI debut 10th January 1959 was in a home match against Petworth. He was a goalkeeper, tall and well built, he was a good asset for the Club, as a player and also as a member of the committee.

LAURIE ETHERIDGE born in Nutbourne 12th September 1942. He attended Schools in Nutbourne, Pulborough and Thakeham at Rydon. On leaving School he worked as an apprentice mechanic for Nutbourne garage, he then went to British Rail for a short period and then to Hall & Co. In 1966 he became a professional speedway rider, he was at Raleigh for about 18 months, he then rode for Hackney, Crayford and Canterbury. In 1975 he won the National riders championship. He rode in South Africa for 2 years. Laurie represented England on a number of occasions and rode in several different countries. In 1984 he finished his speedway career and went to work for Saunders Specialised Services, he still works part time for them. He made his 2nd XI debut 6th April 1963 at Balls Cross, his 1st XI debut was against Portfield Reserves 30th November 1963. He was a goalkeeper, not that tall, but he was brave and a good shot stopper. He never played a lot of matches as he was often away riding. He lives in Nutbourne.

MICK WALLIS born in Petworth 25th February 1945. He went to St. Margaret's convent School in Midhurst and then The Weald in Billingshurst. He went to work in Saville Row in London as a trainee tailor, but did not stay long. Mick then went into the film industry, starting at the bottom, he worked his way up and is now a producer and is involved in making films for television. He joined 'The Robins' at the start of the 1967-1968 season and made his 1st XI debut against Wittering 26th September 1967. He was a goalkeeper, but he did not look like one, he was slim and not that tall, but looks are deceiving, he was very good, he was agile and had great reflexes, he became a regular first team player. He played for Petworth, Midhurst and Northchapel. Mick lives in Birdham, near Chichester.

ROBIN THOMPSETT born in Pulborough 21st October 1942. He attended the local St. Mary's School, before going to The Weald and he moved on to go to Horsham Technical College. His working life started at Spiro Gills, in the inspection department, he then became an estimator. When the firm closed down, he went to work for Horsham Salts Health Care in the town, he still works part time there. He played his 1st game against Broadbridge Heath 19th September 1959, his 1st XI debut was against Wittering 1-12 1962. Robin usually played on the left wing, he was mainly in the 2nd XI and played very well for them, he scored a few goals, but made goals for other players. He lives in Gay Street.

1970/71 Season Players

COLIN CARTER was born on the 20th June 1952 in Chichester. He attended St Marys School and then The Weald. His first job was for Ross Chickens in Cootham, then for Spiro Gills for several years. Colin first played for the Club in 1966. He established himself in the first XI during the 1968-69 season. When the side won the West Sussex League Division 1 title, he only missed one game. A superb goalkeeper, the best I ever played with, Colin had great hands. Anything played into the penalty area he made his ball. Very agile and a good shot stopper, he gave the defence confidence. He went on to play for Worthing. He moved to Staffordshire and played for Stafford and West Midland All Stars, a semi-professional side. Colin is now back and living in the village.

TERRY HATCHARD (HERB) was born in Stane Street Close in Pulborough on the 2nd Sept 1947. He went to St Mary's School and The Weald. He started work as an electrician for Allfrey's, a local builder, then worked for Lintots, a Horsham company, before moving on to Hoad & Taylor. Terry made his debut for the Club in October 1961. He played in several positions before he settled to play at full back. He was in side that won promotion to the Premier League. A tough tackling full back, he was very quick and not many wingers got the better of him. A loyal one Club man, Terry now lives in Billingshurst and comes to watch 'The Robins' play.

NIGEL POPE was born in Handcross in 1944. On moving to Storrington, he attended the local Primary School and Rydon County Secondary School in Thakeham. His first job was for Spiro Gills, where he did his apprenticeship and stayed for many years, before moving to Born Heaters, who became Boustad International Heaters. Nigel made his first team debut in 1963, against Southbourne. He could play as full back or centre half. A big man, Nigel was good in the air, a fearless tackler and gave opposing forwards a hard time. He was in the side that won promotion to the Premier League. He left the Club in 1973 to play for Rustington for two years and became their manager for a time. He came back to play for us in 1980 and stayed until 1982. He now lives in Angmering.

MICHAEL BROWN was born in Croydon on 12th March 1945. He went to St Marys School, The Weald and Crawley College, then to work for Seeboard and later London Electricity, where he became a director. He took early retirement in 1997. He first played for the Club in 1961, making his first XI debut against Yapton 4th September

1963. He retired from playing in 1977. In his early years he was a forward and scored a lot of goals, then later played at full back. He was quick and a hard tackler who liked to get forward and was in the side that won the West Sussex League Division 1 title and also team that played in Horsham and District League Division 5 Charity Cup Final in 1972. Mike now lives in Sutton, near Bignor.

TONY LEADBEATTER born Chichester 16th April 1939, attended St Marys School and Midhurst Grammar School. He started work for Gray and Rowsell in Bury but left after about nine months to work for Spiro Gills as an apprentice welder, where he spent many years. The last 20 or so years of his working life were spent with Royal Mail Pulborough branch. There is no record of when Tony first played for 'The Robins' but he thinks it was 1955. He did National Service in the army with the REME, where he played a good standard of football. He returned to play for us until hanging up his boots at the end of the 1981-82 season. In his younger days he played as an inside forward, a skilful player, who scored his share of goals. Tony was then converted to become a central defender, with great success. Good in the air and the best tackler in the side, he had the ability to bring the ball out of defence and set moves going. He was injured and sadly unable to play in the last game of the season at Bognor. Tony played for the West Sussex League side and had one season playing for Fittleworth. He lives in Findon.

TERRY ROBERTS was born on 2nd November 1947 in The Moat in Pulborough. He went to St Mary's School and The Weald. While going to Bognor College he started work for Hamilton & Cole, a local shop, as an apprentice electrician. After many years he became a director and eventually purchased the company, which he sold and retired in July 2004. He signed on for the Club in the 1963-64 season and made his first XI debut against Southbourne. He became a regular first team player in 1968. Rob was a half back or midfield player, not the tallest, but was good in the air, a fierce competitor and a good ball winner who never gave up and kept the side motivated. He was part of the side that won the West Sussex League Division 1 title, captain of both first and second teams and also served on the committee. Rob retired from playing in 1983. He loved running and was co-founder of

Fittleworth Flyers Running Club; he ran in the London Marathon. He still lives locally.

MICHAEL LEADBEATTER (JIM) was born in The Moat Pulborough on 26th March 1942. He went to St Mary's School then Rydon County Secondary. Jim would cycle to play for the School team in the morning, then cycle back to play for Pulborough second XI in the afternoon. His working life started at Spiro Gills, as an apprentice welder, where he stayed for a good many years. He also worked for Royal Mail and finished his working days as a security officer at Gatwick Airport. He first played for the Club in the 1956-57 season and soon established himself in the first XI. He played as an inside forward, a good goal scorer and a skilful player. In the late 60s and early 70s he became a more defensive player and held the midfield together, a strong tackler and good on the ball, he rarely gave it away. He was captain of the side and also a committee member. Jim was in the team that won promotion to the premier League. In his younger days he was asked to play for Arundel but stayed with us. He played for the West Sussex League side. He was assistant manager for the second XI at one time and manager of it for a short period. He lives in Findon.

BRIAN HUFFER was born in Bognor in 1948, attended Primary School in Storrington, then went to Worthing Technical College and Brighton College. Brian became a construction manager and spent about five years in the Middle East; he now owns his own construction company. He made his debut for 'The Robins' on 1st October 1967, against Southbourne and played his last game for us in 1972. Brian played in midfield, an excellent player, he had the ability to beat opponents and create chances for the team, he was also a good goal scorer, he had the skill to change games. He was a good team player, it was a big loss to the side when he moved on. He played for Storrington. Brian was also a very good cricketer and now enjoys his golf. He lives in Brighton. He was in the side that won promotion to the Premier League.

TREVOR WELLS was born in 1952 at Bignor Park, near Sutton. After moving to Pulborough he went to St Mary's School and Collyer's School in Horsham. On leaving he went to work for Redifon in Crawley, where he remained for a number of years. Trev was a computer expert and later went freelance. He joined the Club in 1961 and his first game was against Lavant reserves. His first XI debut was against Wigmore Reserves 18th April 1968. He left the Club in 1974, another loss to the team. Trev played wide on the right, was very quick, with the ability to beat defenders and set up chances for the team. He was very fit and could run all day. He was in the side that won the West Sussex League Division 1 title. He loved running and ran in marathons, including the London Marathon. Trevor now lives in Surrey.

GLEN LEWIS was born in Stane Street Close, Pulborough on 5th of April 1947. He attended St Mary's School. At the age of eight he went to live in Malta for three years, when his father, who was in the navy, was posted there. In 1958 he returned to live in the village and went to The Weald School in Billingshurst. He started work as an apprentice welder at Spiro Gills, where stayed for about thirty years. When the firm closed, he went to work in Billingshurst for a while. Glen made his debut for 'The Robins' on 28th November 1959, against Henfield Reserves and made his first XI debut against Shippams Athletic 23rd September 1961. He started of playing on the wing but soon established himself as a centre forward. Glen was the complete forward, a superb header of the ball, fast, brave, sometimes too brave for his own good, a prolific goal scorer and a good team player. He was captain of the side that won promotion to the Premier League and the best forward I had the pleasure of playing with. He was a regular player for the West Sussex League side and played several times for the Sussex intermediate team. He could have played at a higher level if he had chosen to. He decided to retire at the end of the 1979-80 season, a huge loss to the club; players of that quality don't come around very often. He played for Petworth for half a season. He still lives in the village.

GERALD CLARK (GERRY) was born in Shoreham on 14th October 1952, went to Coldwaltham Primary School and Worthing Technical college before studying at Croydon College. He did his apprenticeship with APV in Crawley, then became a brewery proposal officer, before working for Recardo engineers. He made his first debut against Lancing and Sompting Legion 14th December 1968 and left the Club at the end of the 1971-72 season. Gerry played wide on the left, had a good left foot, was quick, could beat a defender and scored his share of goals. He was in the side that was promoted after winning the West Sussex League Division 1 title in 1971. He played for Petworth and Watersfield, where he was manager for 2 years. He lives in Shoreham.

GEOFF UPJOHN was born in Shoreham in 1944. He went to St Mary's School in Pulborough and then The Weald. He started work as an apprentice draughtsman at Spiro Gills. After 2 years he left and joined British Telecom, where he stayed for 34 years. He also worked for IBM as European Service Manager for 5 years. He made his second XI debut 2nd September 1961 against Birdham and his 1st XI debut against Lavant on 30th September 1961. He could play anywhere in the forward line, was not the quickest but was very skilful and a good header of a ball. He had the knack of being in the right place and scored many goals. Geoff was a good Club man and served on the committee. He was part of the squad which won the West Sussex League Division 1 title. He also played in the Horsham & District League Division 5 Charity Cup Final in 1972. He played for Crawley and Fittleworth. He lives in Hampshire.

GLEN FALLOWFIELD (BUSTER) was a Manchester lad who came to live in Pulborough and lodged at the Rose & Crown. He made his first team debut against Portfield 6-9-1969 and scored. Not the greatest of team players, he wanted to score goals and playing up front in a good side, had many chances to score and usually took them. He was very quick and direct. He was in the side that was promoted to the Premier Division and also played in the Horsham & District League Division 5 Charity Cup Final.

I can vaguely remember the team members and some of our wives and girlfriends visiting some of the local pubs during the evening. A good night was had by everyone, including our supporters.

This was the best team I was fortunate enough to play with. Many of us had grown up together and we had a great team spirit. We never knew when we were beaten, everyone knew their position and the team played some very fine football. We had one of the best goalkeepers in the league in Colin, who gave us confidence and was excellent in everything he did. We used 3 full-backs during the season – Nigel, Mike and Herb – all tough tackling players who knew their main task was to stop the opposition winger getting into the game. They were also quick and got forward when possible. Too many full backs today are too interested in going forward and not that good at defending; the three of them were good defenders.

Our two central defenders were Tony and myself. We were probably the smallest partnership in the league, but we had a good understanding. We had both played in midfield in our earlier days, so we had the ability to bring the ball out of defence and use it well. Tony was the best tackler in the club and a fine header of the ball. I was quick and could read the game well, so we formed an important partnership at the heart of our defence.

In central midfield we had Rob, Jim and Brian – a good combination. Rob was one of the smallest players in the league, but he was good in the air, a strong tackler, a fierce competitor and very vocal. Jim played in front of the back four and gave us protection; he was calm, a fine header and read the game well. He had also played in midfield in his younger days and was a skilful player. Brian was the complete midfield player; going forward he had the ability to beat his man, he had a fine range of passing, could spot an opening and deliver defence-splitting balls and scored his share of goals.

The two wide players in midfield were Trevor and Gerry. Trev was very quick and tricky, able to go past the opposition and create chances for the team. He was fantastically fit and could run all day, which he did for us. Gerry played on the opposite flank; he had a good turn of pace, could beat his full back and deliver good crosses into the penalty area. Gerry scored some important goals for us. They were two young lads who gave the team pace and energy.

We played with two main strikers. Glen, who was our skipper, was the best forward I had the pleasure of playing with. He was brilliant in the air, scoring some great goals. Glen had the

Match Report 1-5-1971
Pulborough have made it, they are the first division champions

Pulborough are champions of the West Sussex Football League's first division. A narrow win over Bognor Reserves on Saturday gave them the title on goal-average over Lavant.

The elevation to the premier division is the first honour achieved by the club since 1952, and the occasion was accorded all the enthusiasm and tension of a cup-final.

During the first half it was Bognor who played the better football and the visitors seemed unable to capture the flair and creativeness they had displayed in so many of their season's games. After the interval Pulborough gradually began to dominate, and their loyal and vocal supporters began to sense victory. Bognor's defence suddenly seemed shaky and their right-back was booked after three warnings by the referee. Then, at last, the goal came. Fallowfield was put through on the left and, despite mis-hitting his shot, still managed to steer the ball into the net. Pulborough held onto their lead for the last ten minutes to clinch the championship. Champagne in the dressing room marked the start of the celebrations, which continued later in the evening, during which players and supporters packed into the club's headquarters at the Red Lion, Pulborough.

C. Carter, T. Hatchard, M. Hatchard, J. Leadbeatter, N. Pope, B. Huffer, T. Roberts, T. Wells, G. Clark, G. Lewis (capt), G. Fallowfield. Sub G. Upjohn.

ability to beat players and had a had a powerful shot. He also had the skill to hold the ball up and create chances for his team; he was a great team player. Buster was our other striker. He was not the biggest, but he was quick and had the ability to score goals. He did not always get involved in the build-up, but when chances came to score he took them. Glen and Buster were a formidable partnership up front. Geoff came in if we had injuries and was our sub on several occasions. He played up front, good in the air, scored plenty of goals and always seemed to be in the right place for tap-ins and rebounds. Others who played that year were R. Branch, R. Czarnecki, J. Harrison, N. Hoffman, T. Jones, A. Richardson.

Our venture into to the Premier Division was going to be hard. Some of the teams we played in the 1970s would go on to play County League football; Midhurst, Pagham, Selsey and Wick did. We also had to play against the County reserve sides of Arundel, Bognor, Chichester, Littlehampton and Southwick, which meant that most weeks we were up against players with County League experience. Playing those teams, meant that you were playing on good grounds, with good facilities.

We made a good start, beating Chichester Reserves in our first home match of the season by 4 goals to 2. Despite being thrashed by Selsey in our next match, we were unbeaten in our next 4, winning 3 and drawing 1. I remember an evening match at home, against a strong Horsham Olympic side; we played really well and knocked in 5 goals. We had a couple of good results in the Sussex Intermediate Cup, beating Cuckfield 7-1 and in the next round Hanover Athletic 4-3, but our run came to an end when we lost to a good Littlehampton Town Reserve side 1-0 AET. We had two heavy losses when we came up against Midhurst. The end of the season saw us finish in 13th place.

The 1972/73 season was to be a difficult one, we had lost 5 of the players from the 1970/71 season. Losing the first 4 games knocked our confidence. The new look side was not good enough to play in the Premier League. We had some close games where we only lost by the odd goal, but there were times when we were outclassed. After two seasons in the top flight, we were relegated back to Division 1.

26-9-1970 vs Hunston

A superb hat-trick by skipper Glen Lewis brought Pulborough a WSL Div 1 win on Saturday at Hunston. The first goal came after keeper Carter threw the ball to left-back Brown, he carried the ball up field before finding Lewis, who made ground to beat the keeper with a ferocious shot. Fallowfield soon increased the score in the second half with a close range shot. And the third goal was a gem. Outside-right Wells made the running before sliding the ball to the unmarked Lewis, who swivelled and hit a shot the keeper hardly saw. With J. Leadbeatter in particularly fine form in mid-field the result was never in doubt, and near the end Lewis completed his hat-trick with a header from full-back Pope's cross.

Match Report 19-4-1972
Keatings win cup-final thriller in the last minute of extra time

Thomas Keatings 2 Pulborough 1

In a hard-fought and exciting West Sussex League Division 5 Cup final at Queen Street. Thomas Keating, the works team from Billingshurst, in their first season of football, defeated Pulborough in the last minute of extra time. In a game dominated by defences, and marred by many offsides, Pulborough had the edge in the first half down the slope, but it was not until the 36th minute, after several near-misses that they took the lead. After an inter-passing movement on the left wing, followed by a low cross into the goalmouth, centre-forward Geoff Upjohn side-footed home. In the second half Keatings, now with the advantage of the slope, attacked incessantly and in the 77th minute the Pulborough goalkeeper, harried by D. Heslop, dropped the ball, it ran loose to A. Puttick, who shot into the empty net. In the last ten minutes Pulborough almost scored through inside-left Fallowfield, and Keatings' Charman and Heslop had efforts saved by good goalkeeping. In the first period of extra time Pulborough, playing down the slope, had most chances, but failed to capitalise on them, with Keatings using offside tactics.

Pulborough FC v Portsmouth ex-Professionals – Sunday 22nd April 1973
PFC players from left: Nigel Pope, Tony Leadbeatter, Trevor Wells, Terry Hatchard.

'Pulborough striker "Twiggy" Branch has a go during Sunday's charity match with Portsmouth FC ex-professionals side, but it was Kevin Turner who got the ball into the net for the locals. They went down 3-1 however, to a hat-trick by McClelland in the match, which raised about £30 for Pulborough FC funds.'

The highlight of the year was a match against Portsmouth ex-Professionals in a Charity match, played on the Sunday 15th April 1973. The Club had 500 programmes printed and they were given out on the day free. Unfortunately, I could not find anyone who had one, so I am not able to give the names of all the Portsmouth players. It was a nice day and a large crowd turned up to watch the match. Anthea Askey, the daughter of Arthur Askey was invited to meet the teams and to start the match. I remember walking to the half way line for the toss and looking up at their skipper, 'Big Dougie Reid'. As we shook hands I realised just how big he was; he was about a foot taller than me!

Another big man was Ron Tindall, who had been the manager of Portsmouth at one time and was an ex-Chelsea player. The majority of their players were in their late forties and some were in their fifties. They were far superior, even at their age. They were obviously not as quick or mobile as in their playing days, but they always found space and had so much time

Pulborough v Petworth 18th November 1972
PFC players from left: Terry Roberts, Graham Hill, Len Hookey (goalie) Mick Hatchard.

Pulborough win at last
Pulborough 3 Petworth 2

Pulborough pulled off their first division West Sussex league win of the season on Saturday when they entertained Petworth.

Only after the home side had withstood several Petworth attacks were they able to press forward themselves and midway through the first half they were awarded a free kick.

Pope's lofted drive was flicked on by Upjohn for Ned Turner to give the keeper no chance.

Pulborough gained confidence but the visitors got on terms when J Staker hammered the ball home.

The home side then raised their game and forced a corner and from a 'Twiggy' Branch corner D Stenning put them ahead again.

'Snuffer' Hill made it three when his shot was not cleared but Petworth got lucky when G Thomas fooled A Leadbeatter with a hurried back-pass and the ball trickled over the line for an own goal.

on the ball. They made the game look easy and were always in the right place at the right time. We gave them a good game, but they were always in charge and if they needed to, they could have beaten us without breaking sweat. It was an eye-opener and you realised just how good you had to be to become a professional footballer. It was a great experience for us, one which we all enjoyed, as did the spectators. Our team that day was: M. Pattenden, T. Roberts, G. Hill, M. Hatchard, N. Pope, T. Wells, A. Leadbeatter, K. Turner, N. Turner, G. Lewis, R. Branch, D. Stenning, T. Hatchard, M. Brown. I just remembered, we lost by 3 goals to 1 and J. McClelland scored all 3 for Portsmouth.

The AGM for the 1973/74 season was held at the Red Lion on Friday 6th July 1973. The Treasurer's report stated that there was a balance of £66-20p. The solvent position of the club was mainly due to the fundraising activities and the charity match against Portsmouth ex-Professionals, which netted £34-67p. A vote of thanks was recorded to Mr L. Greenfield (Toby) for over 20 years as our chairman. The new chairman was Mr B. Thayre. The side were to have a poor season, they finished up in 11th place. On the positive side, two young lads had broken into the team. Bob Chandler and Nick Bainbridge were going to be an asset to the club.

The 1974/75 AGM was to be an important one. The Treasurer reported a balance of £183-67p, largely due to the two dances run by the club and the competition tickets sold by Mr P. Chapman. The meeting was important, because it was proposed by Mr T. Roberts that the club colours be changed from our traditional red to yellow shirts with green shorts and green socks. The motion was carried by 12 votes to 10. This is the one and only time that the

Pulborough FC 1973/74: *back row from left* Dave Stenning, Mick Hatchard, Mick Pattenden, Graham Hill, Glen Lewis, Tony Leadbeatter. *Front row* Neil Turner, Roland Branch, Nick Bainbridge, Terry Roberts, Trevor Wells.

side played in anything other than red and it was probably a mistake, since we have always been known as 'The Robins'. The second XI were still to play in red. The meeting also looked at the possibility of trying to engage the services of a coach/manager.

There were some incidents during the 1960s and early 1970s that were not particularly funny at the time but in the dressing room after the game, or on the way home, made you smile.

I do not remember who we played, but I do recall this incident. Glen was not the type of player who got upset at a bit of rough treatment, he could look after himself. But in this game the defender set out right from the first whistle to foul him at every opportunity, even when he was nowhere near the ball. The referee was weak and did nothing to stop the defender committing fouls. After yet another foul, Glen snapped and went after him. Now the defender was in full flight, tearing up the pitch, with Glen in hot pursuit. Luckily for him the game was stopped before Glen got to him. I don't think either player was booked. It was not funny at the time, but we had a laugh later on, to see this guy running away after kicking Glen all the match.

Another incident involved Tony. I remember it well, because in all the time I played for Pulborough, he was the only player I can think of that was sent off. It was in an away game at Graylingwell. Tony fouled one of their players and the referee called him over, booked him and asked for his name and how to spell it. Tony walked away, but the referee called him back and asked him how he spelt his name, Tony replied 'I just bloody well told you!' With that, the ref sent Tony off. We all said he was very unlucky and that had the referee been able to spell, he would have stayed on the pitch!

There was another incident in which I was involved, but knew very little about. I had just brought an opposition player down, knowing it was a foul, so I just trotted off up the pitch. On hearing a shout, I turned around to see Herb grappling with the man I had just fouled. One of their players said, 'What's up with that guy?' The reply from one of our team was 'That guy was chasing after his brother.' Again, I don't think anyone was booked. In our era players fouled and got fouled and you just got on with the game; it was hard and physical but we just accepted it.

1975/76 AGM Minutes

Election of Officers. President Mr V. Corden. Proposed J. Leadbeatter, seconded L. Greenfield. Chairman Mr A. Payne. Proposed V. Corden seconded C. Parsons. Secretary T. Roberts. Proposed M. Jupp, seconded J. Stewart. Treasurer C. Parsons. Proposed L. Greenfield, seconded J. Leadbeatter. Team Secretary D. Smith. Proposed L. Greenfield, seconded J. Gallagher. Committee Mr J. Stewart, Mr J. Philpot, Mr M. Ralph, Mr A. Jupp. Linesman Mr L. Greenfield (first) Mr A. Payne (seconds). Subscriptions increased to £2 per year and home match fees 50p, half price for those still at School.

Committee meeting at Red Lion 14th July. Mr M. Hatchard to manage both teams. Second XI to play in all blue. A sponsored jog around the recreation ground was decided and members of the cricket, rugby and stoolball Club were invited to take part. It was proposed by Mr J. Philpot and seconded by Mr A. Payne, that Mr L. Greenfield and Mr M. Browning become life members of the Club.

West Sussex League Champions Division Five Central 1977/78 *back row from left* Martin Pepper, Mick Ruff, Geoff Messenger, Guy Smith, Bob Backhouse, Graham Hill, John Norman, John Jupp. *Front row* Malcolm Jupp, Dave Stenning, Terry Hatchard, Lee Rout, Colin Spain.

Pulborough FC 1981/82 *back row from left* Toby Greenfield (chairman), Tim Wilkins, Mick Ruff, Malcolm Jupp, Graham Hill, Colin Spain, Andy Kynoch, Mick Hatchard (manager). *Front row* Terry Roberts, Dave Rhoder, John Jupp, Steve Leadbeatter, Colin Hutton, Bob Hewitt.

Although I had a year of experience managing the second XI and had taken several training sessions when Mick was away on business, it was a tough challenge to manage both teams. It was going to be a hard season for the 1st XI, we had only finished in 4th place but were put into the Premier Division. The task was made even harder by the loss of Glen Lewis and Bob Chandler. Glen had decided to call time on his very fine playing career. Over the years he had suffered some head injuries, due to his own bravery and, now in his thirties, he decided to retire. This was a huge blow to myself and the club; he was one of the finest players ever to play for PFC. Bob was one of our best young players but was now living and working in Horsham. Bob and I spoke and he explained that he would not be able to get to training and did not think it right to play for the team if he could not train with them. So before the season had even started we had lost our best forward and our best midfield player. The season went pretty much as I expected; we were not good enough to play at that level. We had a couple of old hands still playing, but their best days had gone. I brought in 3 or 4 younger lads from the second XI, but they had no experience of playing in intermediate football. I could not fault the team's effort, but we were not good enough defensively. We conceded 94 goals; it was a mistake putting us in the Premier Division.

During the season a few of the lads kept asking me if I would arrange a match between the current side and the side of 1970/71 that won the West Sussex League Division 1 title. I kept telling them that the guys from that era were mostly in their thirties and had retired from playing and that I did not know where some of them now lived. But after more pressure from the lads, I eventually said that I would try to track down the players and see if they were willing to play. The only two players I was not able to get in touch with were Geoff Upjohn and Glen Fallowfield; all the others said they would be happy just to get together again. They were not going to be as fit as they would like, but they looked forward to playing as a team again. Some of us had not seen each other for several years and had not played together as a team for about 9 years. Tony Leadbeatter and Terry Roberts were still playing for the second XI, but I think the rest of us had stopped playing. I got the impression that the current team thought they would beat the old team without too much trouble. After all, they were fitter and faster than us...

SATURDAY 25th APRIL 1981 'THE BIG MATCH'
1970/71 Division 1 winners (Pulborough FC)
versus 1980/81 Pulborough FC First XI
Pulborough Recreation Ground
K.O. 3pm. Referee E. Blake

1970/71 team *ages in brackets* Colin Carter (29), Terry Hatchard (34), Nigel Pope (37), Mick Hatchard (38), Tony Leadbeatter (42), Terry Roberts (34), Jim Leadbeatter (39), Brian Huffer (33), Trevor Wells (29), Glen Lewis (34), Gerald Clark (29), Michael Brown (36).

1980-1981 team: Malcolm Jupp, Steve Nicholls, Colin Spain, David Stenning, Michael Ruff, Colin Hutton, David Smith, David Scott, D. Richardson, Robert Hewitt, G. Edwards, John Jupp.

They were in for a shock. Apart from the first 15 or 20 minutes, when we were put under pressure and still trying to get our understanding back, we were reasonably comfortable. We started to get organised and slowly got into the game, got our passing going and were creating chances, while defensively we were not in too much trouble. Although we tired in the last 15 minutes, we were determined not to concede any goals. We won by 4 goals to nil. I don't think the 1980/81 side realised how good we were in our prime. Even though we had not played together for many years and were slower, we still had the skill and know-how to play as a team. It was good to see old friends and enjoy playing as a team again.

On Friday April 24th, the new Pulborough Sports and Social Club and its new pavilion was officially opened. If we thought that going down to Division 1 was going to be a little easier, we were mistaken; it was still a very good standard of football. We continued to struggle over the next 3 years. We did not have anyone who could score goals consistently. If you don't take your chances when they come, you are not going to win games. We were quite a small side and often lost out to more physical teams.

The 1983/84 season illustrated our lack of goal scoring ability. In 28 League matches we only scored 26 goals. Players make mistakes and, looking back, I think I did as well. When the team is losing most of its games, you try to change things. You have to try different players and make positional changes to try and get results. Maybe I should not have altered the team quite so often. It was difficult knowing the team was not good enough to play at that level. Although the 1983/84 season was a poor one, at the end of the season we were invited to enter the Marley Cup, which was run by Storrington FC. To our surprise we won the cup.

I remember blowing my top in the dressing room before the final. I had a rule that no one should drink alcohol on the day of a match and that if anybody turned up the worse for drink, they would not play. John Geddes, who was a teacher at Windlesham House School, had arrived, unbeknown to me, not felling well. The team went out to warm up, then someone came in and told me that John had been sick and was pretty rough. I got him in and he admitted that he had been to a farewell party to say goodbye to a friend who was leaving the area and had a bit too much to drink. In normal circumstances I would not have played him but we did not have our strongest team that day, so I told John that I did not care how bad he felt, he had let me and the team down, so he was bloody well going to play and play for his teammates. [I think my language may have been a bit stronger

than what I have written.] Well, John played the game of his life and was man of the match! He apologised afterwards and I told him that if he played like that, he could have a drink now and again, but not to let me know! I can't recall who we played in the final, but our team was: P. Gibson, M. Osborne, M. Ruff, J. Jupp, C. Spain, T. Roberts, C. Hutton, J. Geddes, D. King, P. Bird, D. Fry, Subs M. Jupp, T. Blunden.

During the course of the 1983/84 season, I knew the side needed some new blood, so I started to look for a few new players to bring to the club. Two players joined us that season, Paul Gibson and Dave King. They improved the team and over the next few years would be important players for us. I remember Paul turning up one evening while we were training. He introduced himself and said that he was now living in Pulborough and wanted to start playing again, that he had not played for some time, due to work commitments and was a goalkeeper. I asked him to come along to our next training session. I put Paul through a goalkeeping routine, but within two minutes I could see that he was very good and that we had signed a class player. Dave signed on and I soon realised that he was going to be an important player for us. He was different from the other midfield players we had.

A Change of Fortune

Stepping down to Division 2 would give us the opportunity to rebuild the side but, before the league games had started, I had news that two of my best forwards had been spoken to by a senior club and persuaded to go and play for them. To say that I was angry was an understatement. They had signed on, played in our friendly matches and were penciled in to play in our first league match. I was annoyed with them for leaving it so late. I had no time to replace them and I was angry that the man who had enticed them away was a former player who was still living in the village. Had the players informed me earlier, before we began our friendly matches, I would have wished them all the best, but to find out just as our league programme commenced showed a lack of respect to both me and the club.

During our successful Marley Cup campaign at the end of the previous season, I had seen a player who was playing for one of our rivals. I made some inquires and was told that his name was Martin Harrison and that he was living in Pulborough. I got in touch with him and asked if he would be interested in playing for Pulborough in the coming season. He wasn't that keen to start with, but I persuaded him to come along and train with us and then decide if he wanted to join us. The session went well and he signed for us. He was to be a big player for the side. I later learnt from his father that Martin could hardly walk for several days after his first training session, but I think he understood that the fitter he the better a player he would be.

The side was taking shape. In Paul Gibson we had a class goalkeeper, Andy Kynoch was still playing well, Mike Osborne and Colin Spain had settled down, Mick Ruff was fulfilling the potential he showed as a young man, Colin Hutton was blossoming and enjoying his free role and Dave King, with his experience, was holding the midfield together. I brought in Dave Rhoder and Steve Leadbeatter from the second XI and they were playing well, Dave Scott had joined us from Storrington and had made an impact, Richard James was able to play in

Pulborough FC line-up before their 10th successive win against Partridge Green 25th January 1986
Back row from left Mick Hatchard (manager), Peter Bird, Kim Furlonger, Andy Kynoch, Paul Gibson, Richard James, Roger Jupp, Dave King. *Front row* Colin Hutton, Martin Harrison, Mick Ruff (captain), Steve Leadbeatter, Nick Bainbridge, Colin Spain.

different positions, Martin Harrison was leading the line brilliantly and in Peter Bird and Tim Hatchard we had two young lads who were going to be important players for the club.

By the middle of October the team was starting to gel and were playing well. The biggest problem I had all season concerned Tim. He was scoring goals for fun in the second XI, including 7 on 2 occasions, 6 on another and 3 hat-tricks. At any other time he would have been in the first as a regular, but because the team were playing well and getting results, it was difficult to change the side. The team just missed out on promotion, finishing in 3rd place. The team played well to reach the final of the Chichester Charity Cup, beating Warnham, Rudgwick and Felpham on our way to the semi-final. Rustington were our opponents and we had to play on their ground. The score after extra-time was 0-0. The replay was three days later, on Tuesday evening. There was a large crowd and the team did not disappoint the home fans. We played some fine football and 2 goals from Martin saw us win by 2 goals to nil.

The Cup Final was against South Bersted and was played on the Rusting ground. As always we took a lot of supporters and there was a good atmosphere. The game itself was a tense one, with defences mainly on top. There was nothing between the sides and either team could have won. Unfortunately for us, they nicked a goal and managed to hold on, despite being put under great pressure. Our team that day was: Paul Gibson, Mick Osborne, Andy Kynoch, Mick Ruff, Colin Spain, Dave Rhoder, Colin Hutton, Dave King, Tim Hatchard, Martin Harrison, Dave Scott, subs Peter Bird and Richard James.

The 1985/86 season was one of our best for several years. The side had been strengthened when Kim Furlonger joined. I now had a squad of 16 players all good enough to play in the first XI.

Having got the players, I now had to get them to accept my vision of how I wanted them to play. They were good individually, but we had to play as a team. I wanted the team to keep possession and build from the back and bring the midfield into the game, so we could create chances for the forwards.

25th January 1986

Division Two North leaders are now Pulborough after their 10th win in as many league matches, a deserved if flattering 4-0 success at home to Partridge Green. With both defences pushing up towards the halfway line there was little flowing football, the Green having the better of the exchanges territorially but lacking conviction when scoring chances came. In contrast, Nick Bainbridge punished a mistake in fine style to put Pulborough ahead after 25 min and the away team's hopes were finally killed off when they conceded three goals in the last four minutes. Martin Harrison directed a fine header beyond Jimmy Lister's reach and then Peter Bird got two goals.

19th April 1986

Pulborough are champions of Division Two North following a convincing 5-0 win against lowly Rudgwick. They scored four times in a devastating 20 minute burst during the first half, Martin Harrison getting two and Colin Hutton and Peter Bird one each. Pulborough, continuing to press during the second half, managed only one goal, by Nick Bainbridge, who converted from 6 yards.

Pulborough had earlier beaten Wisborough Green 2-0, scoring half-way through the first period when Kim Furlonger thundered in a shot from 25 yards. A second goal minutes later from Martin Harrison strengthened the lead. Wisborough Green rallied in the second half but made little progress against a solid defence.

24th April 1986 – slick Pulborough remain unbeaten

Pulborough football team, champions of the West Sussex League Division Two North, remain unbeaten for the season following their 4-1 win over Steyning Old Grammarians. In doing so they scored their 100th league goal of the season. Martin Harrison and Nick Bainbridge gave Pulborough a two-goal half-time lead and the same players scored again in the second half. After the game, Pulborough captain Mick Ruff was presented with the Division Two North Championship Shield.

So many sides just hit long balls and missed out their midfield. When that happens, more often than not the ball just comes straight back. The players adapted really well and adopted the style I asked them to play.

The team played some great football during the season and got their reward. The side won the West Sussex League Division 2 North title without losing a game; they won 18 and drew 4. In 22 games we scored 77 goals and only conceded 21, which showed that we were a fine all-round team, able to score freely but giving very little away defensively. We were not a big side, but the guys were very good in the air. The team was really competitive and I think some other teams were intimidated by the way we put them under pressure. Most sides were not able to compete with us when we hit top form, our passing game was great to watch and our one- and two-touch football was difficult to stop.

Our supporters were very happy with the football they had watched and I even had some referees telling me what a fine team we were. We only lost 2 games that season: the first was a Sussex Junior Cup match against Sunallon, who cancelled their first team fixture on the morning of the match and brought most of them down to play us. It was not very sporting of them and left a bad taste in the mouth, but they didn't care. We beat their usual second XI home and away.

**Pulborough FC 1985/86 season – Division 2 North Champions,
Marley Cup Winners and Chichester Charity Cup Finalists**
Back row l to r Colin Spain, Peter Bird, Kim Furlonger, Paul Gibson,
Dave King, Dave Rhoder, Dave Lidbetter, Mick Hatchard.
Front row Trevor Blunden, Martin Harrison, Steve Leadbeatter,
Colin Hutton, Nick Bainbridge, Andy Kynoch.

The second match we lost was in the final of the Chichester Charity Cup, a match we could quite easily have won, but it was not to be. We ended the season on a high note by winning the Marley Cup. At the end of the season we had won our Division, reached the final of the Chichester Charity Cup and won the Marley Cup, a successful year for the club.

Chichester Charity Cup 1985-86

A CROWD OF OVER 200 turned up at Graylingwell Hospital's ground to watch the match of the champions and what a wonderful final it turned out to be. Both clubs were looking for the double, having just won the championships of Division II South and North respectively. At the end of a dramatic two hours of nail-biting cup-tie football, it was Felpham who eventually proved themselves to be the top junior side in West Sussex football.

This was Felpham's third visit to the Hospital's ground. A four-goal starter in the League followed by five in an earlier round of the cup, which also went into extra-time and another win on Monday will surely make this their favourite ground.

But it had looked like turning sour for United at one stage. With a 3-1 lead until well into the second half and the chance of another which Nick Bainbridge scooped over the top soon after, Pulborough must still be kicking themselves for letting it slip. Pulborough were certainly the neater, methodical side for much of the game. But Felpham, although looking vulnerable at times at the back, had three powerful front runners, so that goals at both ends always seemed on the cards. In fact, there could have been several more at either end. Although there were a total of five bookings handed out by Referee Morris, most of the these were for over-exuberance. It was never a dirty game, though hard fought, with Pulborough claiming three cautions to Felpham's two.

Les Bromley opened the scoring for Felpham, but a mistake by United's Nigel Lambert let Steve Leadbeatter in to equalise. Martin Harrison made it 2-1 to Pulborough after cutting in from the right and when the diminutive Colin Hutton, from Guy Harwood's successful racing stable, hooked in the third goal the whole of Pulborough must have thought they were on another winner. But suddenly Bromley burst through the middle for his second goal and up came John Latham from the back to score with a downward header off a free kick and United were back on level terms. Pulborough could never quite recover from that shock in extra-time, though only some heroics from Lambert kept them out as the excitement mounted. Eventually it was Pulborough who cracked when defender Kim Furlonger headed into his own net. Their defence was in complete disarray as Andy White nipped in to make it five, though a late goal from Peter Bird to complete the scoring was no more than they deserved. The winners were presented with the trophy, on behalf of the League by Mick Browning, the former England Amateur International and the "man of the match" award went to Felpham's Les Bromley.

Woman and Bicycle Stop Match

I believe it was in the 1980s, in a home match, that the incident occurred, it was the strangest thing I had seen during my time in football. I was standing in my usual position on the halfway line, when I happened to turn and look towards Pocket Park and just emerging was a woman pushing her bicycle, I did not take any notice, but about 30 seconds later, the woman was strolling through the middle of the football pitch, still pushing her bicycle. Despite the fact that there were 22 players and a referee on the pitch, she calmly kept walking. The referee had to stop the game, by now players and supporters were telling her to get of the pitch, she was completely oblivious to the abuse she was now getting. She ignored everyone and continued on until she was off the pitch. No one seemed to know who the woman was, I had never heard of a match being stopped because of a woman and her bicycle!

Pulborough Football Club AGM, held in the Sports and Social Club Tuesday 17th June 1986. Last meetings minutes read and signed by Mr A. Payne. Treasurer's report, to follow at a later date due to late arrival of money. Chairman's report. 1st team came 1st in Division 2 North, runners up for the Chichester Charity Cup and winners of the Marley Trophy. The 2nd team were 3rd in Division 4 Central. Thanks were given to Lil Rhoder for washing the kits and for the teas and food provided and for Vanessa Cordingly for doing the Secretary job again. The atmosphere in the Club is as good as ever. Committee. President Mr V. Corden, ppd T. Greenfield, scd J. Stewart. Vice Presidents, approaching G. Harwood. Chairman Mr. A. Payne, ppd J. Rhoder, scd R. Jupp. Treasurer Mr C. Parsons, ppd J. Stewart, scd M. Hatchard. Secretary Sally Goodchild ppd P. Goodchild, scd M. Hatchard. Team Secretary to be decided. Linesman 1st team A. Payne ppd T. Greenfield, scd S. Hurst, 2nd XI M. Ralph ppd P. Goodchild, scd S. Hurst. Sports & Social Club Trust J. Rhoder ppd L. Adsett, scd T. Greenfield. Sports & Social Club representatives L. Adsett & J. Stewart, ppd T. Greenfield, scd M. Hatchard. 1st Team Manager M. Hatchard. 2nd Team Manager to be decided. A.O.B. Kit 1st O.K. 2nds to be decided. Subs proposed by S. Hurst and seconded by J. Jupp will be £10. Match fees Home £1-50, Away £1.00, Juniors 75p and 50p. Subs due by 30th September.

Players meeting Tuesday 22nd July, pitch talked about at players meeting. Programmes, being dealt with. Proposal, in future A.G.M. to be held on Monday nights, committee meeting once a month. Letter to Mrs Lil Rhoder thanking her for all she has done.

The next six seasons saw the team back to playing intermediate football in Division 1. It was always going to be hard in a higher standard of football. The 1986/87 season was an up and down one. We were not consistent. We would have 2 or 3 wins and then a few bad results. We did not score enough goals and we let in far too many. Nevertheless, finishing in 7th place was satisfactory in our first season in Division 1.

The following season 1987/88 was similar. The team got off to a terrible start, our first 5 League matches produced just 1 point, with 4 losses and 1 draw. Things then improved and we had a good result against Emsworth, with Kevin Taylor scoring 3. We then lost to a very good Old Collyerians side. We had 2 games against Ashington, home and away, which saw us score 5 goals in each match and Martin Harrison scored hat-tricks in both games.

To illustrate how our season had gone, 2 games showed the best and the worst of it. Our home match against Old Collyerians was the opportunity to get revenge for losing to them earlier in the season. The team were brilliant that day, the best they had played for a couple of years. Everyone played to their maximum and we won 7-0. Had their goalkeeper not been in fine form we would have doubled our score. Our passing and one and two touch football was too much for them; they couldn't get near us. In our last game of the season we played Milland. We had a slightly different side that day but we were absolutely hopeless. We kept giving the ball away, couldn't deal with their long ball tactics and lost by 9 goals to nil. It was an embarrassing afternoon. From the sublime to the ridiculous in 2 matches summed up the season. We did get to the final of the Marley Cup, but lost to a very strong Storrington side.

There was big disappointment before the 1988/89 season had even started. Paul Gibson informed me that he was not able to play for the club anymore as he was leaving the area because of his work. This was a huge blow, as anyone who knows about football will tell you, a class goalkeeper is hard to replace. In my opinion he is worth between 6 and 10 points a season. On the plus side, Dave Smith had returned and I gave a young Dean Lewis a run in the first XI. For one reason or another I was not able to select the strongest team, it was the end of November before I had them all available but, despite this, we made a good start. Up to the middle of December we had lost only 1 League match, with 5 wins and 2 draws.

The second half of the season saw us lose 10 matches. Towards the end of the season there were injuries, which disrupted the team. We were knocked out of the Malcolm Simmonds

Pulborough FC 1986/7 *back row left to right* Dave Rhoder, Peter Bird, Martin Harrison, Albert Payne (chairman), Paul Gibson, Mick Hatchard (manager), Steve Leadbeatter, Andy Kynoch, Kim Furlonger.
Front row Dave King, Colin Hutton, Colin Spain, Nick Bainbridge, Kevin Taylor, Mick Ruff.

Cup in the first round but had a great run in the Sussex Intermediate Cup; we drew with Wittering and in the replay beat them 7-0, with six players scoring. We then beat Durrington 2-0. This gave us an away fixture against Ringmer, who were in a better league than us and we were given no chance of getting a result.

It was a long trip, so we went by coach, which also gave our supporters the opportunity to travel with us. It had rained for most of the week and when we arrived the pitch was in poor condition. It was touch-and-go as to whether the game would be played. A discussion with the referee and both managers took place. I asked for the game to be played. Conditions were the same for both sides, I said, and we had travelled a long way. It was agreed to start the game but that if the pitch got any worse it would be called off.

Apart from Martin Harrison, who was injured, we were at full strength. We were under pressure for most of the game but we defended really well and restricted them to half chances. On the break we were dangerous and had the two best chances to win the game. A goalless draw was a great result. The replay was a week later. Dave Smith had been injured in the first match and was not fit to play, Dave King was also not able to play, but Martin was back. The team put in a terrific performance. We outplayed them and defeated them 5-2. Martin scored 3 and Nick Bainbridge and Dean Lewis got one each.

We then had a home tie against our old rivals Rustington Town. With Kim Furlonger not available, the back four had to be changed. There was a good crowd and they saw a fine match. There was little to choose between the sides and the game went into extra-time. We were the fitter side and finally we won by 3 goals to 1; Dave Smith 2 and Nick Bainbridge 1 were our scorers. We were drawn to play Steyning Old Grammarians in the quarter-final. They were a very good side, with several ex-County League players in their side but, with home advantage, I was confident we could progress to the semi-final. Alas it was not to be... a goalkeeping error early in the game was a setback. We started to chase the game and a very experienced side were able to ride out the pressure. We reached the final of the Marley Cup but lost to a strong West Chiltington side.

The following season 1989/90, was a difficult one. Three players had moved on and the side was probably changed more than it should have been. When a side is losing and not playing well, as a manager you have to try to improve things. I used 26 players during the season. We conceded just 44 goals in 26 league matches but only scored 41. This was the main reason we struggled to make an impact.

I had informed the club before the season started that it was going to be my last, so I left in 1990. Things had changed off the field that year. Mr Albert Payne, who had been Chairman for the last 10 years, did not want to carry on. Mr Tony Petras was elected as Chairman, Miss Colleen Richards was the new Secretary and Mr John Stewart and Mr M.J. Leadbeatter were joint managers of the second XI.

Back to Division 4 in 1985/86, the side played quite well and finished in 3rd spot and were promoted. The goals were shared around, with 12 players getting on the score-sheet.

In 1986-/87 we were in Division 3 Central and the side finished in 4th position. They were not as good defensively and goals were harder to come by, but it was not a bad season.

In 1987/88 the side were very poor and were relegated.

1988/89 was a successful one. In Mike Osborne, Frank Rhoder and brothers Colin and Steve Merriot they had some old heads and with young Simon Harrison and Ant Leadbeatter fulfilling their potential, the side was a more solid unit and only 35 goals were conceded. With Colin Hutton pulling the strings in midfield, chances were being created. Tim Hatchard was the first to acknowledge that without the team creating chances he would not have scored 34 goals that season. In John Stewart and Jim Leadbeatter the side had two good managers. They were runners-up and were promoted back to Division 3.

Now playing in Division 3 Central, the 1989/90 season was a little tougher, but the side performed well and finished 4th. The team remained much the same as the previous couple of years; hat-tricks were scored by Graham Blunden, Richard Streeter, Tim Hatchard and Kevin Taylor.

Match Reports 1965-80

18-12-1965 vs Felpham United

When Pulborough received Felpham United in a West Sussex Division 1 match on Saturday, the sides played some excellent football despite the atrocious conditions. After a goalmouth melee Pulborough went ahead through Upjohn and then added to their tally when Lewis scored a well-deserved goal. Felpham reduced the arrears through their outside-right. Combined work by defence and attack brought Pulborough a third goal through J. Leadbeatter, and although Felpham pulled another back they never really looked dangerous against the home side. Brown finally made it four for Pulborough with a 20-yard shot but they should have netted more. Pulborough linkmen M. Hatchard and J. Leadbeatter were supplied by the defence and kept their forwards on the move.

Pulborough: G. Loomes, G. Mason, C. Hamilton, T. Roberts, N. Pope, A. Leadbeatter (capt), M. Brown, M. Hatchard, G. Lewis, J. Leadbeatter, G. Upjohn.

2-10-1965 vs Selsey A

Pulborough pulled off a convincing four goal win over Selsey A in the first round of the Sussex Intermediate cup on Saturday. With five changes – three positional – the whole team worked harder than they have done previously this season. After being a goal down in the opening minutes, Pulborough quickly equalised when Lewis headed the ball on to Maybee, who nodded it down for the incoming Chapman to slam it into the roof of the net. A. Leadbeatter had his shot deflected into the goal for the second. Maybee held off the challenge of two Selsey defenders to crack in a terrific left-footer for number 3, but Selsey replied when their centre-forward capped a good run by scoring. Then Maybee was pulled down and G. Lewis converted the penalty-kick. Lewis and Chapman added two more, following good moves, before J. Leadbeatter left the Selsey goalkeeper standing when he slammed the ball home from 20 yards out. The Selsey centre-forward scored his second following a half-clearance. Lewis was robbed of his hat-trick by the final whistle, which shrilled as his shot was about to enter the net.

11-12-1965 vs Petworth

When Pulborough entertained Petworth in this West Sussex first division match on Saturday there were plenty of goals. Petworth scored first but Pulborough quickly equalised with a goal from Upjohn. Petworth went ahead again, only for the home side to level again after good play from J. Leadbeatter and G. Lewis. Pulborough then added four more – three from Lewis and another from M. Hatchard. After the interval the home side were three goals up but strong pressure from the Petworth forwards resulted in the scores being even at the end of 90 minutes.

Pulborough: P. Goodsell, G. Mason, C. Hamilton, T. Roberts, N. Pope, A. Leadbeatter, M. Brown, J. Leadbeatter, G. Lewis, M. Hatchard, G. Upjohn.

15-1-1966 vs South Bersted

On a frozen, snow-covered pitch, Pulborough played much better than in previous weeks in their West Sussex League game with South Bersted on Saturday. Playing some good attacking football, they tested their opponents' defence and only the goalkeeper kept them out. But South Bersted scored first when they broke away. Pulborough replied when J. Leadbeatter's shot was deflected into the net and Upjohn's corner-kick, swinging in, resulted in the second. After the interval a fine drive by Brown beat the goalkeeper for number 3. Some fine football from Lewis went unrewarded but Brown forced home the fourth. The defence backed up the forwards well and kept them well supplied with passes and, after a fine solo run, J. Leadbeatter beat the diving goalkeeper to make it five for Pulborough. In the last quarter of an hour, Pulborough kept up the pressure and forced several corners. From one of these a Davis pass was hit home by Upjohn.

Pulborough: G. Loomes, G. Mason, C. Hamilton, A. Leadbeatter (capt), N. Pope, B. Davis, M. Brown, M. Hatchard, G. Lewis, J. Leadbeatter, G. Upjohn.

5-2-1966 vs Wick

Pulborough's defenders scored three of the side's four goals in this first division West Sussex League at Wick on Saturday. Pulborough were lucky to prevent the home side scoring in a goal 5 less first half, but afterwards they settled down and left half Davis put them ahead when he collected the ball and lobbed it home from 30 yards following a corner-kick. After this encouragement centre-forward Lewis broke through to drive home a shot from 25 yards. Skipper A. Leadbeatter, playing well from his new position of right half, instilled a good deal of zest into his team. Collecting a pass from Pope, he added No 3 with a left-foot drive. Pulborough's defence played excellently to deal competently with several dangerous attacks and right-back G. Mason added the final goal from the penalty spot.

Pulborough: G. Loomes, G. Mason, C. Hamilton, A. Leadbeatter, N. Pope, B. Davis, M. Brown, T. Roberts, G. Lewis, J. Leadbeatter, G. Upjohn.

26-3-1966 vs Portfield

Pulborough centre-forward G. Lewis scored eight goals in his side's runaway win over Portfield in the West Sussex League on Saturday. Taking almost every opportunity that came, he scored four in the first 30 minutes. Pulborough centre half, Pope, after being was injured, was moved to the right wing, R. Maybee, replacing him, put real zest into the play along the right flank, from which several goals came. After the second half had started with a storming shot by M. Hatchard which brought a magnificent goal, the defence got in on the goal-scoring act with two well-taken goals from A. Leadbeatter and B. Davis. After this it was one way traffic and goals were added from Lewis and Upjohn. J. Leadbeatter and M. Hatchard laid on many chances to the forwards and these were mostly taken.

Pulborough: G. Loomes, G. Mason, P, Chapman, A. Leadbeatter, N. Pope, B. Davis, R. Maybee, M. Hatchard, G. Lewis, J. Leadbeatter, G. Upjohn.

22-1-1966 PFC Reserves vs Graffham

Pulborough Reserves left-winger P. Chapman scored half his side's half-dozen goals in their West Sussex League game with Graffham Reserves on Saturday. They were cheered on by the first eleven, whose game was postponed. The Pulborough forwards settled down after a goal from D. Hollins, who also added their second goal from a good cross by J. Stewart. But the home forwards did not have it all their own way, and sever al Graffham attacks only broke down at the last minute. Pulborough link-men P. Goodsell and A. Spain played well, and a move started by Goodsell was rounded off by J. Waliston for their third goal. After the interval the home side went further ahead through P. Chapman, who added another from J. Stewart's cross. A. Spain using his wings well, was just wide with a long shot on a return pass from Chapman, who completed his hat-trick by banging home Stewart's centre.

Pulborough Res: L. Etheridge, M. Leadbeatter, A. Puttock, P. Goodsell, T. Hatchard, A. Spain, J. Stewart, T. Roberts, D. Hollins, J. Waliston. P. Chapman.

24-9-1966 vs Slindon

Pulborough won their 1st division WSL match with Slindon on Saturday despite missing a penalty. They attacked from the start, but a Lewis 'goal' was judged offside by the visiting linesman. The defence prompted the attack constantly, and from one such move Upjohn put the ball through for Lewis to net with a tremendous shot. Slindon equalised following a defensive slip. In the second half Pulborough tightened their defence, and the attack forced several corners. After missing a penalty, Lewis scored the winner from a Leadbeatter corner with a chip over the unsighted defence.

PFC. L. Hookey, P. Chapman, B. Davis, J. Leadbeatter, N. Pope, A. Leadbeatter, G. Parker, M. Hatchard, G. Lewis, M, Baker, G. Upjohn.

1-10-1966 vs Worthing Reserves

Pulborough started their Sussex Intermediate Cup tie with the zest of champions on Saturday, but the superior fitness of Worthing Reserves proved too much for them in the end. Worthing took the lead after a defensive slip and made it two just minutes later. Pulborough pressed hard, but on another breakaway Worthing were soon 3 up. Just before the interval Pulborough pulled a goal back when a defender's clearance was hit back into the net by Parker. After the interval Pulborough further reduced the arrears when Upjohn hit home a Baker pass as they piled on the pressure, shots from the Leadbeatter brothers were narrowly wide. Worthing gradually wore down the Pulborough offensive and fought their way back into the game. Welland, centre forward scored 4 goals, a hat-trick with his head. Pulborough were unlucky with several shots and had some doubtful decisions given against them.

Pulborough: L. Hookey, P. Chapman, B. Davis, J. Leadbeatter, N. Pope, A. Leadbeatter (capt), G. Parker, M. Hatchard, G. Lewis, M. Baker, G. Upjohn.

15-10-1966 vs Felpham

Pulborough's linkmen played a big part in their side's easy 1ˢᵗ division WSL win over visiting Felpham United. But the visitor s should have scored first before the home side settled down to some entertaining football. The Pulborough defence cleared many attacks by gaining possession of the ball and prompting to forwards via the linkmen. The home side let the ball do the work, and were 2 up at the interval through inside left Baker. After the resumption Baker completed his hat-trick by driving home a Lewis header following a corner. Continual pressure by Pulborough brought the 4ᵗʰ goal, when a combined attack ended with Lewis driving home a Parker pass, Baker notched his 4ᵗʰ goal when he netted a free-kick from just outside the area.

PFC team L. Hookey, P. Chapman, B. Davis, J. Leadbeatter, N. Pope, A. Leadbeatter, G. Parker, T. Roberts, G. Lewis, M. Baker, G. Upjohn.

5-11-1966 vs Arundel Reserves

After holding Arundel with only 10 men in the first half, Pulborough turned on the heat in the second to win this Malcolm Simmons Cup game on Saturday. They went ahead before the interval when Lewis intercepted a back pass and placed it wide of the keeper. After the resumption when they were back to full strength, Chapman made it 2 when a defender handled the ball to save a certain Upjohn goal, Baker made no mistake from the spot. Baker added his second by driving home a fine Upjohn cross. Although Arundel reduced the arrears, Pulborough were well on top, and Upjohn put M. Hatchard away, he beat 2 men before driving home a scorching shot. Outstanding work by the defence, in which young T. Hatchard made his debut, inspired the forwards, and Lewis made it 6 from M. Hatchard's pass. The same player made it 7 off a defender, and Upjohn's cross was netted with an overhead kick by Baker.

PFC team G. Loomes, T. Hatchard, B. Davis, J. Leadbeatter, N. Pope, A. Leadbeatter, G. Upjohn, M. Hatchard , G. Lewis, M. Baker, P. Chapman.

19-11-1966 vs Wittering & Birdham United

Pulborough started their West Sussex League division 1 game at Wittering on Saturday rather shakily and were 2 goals down against their unbeaten opponents. They pulled one back when the ball was cleared up-field to Upjohn and he crossed to Chapman who headed home. Pulborough again became lax after this, but a fine shot by Upjohn that hit the bar went close before the interval. After the break, Wittering went further ahead when their outside left netted after a goalmouth melee. The visitors then settled down and Leadbeatter made a fine solo run down the wing before crossing the ball for Baker to net. Minutes later Baker flicked the ball past the Wittering keeper from Lewis's lob. But Wittering regained the lead when their right half scored from 20 yards. After this Pulborough really piled on the pressure, and a minute from time J. Leadbeatter snatched a point after beating two defenders from a Baker pass.

10-12-1966 vs Wick

A strong finish by Pulborough which brought all their 6 goals in the last half hour enabled them to pull off a surprise West Sussex League win at Wick. Wick attacked for most of the first half and the visiting defence did well to concede only 2 goals. In the second half Pulborough put on the pressure and, from a corner from Upjohn, Baker converted. A minute later Lewis levelled the scores from an Upjohn cross. Lewis hit number 3, after a good run, as Pulborough dominated the game with 10 minutes to go. After a fine run and pass from Parker, Baker placed the ball wide of the keeper for the 4th. Baker completed his hat-trick by driving home a fine shot. Later, when the ball was cleared up to Baker, he put M. Hatchard through, who completed Pulborough's half dozen at the second attempt.

PFC G. Loomes, T. Hatchard, G. Mason, J. Leadbeatter, N. Pope, B. Davis, G. Parker, M. Hatchard, G. Lewis, M. Baker, G. Upjohn.

19-9-1970 vs Bognor Reserves

Pulborough notched up their fourth West Sussex League Division 1 victory of the season when they beat Bognor Reserves 4-1. They began shakily, however, and found themselves a goal down after 20 minutes. The home sides reply came from the penalty spot, Lewis made a mistake with his shot after Clark had been brought down. Pulborough took the lead soon afterwards when J. Leadbeatter headed home a free-kick and Bognor received an even bigger setback shortly before the interval when their inside-left was sent off, apparently for using bad language. Pulborough capitalised on their opponents' misfortune when Fallowfield ran on to take a through ball from Clark and chip it over the advancing goalkeeper. Pulborough dominated the second half and played some splendid football. Lewis scored the fourth with a fine drive.

PFC C. Carter, N. Pope, M. Brow n, M. Hatchard, A. Leadbeatter, J. Leadbeatter, T. Wells, B. Huffer, G. Fallowfield, G. Lewis, G. Clark, sub T. Roberts.

3-10-1970 vs East Preston

Pulborough lost their unbeaten home record when they went down by the odd goal in 5 to East Preston in Saturday's WSL D1 fixture. The visitors took an early lead, but Pulborough equalised when Lewis rounded the keeper and shot into an empty net. They should have gone ahead, but 2 Fallowfield drives were brilliantly saved and Wells headed over the bar from close range. After the interval Pulborough's Lewis scored from the penalty spot after a defender had handled the ball. But the visitors equalised from a corner kick. Then East Preston sent a stream of long balls down the middle, and had keeper Carter in some trouble. With 5 minutes to go he collided with an opposing striker and was carried off. Fallowfield substituted in goal and, in the last minute, watched the ball sail into the net while standing 5 yards off his line.

10-10-1970 vs South Bersted

Pulborough conceded both WSL D1 points to South Bersted on Saturday. There was an ominous start to the game, when only 9 Pulborough players had arrived, but they held firm until Clark and Wells arrived. Pulborough played well at this stage, and Clark put them ahead. Just before half time, South Bersted missed a penalty. When the home side equalised after the interval, Pulborough's game went to pieces, passing movements broke down, and simple chances were squandered. They paid the inevitable price of frittered chances when the South Bersted centre forward scored the winning goal. But then they missed another penalty.

17-10-1970 vs APV

A Pulborough forward line, sharper than for several weeks, crashed 5 goals past APV keeper in the 2nd round of the Sussex Intermediate Cup on Saturday. APV controlled the mid-field for long spells, but their finishing never achieved the success their build -up play promised. The home side took the lead through J. Leadbeatter, after good work with Lewis. Upjohn made it 2 with a header from a Fallowfield corner. Lewis and Fallowfield combined to create Pulborough's 3rd for Lewis, and Fallowfield scored number 4 with a shot from an acute angle. After the interval APV reduced the arrears during a defensive mix up. But the result was never in doubt and Fallowfield scored a 5th following a fine run by Clark. The only change to the normal squad was that J. Harrison played in goal for the injured Carter.

24-10-1970 vs Graylingwell

Pulborough's Glen Lewis scored 3 times as the home side revelled in the final 15 minutes in

Saturday's WSL D1 game with visiting Graylingwell. In the first half Pulborough made most of the running and a quick ball out of defence was pushed through for Lewis to score. Upjohn was then put through and his cross was headed home by Clark. After the break the visitors hit back to reduce the arrears, and only good work by M. Hatchard and keeper Carter kept the opposition at bay. In the last 15 minutes, it was all Pulborough, and Lewis hammered home the 3rd from close range, and completed his hat-trick from the spot after being brought down. Following a throw in and good running by Upjohn, Lewis's shot on the turn beat the goalkeeper, and just before the end Fallowfield made it 6.

7-11-1970 vs Rustington

A scrambled goal just before the end of Saturday's WSL D1 game at Rustington cost Pulborough a point. They opened the scoring when Clark squeezed the ball past the keeper, after good work by Lewis. But Pulborough paid for midfield gaps when Rustington equalised through their inside left. The midfield link was repaired in the second half, when Wells was moved back. Pulborough then got on top to create some moves, with Fallowfield and Lewis coming close. A break by Wells down the right, and a well-judged cross was excellently headed home by Fallowfield to give the visitors the lead. Pulborough looked certain of 2 points until a goalmouth scramble resulted in Rustington gaining a well-deserved point.

14-11-1970 vs Lavant

Pulborough were in fine form on Saturday when they beat visiting Lavant to reach the 3rd round of the Sussex Intermediate Cup. Both sides found difficulty in controlling the ball on the greasy surface but Lavant took the lead after half an hour. Their inside-left, running in from deep, outwitted Pulborough's offside trap before stroking the ball into the corner of the net. Just before half time, Pulborough equalised, when Lewis slid home a cross. As Pulborough's confidence grew Lewis and Huffer were unlucky not to score at least 3 goals. Fallowfield finally added the 2nd with a close range drive and, with 6 minutes left to go, Pope the full back crashed in the 3rd following a corner kick. Seconds before the final whistle, Carter saved a penalty.

21-11-1970 v East Preston

Top Division 1 WSL goalscorers Pulborough added another 4 to their tally when they disposed of East Preston on Saturday. Roberts put them ahead after 10 minutes but only a superb save from Carter, just on half time, prevented an East Preston equaliser. In the second half Pulborough went further ahead through Lewis, after good work by Huffer and Upjohn. Upjohn himself scored soon afterwards. East Preston pulled one back but Lewis restored the lead with a header.

28-11-1970 vs Arundel

In Saturday's Malcolm Simmonds cup tie, Arundel, currently WSL leaders, started as clear favourites against leading Division 1 goalscorers Pulborough. But they had to fight all the way before finally going through to the next round. Arundel took the lead after 15 minutes, when the inside-left's hard, low shot went in off the inside of a post. Shortly afterwards the ball struck the arm of Pulborough centre half A. Leadbeatter and, despite protest, the referee awarded a penalty, centre forward Allan making no mistake with his spot kick. Pulborough hit back and were rewarded when Roberts netted a Huffer cross. In the second half Huffer almost equalised for Pulborough when the best shot of the game was inched over the the bar by the Arundel keeper.

PFC team: C. Carter, N. Pope, M. Hatchard, A. Leadbeatter, M. Brown, T. Wells, B. Huffer, J. Leadbeatter, G. Lewis, G. Fallowfield, T. Roberts.

5-12-1970 v Chichester

After a shocking 1st half display, Pulborough pulled themselves together in time to defeat a poor Chichester side in Saturday's WSL D1 fixture. Late in the first half Chichester's outside right, was allowed to lob the ball over the hands of stranded keeper Carter. After the break, however, Pulborough's play became more positive, and Fallowfield levelled the scores with a left foot drive, Clark then added a 2nd, finding space for himself Fallowfield scored a 3rd, and topped off a fine display with a third goal, in the last few minutes a defensive error left Lewis to crack in Pulborough's 5th.

12-12-1970 v Rudgwick

When Pulborough received Rudgwick in the 3rd round of the Sussex Intermediate Cup on

Saturday, the local derby lived up to expectations. More than a hundred spectators were treated to goals and plenty of excitement. Pulborough were on top in the early stages and a Fallowfield shot bounced off the keeper before a defender headed into his own net. As the home side slackened off, Rudgwick equalised. In the second half it was Rudgwick's turn to take the initiative and their outside right scored. But as Pulborough fought their way back into the game, Lewis and Fallowfield had shots well saved by the keeper. Lewis finally levelled the scores with a header when Clark crossed accurately from the right. Clark's glancing header from a Huffer free kick gave Pulborough the lead again and Clark rounded off a great display when his pass was cracked in by Lewis.

19-12-1970 v Littlehampton Reserves

The absence of injured first team players, no subs, and a strong Littlehampton side led to Pulborough being outplayed in Saturday's WSL D1 game. After Pulborough had missed several chances Littlehampton scored and when Brown was injured Pulborough were down to ten men. The home side exploited the weakened left flank and soon increased their lead, before running their score up to 6. Pulborough came closest to scoring when Lewis hit the bar.

2-1-1971 v Graffham

Missed chances cost Pulborough Reserves a point when they visited Graffham in frosty conditions for Saturday's West Sussex League game. They always looked dangerous and created many chances. After a few minutes played, a long through ball found Trefor Jones and he gave the keeper no chance with his fierce shot. Mick Pattenden, who was giving a great display in goal, was then penalised and Graffham levelled the score from the spot. Geoff Upjohn and Richard Czarnecki hit the woodwork. After the interval the visitors lost their composure and during heavy pressure skipper John Habgood handled for Graffham to once again score with a well-taken spot kick. This stirred Pulborough and continued pressure on the icy pitch brought a reward, the Graffham defence could only scramble the ball away as far as Tony Leadbeatter and he slammed it into the he top corner of the net to snatch a point.

PFC team M. Pattenden, A. Leadbeatter, P. Chapman, J. Jupp, J. Habgood, B. Davis, A. Richardson, R. Czarnecki, T. Jones, G. Upjohn, R. Branch, sub M. Leadbeatter.

9-1-1971 vs Storrington

The expected thriller resulted on Saturday when Storrington and Pulborough met for the first time in recent years in the Sussex Intermediate Cup. After Pulborough had taken an early lead through Huffer, Storrington fought back with goals by Searle, Dodsworth and Connor. Storrington then made the mistake of relaxing and Pulborough pulled themselves back into the game with 2 goals by Lewis. In extra time, with both teams tiring, Storrington soon went ahead through Connor but again Pulborough equalised with a header by Huffer. Hero Connor scored the winner for Storrington from ten yards in the last minute of extra time, much to the relief of the crowd of about 250.

16-1-1971 vs Rogate

After winning the previous weeks West Sussex League rehearsal 4-2 Pulborough Reserves went down in their Division 5 Charity Cup tie by the odd goal on Saturday. Rogate had a completely changed team on this occasion, including a centre forward who relied on his weight to get him through. He put them ahead from a through ball, but when they hit back Pulborough's finishing let them down. Rogate added a second following a goal-mouth scramble. But the home side were now settling down together and producing some good moves and when John Stewart pushed the ball back for Geoff Upjohn, he slammed one in from fully 30 yards. After the interval Pulborough pressed and when a shot from Trevor Wells was blocked Alan Richardson equalised from an almost impossible angle. Their revival proved in vain, however, when Rogate scored the winner with a well taken header from a corner.

PFC: John Harrison, John Jupp, Peter Chapman, Melvin Leadbeatter, John Habgood, Basil Davis, Alan Richardson, Richard Czarnecki, Trevor Wells, Geoff Upjohn, John Stewart, sub Trefor Jones.

3-4-1971 vs Wigmore

Pulborough's 7 goals at Wigmore in Saturday's league game brought their total to more than 100 this season. Lewis put them ahead with a deflected shot and Fallowfield made it 2. Wells added the 3rd from fully 40 yards. In the second half, Clark increased the lead before Fallowfield completed his hat-trick, and Lewis completed the scoring.

29-9-1979 vs Stedham

In an exciting West Sussex League Division 1 game, Pulborough drew with Stedham 2-2 on Saturday, after being two goals down. Stedham played some masterly football in the first half but Pulborough hit back with goals from John Jupp and Glen Lewis to make it 2-2 at half time. The second half was fast and flowing but there was no further score.

20-10-1979 vs Slinfold

From being two goals down, Pulborough stormed back to win 3-2 against Slinfold in Saturday's division 1 match. A Roberts own goal gave Slinfold the lead and Sparling put the visitors further ahead early in the second half after good work by Haines. A header from Glen Lewis and a shot by Andy Kynoch brought Pulborough level and in the closing minutes Kynoch slammed home the winner.

15-9-1979 vs Watersfield

Watersfield offered little resistance to Pulborough, who won 5-1 on Saturday after taking the lead through Glen Lewis. By half time they were 3-0 up, with Lewis getting 2 more and despite a temporary recovery by Watersfield in the second half, Pulborough went further ahead through John Jupp. Harper scored a consolation for the home team but Pulborough made it 5-1 when Nick Bainbridge nodded in a Lewis cross.

29-9-1979 vs Stedham

In an exciting West Sussex League Division 1 game, Pulborough drew with Stedham 2-2 on Saturday after being 2 goals down. Stedham played some masterly football in the first half but Pulborough hit back with goals from John Jupp and Glen Lewis made it 2-2 at half time. The second half was fast and flowing but there was no further score.

20-10-1979 vs Slinfold

From being 2 goals down, Pulborough stormed back to win 3-2 against Slinfold in Saturday's division 1 match. A Roberts own goal gave Slinfold the lead and Sparling put the visitors further ahead early in the second half after good

work by Haines. A header from Glen Lewis and a shot by Andy Kynoch brought Pulborough level and, in the closing minutes, Kynoch slammed home the winner.

3-11-1979 vs Petworth

Pulborough's never-say-die attitude earned them a 3-2 victory over Petworth in Saturday's Division 1 match. Kitchener opened the scoring for Petworth after racing through the home defence and then put the visitors two up. Glen Lewis pulled one back for Pulborough before the break and Bob Chandler equalised with a shot that flew past Vickery. Man-of-the match Lewis scored the winner with the Petworth defence in disarray.

10-11-1979 vs Barns Green

Pulborough gave away a late goal to draw 3-3 with Barns Green in Saturday's Division 1 clash. After 20 minutes Barns Green were 2-up but goals from Glen Lewis (penalty) and Andy Kynoch (2) gave Pulborough a 3-2 advantage at the break. Dumbrill missed a penalty for the home side but made amends with the late equaliser.

13-9 1980 vs Lavant

Pulborough, after going in at half time 2-1 down to Lavant, fought back to win 3-2 in the FC Lane Electronics Premier Division. Lavant went 2-up with well-taken chances but a diving header by Tim Wilkens put Pulborough back in the game. In the second half a fighting display by the premiership newcomers led to goals from Nick Bainbridge and a young Dave Smith gave them a deserved victory.

6-12-1980 vs Sunallon

Sunallon were glad to hang on to both premier league points following a spirited Pulborough comeback to make the score 2-1 on Saturday. Despite having nearly all the play in the first half, they only had M. Jones fine individual goal to show for it at the break. But early in the second half Nick Taylor fired home number two from the edge of the box. Unfortunately Sunallon then relaxed and allowed Pulborough back into the game. John Jupp pulled a goal back 10 minutes from time and only stout defensive work and fine goalkeeping from Lockyer enabled Sunallon to hold onto two points.

Players from the 1970s & 80s

ROBERT CHANDLER (BOB) was born in Shoreham 24th February 1958. He went to the local Primary School in Pulborough and then to Collyer's in Horsham. On leaving he went to work for Sun Alliance in Horsham. He now earns his living with Royal Mail and has been with them for a number of years. He played a few games for the Colts, a side which played some friendly matches. He joined the senior side at the start of the 1973/74 season and his first game was for the 2nd XI 15th September 1973 versus Northchapel, he then broke into the 1st XI and his first game for them was against Sidlesham 6th October 1973. Bob soon established himself in the team. He was an inside forward, or in today's football terminology a midfield player. He was tall and lean and soon adapted to the rigours of playing against bigger opponents. He was an intelligent and skilful player, who had a good range of passing. Bob left at the end of the l978-79 season, he did not want to leave, but he was working and now living in Horsham so played for his firm Sunallon. He still lives in Horsham.

ROBERT HEWITT (BOB) born 29th January 1946, in Burnley, Lancashire. He went to Hargher Clough School and then to Rosegrove Secondary Modern. He attended Burnley Municipal College and became a tool maker. Aged 22 he went to live in Jersey for 7 years, he had short spells in two or three jobs, before tacking a position with R.C.A. On returning to England he worked for Spiro Gills as an estimator, Bob then moved on to be a sales manager and Finally he was sales director for the company. He joined the Club in 1975 and his first XI debut 27th December 1975, was at Barns Green. He played in the forward line, although not a great goal scorer, he got his share of goals. He was one of the fittest players in the Club and always gave everything when he played and was not happy if others did not give the same commitment, with his work rate and movement he made space for others. Bob lives in Pulborough and he still runs to keep fit. He played for West Chiltington.

TIM WILKENS was born in Horsham on 29th September 1959. He attended school at Oxford Road, Arunside and Forest. On leaving he went to work as an apprentice compositor with the West Sussex County Times. He had several other jobs after that. He now works with people who have Alzheimer's Disease in the West Sussex area, making sure they have all the help they require, a rewarding and important position. Tim joined the Club during the 1977-78 season and made debut when he came on as a sub for the first team on 1st October 1977 against Bosham. He soon established himself in the first XI. He was versatile and could play in midfield or defence. He was a very aggressive player, never one to shirk a tackle, a good ball winner and a good header, someone you were pleased to have on your side. He was fit and quick and could run all day, a good Club man and popular. He also played for Slinfold, Broadbridge Heath and Horsham Olympic where he is the manager and has been for several seasons. He lives in Horsham.

ROWLAND BRANCH (TWIGGY) was born in Ashurst on 15th April 1953. On moving to Pulborough, he went to St. Mary's School and then The Weald in Billingshurst. On leaving School he worked for Daux Builders in Billingshurst, as an apprentice and in 1972 became self-employed. He joined the Club during the 1969-70 season and played his first game for the second XI on 14th March 1970 against Amberley. His first game for the first XI was when he came on as a sub on 20th February 1971 against Wigmore Athletic. Until 1974-75 Twiggy played in the forward line, but then settled down and played as a full back. He was quick and aggressive, never one to pull out of a tackle and good in the air; a very committed player, he always gave everything when he played. He also played for Billingshurst and now lives in Wisborough Green.

PAUL GIBSON was born in Hong Kong in 1962. He then moved to New Zealand before coming to live in England. In 1976 he attended The Weald School in Billingshurst and went on to college in West Bromwich in the Midlands. On leaving college he went to work for the Metropolitan Police, as a photographer, an occupation he is still in today. He joined 'The Robins' at the start of the 1983-84 season and made his first XI debut against Lancing & Sompting Legion on 1st October 1983. Paul was a first class goalkeeper, the best I had the fortune to manage. He was not that tall for a keeper, being around five foot ten, but was powerfully built and could dominate the penalty area, coming out for crosses and corner kicks and not afraid to go down at players' feet. He gave the defence confidence. He gained two losers medals in 1984-85 and 1985-86, when the team reached the Finals of the West Sussex League, Chichester Charity Cup. In 1985-86 he won a winners medal when the team won the West Sussex League Division 2 North title, the same year he was in the side that won the Marley Cup. Paul played for the West Sussex League intermediate team and also the Junior XI. When Paul had to move away because of his work it was a huge loss to the Club, class goalkeepers are very hard to find. He also played for Horsham, Billingshurst and Storrington. Paul now lives in Berkshire.

MICHAEL OSBORNE (OSSIE) was born in Winchester in 1961. He moved to Pulborough in 1974 and he went to The Weald School in Billingshurst. In 1976 he started work as an apprentice electrician for Allfrey's, a local firm. He is now a self-employed electrician and lives in the Worthing area. Mike joined the Club at the start of the 1978-79 season and made his first appearance against Harting, coming on as a substitute for the second XI on 7th October 1978. He made his first XI debut against Manor Athletic on 22nd January 1983, coming on as a substitute. He was usually played as a full back. Although not the quickest, he was a very sound defender and always tried to keep it simple, a good team player. Mike was in the squad that won the Marley Cup in 1984. In 1985 he was in the team that reached the Final of the West Sussex League, Chichester Charity Cup. He played into his thirties and was a one-club man.

COLIN SPAIN was born in Pulborough 4th January 1961. He went to School in North Heath and The Weald in Billingshurst. He attended Chichester College, taking a course in business studies, then went to work at the County Court in Horsham. Colin then went to live in Bridgend, South Wales, where he works as Senior Personal Injury claims underwriter for HCC Insurance. He made his Club debut on 26th November 1977, when he came on as a substitute for the second XI against Loxwood and made his first XI debut against Fernhurst on 7th October 1978. Colin played in several different positions for the Club, including goalkeeper, he established himself in the first XI during the 1980-81 season. He settled down to play as a full back, could play on both sides, was quick and a good asset for the side. He got a medal in the 1984-85 season when the team reached the Final of the West Sussex League, Chichester Charity Cup and the next season when the team played in the same competition. He was part of the squad that won the West Sussex League Division 2 North title in 1985-86. He also won a medal when the second XI won the West Sussex League Division 5 central title. Colin assisted me in running the junior team, before eventually taking over, he was also a qualified referee.

ANDY KYNOCH born 16th November 1957 in Windsor. He attended North Nolms School and then went on to Collyer's School in Horsham. On leaving he went into the aviation industry and is now Director of Airport Consumer Services for Europe and the Middle East. In 1969 while at Collyer's he was captain of the School under-12 side. In 1970 he was in the squad for North West Sussex under 14s, from 1970 to 1975 he represented Sussex Schoolboys at under 15 and under 19. He played for Brighton & Hove youth team when Brian Clough was manager of Brighton. Andy joined the Club at the start of the 1976-77 season and made his first XI debut on 18th September 1976 against Chichester Hospitals. He played on the left hand side, either as a full back or in midfield. He was powerfully built but not the tallest, he had a great left foot and could hit long raking passes and also scored with some powerful shots. He was not the quickest but was quite skilful and always gave of his best. He won medals in 1984-85 and 1985-86 when the team reached the Finals of the West Sussex League Chichester Charity Cup. In 1985-86 he was part of the squad that won the West Sussex League Division 2 North title. He was in the squad that won the Marley Cup in 1984. Andy represented the West Sussex League side. In 1990 he became player/manager of the Club, resigning from this post in 1992. He played for Roffey, Old Collyerians and Horsham Olympic. He was a popular member of the Club, as a player, manager and committee member. He lives in Ashington.

KIM FURLONGER (SHAGGER) was born in Storrington 8th October 1962. He went to the local Primary School, then Rydon School in Thakeham and finished his schooldays at Steyning Grammar. Kim worked for Paula Rosa on leaving School and stayed there for many years; he is now self-employed. He joined 'The Robins' at the start of the 1985-86 season and made his first XI debut on 7th September 1985 against Horsham Olympic and quickly became a first team regular. A talented footballer who could have played in midfield but became a central defender, he was good in the air, strong in the tackle and had the ability to bring the ball out of defence to set moves going. He also had a powerful shot. Kim represented the West Sussex League side. He was a member of the squad that won the West Sussex League Division 2 North championship. He was in the side that reached the Final of the West Sussex League, Chichester Charity Cup. He retired from playing during the 1990-91 season. Kim also played for Storrington, where he now lives.

DAVID RHODER (ZOONEY) was born in Pulborough 13th March 1962. He went to St. Mary's School and The Weald School in Billingshurst. He started work on local building sites and did so for several years before going to work for British Rail. He joined the Club in 1977 and played his first game for the second XI on 10th September 1977, against Stedham. His first XI debut was against Watersfield 15th September 1979. Dave played as a central defender, was good in the air, a tenacious tackler, too brave for his own good at times and better on the ground than some people gave him credit for. On 25th September 1982 he suffered an horrific injury, the worst broken leg I have ever seen. Most players would have retired after such an injury but he came back and resumed playing in 1984. In 1994 he sustained another badly broken leg. In 1984-85 and 1985-86 he was in the side that reached the Final of the West Sussex League, Chichester Charity Cup. In the same year he was in the squad that won the West Sussex League Division 2 North title. He was a good Club man. He played for Billingshurst for a season. He lives in Pulborough.

MICK RUFF was born in Amberley 11th October 1955. He attended Amberley Primary School then Rydon county secondary and finished up at The Weald School in Billingshurst. His working life started at Spiro Gills in the sheet metal shop, as an apprentice. He has been with his present company SOGAT for a number of years. He came to the Club at the start of the 1971-72 season and made his debut for the second XI on 18th September 1971 when he came on as a sub against Lurgashall, his first XI debut 18th March 1972 was against Southwick. In his early years he played in the back four. In 1974 he broke his leg and didn't start playing again until 1976. Mick became a regular in the first team in 1981, still in the defence, but he played a few games in midfield. He was not the quickest but had a good football brain and the ability to read the game,

break up moves and bring the ball out of defence to set the team going forward. He was a very good player. He was in the West Sussex League Chichester Charity Cup Final side and won a losers trophy in 1985. The following year he won a winners medal when the team won the West Sussex League Division 2 North title and also a medal when the team again reached the Final of the Chichester Charity Cup. He was in the side that won the Marley Cup the same year. Mick lives just outside Billingshurst.

STEVE LEADBEATTER was born in Pulborough on 23rd July 1964. He attended St. Mary's School and The Weald in Billingshurst. Steve went to work for British Gas and is still with them today. He joined 'The Robins' in 1980 and played his first game for the second team on 6th September 1980 against North Holmwood and scored his first goal for the club. He made his first XI debut when he came on as a sub against Emsworth on 29th November 1980 and on 6th December 1980 was selected to start for the side. He became a regular in the side during the 1981-82 season. Steve was a right sided midfield player, very quick, and with his pace and dribbling skills he created chances for the team as well as scoring his share of goals. He was an intelligent player who had an important role in the way the team played. Both I and the rest of the side had respect for the way he played. In 1983 he broke his leg and did not resume playing until 1984. In the 1985-86 season Steve was in the squad that won the West Sussex League Division 2 North Championship and reached the Final of the West Sussex League Chichester Charity Cup. Steve was a loyal one-Club man. He lives in Bramber.

COLIN HUTTON (ARCHIE) a proud Scot, was born in Hamilton on 28th October 1953. He went to Glen Lee School and Hamilton Academy. At the age of 12 he played for Wisham Junior side, the same Club that Kenny Dalglish played for as a junior. He then played for Hamilton Avondale. On leaving School he went to work as an apprentice for Mr. Buick at his Newbury racing stables. On moving to Sussex he worked at the very successful racing stables in Pulborough for Mr. Harwood. He left there and went to the Arundel stables of Mr. Dunlop. Archie joined the Club in 1977, his first game was for the second XI against Loxwood 15th January 1977. His first XI debut was against Graffham 9th September 1978. He was a midfield player with a lot of talent who could beat opponents with his dribbling. He was given a free role when we were in possession to get forward, create chances and score goals. At his best he was difficult to stop. He left the Club in 1995. He played for Lambourne FC and also Watersfield. Archie lives in Rustington.

PHIL GORING was born in Crawley on 13th October 1959. He attended Thomas Bennet School there. On leaving he went into the building trade, working for Longley's, a local firm. After several years with them he became self-employed and now runs his own company, based in Watersfield. He played for several different Clubs, including, Desmond Anderson, Stone Platt and Mallory Batteries. Phil joined us in 1984 and made his second team debut on 29th December 1984 against Barns Green; his first XI debut was against Slinfold on 2nd March 1985. He was a big man, good in the air and strong in the tackle, a ball winner, who could intimidate the opposition. Owing to work commitments he only played for one season. Phil lives in Watersfield.

TIM HATCHARD was born 7th November 1966 in Pulborough. He went to St. Mary's School and The Weald in Billingshurst. On leaving he went to work for a nursery in Mare Hill, then Mason's nursery, then spent time at Riverside Concrete. He now works in the office for Royal Mail at the Pulborough branch. He first played for the under 11 junior side and came through the other age groups to play for the senior sides. His first game for the second XI was against Lurgashall on 4th September 1982. He then took a year out and began again in 1984. He made his first team debut 29th December 1984 against Old Collyerians. Tim was in the team that reached the Final of the West Sussex League Chichester Charity Cup in the 1984-85 season. That season he scored 41 goals, mainly for the second XI, as he was not always available to play. He was not able to play the following season. He resumed in 1986. He played centre forward most of the time, he always worked for the team. To score 20 plus goals virtually every season is good in any standard of football. He had the ability to score goals from anywhere on the pitch. He had his best seasons in the 1990s and in the 1993-94 season scored 48 goals. Tim had knee problems and after two operations had to call it a day and gave up playing in 1996. He lives in Rustington.

DAVE SMITH [see Managers].

NICK BAINBRIDGE was born in London 13th May 1958. On moving to Pulborough he attended St.

Mary's School and Collyer's in Horsham. On leaving there in 1976 he began working for Friends Provident and stayed there for the next 17 years. He is a financial adviser and owns his own company based in Dorset. He joined the Club at the start of the 1973-74 season, his debut came on 21st August 1973 against Storrington. He played wide on the left, as a winger going forward and dropping back into midfield when we were defending. Nick was skilful and very quick, able to beat defenders with ease. For a winger he scored a lot of goals, his best season was in 1979-80, when he got 19 goals and 3 hat-tricks. He created many chances for his teammates. From 1982 to 1985 he stopped playing and resumed again at the start of the 1985-86 season. He was in the side that reached the Final of the West Sussex League Chichester Charity Cup in 1986 and was in the squad that won the West Sussex League Division 2 North title the same year. That season he was selected for the West Sussex League side. Nick played for Horsham YMCA for a spell. He lives in Broadstone, in Dorset.

MARTIN HARRISON (HARRY) was born in Cootham, near Storrington on 21st March 1964. He attended the local School in Spierbridge Road and then Steyning Grammar School. His working life began when he went to the Storrington firm Lanceleys, as an apprentice plumber. He then had a short spell with Merriworth builders, before going self employed. In 1993 he joined the Mitie company, where he is still employed today. He joined 'The Robins' at the start of the 1984-85 season and played his first game for the Club against Sunallon on 1st September 1984 and scored on his debut. He played as a striker, he was not the tallest, but he was well built and powerful. Harry was a good header of the ball and great at holding the ball up and bringing others into play and creating chances for them. He was a very fine goal scorer in his own right. He put opposing defenders under pressure, and forced mistakes from them. He was in the team that reached the Final of the West Sussex League Chichester Charity Cup in 1984-85 and 1985-86. He was in the squad that won the West Sussex League Division 2 North title in 1985-86. The same season he was selected to represent the West Sussex League side. He left the Club at the end of the 1988-89 season. Harry played for Storrington, Billingshurst, West Chiltington and Storrington Priory. He lives in Pagham.

PETER BIRD was born in Canada in 1967. On returning to Pulborough he went to St. Mary's School and The Weald in Billingshurst. He worked for Tesla engineering for several years and is now at Travis Perkins. Peter came through the ranks, first playing for the under-11 junior side and progressing into the senior sides. He joined the Club at the start of the 1983-84 season and played his first for the second XI 3rd September 1983 against Lurgashall, when he came on as a sub. His first team debut was against Lavant 14th January 1984 when he again came on as a sub. He was a forward, a very good all round player, strong and aggressive, a fine goal scorer, who struck up a good partnership with Harry. He was in the squad that reached the Final of the West Sussex League Chichester Charity Cup in 1985. The next year he was in the team that again reached the Final of the same competition and won the West Sussex League Division 2 North title. He played for Ashington, Storrington and East Preston.

RICHARD JAMES (DICKIE) first came to the Club in 1978. He made his second team debut 30th September 1978 and his first XI debut 23rd December 1978 against Slinfold. He started off playing in goal but after several years decided that he wanted to play on the field and was used as a striker. He was good in both positions but had he concentrated on one or the other he could have become very good. He was in the squad that reached the Final of the West Sussex League Chichester Charity Cup in 1984/5 and 1985/6 when the squad also won the West Sussex League Division 2 North title.

DAVE SCOTT was a Storrington lad who joined us in 1980. He made his debut for the second XI against Wisborough Green on 20th September 1980 and played his first XI game 31st January 1981 against Slinfold, when he came on as a sub. He was a big man, over 6 feet tall and well built, played on the left wing position, being a naturally left footed player who had the pace and ability to beat players, score goals and create chances for the team. Dave was in the team that reached the Final of the West Sussex League Chichester Charity Cup in 1985. He played for Storrington and West Chiltington.

DAVE LIDBETTER was born in Pulborough on 23rd October 1965. He attended St. Mary's School in the village before going on to The Weald in Billingshurst. On leaving School he went to work for Paula Rosa, a kitchen company in Storrington. He joined 'The Robins' in 1985. His first game for the second team was against Stedham Reserves, 31st August 1985, when he came on as a sub. His first XI debut was against Sidlesham Reserves 7th December 1985. After playing in midfield for a while, he settled down at right back. Dave was a strong, well-built man who was not afraid to get tackles in and break up attacks. He also got forward at every opportunity to help when we were attacking. Pulborough was his only Club. He was also a very good rugby player and turned out for the local rugby side. He lives in Storrington.

DAVE KING was born 26th May 1957 in Kilwinning, Scotland. He went to school in Kilburnie, first to St Bridgend and then Ladyland. In 1973 he enlisted in the Royal Air Force and served for 5 years. He then moved down to live in Sussex. In 1979 he went to work at Spiro Gills, leaving there in 1993. He worked in Storrington for GRS Engineering for 10 years, then had a short spell with the Body Shop in Littlehampton. In 2005 he returned to live in Milton-by-Kildary in Scotland. He found work with the Johnson Lift Scan Scotland Company and is still there today. He played football for Ford Prison and Bilsham United. Dave joined us at the start of the 1983-84 season and made his 1st XI debut 3rd September 1983, against East Preston Reserves. He was in the side that reached the Final of the West Sussex League Chichester Charity Cup in 1985 and 1986, when they also won the West Sussex League Division 2 North title. Dave was a midfield player, was strong and stocky and played a more defensive role, so others could go forward, he was good in the air, strong in the tackle and a good passer, he was my Captain and well respected by the team.

Results 1960 – 1989

WSL DIVISION 2, 1960/61

27-8-1960 [A] **Lavant** (W 2-1) A Leadbeatter 1, J Leadbeatter 1

3-9-1960 [A] **Sidlesham** (L 0-1)

10-9-1960 [A] **Bosham** (W 3-0) T Cousins 1, K Handley 1, J Leadbeatter 1

17-9-1960 [A] **Selsey** (L 2-3)

24-9-1960 [H] **Chidham** (W 3-0)

1-10-1960 SJC [A] **Loxwood Utd** (W 6-0) M Hatchard 3

8-10-1960 [H] **Aldingbourne** (W 11-2)

15-10-1960 SJC [A] **Hammer Utd** (W 6-4)

22-10-1960 [H] **Shippams Athletic** (L 3-4)

29-10-1960 [A] **Felpham Utd** (W 3-2)

5-11-1960 SJC [H] **Clymping** (W 5-0)

12-11-1960 [A] **Rustington** (D 1-1)

19-11-1960 [A] **Aldingbourne** (W 6-3)

26-11-1960 SJC [A] **Storrington** (L 0-3)

3-12-1960 [H] **Lavant** (W 5-1)

10-12-1960 [H] **Bosham** (W 7-4)

27-12-1960 [H] **Graffham** (L 0-6)

31-12-1960 [A] **Graffham** (L 1-8)

14-1-1961 [A] **Shippams Athletic** (L 5-7)

21-1-1961 [H] **Pagham** (L 1-7)

4-2-1961 [H] **Emsworth** (W 5-0)

11-2-1961 [A] **Pagham** (L 0-3)

18-2-1961 [H] **Sidlesham** (L 0-2)

25-2-1961 [H] **Chidham** (W 6-1)

4-3-1961 [H] **Rustington** (L 2-4)

18-3-1961 [H] **Felpham Utd** (L 1-4)

25-3-1961 [A] **Emsworth** (L 0-6)

1-4-1961 [H] **Selsey** (L 0-2)

8-4-1961 [A] **Wick** (L 0-4)

11-4-1961 [H] **Wick** (L 1-2)

19-4-1961 [H] **Midhurst & Easebourne Utd Res** (W 9-2)

26-4-1961 [A] **Midhurst & Easebourne Utd Res** (L 2-4)

P28 | W11 | D1 | L16 | GF79 | GA84 | 24pts | 11th

WSL DIVISION 2, 1961/62

2-9-1961 [A] **Sidlesham** (L 1-2) M Hatchard 1

9-9-1961 [A] **Bosham** (L 2-5) M Brown 1, G Johnson 1

16-9-1961 [A] **Boxgrove Sports** (W 4-2) P Chapman 4

23-9-1961 [A] **Shippams Athletic** (W 2-1) P Chapman 1, J Leadbeatter 1

30-9-1961 [A] **Lavant** (L 1-4) G Burletson 1

7-10-1961 [H] **Bosham** (L 2-3) P Chapman 1, J Leadbeatter 1

14-10-1961 SJC [H] **Longleys** (W 4-2) J Leadbeatter 2, P Chapman 1, A Leadbeatter 1

21-10-1961 [H] **Wittering & Birdham Utd** (L 2-4) J Leadbeatter 2

28-10-1961 [A] **Rustington** (L 2-5) G Upjohn 1, OG 1

4-11-1961 SJC [H] **Pagham** (L 1-6) J Leadbeatter 1

11-11-1961 CCC [A] **West Dean** (W 9-2) A Leadbeatter 4, J Leadbeatter 4, D Madgett 1

18-11-1961 [H] **Emsworth** (W 4-2) K Handley 1, D Madgett 1, A Smith 1, G Upjohn 1

25-11-1961 [A] **Felpham Utd** (L 0-3)

2-12-1961 [H] **Lavant** (W 7-2) K Handley 3, M Hatchard 1, D Madgett 1, G Upjohn 1, OG 1

9-12-1961 [A] **Pagham** (D 1-1) M Hatchard 1

16-12-1961 [H] **Rustington** (W 3-1) A Leadbeatter 2, Madgett 1

30-12-1961 CCC [H] **Felpham Utd** (W 4-1) K Handley 2, A Leadbeatter 2

13-1-1962 [H] **Shippams Athletic** (W 4-0) G Lewis 2, M Hayler 1, G Upjohn 1

20-1-1962 [A] **Wittering & Birdham Utd** (W 4-3) K Handley 2, J Leadbeatter 1, G Upjohn 1

27-1-1962 CCC [A] **Yapton** (L 2-5) J Leadbeatter 1, D Madgett 1

3-2-1962 [H] **Boxgrove Sports** (L 2-3) M Hatchard 2

10-2-1962 [A] **Graffham** (W 6-4) A Leadbeatter 2, D Madgett 2, K Handley 1, G Upjohn 1

17-2-1962 [H] **Pagham** (L 1-2) K Handley 1

24-2-1962 [A] **Midhurst & Easebourne Utd Res** (L 2-6) M Hayler 1, A Leadbeatter 1

3-3-1962 [H] **Midhurst & Easebourne Utd Res** L1-4) K Handley 1

10-3-1962 [H] **Felpham Utd** (L 1-5) A Leadbeatter 1

17-3-1962 [A] **Stedham Utd** (L 3-4) J Leadbeatter 1, D Madgett 1, R Maybee 1

31-3-1962 [A] **Emsworth** (L 1-3) K Handley 1

7-4-1962 [H] **Graffham** (W 6-1) J Leadbeatter 2, L Hamilton 1, A Leadbeatter 1, D Madgett 1, G Upjohn 1

25-4-1962 [H] **Stedham Utd** (W 2-1) A Leadbeatter 1, G Lewis 1

28-4-1962 [H] **Sidlesham** (L 0-7)

P26 | W10 | D1 | L15 | GF66 | GA80 | 21pts | 9th

WSL DIVISION 2, 1962/63

1-9-1962 [A] **Sidlesham** (L 1-2) P Chapman 1

8-9-1962 [A] **Wittering Utd** (D 1-1) J Leadbeatter 1

15-9-1962 [A] **Emsworth Res** (W 5-2) P Chapman 2, J Leadbeatter 1, G Lewis 1, OG 1

22-9-1962 [A] **Yapton** (L 0-2)

6-10-1962 [H] **Selsey A** (W 3-2) P Chapman 1, J Leadbeatter 1, A Smith 1

13-10-1962 SJC [A] **Portfield Res** (L 1-2) G Lewis 1

20-10-1962 [H] **Bosham** (L 2-3) A Leadbeatter 1, G Upjohn 1

27-10-1962 [A] **Graffham** (W 2-1) G Lewis 2

3-11-1962 [A] **Selsey A** (L 1-6) P Chapman 1

10-11-1962 [H] **Bosham** (W 3-1) L Hamilton 1, R Maybee 1, G Upjohn 1

17-11-1962 [H] **Wittering Utd** (L 3-6) G Lewis 2, J Leadbeatter 1

24-11-1962 [H] **Emsworth Res** (W 7-4)

1-12-1962 CCC [A] **Wittering Utd** (W 3-2) G Lewis 2, G Upjohn 1

8-12-1962 [H] **Graffham** (W 2-1) J Leadbeatter 1, G Upjohn 1 [game abandoned after 71 minutes]

15-12-1962 [A] **Chichester B** (L 0-2)

22-12-1962 [A] **Lavant** (W 9-1) G Lewis 3, J Leadbeatter 2, B List 2, G Upjohn 1, OG 1

2-3-1963 [H] **Lavant** (L 0-3)

9-3-1963 [H] **Rustington** (W 5-0) G Upjohn 2, A Leadbeatter 1, J Leadbeatter 1, B List 1

16-3-1963 [A] **Fernhurst** (W 5-3) A Leadbeatter 1, G Lewis 1, R Thompsett 1, G Upjohn 1, OG 1

23-3-1963 [H] **Midhurst & Easebourne Utd Res** (W 3-1) J Leadbeatter 2, G Upjohn 1

30-3-1963 [A] **Rustington** (W 3-1) J Leadbeatter 2, G Upjohn 1

6-4-1963 [H] **Sidlesham** (W 2-1) R Maybee 1, G Upjohn 1

12-4-1963 [A] **Midhurst & Easebourne Utd-Res** (D 0-0)

13-4-1963 [H] **Chichester B** (W 2-1) B List 2

27-4-1963 [H] **Fernhurst** (W 9-0) G Upjohn 4, J Leadbeatter 2, B List 2, A Leadbeatter 1

1-5-1963 [H] **Pagham** (D 3-3) G Lewis 1, R Maybee 1, G Upjohn 1

4-5-1963 [H] **Yapton** (W 5-1) B List 2, J Leadbeatter 1, G Lewis 1, G Upjohn 1

18-5-1963 [A] **Pagham** (L 0-2)

P26 | W15 | D3 | L8 | GF76 | GA50 | 33pts | 4th

WSL DIVISION 2, 1963/64

4-9-1963 [A] **Yapton** (D 1-1) T Roberts 1 [abandoned after 80 mins]

14-9-1963 [A] **Southbourne** (D 3-3) M Brown 1, L Hookey 1, A Leadbeatter 1

21-9-1963 [A] **Selsey** A (L 0-3)

28-9-1963 SJC [H] **Ashington** (W 5-1) T Funnell 3, A Leadbeatter 1, G Lewis 1

5-10-1963 [H] **Bognor Training College** (W 4-1) T Roberts 2, R Maybee 1, G Upjohn 1

12-10-1963 SJC [A] **Sompting** (W 7-1) G Lewis 3, T Funnell 2, A Leadbeatter 1, J Leadbeatter 1

19-10-1963 [H] **Southbourne** (W 6-3) G Upjohn 3, G Lewis 2, J Leadbeatter 1

26-10-1963 [A] **Wittering Utd** (D 3-3) J Leadbeatter 1, G Lewis 1, G Upjohn 1

2-11-1963 SJC [H] **Durrington Athletic** W 6-3) T Funnell 3, Lewis 2, A Leadbeatter 1

9-11-1963 [A] **Lavant** (L 4-8) G Upjohn 3, R Maybee 1

16-11-1963 [H] **Wittering Utd** (L 4-5) T Funnell 1, G Lewis 1, R Maybee 1, G Upjohn 1

23-11-1963 SJC [A] **Wittering Utd** (L 4-5) G Lewis 1, R Maybee 1, G Upjohn 1, 1?

30-11-1963 [H] **Portfield Res** (W 7-2) T Funnell 2, G Upjohn 2, J Leadbeatter 1, G Lewis 1, 1?

7-12-1963 [H] **Lavant** (L 3-6) R Jones 1, A Leadbeatter 1, G Upjohn 1

14-12-1963 [A] **Bosham** (W 4-3) Upjohn 2, Funnell 1, R Jones 1

21-12-1963 [H] **Midhurst & Easebourne Utd Res** (W 3-2) R Maybee 1, M Stewart 1, G Upjohn 1

28-12-1963 [A] **Chichester B** (W 6-0) J Leadbeatter 2, T Funnell 1, G Lewis 1, G Upjohn 1, 1?

4-1-1964 [A] **Midhurst & Easebourne Utd Res** (W 6-4) J Leadbeatter 2, A Leadbeatter 1, G Lewis 1, A Spain 1, G Upjohnl

11-1-1964 [H] **Chichester B** (W 11-0) T Funnell 4, G Lewis 3, A Leadbeatter 2, J Leadbeatter 2

18-1-1964 CCC [A] **Sidlesham Res** (W 10-1) T Funnell 3, G Lewis 3, G Upjohn 2, J Leadbeatter 1, R Maybee 1

25-1-1964 [H] **Selsey** A (L 1-3) A Leadbeatter 1

1-2-1964 [H] **Emsworth Res** (W 2-1) T Funnell 1, R Maybee 1

8-2-1964 [H] **Arundel** A (W 5-2)

15-2-1964 CCC [A] **Lavant** (L 2-5) T Funnell 1, J Leadbeatter 1

22-2-1964 [A] **Graffham** (W 4-1) T Funnell 2, A Leadbeatter 1, J Leadbeatter 1

29-2-1964 [A] **Emsworth Res** (W 3-1) T Funnell 3

7-3-1964 [A] **Bognor Training College** (L 0-1)

14-3-1964 [H] **Yapton** (W 5-2) G Lewis 3, T Funnell 1, 1?

23-3-1964 [H] **Bosham** no result

28-3-1964 [H] **Graffham** (W 3-1) J Leadbeatter 2, T Funnell 1

7-4-1964 [A] **Arundel** A no result

11-4-1964 [A] **Portfield Res** (D 2-2) T Funnell 2

P26 | W14 | D4 | L8 | GF95 | GA64 | 32pts | 5th

WSL DIVISION 2, 1964/65

5-9-1964 [A] **Southbourne** Sports (W 3-2) A Leadbeatter 1, J Leadbeatter 1, G Upjohn 1

12-9-1964 [A] **South Bersted** (L 1-4) J Leadbeatter 1

19-9-1964 [A] **Lavant** (W 7-2) G Upjohn 4, M Brown 1, A Leadbeatter 1 G Lewis 1

26-9-1964 [A] **Bognor Training College** (W 4-2) A Leadbeatter 2, J Leadbeatter 1, G Lewis 1

3-10-1964 [H] **Emsworth Res** (W 5-3) J Leadbeatter 2, M Brown 1, A Leadbeatter 1, R Maybee 1

10-10-1964 SJC [A] **Rustington Res** (L 1-6) T Funnell 1

17-10-1964 [A] **Emsworth Res** (W 5-1) G Upjohn 3, T Funnell 1, J Leadbeatter 1

24-10-1964 [A] **Hunston Utd** (W 4-3) G Lewis 2, Upjohn 1, OG 1

31-10-1964 [H] **Chichester B** (W 7-1) P Chapman 3, G Upjohn 2, M Brown 1, J Leadbeatter 1

7-11-1964 CCC [A] **Littlehampton** A (W 9-2) P Chapman 3, J Leadbeatter 2, G Upjohn 2, M Brown 1, A Leadbeatter 1

14-11-1964 [A] **Bosham** (W 6-1) A Leadbeatter 2, J Leadbeatter 2, P Chapman 1, G Upjohn 1

21-11-1964 [H] **Bognor Training College** (L 1-2) J Leadbeatter 1

28-11-1964 [H] **Hunston Utd** (W 4-2) P Chapman 1, J Leadbeatter 1, G Lewis 1, G Upjohn 1

12-12-1964 CCC [H] **Chichester B** (W 5-2) G Upjohn 3, G Lewis 2

19-12-1964 [H] **Southbourne** Sports (W 6-1) M Brown 2, J Leadbeatter 2, G Lewis 1, G Upjohn 1

2-1-1965 [H] **Graffham** (W 3-2) M Brown 1, A Leadbeatter 1, OG1

9-1-1965 [A] **Graffham** (L 1-7) M Brown 1

16-1-1965 [H] **Slindon** (L 0-1)

23-1-1965 [A] **Chichester B** (W 8-1) G Upjohn 3, R Maybee 2, J Leadbeatter 1, G Lewis 1, 1?

30-1-1965 [H] **Lavant** D2-2) J Leadbeatter 1, R Maybee 1

6-2-1965 [A] **Petworth** (D 1-1) M Brown 1

13-2-1965 CCC [H] **Portfield** (L 0-4)

20-2-1965 [A] **Graylingwell** (W 2-0) A Spain 1, G Upjohn 1

27-2-1965 [A] **Yapton** (D 1-1) G Upjohn 1

13-3-1965 [H] **South Bersted** (W 3-1) G Lewis 2, R Maybee 1

20-3-1965 [H] **Petworth** (L 2-5) A Spain 1, G Upjohn 1

30-3-1965 [A] **Slindon** (W 2-1) G Lewis 1, R Maybee 1

10-4-1965 [H] **Yapton** (L 1-4) [A] Leadbeatter 1

17-4-1965 [H] **Graylingwell** (W 2-1) G Lewis 1, G Upjohn 1

P26 | W17 | D3 | L6 | GF81 | GA52 | 37pts | 3rd

WSL DIVISION 1, 1965/66

4-9-1965 [A] **Graylingwell** (L 0-6)

11-9-1965 [H] **Wittering Utd** (W 7-2) R Maybee 2, G Upjohn 2, A Leadbeatter 1, J Leadbeatter 1, G Lewis 1

18-9-1965 [A] **Portfield** (D 1-1) G Lewis 1

25-9-1965 [H] **Graylingwell** (L 3-5) J Leadbeatter 1, R Maybee 1, G Upjohn 1

2-10-1965 SIC [A] **Selsey** (W 7-3) P Chapman 2, G Lewis 2, A Leadbeatter 1, J Leadbeatter 1, R Maybee 1

9-10-1965 [H] **Yapton** (L 1-5) J Leadbeatter 1

16-10-1965 SIC [H] **Yapton** (L 3-4) P Chapman 1, G Lewis 1, G Upjohn,

23-10-1965 [A] **Ferring Res** (L 1-2) G Lewis 1

30-10-1965 [A] **South Bersted** (W 9-2) G Lewis 3, P Chapman 2, G Upjohn 2, A Leadbeatter 1, OG 1

6-11-1965 [H] **Lavant** (L 0-1)

13-11-1965 [H] **Ferring Res** (L 4-8) G Lewis 3, A Leadbeatter 1

20-11-1965 [A] **Yapton** (W 5-3) G Lewis 2, P Chapman 1, G Upjohn 1, 1?

27-11-1965 [H] **Bognor Training College** (L 2-4) P Chapman 1, M Hatchard 1

4-12-1965 WSBC [A] **Midhurst & Easebourne Utd** (L 2-9) M Brown 1, G Upjohn 1

11-12-1965 [H] **Petworth** (D 6-6) G Lewis 4, M Hatchard 1, G Upjohn 1

18-12-1965 [A] **Felpham Utd** (W 4-2) M Brown 1, J Leadbeatter 1, G Lewis 1, G Upjohn 1

1-1-1966 [A] **Slindon** (L 0-3

8-1-1966 [H] **Felpham Utd** (D 2-2) G Lewis 1, G Upjohn 1

15-1-1966 [H] **South Bersted** (W 6-1) M Brown 2, J Leadbeatter 2, G Upjohn 2

29-1-1966 [H] **Wick** A (W 4-1) J Leadbeatter 2, G Lewis 1, G Upjohn 1

5-2-1966 [A] **Wick A** (W 4-0) B Davis 1, A Leadbeatter 1, G Lewis 1, G Mason 1

12-2-1966 [H] **Horsham Olympic** (L 0-1)

19-2-1966 [A] **Horsham Olympic** (L 2-4) M Hatchard 1, G Lewis 1

12-3-1966 [A] **Wittering Utd** (L 1-6) J Leadbeatter 1

26-3-1966 [H] **Portfield** W15-1) G Lewis 8, G Upjohn 2, B Davis 1, M Hatchard 1, A Leadbeatter 1, OG 2

9-4-1966 [A] **Petworth** (L 0-3)

16-4-1966 [H] **Slindon** (L 1-4) G Upjohn 1

P24 | W8 | D3 | L13 | GF79 | GA77 | 19pts | 8ᵗʰ

WSL DIVISION 1, 1966/67

3-9-1966 [A] **Portfield Res** (D 3-3) M Baker 3

10-9-1966 [A] **South Bersted** (W 4-1) G Parker 3, G Lewis 1

17-9-1966 [H] **Wittering & Birdham Utd** (L 3-4) M Baker 1, G Lewis 1, G Parker 1

24-9-1966 [H] **Slindon** (W 2-1) G Lewis 2

1-10-1966 SIC [H] **Worthing Res** (L 2-7) G Parker 1, G Upjohn 1

15-10-1966 [H] **Felpham Utd** (W 5-0) M Baker 4, G Lewis 1

22-10-1966 [H] **Bognor Training College** (L 1-6) M Hatchard 1

5-11-1966 MSC [H] **Arundel A** (W 8-3) M Baker 3, G Lewis 2, P Chapman 1, M Hatchard 1, 1?

19-11-1966 [A] **Wittering & Birdham Utd** (D 4-4) M Baker 2, P Chapman 1, J Leadbeatter 1

26-11-1966 [H] **Ferring Res** (W 4-2) M Baker 3, J Leadbeatter 1

3-12-1966 [H] **South Bersted** (L 1-3) M Baker 1

10-12-1966 [A] **Wick A** (W 6-2) M Baker 3, Lewis 2, M Hatchard 1

31-12-1966 [H] **Petworth** (L 4-6) G Lewis 3, M Baker 1

14-1-1967 [H] **Horsham Olympic** (W 3-2) G Parker 2, M Baker 1

21-1-1967 [A] **Yapton** (L 2-4) M Baker 1, M Hatchard 1

28-1-1967 [H] **Portfield Res** (L 4-6) G Lewis 3, G Upjohn 1

11-2-1967 MSC [A] **Pagham** (L 0-6)

18-2-1967 [A] **Slindon** (W 3-0) G Lewis 2, G Upjohn 1

25-2-1967 [A] **Ferring Res** (D 2-2) G Lewis 1, G Upjohn 1

4-3-1967 [A] **Horsham Olympic** (D 2-2) G Lewis 1, G Upjohn 1

11-3-1967 [H] **Wick A** (W 6-1) J Leadbeatter 3, Upjohn 2, Lewis 1

18-3-1967 [A] **Bognor TC** (L 3-4) M Baker 1, J Leadbeatter 1, G Upjohn 1

25-3-1967 [H] **Yapton** (L 1-3) G Lewis 1

1-4-1967 [A] **Graylingwell** (L 4-5) M Brown 1, P Chapman 1, M Hatchard 1, 1?

8-4-1967 [A] **Felpham Utd** (W 2-1) G Lewis 2

15-4-1967 [A] **Petworth** (L 3-4) M Hatchard 1, G Upjohn 1, OG 1

29-4-1967 [H] **Graylingwell** (L 0-5)

P24 | W9 | D4 | L11 | GF72 | GA71 | 22pts | 8ᵗʰ

WSL DIVISION 1, 1967/68

2-9-1967 [H] **Wittering & Birdham Utd** (L 2-5) Lewis 1, Upjohn 1

9-9-1967 [H] **Emsworth** (W 4-3) Upjohn 2, M Brown 1, Hayler 1

16-9-1967 [A] **Portfield Res** (W 7-3) G Lewis 3, G Upjohn 2, M Hatchard 1, J Leadbeatter 1

23-9-1967 [H] **Yapton** (W 7-1) Lewis 4, M Hatchard 2, M Brown 1

30-9-1967 [A] **Wigmore Athletic** (W 4-2) G Lewis 2, G Upjohn 2

7-10-1967 [H] **Southbourne** (D 2-2) T Roberts 2

21-10-1967 MSC [H] **Billingshurst** (L 1-2) M Hatchard 1

28-10-1967 SIC [H] **Tarring** (W 7-3) Lewis 3, Huffer 2, Upjohn 2

4-11-1967 [A] **Yapton** (W 4-2) Lewis 2, Hatchard 1, Leadbeatter 1

11-11-1967 SIC [A] **Sompting** (L 2-3) G Lewis 2

18-11-1967 [H] **Graylingwell** (L 4-6) M Hayler 1, B Huffer 1, G Lewis 1, G Upjohn 1

25-11-1967 [A] **Southbourne** (D 2-2) G Lewis 2

2-12-1967 [A] **Slindon** (W 12-0) G Lewis 7, A Leadbeatter 2, L Hookey 1, B Huffer 1, G Upjohn 1

16-12-1967 [A] **Wittering & Birdham Utd** (D 3-3) G Lewis 2, M Hatchard 1

30-12-1967 [H] **Wick A** (W 3-2) G Upjohn 2, M Hatchard 1

6-1-1968 [A] **Angmering** (W 3-2) G Lewis 2, M Hatchard 1

20-1-1968 **Ferring Res** (L 2-3) G Lewis 1, G Upjohn 1

27-1-1968 [A] **Graylingwell** (D 2-2) A Leadbeatter 1, G Upjohn 1

10-2-1968 [A] **Angmering** (W 2-1) M Hatchard 1, G Lewis 1

17-2-1968 [H] **Slindon** (W 7-1) G Lewis 3, B Huffer 2, J Leadbeatter 1, T Roberts 1

24-2-1968 [A] **Emsworth** (W 3-2) G Lewis 2, D Lidbetter 1

2-3-1968 [A] **Wick A** (W 5-3) G Lewis 3, A Leadbeatter 1, 1?

9-3-1968 [H] **Portfield Res** (D 4-4) B Huffer 2, G Lewis 2

16-3-1968 [H] **Ferring Res** (W 5-1) B Huffer 1, G Lewis 1, D Lidbetter 1, 2?

30-3-1968 [A] **Rudgwick** (L 1-2) G Lewis 1

6-4-1968 [A] **Horsham Olympic** (L 0-3)

13-4-1968 [H] **Horsham Olympic** (L 0-2)

20-4-1968 [A] **Wigmore Athletic** (W 4-2) B Huffer 2, G Lewis 2

27-4-1968 [H] **Rudgwick** (W 4-1) Lewis 2, M Hatchard 1, Upjohn 1

P26 | W15 | D5 | L6 | GF96 | GA60 | 35pts | 4ᵗʰ

WSL DIVISION 1, 1968/69

7-9-1968 [A] **Portfield Res** (W 2-0) B Huffer 1, G Lewis 1

14-9-1968 [H] **Ferring R** (W 5-2) Lewis 3, G Clark 1, R Phillips 1

28-9-1968 [H] **Wigmore Ath R** (W 2-0) B Huffer 1, R Phillips 1

5-10-1968 MSC [A] **Southbourne** (L 0-6)

12-10-1968 [A] **Lancing & Sompting Legion** (L 2-3) M Hatchard 1, G Upjohn 1

19-10-1968 SIC [A] **Nuthurst** (W 3-1) B Huffer 1, G Lewis 1, G Upjohn 1

26-10-1968 [A] **Emsworth** (W 1-0) B Huffer 1

2-11-1968 SIC [A] **Worthing Res** (D 2-2) AET G Lewis 2

9-11-1968 SIC Replay [H] **Worthing Res** B Huffer 1, 1

16-11-1968 SIC [A] **Horsham Olympic** (L 1-6) G Upjohn 1

23-11-1968 [H] **Angmering** (W 2-0) G Lewis 1, G Upjohn 1

30-11-1968 [A] **Southbourne** (L 1-5) B Huffer 1

7-12-1968 [H] **Wittering Utd** (L 1-2) G Lewis 1

14-12-1968 [H] **Lancing & Sompting Legion** (L 3-4) B Huffer 1, J Leadbeatter 1, G Lewis 1

21-12-1968 [H] **Yapton** (W 2-1) B Huffer 1, G Lewis 1

4-1-1969 [A] **Bosham** (W 9-1) G Lewis 3, B Huffer 2, G Upjohn 2, J Leadbeatter 1, T Roberts 1

11-1-1969 [A] **Littlehampton Res** (W 6-2) G Lewis 5, 1?

18-1-1969 [H] **Hunston Utd** (L 3-5) G Lewis 2, J Leadbeatter 1

25-1-1969 **Bognor Res** (W 3-2) G Upjohn 2, B Huffer 1

22-2-1969 [H] **Bosham** (W 7-1) G Lewis 4, B Huffer 1, G Upjohn 1, T Wells 1

1-3-1969 [H] **Southbourne** (W 3-2) G Lewis 1, D Stenning 1, G Upjohn 1

8-3-1969 [H] **Rudgwick** (W 4-0) Upjohn 2, G Clark 1, G Lewis 1

22-3-1969 [H] **Bognor Res** (W 2-0) B Huffer 1, G Lewis 1

29-3-1969 [A] **Emsworth** (L 2-3) B Huffer 1, R Phillips 1

5-4-1969 [H] **Portfield Res** (W 6-1) G Lewis 3, M Bailey 1, G Clark 1, R Phillips 1

7-4-1969 [A] **Ferring Res** (W 5-0) G Lewis 2, G Clark 1, M Hatchard 1, T Roberts 1

10-4-1969 [H] **Littlehampton Res** (W 4-1) G Upjohn 2, G Lewis 1

12-4-1969 [A] **Hunston Utd** (L 2-3) G Clark 1, G Upjohn 1

15-4-1969 [A] **Rudgwick** (W 3-0) Lewis 1, T Roberts 1, Upjohn 1

17-4-1969 [A] **Yapton** (D 0-0) abandoned after 81 minutes

19-4-1969 [A] **Wigmore Athletic Res** (D 2-2) Lewis 1, R Phillips 1

26-4-1969 [A] **Angmering** (W 2-1

28-4-1969 [A] **Wittering Utd** (L 2-6)

P28 | W18 | D2 | L8 | GF86 | GA47 | 38pts | 4ᵗʰ

WSL DIVISION 1, 1969/70

30-8-1969 [A] **Bognor Res** (L 0-3)

1-9-1969 [A] **Hunston Utd** (W 6-3) R Phillips 3, G Fallowfield 2, G Upjohn 1

6-9-1969 [H] **Portfield Res** (W 3-2) G Fallowfield 2, G Upjohn 1

13-9-1969 [H] **Rudgwick** (L 2-4) G Fallowfield 1, R Phillips 1

20-9-1969 [A] **Sweetlands Sports** (L 2-4) R Phillips 1, Upjohn 1

27-9-1969 [A] **Wigmore Athletic Res** (L 0-2)

4-10-1969 MSC [A] **Angmering** (W 5-1) G Fallowfield 3, G Clark 1, G Upjohn 1

11-10-1969 [H] **Angmering** (W 3-1) Fallowfield 2, M Hatchard 1

18-10-1969 [H] **Chichester City 3rds** (L 0-1)

25-10-1969 [H] **Littlehampton Town Res** (W 6-1) G Fallowfield 2, G Lewis 2, G Clark 1, G Upjohn 1

1-11-1969 [A] **East Preston** (D 2-2) G Fallowfield 2

8-11-1969 [H] **Yapton** (W 2-1) G Clark 1, G Fallowfield 1

15-11-1969 SIC [A] **Shoreham Boys Club** (W 7-1) G Fallowfield 2, G Lewis 2, G Upjohn 2, T Roberts 1

22-11-1969 MSC [H] **Hunston Utd** (W 4-0) G Fallowfield 2, G Lewis 1, T Roberts 1

29-11-1969 [A] **Emsworth** (L 1-4) G Lewis 1

6-12-1969 [A] **Lancing & Sompting Legion** (L 0-4)

13-12-1969 SIC [A] **Midhurst & Easebourne Utd** (L 2-3) G Fallowfield 1, M Hatchard 1

20-12-1969 MSC [H] **Southwick Res** (D 3-3) G Fallowfield 1, M Hatchard 1, G Upjohn 1

27-12-1969 [A] **Yapton** (W 3-1) M Bailey 2, G Fallowfield 1

3-1-1970 [H] **Wigmore Athletic Res** (W 7-2) M Hatchard 2, G Upjohn 2, G Fallowfield 1, G Lewis 1

10-1-1970 [A] **Graylingwell** (W 3-1) Lewis 1, Upjohn 1, T Wells 1

24-1-1970 [A] **Angmering** (D 2-2) M Hatchard 1, G Lewis 1

31-1-1970 [H] **Hunston Utd** (W 3-2) G Fallowfield 1, M Hatchard 1, T Wells 1

7-2-1970 MSC replay [A] **Southwick Res** (L 0-7)

21-2-1970 [A] **Portfield Res** (W 1-0) G Lewis 1

7-3-1970 [H] **Graylingwell** (W 2-0) G Fallowfield 1, G Lewis 1

14-3-1970 [H] **Lancing & Sompting Legion** (L 3-4) M Brown 1, G Lewis 1, T Wells 1

21-3-1970 [H] **Emsworth** (L 0-3)

28-3-1970 [A] **Chichester City 3rds** (W 2-1) N Pope 1, T Wells 1

4-4-1970 [A] **Littlehampton Town Res**, D 1-1) G Lewis 1

11-4-1970 [H] **East Preston** (W 3-2) G Fallowfield 1, M Hatchard 1, G Lewis 1

15-4-1970 [A] **Rudgwick** (L 0-2)

18-4-1970 [H] **Bognor Res** (L 2-4)

25-4-1970 [H] **Sweetlands Sports** (W 2-1) M Bailey 1, G Lewis 1

P28 | W14 | D3 | L11 | GF61 | GA59 | 31pts | 6th

WSL DIVISION 1, 1970/71

29-8-1970 [H] **Littlehampton Town Res** (W 3-2)

1-9-1970 H **APV Res** (D 0-0)

5-9-1970 [H] **South Bersted** (W 12-0)

12-9-1970 [A] **Lavant** (L 3-6)

19-9-1970 **Bognor Res** (W 4-1) G Lewis 2, G Fallowfield 1, J Leadbeatter 1

26-9-1970 [A] **Hunston Utd** (W 4-0) G Lewis 3, G Fallowfield 1

3-10-1970 [A] **East Preston** (L 2-3) G Lewis 2

10-10-1970 [A] **South Bersted** (L 1-2) G Clark 1

17-10-1970 SIC [H] **APV Res** (W 5-2) G Fallowfield 2, J Leadbeatter 1, G Lewis 1, G Upjohn 1

24-10-1970 [H] **Graylingwell** (W 6-1) G Lewis 4, G Clark 1, G Fallowfield 1

7-11-1970 [A] **Rustington** (L 2-1) Clark, Fallowfield

14-11-1970 SIC [H] **Lavant** (W 3-1) Lewis, Fallowfield, Pope

21-11-1970 [A] **East Preston** (W 4-1) Roberts, Lewis, Huffer, Upjohn

28-11-1970 MSC [A] **Arundel Res** (L 2-1) Lewis

12-12-1970 SIC [A] **Rudgwick** (W 4-2)

19-12-1970 [A] **Littlehampton Town Res** (L 0-6)

9-1-1971 SIC [A] **Storrington** (L 4-5) AET B Huffer 2, G Lewis 2

16-1-1971 [A] **Graylingwell** (W 6-0) M Brown 3, G Clark 1, G Lewis 1, OG 1

23-1-1971 [H] **Rudgwick** (W 3-2)

30-1-1971 [H] **Chichester City 3rds** (W 2-0) G Lewis 1, OG 1

6-2-1971 [A] **APV Res** (W 6-1) G Fallowfield 2, M Brown 1, G Clark 1, B Huffer 1, G Lewis 1

13-2-1971 [H] **Hunston Utd** (W 5-0)

20-2-1971 [H] **Wigmore Athletic Res** (W 6-3)

27-2-1971 [A] **Lancing & Sompting Legion** (D 0-0)

6-3-1971 [H] **Rustington** (W 3-0) G Clark 1, G Fallowfield 1, B Huffer 1

13-3-1971 [H] **Lavant** (D 2-2)

20-3-1971 [A] **Billingshurst** (W 4-0) G Fallowfield 2, G Lewis 2

27-3-1971 [A] **Portfield Res** (W 10-1)

3-4-1971 [A] **Wigmore Athletic Res** (W 7-0)

10-4-1971 [H] **Portfield Res** (W 2-0) G Clark 1, G Lewis 1

17-4-1971 [H] **Billingshurst** (W 5-2) G Fallowfield 3, G Clark 2

20-4-1971 [H] **Lancing & Sompting Legion** (D 1-1) Fallowfield 1

24-4-1971 [A] **Rudgwick** (W 1-0) G Fallowfield 1

1-5-1971 [A] **Bognor Res** (W 1-0) G Fallowfield 1

P30 | W21 | D5 | L4 | GF110 | GA37 | 47pts | 1st

WSL PREMIER DIVISION 1971/72

28-8-1971 [H] **Chichester City Res** (W 4-2)

4-9-1971 [H] **Selsey Res** (L 0-6)

7-9-1971 [H] **Horsham Olympic** (W 5-0)

11-9-1971 [H] **Sweetlands** (W 3-0)

14-9-1971 [H] **Petworth** (D 3-3) G Lewis 3

18-9-1971 [H] **Wittering & Birdham Utd** (W 4-1)

25-9-1971 MSC [A] **Arundel Res** (L 2-6) G Upjohn 2

2-10-1971 [H] **Lavant** (D 2-2) G Lewis 1, G Upjohn 1

9-10-1971 [A] **Stedham Utd** (D 4-4)

16-10-1971 SIC [H] **Cuckfield** (W 7-1)

23-10-1971 [H] **Littlehampton Town Res** (L 1-3)

6-11-1971 [H] **Sweetlands** (D 1-1)

13-11-1971 SIC [H] **Hanover Athletic** (W 4-3) G Fallowfield 2, B Huffer 1, J Leadbeatter 1

20-11-1971 [A] **Wittering & Birdham Utd** (W 4-0)

27-11-1971 [H] **Sidlesham** (D 2-2) G Lewis 1, G Upjohn 1

4-12-1971 [A] **Chichester City Res** (D 1-1)

11-12-1971 SIC [H] **Littlehampton Town Res** (L 0-1) AET

18-12-1971 [A] **Midhurst & Easebourne Utd** (L 0-6)

1-1-1972 [A] **Lavant** (L 2-4)

8-1-1972 [A] **Bognor Training College** (L 1-4)

15-1-1972 [H] **Midhurst & Easebourne Utd** (L 1-5)

22-1-1972 [A] **Sidlesham** (D 1-1) G Upjohn 1

5-2-1972 [H] **Stedham Utd** (L 0-4)

19-2-1972 [A] **Littlehampton Town Res** (D 1-1)

26-2-1972 [A] **Selsey Res** (L 0-1)

4-3-1972 [H] **Arundel Res** (L 0-2)

11-3-1972 [A] **Petworth** (W 4-1)

18-3-1972 [A] **Southwick Res** (L 1-3)

25-3-1972 [H] **Southwick Res** (D 1-1)

8-4-1972 [A] **Corocraft Pegasus** (L 1-2)

13-4-1972 [A] **Arundel Res** (L 0-3)

15-4-1972 [H] **Corocraft Pegasus** (L 1-3)

20-4-1972 [A] **Horsham Olympic** (L 0-6)

24-4-1972 [H] **Bognor Training College** (D 1-1)

P30 | W6 | D10 | L14 | GF49 | GA73 | 22pts | 13th

WSL PREMIER DIVISION 1972/73

2-9-1972 [H] **Wittering & Birdham Utd** (L 2-4)

9-9-1972 [H] **Sunallon** (L 2-3)

16-9-1972 [H] **Selsey Res** (L 2-3)

23-9-1972 [A] **Ferring** (L 3-6)

30-9-1972 **MSC** [H] **Selsey** Rs (W 2-0) A Richardson 1, Upjohn 1

7-10-1972 [H] **Sidlesham** (D 1-1) G Lewis 1

14-10-1972 **SIC** [A] **Stone Platt** (W 2-1) Lewis 1, A Richardson 1

28-10-1972 [H] **Bognor Training College** (L 1-5)

4-11-1972 [A] **Midhurst & Easebourne Utd** (L 0-4)

11-11-1972 **SIC** [A] **Inland Revenue** (W 1-0) G Lewis 1

18-11-1972 [H] **Petworth** (W 3-2) Hill 1, Stenning 1, N Turner 1

25-11-1972 **MSC** [H] **Midhurst & Easebourne Utd** (L 1-3)

2-12-1972 [A] **Sidlesham** (L 1-5)

9-12-1972 **SIC** [H] **Midhurst & Easebourne Utd** (L 1-7) Lewis 1

16-12-1972 [H] **Ferring** (W 2-1) R Branch 1, G Lewis 1

23-12-1972 [A] **Lancing & Sompting Legion** (L 1-6)

30-12-1972 [A] **Arundel Res** (L 0-4)

6-1-1973 [H] **Corocraft Pegasus** (L 3-4) Hill 1, Lewis 1, Upjohn 1

13-1-1973 [A] **Wittering & Birdham Utd** (L 0-4)

20-1-1973 [A] **Petworth** (L 1-2)

27-1-1973 [H] **Midhurst & Easebourne Utd** (L 0-9)

3-2-1973 [A] **Selsey Res** (D 2-2)

10-2-1973 [H] **Lancing & Sompting Legion** (L 1-2)

17-2-1973 [A] **Stedham Utd** (L 1-6)

24-2-1973 [H] **Arundel Res** (W 2-1) G Lewis 2

3-3-1973 [A] **Bognor Training College** (L 0-8)

10-3-1973 [A] **Corocraft Pegasus** (L 0-4)

17-3-1973 [H] **Horsham Olympic** (L 1-2) OG 1

24-3-1973 [A] **Horsham Olympic** (L 2-7)

16-4-1973 [A] **Sunallon** (L 0-4)

18-4-1973 [H] **Stedham Utd** (L 1-9)

P26 | W3 | D2 | L21 | GF31 | GA108 | 8pts | 13th

WSL DIVISION 1, 1973/74

8-9-1973 [H] **Graylingwell** (L 1-4)

15-9-1973 [A] **South Bersted** (W 3-0) G Lewis 1, K Turner 1, G Upjohn 1

29-9-1973 [H] **Rudgwick** (W 2-1)

6-10-1973 **MSC** [H] **Sidlesham** (W 3-2) R Chandler 1, M Hatchard 1, G Lewis 1

13- 10-1973 [A] **Lavant** (L 2-4) N Bainbridge 1, T Wells 1

20-10-1973 [H] **Southbourne** (W 3-2) R Branch 1, G Upjohn 1, T Wells 1

27-10-1973 [H] **South Bersted** (D 0-0)

3-11-1973 [A] **Storrington** (L 1-2)

10-11-1973 [A] **Graylingwell** (L 1-4)

17-11-1973 **MSC** [H] **South Bersted** (L 3-5) G Lewis 1, K Turner 1, T Wells 1

24-11-1973 [A] **Rudgwick** (L 1-2)

1-12-1973 [A] **Southbourne** (W 3-1)

8-12-1973 [H] **Inland Revenue** (L 0-4)

15-12-1973 [H] **Barns Green** (L 2-6)

22-12-1973 [H] **Lavant** (L 2-7)

29-12-1973 [A] **Billingshurst** (L 1-3)

2-2-1974 [A] **Inland Revenue** (L 1-5)

16-2-1974 [A] **Rustington** (L 2-3)

23-2-1974 [A] **Broadbridge Heath** (L 0-3)

2-3-1974 [A] **Barns Green** (L 2-8)

9-3-1974 [H] **Billingshurst** (L 0-1)

23-3-1974 [H] **Storrington** (D 3-3)

30-3-1974 [H] **East Preston** (L 5-6)

6-4-1974 [A] **East Preston** (D 4-4)

17-4-1974 [H] **Broadbridge Heath** (L 2-6)

20-4-1974 [H] **Rustington** (L 2-5)

P24 | W4 | D3 | L17 | GF43 | GA84 | 11pts | 11th

WSL DIVISION 1, 1974/75

14-0-1974 [H] **Midway** (L 1-4)

21-9-1974 [H] **Rustington** (D 0-0)

28-9-1974 [H] **Chichester** Hospitals (W 3-1)

12-10-1974 [H] **Storrington** (L 2-4)

19-10-1974 [A] **Lavant** (L 2-7)

26-10-1974 [A] **Chichester** Hospitals (W 3-2)

2-11-1974 **MSC** [A] **Rustington** (L 1-2)

9-11-1974 [H] **Rudgwick** (D 2-2)

30-11-1974 [H] **Newtown** (W 3-2)

7-12-1974 [A] **Broadbridge Heath** (L 0-2)

14-12-1974 [H] **Hunston** (W 2-0)

21-12-1974 [A] **Rudgwick** (W 4-1)

28-12-1974 [A] **East Preston** (L 1-5)

4-1-1975 [H] **Ferring** (L 1-4)

11-1-1975 [H] **East Preston** (L 0-1)

1-2-1975 [A] **Inland Revenue** (L 0-3)

8-2-1975 [H] **Broadbridge Heath** (L 0-2)

22-2-1975 [A] **Midway** (L 0-1)

15-3-1975 [H] **Inland Revenue** (L 3-4)

22-3-1975 [A] **Hunston** (L 2-8)

5-4-1975 [A] **South Bersted** (L 1-3)

12-4-1975 [H] **South Bersted** (L 1-3)

15-4-1975 [H] **Barns Green** (D 2-2)

19-4-1975 [A] **Rustington** (L 1-4)

22-4-1975 [A] **Newtown** (L 0-3)

26-4-1975 [H] **Lavant** (L 0-8)

29-4-1975 [A] **Barns Green** (W 3-2)

9-5-1975 [A] **Ferring** (D 0-0)

P26 | W6 | D4 | L16 | GF32 | GA73 | 16pts | 12th

WSL DIVISION 1, 1975/76

6-9-1975 [H] **Chichester** Hospital (W 5-3) Lewis 3, Bainbridge 2

9-9-1975 [A] **Horsham Olympic** (W 3-1) Bainbridge 2, Lewis 1

13-9-1975 [A] **Rustington** (L 1-4) N Bainbridge 1

20-9-1975 **MSC** [H] **Midway** (D 3-3 AET) N Bainbridge 2, A Leadbeatter 1

4-10-1975 [H] **Rudgwick** (W 1-0) G Lewis 1

11-10-1975 **SIC** [A] **Storrington** (L 2-4) T Hatchard 1, G Lewis 1

18-10-1975 [A] **East Preston** (L 0-4)

25-10-1975 [H] **Ferring** (W 3-2) J Leadbeatter 1, G Lewis 1, ?1

1-11-1975 [H] **Summerley Park Rangers** (L 0-2)

8-11-1975 [A] **Rudgwick** (L 2-3) N Bainbridge 1, G Lewis 1

22-11-1975 [H] **Broadbridge Heath** (L 1-5) G Lewis 1

29-11-1975 [A] **Watersfield** (L 4-5) G Lewis 4

6-12-1975 **MSC Replay** [A] **Midway** (L 0-3)

13-12-1975 [H] **Barns Green** (W 3-0) G Lewis 2, G Keast 1

27-12-1975 [A] **Barns Green** (W 3-2) R Chandler 1, G Lewis 1, OG1

3-1-1976 [A] **Summerley Park Rangers** (L 2-4) N Bainbridge 2

10-1-1976 [H] **East Preston** (W 4-3) N Bainbridge 2, R Hewitt 1, G Lewis 1

24-1-1976 [A] **Ferring** (L 1-4) G Lewis 1

31-1-1976 [A] **Rustington** (L 0-2)

7-2-1976 [A] **Billingshurst** (D 2-2) J Jupp 1, G Lewis 1

14-2-1976 [A] **Chichester** Hospital (L 1-2) OG 1

21-2-1976 [H] **Billingshurst** (W 1-0) N Bainbridge 1

28-2-1976 [A] **Horsham Olympic** (D 1-1) R Hewitt 1

6-3-1976 [A] **Broadbridge Heath** (L 0-4)

3-4-1976 [H] **Watersfield** (W 3-1) N Bainbridge 1, G Lewis 1, OG1

P22 | W9 | D2 | L11 | GF41 | GA54 | 20pts | 7th

WSL DIVISION 1, 1976/77

18-9-1976 [H] **Chichester** Hospital (W 6-1) G Lewis 4, N Bainbridge 1, Wiseman 1

25-9-1976 [A] **East Preston** (L 2-5) G Lewis 2

2-10-1976 **MSC** [H] **Midhurst & Easebourne Utd** (L 0-6)

9-10-1976 **SIC** [A] **Slinfold** (W 5-2) R Hewitt 2, N Bainbridge 1, R Chandler 1, G Lewis 1

16-10-1976 [H] **Hunston** (L 3-4) J Jupp 1, M Jupp 1, G Lewis 1

23-10-1976 [A] **Stedham Utd** (L 0-4)

30-10-1976 [H] **Horsham Olympic** (L 0-1)

20-11-1976 [H] **Sidlesham** (W 5-0) M Jupp 2, G Lewis 1, Wiseman 1, OG 1

27-11-1976 **SIC** [A] **Excess Sports** (L 1-4) G Lewis 1

4-12-1976 [A] **Watersfield** (W 5-0) G Lewis 4, OG 1

11-12-1976 [A] **Summerley Park Rangers** (L 3-4) N Bainbridge 2, G Lewis 1

8-1-1977 [H] **Slinfold** (W 4-1) G Lewis 4

15-1-1977 [A] **Hunston** (L 5-6) A Kynoch 2, R Hewitt 1, G Lewis 1, OG 1

29-1-1977 [H] **East Preston** (W 4-1) N Bainbridge 2, R Chandler 1, A Kynoch 1

5-2-1977 [H] **Henfield Athletic** (D 2-2) R Hewitt 2

19-2-1977 [H] **Billingshurst** (W 2-0) N Bainbridge 2

26-2-1977 [A] **Barns Green** (D 3-3) G Lewis 2, N Bainbridge 1

5-3-1977 [A] **Slinfold** (W 4-1) R Chandler 1, M Hatchard 1, A Kynoch 1, G Lewis 1

12-3-1977 [H] **Summerley Park Rangers** (W 2-0) N Bainbridge 1, C Hutton 1

19-3-1977 [A] **Sidlesham** (W 3-1) R Hewitt 1, Kynoch 1, Lewis 1

26-3-1977 [H] **Watersfield** (W 3-1) N Bainbridge 1, R Hewitt 1, A Kynoch 1

2-4-1977 [A] **Henfield Athletic** (W 2-1) G Lewis 2

9-4-1977 [A] **Chichester** Hospital (W 3-1) Bainbridge 2, Hewitt 1

11-4-1977 [H] **Stedham Utd** (W 4-0) G Lewis 2, N Bainbridge 1, R Hewitt 1

16-4-1977 [A] **Billingshurst** (L 0-1)

26-4-1977 [H] **Barns Green** (W 4-1) G Lewis 2, N Bainbridge 1, R Hewitt 1

30-4-1977 [A] **Horsham Olympic** (W 3-2) Bainbridge 2, Hewitt 1

P24 | W15 | D2 | L7 | GF72 | GA42 | 32pts | 4th

WSL DIVISION 1, 1977/78

10-9-1977 [A] **Stedham Utd** (L 2-3) R Hewitt 1, G Lewis 1

17-9-1977 [H] **Barns Green** (L 1-2) R Hewitt 1

24-9-1977 **SIC** [H] **Beecham Sports** (W 2-1) N Bainbridge 1, R Hewitt 1

1-10-1977 [H] **Bosham** (L 0-2)

8-10-1977 **SIC** [A] **Brighton Insurance** (L 1-3) C Fordham 1

15-10-1977 [H] **Billingshurst** (W 5-0) N Bainbridge 2, R Chandler 1, R Hewitt 1, A Kynoch 1

22-10-1977 [A] **Slinfold** (W 6-1) C Fordham 4, N Bainbridge 1, R Hewitt 1

29-10-1977 [H] **Fernhurst** (D 4-4) N Bainbridge 1, C Fordham 1, R Hewitt 1, A Kynoch 1

5-11-1977 **MSC** [H] **Emsworth** (L 2-4) C Fordham 1, G Lewis 1

12-11-1977 [A] **Barns Green** (W 3-2) N Bainbridge 2, OG 1

19-11-1977 [A] **Billingshurst** (W 5-1) C Fordham 2, R Hewitt 2, N Bainbridge 1

3-12-1977 [H] **Stedham Utd** (L 2-4) N Bainbridge 1, R Hewitt 1

10-12-1977 [H] **Slinfold** (L 1-3) R Hewitt 1

17-12-1977 [A] **Fernhurst** (L 0-4)

31-12-1977 [A] **Bosham** (L 3-4) R Chandler 1, R Hewitt 1, OG1

7-1-1978 [H] **Ferring** (W 3-1) G Lewis 2, C Fordham 1

21-1-1978 [A] **Watersfield** (W 3-3) C Fordham 1, G Lewis 1, OG1

25-2-1978 [A] **Ferring** (L 3-4) C Fordham 1, R Hewitt 1, Lewis 1

4-3-1978 [A] **Old Collyerians** but played at Pulborough (W 4-2) N Bainbridge 2, C Fordham 1, A Kynoch 1

11-3-1978 [H] **Old Collyerians** (W 2-1) OG 2

18-3-1978 [A] **Sidlesham** (L 0-2)

25-3-1978 [H] **Horsham Olympic** (W 2-0) N Bainbridge 2

27-3-1978 [H] **Sidlesham** (D 2-2)

8-4-1978 [A] **Watersfield** (D 0-0)

18-4-1978 [A] **Horsham Olympic** (L 2-4) R Hewitt 1, G Lewis 1

P22 | W8 | D4 | L10 | GF53 | GA49 | 20pts | 9th

WSL DIVISION 1, 1978/79

9-9-1978 [A] **Graffham** (W 4-2) N Bainbridge 1, C Fordham 1, R Hewitt 1, G Lewis 1

16-9-1978 [A] **Slindon** (L 0-2)

23-9-1978 [A] **Old Collyerians** (D 2-2) N Bainbridge 1, OG 1

30-9-1978 **SIC** [A] **Barns Green** (L 1-3) R Chandler 1

7-10-1978 [H] **Fernhurst Sports** (D 1-1) C Hutton 1

28-10-1978 **MSC** [A] **Excess Sports** (L 2-3) N Bainbridge 2

4-11-1978 [H] **Excess Sports** (L 2-3) R Hewitt 1, M Pepper 1

11-11-1978 [H] **Graffham** (D 2-2)

18-11-1978 [H] **Horsham Olympic** (W 3-0) N Bainbridge 3

25-11-1978 [A] **Stedham Utd** (L 0-3)

2-12-1978 [A] **Barns Green** (L 1-6) R Hewitt 1

9-12-1978 [H] **Stedham Utd** (W 2-0) N Bainbridge 1, R Hewitt 1

16-12-1978 [A] **Fernhurst Sports** (L 1-6) R Chandler 1

23-12-1978 [H] **Slinfold** (L 3-4) N Bainbridge 2, R Branch 1

30-12-1978 [A] **Excess Sports** (L 0-5)

3-2-1979 [A] **Petworth** (L 2-5)

10-2-1979 [A] **Slinfold** (W 6-2) C Fordham 2, G Lewis 2, R Hewitt 1, D Stenning 1

24-2-1979 [H] **Barns Green** (D 4-4) G Lewis 2, N Bainbridge 1, R Hewitt 1

3-3-1979 [A] **Watersfield** (W 4-1) G Lewis 3, N Bainbridge 1

17-3-1979 [H] **Petworth** (W 2-1) R Chandler 1, C Fordham 1

24-3-1979 [A] **Horsham Olympic** (W 2-0)

7-4-1979 [H] **Watersfield** (L 0-3)

14-4-1979 [H] **Slindon** (L 0-8)

19-4-1979 [H] **Old Collyerians** (L 0-1)

P22 | W7 | D4 | L11 | GF41 | GA61 | 18pts | 9th

WSL DIVISION 1, 1979/80

8-9-1979 [A] **Graffham** (L 1-5) R Hewitt 1

15-9-1979 [A] **Watersfield** (W 5-1) G Lewis 3, N Bainbridge 1, J Jupp 1

22-9-1979 **MSC** [H] **Rustington** (W 2-1) N Bainbridge 1, J Jupp 1

29-9-1979 [H] **Stedham Utd** (D 2-2) J Jupp 1, G Lewis 1

13-10-1979 **SIC** [A] **APV** (L 1-7) N Bainbridge 1

20-10-1979 [H] **Slinfold** (W 3-2) A Kynoch 2, G Lewis 1

27-10-1979 [A] **Bosham** (L 0-3)

3-11-1979 [H] **Petworth** (W 3-2) G Lewis 2, R Chandler 1

10-11-1979 [A] **Barns Green** (D 3-3) A Kynoch 2, G Lewis 1

17-11-1979 **MSC** [A] **Sidlesham** (L 1-3) N Bainbridge 1

24-11-1979 [A] **Stedham Utd** (W 5-1) G Lewis 2, N Bainbridge 1, Chandler 1, C Hutton 1

1-12-1979 [H] **Bourne Park Rangers** (L 0-3)

8-12-1979 [A] **Hunston Utd** (W 4-3) N Bainbridge 3, G Lewis 1

22-12-1979 [A] **Slinfold** (W 4-3) N Bainbridge 1, R Chandler 1, J Jupp 1, G Lewis 1

29-12-1979 [H] **N. Holmwood** (D 4-4) N Bainbridge 3, G Lewis 1

5-1-1980 [H] **Bosham** (L 2-6) J Jupp 1, G Lewis 1

12-1-1980 [H] **Graffham** (L 1-2) G Lewis 1

19-1-1980 [A] **Petworth** (W 3-2) R Chandler 1, C Hutton 1, T Wilkins 1

26-1-1980 [A] **North Holmwood** (L 1-3) N Bainbridge 1

16-2-1980 [H] **Hunston Utd** (W 4-1) N Bainbridge 3, J Jupp 1

1-3-1980 [H] **Watersfield** (W 6-1) N Bainbridge 1, R Hewitt 1, C Hutton 1, J Jupp 1, A Kynoch 1, G Lewis 1

15-3-1980 [H] **Barns Green** (W 4-0) G Lewis 3, N Bainbridge 1

5-4-1980 [A] **Bourne Park Rangers** (L 2-5) N Bainbridge 1, C Hutton 1

P20 | W10 | D3 | L7 | GF57 | GA52 | 23pts | 4th

WSL PREMIER DIVISION 1980/81

6-9-1980 [H] **Rustington** (L 0-4)

13-9-1980 [H] **Lavant** (W 3-2) Bainbridge 1, D Smith 1, Wilkins 1

20-9-1980 [H] **Midway** (L 2-6) C Hutton 1, D Smith 1

27-9-1980 MSC [H] **Midway** (L 0-3)

4-10-1980 [A] **Sidlesham** (L 3-5) Bainbridge 1, Hutton 1, Smith 1

11-10-1980 SIC [A] **Midway** (W 3-2) N Bainbridge 1, D Smith 1, C Spain 1

18-10-1980 [A] **Excess Sports** (L 1-5) D Smith 1

25-10-1980 [H] **Fernhurst** (D 5-5) D Saunders 2, N Bainbridge 1, R Hewitt 1, D Smith 1

1-11-1980 [A] **Lancing & Sompting Legion** (W 2-1) D Saunders 2

8-11-1980 SIC [A] **Mile Oak** (L 0-5)

15-11-1980 [H] **Bourne Park Rangers** (L 0-3)

29-11-1980 [A] **Emsworth** (L 1-5) D Saunders 1

6-12-1980 [H] **Sunallon** (L 1-2) J Jupp 1

13-12-1980 [H] **Petworth** (L 1-8) OG 1

27-12-1980 [A] **Rustington** (L 1-2) J Jupp 1

3-1-1981 [A] **Sunallon** (D 1-1) N Bainbridge 1

10-1-1981 [H] **East Preston** (L 2-5) Edwards 1, D Smith 1

17-1-1981 [A] **Bourne Park Rangers** (L 3-6) Edwards 1, J Jupp 1, D Smith 1

24-1-1981 [A] **Fernhurst** (L 1-3) N Bainbridge 1

31-1-1981 [H] **Slinfold** (L 1-3) D Smith 1

7-2-1981 [A] **Petworth** (L 3-4) N Bainbridge 2, OG 1

14-2-1981 [H] **Lancing & Sompting Legion** (L 1-2) N Bainbridge 1

21-2-1981 [A] **Lavant** (W 4-3) Bainbridge 2, Hewitt 1, D Smith 1

28-2-1981 [H] **Sidlesham** (L 1-4) OG 1

21-3-1981 [A] **East Preston** (D 0-0)

28-3-1981 [A] **Midway** (L 1-4) OG 1

11-4-1981 [H] **Emsworth** (D 2-2) J Jupp 1, D Smith 1

18-4-1981 [H] **Excess Sports** (L 1-4) N Bainbridge 1

23-4-1981 [A] **Slinfold** (L 2-5) C Spain 2

P26 | W3 | D4 | L19 | GF43 | GA94 | 10pts | 14th

WSL DIVISION 1, 1981/82

12-9-1981 [H] **Midhurst & Easebourne Utd Res** (D 1-1) OG 1

19-9-1981 MSC [A] **Sidlesham** (L 1-4) M Ruff 1

26-9-1981 SIC [A] **Portslade** (L 0-2)

3-10-1981 [H] **Eastergate Utd** (L 2-8) R Hewitt 2

17-10-1981 [A] **Alfold** (L 1-3) N Bainbridge 1

24-10-1981 [H] **Broadbridge Heath Res** (W 3-2) N Bainbridge 1, C Hutton 1, M Ruff 1

31-10-1981 [A] **Liss Athletic Res** (L 0-5)

7-11-1981 [A] **Bosham** (D 0-0)

14-11-1981 [H] **Liss Athletic R** (D 2-2) S Leadbeatter 1, Wilkins 1

21-11-1981 [A] **North Holmwood** (D 0-0)

28-11-1981 [H] **Stedham Utd** (L 1-4) OG 1

5-12-1981 [A] **Barns Green** (W 5-0) J Dunne 2, S Leadbeatter 2, R Hewitt 1

2-1-1982 [A] **Broadbridge Heath Res** (L 1-2) C Hutton 1

16-1-1982 [A] **Lancing & Sompting Legion** (W 2-1) C Hutton 2

23-1-1982 [H] **North Holmwood** (L 0-2)

30-1-1982 [A] **Eastergate Utd** (L 2-4) J Gallagher 1, C Hutton 1

6-2-1982 [H] **Hunston Utd** (D 1-1) K Blackburn 1

13-2-1982 [H] **Horsham Trinity** (L 2-3) S Hayter 1, C Hutton 1

20-2-1982 [H] **Beechams Sports** (D 1-1) S Freegard 1

27-2-1982 [A] **Stedham Utd** (W 4-0) C Hutton 3, S Leadbeatter 1

6-3-1982 [H] **Lancing & Sompting Legion** (D 1-1) J Dunne 1

13-3-1982 [H] **Horsham Trinity** (L 2-4) C Hutton 1, A Kynoch 1

20-3-1982 [A] **Midhurst & Easebourne Utd Res** (L 3-4) R Hewitt 2, C Hutton 1

27-3-1982 [A] **Hunston Utd** (W 1-0) T Roberts 1

3-4-1982 [H] **Barns Green** (D 1-1) S Leadbeatter 1

10-4-1982 [H] **Bosham** (L 1-2) C Hutton 1

14-4-1982 [A] **Beechams Sports** (W 3-1) R Hewitt 1, C Hutton 1, S Leadbeatter 1

19-4-1982 [H] **Alfold** (L 0-2)

P26 | W6 | D8 | L12 | GF40 | GA54 | 20pts | 12th

WSL DIVISION 1, 1982/83

1-9-1982 [H] **Horsham Trinity** (W 9-2) C Spain 3, C Hutton 2, A Kynoch 1, A Maynard 1, M Ruff 1, D Scott 1

4-9-1982 [H] **Manor Athletic** (D 1-1) A Maynard 1

6-9-1982 [A] **Stedham Utd** (L 1-3) J Gallagher 1

11-9-1982 [H] **Henfield Athletic** (L 0-5)

18-9-1982 MSC [A] **Fernhurst Sports** (L 0-5)

25-9-1982 [H] **Barns Green** (L 1-2) R James 1

2-10-1982 [A] **Alfold** (L 0-1)

9-10-1982 SIC [A] (L 0-5)

16-10-1982 [A] **East Preston Res** (L 0-4)

30-10-1982 [H] **Liss Athletic Res** (L 0-3)

6-11-1982 [H] **Lancing & Sompting Legion** (L 1-3) C Hutton 1

13-11-1982 [A] **Excess Sports** (W 6-5) S Leadbeatter 4, L Rout 1, C Spain 1

27-11-1982 [A] **Lancing & Sompting Legion** (W 4-2) C Hutton 2, S Leadbeatter 1, D Smith 1

18-12-1982 [A] **Slinfold** (W 3-1) J Gallagher 1, R Hewitt 1, Rout 1

3-1-1983 [A] **Liss Athletic Res** (D 2-2) C Hutton 1, L Rout 1

8-1-1983 [H] **Excess Sports** (L 2-5) D Fry 1, S Leadbeatter 1

15-1-1983 [H] **Havant Town Res** (L 1-4) S Leadbeatter 1

22-1-1983 [A] **Manor Athletic** (L 0-2)

29-1-1983 [H] **Storrington Res** (W 3-0) D Fry 1, S Leadbeatter 1, D Smith 1

5-2-1983 [A] **Beechams Sports** (L 1-3) S Leadbeatter 1

19-2-1983 [H] **Alfold** (W 3-2) D Fry 1, R Hewitt 1, C Hutton 1

26-2-1983 [A] **Storrington Res** (W 2-1) C Hutton 1, D Smith 1

5-3-1983 [H] **East Preston Res** (W 1-0) D Smith 1

12-3-1983 [A] **Havant Town Res** (L 0-1)

19-3-1983 [A] **North Holmwood** (L 0-4)

26-3-1983 [H] **North Holmwood** (L 0-4)

2-4-1983 [H] **Stedham Utd** (L 1-4) C Spain 1

4-4-1983 [H] **Slinfold** (W 3-1) Hutton 1, Kynoch 1, Maynard 1

9-4-1983 [H] **Beechams Sports** (D 0-0)

16-4-1983 [A] **Horsham Trinity** (L 0-4)

23-4-1983 [A] **Barns Green** (W 1-0) D Smith I

25-4-1983 [A] **Henfield Athletic** (W 5-2) C Hutton 2, Hassan 1, D Fry 1, D Smith 1

P30 | W11 | D3 | L16 | GF51 | GA71 | 25pts | 13th

WSL DIVISION 1, 1983/84

3-9-1983 [H] **East Preston Res** (D 1-1) S Freegard 1

10-9-1983 [H] **Wittering & Birdham Utd** (L 0-7)

17-9-1983 MSC [A] **Wittering & Birdham Utd** (L 0-6)

24-9-1983 SIC [H] **Broadbridge Heath** (L 0-4)

1-10-1983 [H] **Lancing & Sompting Legion** (L 1-2) R James 1

8-10-1983 [A] **Horsham Trinity** (L 1-2) D King 1

15-10-1983 [A] **Lavant** (L 0-3)

22-10-1983 [H] **Liss Athletic Res** (D 2-2) K Wilby 2

29-10-1983 [A] **Stedham Utd** (L 2-4) K Wilby 1, S Leadbeatter 1

5-11-1983 [H] **Henfield Athletic** (L 1-6) D King 1

12-11-1983 [A] **Horndean Res** (L 1-2) S Leadbeatter 1

19-11-1983 [H] **Billingshurst** (L 0-6)

3-12-1983 [H] **Stedham Utd** (L 1-3) C Hutton 1

10-12-1983 [A] **Emsworth** (L 0-7)

31-12-1983 [A] **Liss Athletic Res** (W 3-2) C Hutton 2, C Spain 1

7-1-1984 [H] **Emsworth** (L 1-5, R Hewitt 1

14-1-1984 [H] **Lavant** (W 2-1) C Hutton 1, M Jupp 1

21-1-1984 [A] **East Preston Res** (L 0-1)

11-2-1984 [H] **Horndean Res** (L 1-4) R Hewitt 1

18-2-1984 [A] **Lancing & Sompting Legion** (L 0-2)

25-2-1984 [H] **Barns Green** (W 2-0) D King 2

3-3-1984 [H] **Excess Sports** (D 1-1) C Hutton 1

17-3-1984 [A] **Henfield Athletic** (L 1-2) J Jupp 1

24-3-1984 [A] **Excess Sports** (L 1-8) C Spain 1

31-3-1984 [H] **Roffey** (L 1-5) M Jupp 1

7-4-1984 [A] **Billingshurst** (L 0-5)

14-4-1984 [A] **Wittering & Birdham Utd** (L 0-4)

17-4-1984 [A] **Barns Green** (W 3-0) M Osborne 2, D Fry 1

21-4-1984 [H] **Horsham Trinity** (L 0-3)

25-4-1984 [A] **Roffey** (L 0-1)

P28 | W4 | D3 | L21 | GF26 | GA89 | 11pts | 14th

WSL DIVISION 2, NORTH 1984/85

1-9-1984 [H] **Sunallon Res** (W 2-1) M Harrison 1, R James 1

8-9-1984 [A] **Graffham** (D 0-0)

15-9-1984 CCC [A] **Warnham** (W 2-1) M Harrison 1, D Scott 1

22-9-1984 SJC [H] **Worthing Central** (W 4-3) C Hutton 2, M Harrison 1, S Leadbeatter 1

29-9-1984 [H] **Slinfold** (L0-1)

6-10-1984 SJC [A] **Mile Oak** R (W 2-1) Harrison 1, S Leadbeatter 1

13-10-1984 [A] **Rudgwick** (W 2-1) M Harrison 1, OG 1

20-10-1984 [H] **North Holmwood** (L 2-3) M Harrison 1, D King 1

27-10-1984 [H] **Old Collyerians** (W 4-0) M Harrison 1, C Hutton 1, S Leadbeatter 1, D Scott 1

3-11-1984 SJC [H] **Sompting Res** (W 2-1) Harrison 1, Hutton 1

17-11-1984 CCC [H] **Rudgwick** (W 3-1) D Scott 2, D King l

1-12-1984 SJC [A] **Sunallon Res** (L 2-6) G Blunden 1, Harrison 1

8-12-1984 [H] **Graffham** (W 2-0) M Harrison 1, D King 1

15-12-1984 [A] **Shipley** (W 1-0) M Harrison 1

22-12-1984 [H] **Rudgwick** (L 1-4) M Harrison 1

29-12-1984 [A] **Old Collyerians** (D 2-2) Kynoch 1, S Leadbeatter 1

5-1-1985 CCC [H] **Felpham Utd** (W 3-0) R James 1, C Spain 1, OG1

26-1-1985 [A] **Partridge Green** (W 2-1) M Harrison 1, R James 1

23-2-1985 [A] **North Holmwood** (D 2-2) M Harrison 1, C Hutton 1

2-3-1985 [A] **Slinfold** (L 1-4) G Blunden 1

9-3-1985 [A] **Warnham** (L 3-6) C Hutton 2, M Harrison 1

16-3-1985 [H] **Shipley** (W 3-0) Goring 1, M Harrison 1, R James 1

23-3-1985 [A] **Alfold** (W 3-1) M Harrison 2, C Hutton 1

30-3-1985 [H] **Horsham Olympic** (D 2-2) M Harrison 1, R James 1

6-4-1985 [H] **Warnham** (W 3-2) Harrison 1, Hutton 1, D Scott 1

8-4-1985 [A] **Sunallon Res** (L 2-3) M Harrison 1, C Hutton 1

13-4-1985 CCC Semi Final [A] **Rustington Res** (D 0-0) AET

16-4-1985 CCC Replay [H] **Rustington Res** (W 2-1) M Harrison 2

20-4-1985 [H] **Alfold** (W 6-1) M Harrison 3, Tim Hatchard 2, C Hutton 1

25-4-1985 [H] **Partridge Green** (W 1-0) Tim Hatchard 1

27-4-1985 [A] **Horsham Olympic** (L 1-2) M Harrison 1

7-5-1985 CCC FINAL [at Rustington] v **South Bersted** (L 1-0)

P22 | W11 | D4 | L7 | GF45 | GA36 | 26pts | 3rd

WSL DIVISION 2, NORTH 1985/86

7-9-1985 [H] **Horsham Olympic** (W 4-2) K Furlonger 2, C Hutton 1, R James 1, S Leadbeatter 1

14-9-1985 [H] **Sunallon** (W 3-0) P Bird 2, C Hutton 1

21-9-1985 SJC [H] **Manor Athletic** (W 4-2) K Furlonger 2, N Bainbridge 1, R James 1

28-9-1985 [H] **North Holmwood** (W 5-3) R James 2, P Bird 1, A Kynoch 1, R Streeter 1

5-10-1985 SJC [H] **Amberley** (W 3-1) R James 2, M Harrison 1

19-10-1985 [A] **Horsham Trinity** (W 4-0) M Harrison 3, R James 1

2-11-1985 SJC [A] **Portslade Res** (W 6-0) M Harrison 2, N Bainbridge 1, P Bird 1, G Blunden 1, M Ruff 1

9-11-1985 CCC [A] **Warnham** (W 3-2) Harrison 2, N Bainbridge 1

16-11-1985 [H] **Rudgwick** (W 5-0) P Bird 2, M Harrison 1, C Hutton 1, S Leadbeatter 1

23-11-1985 [A] **North Holmwood** (W 4-0) N Bainbridge 2, D King 1, S Leadbeatter 1

30-11-1985 [H] **Warnham** (D 4-4) M Harrison 4

7-12-1985 SJC [A] **Sidlesham** R (W 3-0) N Bainbridge 2, R James 1

21-12-1985 [A] **Steyning Old Grammarians** (W 3-1) R James 1, D King 1, C Spain 1

28-12-1985 [H] **Graffham** (W 5-1) N Bainbridge 2, K Furlonger 1, R James 1, M Ruff 1

4-1-1986 SJC [H] **Sunallon Res** (L 0-4)

11-1-1986 CCC [H] **Horsham Olympic** (W 4-1) N Bainbridge 2, P Bird 1, R James 1

25-1-1986 [H] **Partridge Green** (W 4-0) P Bird 2, N Bainbridge 1, M Harrison 1

1-2-1986 [H] **Horsham Trinity** M Harrison 2, K Furlonger 1

8-3-1986 [A] **Graffham** (W 5-2) Harrison 3, C Hutton 1, D King 1

15-3-1986 CCC Semi Final [H] **Hunston Utd** (W 8-1) N Bainbridge 2, Hutton 2, P Bird 1, Harrison 1, S Leadbeatter 1, C Spain 1

22-3-1986 [A] **Wisborough Green** (D 1-1) M Ruff 1

29-3-1986 [A] **Partridge Green** (D 1-1) R James 1

31-3-1986 [A] **Horsham Olympic** (W 3-1) N Bainbridge 1, S Leadbeatter 1

5-4-1986 [A] **Warnham** (W 6-1) R James 3, Harrison 2, Hutton 1

12-4-1986 [A] **Sunallon Res** (W 1-0) N Bainbridge 1

16-4-1986 [H] **Wisborough Green** (W 2-0) N Furlonger 1, M Harrison 1

19-4-1986 [A] **Rudgwick** (W 5-0) M Harrison 2, N Bainbridge 1, P Bird 1, C Hutton 1

26-4-1986 [H] **Steyning Old Grammarians** (W 4-1) N Bainbridge 2, M Harrison 2

30-4-1986 [H] **Shipley** D 0-0

3-5-1986 [A] **Shipley** (W 5-1) R James 3, N Bainbridge 1, P Bird 1

5-5-1986 CCC FINAL [at Graylingwell] v **Felpham Utd** (L 5-4 AET) P Bird 1, M Harrison 1, C Hutton 1, S Leadbeatter 1

P22 | W18 | D4 | L0 | GF77 | GA21 | 40pts | 1st

Unbeaten in league

WSL DIVISION 1, 1986/87

30-8-1986 [A] **Bracklesham** (L 0-2)

6-9-1986 [H] **Felpham Utd** (W 3-1) P Bird 1, K Furlonger 1, M Harrison 1

13-9-1986 [H] **Fernhurst** (W 3-1) P Bird 2, A Kynoch 1

20-9-1986 [A] **Lavant** (D 3-3) P Bird 2, C Hutton 1

27-9-1986 MSC [H] **Emsworth** (W 3-0) P Bird 1, M Harrison 1, C Hutton 1

4-10-1986 [H] **Beecham Sports** (W 5-2) P Bird 2, N Bainbridge 1, C Hutton 1, D Leadbeatter 1

11-10-1986 SIC [A] **Brighton Electric** (W 5-2) N Bainbridge 2, M Harrison 2, P Bird 1

1-11-1986 MSC [A] **Lavant** (L 0-2) AET

8-11-1986 SIC [H] **Shoreham Res** (D 2-2) M Harrison 2

22-11-1986 SIC replay [A] **Shoreham Res** (L 1-2) P Bird 1

29-11-1986 [A] **Milland** (L 1-2) M Harrison 1

6-12-1986 [H] **Lavant** (W 2-0) P Bird 1, M Harrison 1

20-12-1986 [A] **Beecham Sports** (W 3-1) P Bird 1, M Harrison 1, S Leadbeatter 1

27-12-1986 [H] **Bracklesham** (L 1-4) P Bird 1

10-1-1987 [H] **Old Collyerians** (D 2-2) P Bird 1, M Harrison 1

31-1-1987 [A] **Old Collyerians** (L 0-1)

7-2-1987 [H] **Barns Green** (D 0-0)

14-2-1987 [A] **Emsworth** (L 0-2)

21-2-1987 [H] **Milland** (D 1-1) N Bainbridge 1

28-2-1987 [A] **West Sussex Institute of Higher Education** (W 4-3) A Henderson 3, D King 1

7-3-1987 [H] **Emsworth** (D 1-1) S Leadbeatter 1

14-3-1987 [A] **Felpham Utd** (L 0-3)

21-3-1987 [H] **Southwater** (W 2-0) P Bird 2

11-4-1987 [A] **Stedham Utd** (L 2-3) S Leadbeatter 1, C Spain 1

13-4-1987 [H] **Roffey** (W 2-0) M Harrison 1, D King 1

15-4-1987 [A] **Barns Green** (W 4-1) M Harrison 2, D Leadbeatter 1, S Leadbeatter 1

18-4-1987 [A] **Fernhurst** (W 3-0) M Harrison 2, G Blunden 1

20-4-1987 [A] **Roffey** (L 0-1)

22-4-1987 [A] **Southwater** (L 0-2)

25-4-1987 [H] **Stedham Utd** (W 3-0) M Harrison 1, D King 1, S Leadbeatter 1

29-4-1987 [H] **WSIHE** (L 0-3)

P26 | W11 | D5 | L10 | GF45 | GA39 | 27pts | 6th

WSL DIVISION 1, 1987/88

5-9-1987 [A] **Lancing & Sompting Legion** (L 1-2) C Spain 1

12-9-1987 [H] **Rusper** (D 1-1) Tim Hatchard 1

19-9-1987 [H] **Felpham Utd** (L 0-2)

26-9-1987 MSC [A] **North Holmwood** (L 0-2)

3-10-1987 [H] **Lavant** (W 1-0) R James 1

24-10-1987 [A] **Emsworth** (L 0-1)

31-10-1987 [A] **Lavant** (W 3-0) R James 2, M Harrison 1

7-11-1987 [A] **Rusper** (D 1-1) R James 1

21-11-1987 [A] **Barns Green** (D 2-2) M Harrison 1, K Taylor 1

28-11-1987 [H] **Emsworth** (W 5-2) K Taylor 3, N Bainbridge 2

5-12-1987 [A] **Horndean Res** (L 0-3)

12-12-1987 [H] **Lancing & Sompting Legion** (W 3-1) N Bainbridge 1, M Harrison 1, C Hutton 1

19-12-1987 [A] **Old Collyerians** (L 0-5)

9-1-1988 [A] **Steyning Old Grammarians** D 1-1) N Bainbridge 1

23-1-1988 [A] **Stedham Utd** (L 2-3) C Hutton 1, C Staples 1

13-2-1988 [H] **Steyning Old Grammarians** (D 4-4) K Taylor 2, D Leadbeatter 1, F Rhoder 1

20-2-1988 [A] **Milland** (W 1-0) S Leadbeatter 1

27-2-1988 [H] **Barns Green** (W 2-0) C Hutton 1, D Leadbeatter 1

5-3-1988 [H] **Stedham Utd** (L 0-2)

12-3-1988 [H] **Ashington** (W 5-1) M Harrison 3, S Leadbeatter 1, C Staples 1

19-3-1988 [A] **Southwater** (L 2-4) N Bainbridge 2

26-3-1988 [H] **Horndean Res** (D 1-1) N Bainbridge 1

2-4-1988 [A] **Felpham Utd** (L 2-4) M Harrison 2

4-4-1988 [H] **Southwater** (L 0-2)

9-4-1988 [A] **Ashington** (W 5-0) M Harrison 3, N Bainbridge 2

11-4-1988 [H] **Old Collyerians** (W 7-0) M Harrison 2, N Bainbridge 1, S Leadbeatter 1, C Spain 1, K Taylor 1, OG 1

23-4-1988 [H] **Milland** (L 0-9)

P26 | W9 | D6 | L11 | GF49 | GA51 | 24pts | 10th

WSL DIVISION 1, 1989/90

2-9-1989 [H] **Barns Green** (D 0-0)

9-9-1989 [H] **Worthing BCOB** (D 1-1) D Lewis 1

16-9-1989 MSC [A] **Sidlesham** (L 0-6)

23-9-1989 [H] **Worthing Utd** (W 3-2) D Lewis 2, S Leadbeatter 1

30-9-1989 [A] **Eastergate** (D 3-3) D Lewis 2, N Bainbridge 1

7-10-1989 [H] **Sunallon** (D 1-1) Tim Hatchard 1

14-10-1989 SIC [H] **Northbrook** (W 5-3) D Lewis 2, D Rhoder 2, K Furlonger 1

21-10-1989 [A] **Worthing BCOB** (L 2-3) K Furlonger 1, D Lewis 1

28-10-1989 [A] **Cowfold** (L 2-4) D Leadbeatter 1, K Taylor 1

4-11-1989 [H] **Ifield** (L 1-2) OG 1

11-11-1989 SIC [A] **Legal & General** (L 0-2)

18-11-1989 [A] **Barns Green** (W 3-0) Furlonger 1, Ant Leadbeatter 1

25-11-1989 [H] **Alfold** (W 6-1) D Lewis 2, S Whitehead 2, G Blunden 1, K Furlonger 1

2-12-1989 [H] **Cowfold** (L 0-2)

9-2-1989 [H] **Wittering Utd** (L 2-3) D Lewis 2

6-1-1990 [A] **Loxwood** (L 0-3)

13-1-1990 [H] **Lancing & Sompting Legion** (L 0-3)

20-1-1990 [A] **Ifield** (L 2-3) D Lewis 1, G Phur 1

17-2-1990 [A] **Worthing Utd** (L 0-2)

24-2-1990 [A] **Wittering Utd** (L 0-1)

3-3-1990 [A] **Sunallon** (W 2-1) S Cox 1, Ant Leadbeatter 1

10-3-1990 [H] **South Bersted** (W 2-0) K Furlonger 1, K Taylor 1

17-3-1990 [A] **Alfold** (D 1-1) N Spicer 1

31-3-1990 [A] **South Bersted** (L 0-1)

7-4-1990 [H] **Eastergate** (W 5-0) K Taylor 3, D Lewis 2

9-4-1990 [A] **Steyning OG** (D 0-0) 14-4-1990 [H] **Loxwood** (W 3-2) K Taylor 3

16-4-1990 [A] **Lancing & Sompting Legion** (L 1-2) R Streeter 1

25-4-1990 [H] **Steyning OG** (L 1-3) D Lewis 1

P26 | W7 | D6 | L13 | GF41 | GA44 | 20pts | 10th

PULBOROUGH STRUGGLE TO TAKE BOTH POINTS

Pulborough 2, Angmering 1

Pulborough lose after going two up

Pulborough 2, Sompting 3

PULBOROUGH lost Saturday's Sussex Intermediate Cup-tie at Sompting because they only had ten men for most of the match, plus heavy pressure from

Pulborough win a tough and muddy struggle

Yapton 2, Pulborough 4

PULBOROUGH won a tough, muddy and scrappy West Sussex League, Division I game when they visited Yapton on Satur- day.

From a Pope goalkick Upjohn headed the ball on to Lewis, and

Players' Goals and Appearances (accumulated)
Seasons 1959/60 & 60/61

NAME	GAMES	GOALS
ALLFREY	2	1
ANSCOMBE	46	17
ANSELL	13	0
AVES	2	0
BAKER	2	0
BARNETT, A	5	0
BARNETT, P	52	0
BAYLEY	44	0
BISHOP, T	9	0
BJORKOV	16	0
BLACKMAN	2	0
BLAKE	16	0
BOOKER	23	0
BROWN	18	4
BROWN, S	1	0
BRYANT, J	1	0
BRYANT, R	2	0
BURLESTON	98	1
BURMINGHAM	11	0
CARR	10	0
CARTER, G	80	23
CHAPMAN, P	128	29
CHATFIELD	5	1
CLARK, F	39	0
CLARK, J	4	0
CLARK, T	1	0
CLARKE, A	2	0
COLLINS	3	0
COOPER	47	1
COUSINS	59	28
DAVIES	13	2
DILLOWAY	8	0
EDWARDS		0
ELLIOT, R E		0
ELLIOTT, R	31	2
ENTICKNAP	14	2
EVANS	2	0
FINCH	1	0
FORTY	2	0
FROGLEY	112	18
FUNNELL	42	22
GINNAW	31	14
GLOVER	4	0
GODDARD	2	0
GOLDRING	11	0
GOLDSMITH	26	1
GOODSELL, P	34	1
GOODYER	37	7

NAME	GAMES	GOALS
GREENFIELD, A	65	1
GREENFIELD, J	64	0
GREENFIELD, L	2	0
GREENFIELD, S	173	13
GREENING	2	0
GROVER	5	3
HABGOOD	1	0
HAMILTON, L	39	9
HAMILTON, C	25	3
HAMPSHIRE	5	2
HANDLEY	200	73
HARRISON, P	259	125
HATCHARD, M	75	26
HATCHARD, T	8	0
HAWKINS	3	0
HAYLER	18	0
HAYLER, M	27	2
HAYLER, R	11	0
HEASMAN, D	118	34
HEATHER	44	0
HENLEY	20	0
HILTON	37	0
HOGG	1	0
HOLLINGWORTH	2	0
HOLMAN	36	1
HOOKEY	23	0
HORTON	2	0
HOUSE	1	0
JOHNSON	13	3
JONES, R	40	8
KNIGHT	3	0
KOVACS	25	9
LACEY	14	10
LAMMAS	32	0
LARBEY	131	0
LEADBEATTER, A	89	37
LEADBEATTER, F	49	0
LEADBEATTER, J	78	25
LEWERY	3	0
LEWIS, A	15	0
LEWIS, G	28	14
LILLYWHITE	1	0
LIST	22	0
LOOMES	138	0
MACEY	33	30
MADGETT	76	24
MASON	47	0
MAYBEE	184	22
MAYES	1	0
MESSENGER	2	0

NAME	GAMES	GOALS
MULLINGER	2	0
OVENELL	61	1
PADFIELD	2	0
PADWICK	47	0
PARKER, G	31	5
PARRISH	59	3
PARSONS	9	0
PAVEY, C	26	0
PAYNE	2	0
PENFOLD	21	0
POORE	50	0
POPE	35	0
PURNELL	167	2
PUTTOCK	114	4
RAYNOR	197	2
ROBERTS, D	246	45
ROBERTS, E	13	1
ROBERTS, P	194	136
ROBERTS, R	18	2
ROLPH	19	0
ROWLAND, B	91	1
ROWLAND, D	8	0
SARGENT	50	5
SCUTT	80	3
SMITH, A	79	11
SMITH, C	53	1
SOAL	2	0
SPAIN, A	163	3
SPAIN, M	6	1
STENNING	7	0
STENTIFORD	43	9
STEWART, M	20	10
STILLWELL	14	3
SULLIVAN	2	0
SUTER	20	2
THOMPSETT	45	9
TRACY	3	0
UPJOHN	27	11
VEVERINES	38	0
VINCENT, B	5	1
WADEY	1	0
WATKINSON	145	0
WELLS	90	118
WILK	7	0
WILLIAMS	18	0
WILLS	19	4
WOODS	1	0
YOUNG	7	0

Players' Records – Season 1967/68

Goals and Appearances

Player	Apps	1st XI	2nd XI	Goals
Baker, M	13		13	14
Brown, M	27	7	20	13
Carrol, B	4		4	
Carrol, R	17		17	
Carter, C	24		24	
Chapman, P	19	2	17	1
Czarnecki, R	3		3	1
Davis, B	19	4	15	3
Habgood, J	17		17	
Hatchard, M	25	25		10
Hatchard, T	26	26		
Hayler, M	13	6	7	6
Holland, D	26		26	
Hookey, L	29	29		1
Huffer, B	20	20		12
Lake, D	5		5	1
Leadbeatter, A	27	27		6
Lidbetter, D	7	6	1	2
Leadbeatter, J	28	28		2
Leadbeatter, M	19		19	
Lewis, G	29	29		46
Madell, J	4		4	
Pattenden, A	4		4	1
Phillips, R	10		10	4
Pope, N	29	27	2	
Puttock, A	10		10	
Richardson, A	8		8	
Roberts, T	26	25	1	2
Spain, A	9	2	7	
Stuart, J	22		22	13
Upjohn, G	26	25	1	17
Wallis, M	29	29		
Wells, T	20	1	19	10

Goal scorers

Player	Apps	1st XI	2nd XI	Goals
Lewis, G	29	29		46
Upjohn, G	26	25	1	17
Baker, M	13		13	14
Stuart, J	22		22	13
Brown, M	27	7	20	13
Huffer, B	20	20		12
Wells, T	20	1	19	10
Hatchard, M	25	25		10
Leadbeatter, A	27	27		6
Hayler, M	13	6	7	6
Phillips, R	10		10	4
Davis, B	19	4	15	3
Leadbeatter, J	28	28		2
Leadbeatter, D	7	6	1	2
Roberts, T	26	25	1	2
Pattenden, A	4		4	1
Hookey, L	29	29		1
Chapman, P	19	2	17	1
Czarnecki, R	3		3	1
Lake, D	5		5	1

Most Appearances

Player	Apps	1st XI	2nd XI	Goals
Wallis, M	29	29		
Pope, N	29	27	2	
Lewis, G	29	29		46
Hookey, L	29	29		1
Leadbeatter, J	28	28		2
Leadbeatter, A	27	27		6
Brown, M	27	7	20	13
Upjohn, G	26	25	1	17
Roberts, T	26	25	1	2
Hatchard, T	26	26		
Holland, D	26		26	
Hatchard, M	25	25		10
Carter, C	24		24	
Stuart, J	22		22	13
Wells, T	20	1	19	10
Huffer, B	20	20		12

Pulborough FC 1993/94 *back row from left* Colin Spain (linesman), Tony Petras, Dave Rhoder, Steve Leadbeatter, Mick Osborne, Graham Spicer.
Front row Graham Blunden, Nick Zalesny, Steve Buss, Tim Hatchard, Russ Phillips (manager), Joe Myskow, Steve Cox, Danny Streeter.

Pulborough FC 1993/94 *back row from left* Dean Angell, Malcolm Jupp, Alex McGill, Chris Staples, Dave Rhoder, Tony Petras, Darren Downes.
Second row Michael Peacock, Colin Spain, Alan Henderson, Geoff Messenger, Roger Jupp, Steve Leadbeatter, Mick Osborne, Graham Spicer, John Jupp (chairman).
Third row Chris Adsett, Nick Zalesny, Steve Buss, Mark Croft, Russ Phillips (manager), Joe Myskow, Steve Cox, Danny Streeter.
Front row Neil Monahan, Graham Blunden, Tim Hatchard, John Fletcher.

The 1990s

A S I WAS not involved with PFC over the next six years, it is not easy to report on what was happening. I rely on the club archives and what friends have told me about what was going on at the club at the time. It was hoped that over the next few years the side would be able to be more consistent and that, once in a higher division, they would stay there and not be relegated.

Before the start of the 1990/91 season the club advertised for a first team manager. When no applicants came forward, the committee accepted Andy Kynoch's invitation to employ him as caretaker manager for a trial period. As a friend of Andy, I respected his decision to help the club when they could not find a manager, but being a manager is not easy and becoming a player/manager is not something I would recommend to anyone. I felt sorry for him when things were not going that well. The team finished in 10th place.

The first match of the 1990/91 season was against Liss Athletic and resulted in a 4-1 win. The team that day was: M. Harwood, N. Zalesny, J. Jupp, T. Blunden, Ant Leadbeatter, C. Hutton, F. Rhoder, J. Fletcher, C. Merriot, R. Streeter, S. Whitehead, sub R. Jupp. Scorers were S. Whitehead 2, C. Hutton 1, A. Leadbeatter 1. The league matches were disappointing and they just avoided relegation. They had a good run in the Division 3 Charity Cup before finally losing to Sidlesham.

> ### Match report 30-11-1991
> Referee Tony Tester caused fury when he abandoned a soccer match for bad light two minutes before the end - with one side leading 7-1. Players for Horsham Olympic were left fuming as they prepared to celebrate a win over West Sussex League rivals Pulborough. Tony, of Brighton, said Pulborough players threatened to walk off due to "unsafe" light. The League is to rule on a possible replay.

The next season got off to a bad start when Jim Leadbeatter resigned. Colin Hutton agreed to be a manager with John Stewart as back-up. I'm not sure what happened, but Colin Spain was voted in by the committee to be the second team manager. His first game in charge the team lost 9-0; things could only get better. The side selected for that match was M. Croft, S. Harrison, S. Cox, T. Blunden, A. Dumbrill, G. Phur, R. Streeter, N. Baker, J. Fletcher, G. Light, N. Monahan, sub S. Whitehead. Colin resigned as manager in February 1992.

1991/92 was very disappointing, with the team relegated to Division 2. Despite Andy bringing in some new players, the team were not getting results and suffered two heavy defeats in their 2 cup matches. In the Malcolm Simmonds Cup they lost to Sunallon by 11 goals to 1 and in the Sussex Intermediate Cup, Steyning Old Grammarians beat them 10-0.

Andy was to continue as manager for the 1992/93 season. The team started poorly, losing their first 4 league matches, the last one a 7-1 loss to Wittering on 17th October 1992.

At a committee meeting held on 19th October 1992, John Jupp, the Chairman, stated that he had received a phone call from Andy Kynoch regarding his managerial position with the first XI. He had become disillusioned and feeling he was not the right person to motivate the team, tendered his resignation. The committee reluctantly accepted, thanking him for his dedication and expressed the wish that he remain with the club on the committee and concentrate on playing. At this point John Jupp asked Kevin Taylor if he would take over as first XI manager with the assistance of Colin Spain; both agreed. Kevin and Colin were doing their best, but it seemed as though the team was not good enough for most of the season, the best result being a 5-0 win against Lancing & Sompting RBL Reserve, with Tim Hatchard scoring 4. The last 5 matches saw the team win 4 and lose 1, a good end to the season, but it failed to keep the team up and they were relegated and would have to play in Division 3 next year.

In July 1993 Russ Phillips was appointed as manager of the first team. At a Committee Meeting held on 27th September 1993, Cliff Cox expressed concern regarding the penalty points amassed last season and, following a general discussion, it was agreed to send a letter to all players regarding conduct during matches.

Committee Meeting 28-2-1994

A.O.B. Russ Phillips apologised to the Committee for the recent violent behaviour of player X, during a recent match against Alfold, following which he was sent off. Russ Phillips personal recommendation was to terminate the player's registration with the Football Club forthwith and asked the Committee for their views. Following a lengthy discussion, it was unanimously decided to suspend player X from all training and matches until the decision of the Sussex County Football Association was known. John Jupp our Chairman, will advise them of the action taken by the Football Club who are likely to face a substantial fine.

The season saw us playing in Division 3 Central. I think this was the lowest league in which the first team had played but it gave the manager a chance to rebuild the side. One or two new faces were brought in and others were given the opportunity to play regularly for the 1st XI. The team got off to a bad start, losing their first 2 games. The side selected for the first game was, M. Croft, T. Blunden, M. Spicer, G. Spicer, S. Buss, D. Streeter, A. Henderson, N. Zalesny, N. Spicer, T. Hatchard, G. Blunden, subs M. Osborne, J. Fletcher. They got their first result of the season, against Shipley Reserves, a 7-0 win. Then followed a fine win against old rivals Fittleworth in the Bareham Trophy, with Steve Cox getting a hat-trick. Better was to follow when they played Yapton in the Division 3 Charity Cup, with Tim Hatchard netting 5 in an 8-2 win. Two more wins followed, a 5-0 in the Bareham Trophy, Steve scoring another 3, next came a league match against Stedham Reserves, who PFC beat 11-0, with Tim and Dave Smith getting 4 each. Steve Cox got 2 more hat-tricks during the season. Nick Zalesny got in on the act by scoring 4 against East Dean. Tim Hatchard was having a great campaign, scoring 3 hat-tricks, a 4 and 7 in one match against East Dean. By the end of the season he had scored 48 goals. The team lost some silly games and could only finish in 5th place, despite scoring just under 4 goals a game.

It was not easy to get information about the teams in the next few years. Minutes were taken at Committee Meetings, but for one reason or another, no team sheets were recorded and no results or goal scorers were kept. Once again, I had to ask friends who played and what type of football they were playing.

The 1994/95 season was quite a good one, but the team just missed out on promotion by finishing in fourth spot. They had some very big wins in the league. They beat Northchapel 14-2, scorers were Tim Hatchard 5, Ant Leadbeatter 4, Nick Zalesny 2, Dave Smith 1, Kevin Taylor 1 and an own goal. East Dean was a 6-1 win. Tim 4, Steve Buss 1 and Kev 1 scoring. Graffham were beaten 9-0, Dave 4, Darren Downes 2, Tim 1, John Tewsley 1 and Nick 1 were on target. The team had a fine run in the Bareham Trophy, beating Bilsham in the first round and Aldingbourne 3-1 in the next round. In the 3rd round Yapton were disposed of by 5-1, Tim 2, Nick 2 and Darren scoring. Slindon were then beaten 2-1 after extra-time. In the semi-final they drew with Angmering 4-4, Dave (3) and Mike Osborne getting the goals. In the replay at Angmering the score was 1-1 after extra-time; we lost 5-4 on penalties.

Once again the 1995/96 campaign saw the team miss out on promotion. The team fell apart in the last 3 games of the season, gaining just 1 point from those games. As this was the season in which 3 points were awarded for a win, they lost 8 points out of a possible 9 and ended up in 3rd position. There were times when the team played some very good football and heavy defeats were inflicted on Northchapel, the home game being won by 12 goals to 2 (Tim 4, Dave 3, Jason Bailey 2, Steve Cox, Ant Leadbeatter and Danny Streeter were the scorers). The away fixture saw the team win 11-0, with Tim 5, Dave 3, Kev Taylor 2 and Darren scoring. Later in the season Barns Green were thrashed 8-1, with Chris Phillips 3, Dave 3, Dean Angell and Kev scoring. Once again the team were indebted to Tim, who scored 23 goals. Dave had a great season, scoring 16 and showing everyone just how good he was. Chris and Jason also scored hat-tricks. In defence, Ant was outstanding in a defence that only conceded 21 goals.

The team finally gained promotion the next season 1996/97. We had lost Tim for the season, who was out injured, but we had signed on Liam Wadey, who was to have a good season. John Tewsley had also signed and this was a major boost for the team, and with John and Dave Smith in the squad we had two players with senior experience who showed their quality throughout the campaign. The team made a poor start, losing the first 3 games, 2 of which were cup matches. The team improved and two good wins against Fernhurst and Upper Beeding gave them a bit more confidence. We had a tough match away to Partridge Green, who were a physical side and we had to keep our heads. By the end of the game we had three or four players limping off, but we came away with a 6-1 win: Jason 2, Dave 2, Paul Maynard and Kev scoring. In the return match we played some fine football and thrashed them 8-1, Chris Phillips 4, John Tewsley 3 and Liam Wadey being the scorers.

The last game of the season was an away fixture at Wisborough Green, never an easy game in front of their noisy supporters. We played really well and won 7-0, goals coming from Paul Maynard 2, Tony Staples 2, Chris, Nick Zalesny and an own goal. We were champions, the whole squad having played their part, but I thought Ant and Liam at the heart of our defence were outstanding. John and Dave showed their class and 12 different players got on the score sheet.

Players 1 Manager 0

I can't remember who we played against, other than it was an away match. When we arrived at the ground some of the players went to inspect the pitch and as they came back in, I went out. I returned to the dressing room and saw that £1 coins were being handed to Gavin. I asked what was happening and was told that the team were having a flutter on what time the first goal would be scored. I gave him my £1 and said what time I thought the goal would be scored. There was a lot of laughter as I handed my money over.

There was still some chuckling as I started my team talk. I asked them if I had odd socks on, or were my flies undone, but they said no. I finished my talk and out they went, still in a jovial mood. After the match someone asked who had won the money. Gavin said that X had won and with a prediction of 38. I said that was not right, since no goal was scored until the second half. The guys creased up with laughter and I was told that the bet was on how many times I swore during the team talk. I was surprised it was that many. Anyway, the guys had a good laugh at my expense and it showed what a good team spirit we had, which was great.

The less said about the 1997/98 season the better. We lost a few important players and the team did not gel. Losing nine out of our last ten matches spelt trouble and the team were relegated. The side were back in Division 3 Central in 1998/99. It was to be a successful season, with the team being promoted and also reaching the final of the Division 3 Charity Cup. In the cup run they beat Shipley 2-1, Alfold 3-2 and Fernhurst 3-2 after extra-time, this was a replay, the first match was a draw 2-2. In the semi-final Partridge Green were beaten 2-1. In the final we played Yapton, who were a very good team and they won with some comfort. It was no disgrace to lose to such a good team. In the league there were some outstanding performances; Upper Beeding were beaten home and away, 10-2 and 8-1 and Alfold were defeated 7-0. Only 27 goals were conceded in 20 league matches and 61 goals were scored. Unfortunately the goal scorers were not recorded.

We were back to playing intermediate football in 1999/2000 in Division 2 South. Sadly, the side were not up to playing at that standard of football and were relegated. Just 3 games were won and they were knocked out of the cup competitions in the first round. In the Sussex Junior Cup they lost 7-1 to Horsham Olympic, in the Centenary Cup they were defeated by Worthing BCOB 6-2 and in the Chichester Charity Cup Broadbridge Heath beat them 2-0.

Season 1996-1997: Division 3 Central Champions.

Back Row: John Tewsley, Liam Wadey, Mick Osborne, Anthony Leadbeatter, Mick Hatchard (Manager)
Paul Maynard, Dave Clegg, Sean Whitehead.
Front Row: Nick Zalesny, Dave Smith, Steve Buss, Graham Blunden, Kevin Jones.

Season 1998-1999 Promoted to Division 2 South
Division 3 Cup Finalists - Sponsored by John Wadey

Back row: John Jupp (Chairman), Nick Zalesny, Ant Leadbeatter, Unkown, Sean Whitehead.
Stuart Leaney, Liam Wadey, Matt Hall, Steve Buss, Dave Smith (Manager).
Front row: Dave Whitehouse, Matt Parry, Steve Adsett, Kevin Moore, Chris Hall, Unkown

The Squad of 1996-1997

KEVIN JONES was born in Rustington 7th August 1969. He went to Bury Primary School, then St. Phillips Catholic in Arundel and the Phillip Howard School in Barnham. On leaving he worked as a farmer, then became a child social worker, he is now Team Leader for waste and recycling for Horsham District Council. Kev was our goalkeeper, he was short for a keeper but came for balls crossed into the area, he was not afraid to go down at forwards' feet, reliable without being spectacular. He played for a number of Clubs, including, Arundel, Cirencester Town and Watersfield where he was also manager. He is still playing and now lives in Fittleworth.

SEAN WHITEHEAD born in Rustington 11th October 1971. He went to the local St. Mary's School in Pulborough and then to The Weald in Billingshurst. Sean worked for Gammon & Smith for a while, then spent 7 years at Spellman, he has worked for Royal Mail for the last 11 years. He played as a forward sometimes, but was a better goalkeeper. He was the ideal build for a keeper, well over 6 foot tall he was an imposing figure. Pulborough was his only Club and he lives in the village.

ANTHONY LEADBEATTER born 22nd October 1970 in Shoreham. He attended St. Mary's School in Pulborough before going to St. Andrew's in Worthing. He then went to college to study sports. He then took a position at the Trading Standards Department. He is now in the Police Force and is a high ranking Officer. Ant played in several different positions but I think central defender was his best. He was tall and athletic and very fast, a great advantage wherever you play. He was able to bring the ball out of defence and set moves going. Ant was a one Club man, he lives in Worthing.

NICK ZALESNY was born in Chichester 23rd May 1974. He went to the local St. Mary's School in Pulborough and then went on to The Weald in Billingshurst. On leaving School he went to work for Harwood's garage where he did his 6 year apprenticeship. Nick now works for J M Wadey in Bury. He was another one who played in different positions, but settled down to play at fullback. He was not that tall but good in the air and liked to get forward to support the front players. A one Club man, he lives in West Chiltington.

PETER WARDELL was born in Coldwaltham 1st June 1966. He attended Coldwaltham Primary School before moving on to Midhurst Grammar School. His only occupation has been as a self employed carpenter. Pete usually played as a central defender, but I played him as a central midfield player. He was a big man, good in the air and strong in the tackle, he was asked to break up opposition attacks and give the ball to the more attacking players, he did this very well. He also played for Graffham, he lives in Pulborough.

PAUL MAYNARD came to us from Storrington. He was a big strong player and played on the left side of midfield. He was a good solid man to have in the side.

JOHN TEWSLEY was born in Shoreham 18th July 1965. He attended Storrington Primary School and then went to Steyning Grammar School. He played in central midfield and had a great season. John was one of the fittest players in the side, his all round ability stood out, his passing was first class and he got forward to score goals and he was very good when we had to defend. He had a great attitude, always encouraging the rest of the team. He also played senior football for Horsham YMCA and played for Billingshurst and Storrington where he lives.

PAUL SWEENEY came to us from Billingshurst, he played in midfield and was a very aggressive player, someone you wanted on your side and not against you. Paul suffered with injuries from an early age and had surgery to his knees which brought his playing days to an end far too quickly. He played for Loxwood and Billingshurst, where he now lives.

DAVE CLEGG played in midfield, he was short and stocky and was a skilful man in possession of the ball. Dave played senior football.

ANTHONY STAPLES another midfielder, he was a powerful man, a strong tackler and a good ball winner, he was a good man to have on your side. Tony lives in Worthing.

CHRIS PHILLIPS played in the forward line, usually through the centre. He was tall and athletic and very quick, he scored a lot of goals for the Club. Chris played for Horsham, Horsham YMCA, Billingshurst and Loxwood.

DEAN ANGELL was born in Newbury 18th March 1962. He attended Kyntebury the local School and then Park House in Newbury. Leaving School he went to work for Peter Hoblyn as a stable lad, in 1979 he moved to Guy Harwood's racing stables, he is now head lad for Amanda Perrett. Dean played on the right, midfield or forward. He played for Storrington. He lives in Pulborough.

JASON BAILEY was born in Chichester 21st December 1978. He went to St. Mary's School in Pulborough and then went on to The Weald in Billingshurst. He then went to work at the garden centre at Stopham, on leaving there he now works for Ernest Doe gardening centre. Jason played in a number of positions, he was tall, had good ability on the ball and was good in the air, but not the quickest. He played for Horsham YMCA, Plaistow and Alfold. He lives in Pulborough.

GRAHAM BLUNDEN born 20th August 1964 in Shoreham. He went to Billingshurst Primary School and then to The Weald also in Billingshurst. His first job was working for Linfields, he then spent 5 years on a garden farm, he has worked for Crawley Borough Council for the last 28 years. Graham played up front, usually out wide, he was tricky and could go past defenders and scored his share of goals. He lives in Pulborough.

GAVIN CLARK born 28th November 1983 in Chichester. He went to Primary School in Arundel and then to Rydon County Secondary in Thakeham. He then went to work at the Labouring Man pub, he had several other jobs but now has his own company business. Gavin played in midfield, he was not the tallest but he was not afraid to get stuck in and was a skilful player. He lives in Norwich.

MICHAEL OSBORNE, STEVE BUSS LIAM WADEY, DAVE SMITH & KEVIN TAYLOR were also members of this squad.

SEASON 1998-1999
CHANGE KIT SPONSORED BY PSSC

Back row: Martyn Ralph. Steve Adsett. Dave Whitehouse. Sean Whitehead. Stuart Underwood. Mark Wardell. Jim Sears. Stuart Leaney. Front row: John Fletcher. Andy Pavey. Graig jupp. Simon Leadbeatter. Jason Leadbeatter. Graham Blunden.

Results 1990 – 1999

WSL DIVISION 1, 1990/91

1-9-1990 [H] Lavant (L 0-1)

8-9-1990 [H] Sunallon (L 1-2) N. Spicer 1

15-9-1990 [H] South Bersted (L 0-1)

22-9-1990 | MSC [H] Steyning O. G (L 0-4)

29-9-1990 [H] Roffey (W 3-1) P. Bird 1, A. Kynoch 1, S. Leadbeatter 1

6-10-1990 [A] Stedham United (W 1-0) D. Lewis 1

13-10-1990 | SIC [A] Lavant L 1-4) D. Lewis 1

20-10-1990 [A] Worthing B. C. O. B (W 1-0) G. Phur 1

27-10-1990 [A] Barns Green (L 1-2) OG 1. 10-11-1990 [A] Loxwood (L 0-2)

17-11-1990 [H] Amberley (D 0-0)

24-11-1990 [A] Cranleigh (W 6-1) G. Phur 2, P. Bird 1, G. Blunden 1, C. Hutton 1, D. Lewis 1

1-12-1990 [H] Maple Leaf Rangers (D 0-0)

8-12-1990 [A] Emsworth (W 3-0) D. Lewis 3

15-12-1990 [H] Ifield (L 0-2)

22-12-1990 [H] Worthing B. C. O. B (L 0-3)

19-1-1991 [H] Emsworth (D 1-1) D. Lewis 1

26-1-1991 [H] Barns Green (L 1-2) D. Lewis 1

2-2-1991 [A] South Bersted (L 2-3) A. Kynoch 1, D. Lewis 1

16-2-1991 [A] Lavant (L 1-4-D. Lewis 1

23-2-1991 [H] Cranleigh (W 5-1) P. Bird 2, C. Hutton 1, D. Lewis 1, A. Mcgill 1

2-3-1991 [A] Roffey (L 0-5)

9-3-1991 [H] Stedham United (W 1-0) R. Streeter 1

16-3-1991 [A] Maple Leaf Rangers (W 2-0) P. Bird 1, R. Streeter 1

23-3-1991 [A] Amberley (D 1-1) R. Streeter 1

30-3-1991 [H] Loxwood (W 2-1) P. Bird 1, N. Spicer 1

1-4-1991 [A] Cowfold (D 2-2) N. Spicer 1, OG 1

6-4-1991 [A] Sunallon (L 1-5) R. Jupp 1

17-4-1991 [H] Cowfold (D 5-5) D. Lewis 3, P. Bird 1, N. Spicer 1

27-4-1991 [A] Ifield (L 0-3)

P28 | W9 | D6 | L13 | GF40 | GA48 | 24pts | 10th

WSL DIVISION 1, 1991/92

14-9-1991 [H] Horsham Olympic (W 2-1) D. Rhoder 1, R. Streeter 1

21-9-1991 [H] Eastergate (W 3-2) D. King 1, Ant Leadbeatter 1, C. Staples 1

28-9-1991 [A] Stedham United (L 0-1)

5-10-1991 | MSC [A] Sunallon (L 1-11) D. Lewis 1

12-10-1991 | SIC [A] Steyning O. G (L 0-10)

19-10-1991 [H] S. B. Sports (L 1-2) C. Hutton 1

26-10-1991 [A] Worthing B. C. O. B (L 0-1)

2-11-1991 [H] Bracklesham (L 1-4) I. Dumbrill 1

9-11-1991 [A] Eastergate (L 1-2) Tim Hatchard 1

16-11-1991 [A] Ifield (L 1-6) Tim Hatchard 1

23-11-1991 [H] Emsworth (D 2-2) I. Dumbrill 1, M. Osborne 1

30-11-1991 [A] Horsham Olympic (L 1-7) N. Spicer 1, Game abandoned after 88 minutes

7-12-1991 [A] Lavant (L 1-3) C. Hutton 1

21-12-1991 [H] Roffey (L 0-3)

28-12-1991 [A] Cowfold (L 2-3) M. Osborne 1, N. Spicer 1

4-1-1992 [A] S. B. Sports (L 0-5) 18-1-1992 [A] Emsworth (D 1-1) G. Phur 1

25-1-1992 [A] Bracklesham (W 2-0) N. Bainbridge 1, P. Bird 1

1-2-1992 [H] Lavant (D 2-2) N. Bainbridge 1, D. Lewis 1

8-2-1992 [A] Roffey (L 0-5)

15-2-1992 [A] Billinghurst (W 3-2) N. Bainbridge 1, D. Lewis 1, G. Phur 1

22-2-1992 [H] Ifield (L 0-3)

29-2-1992 [H] Stedham United (W 4-3) N. Bainbridge 1, P. Bird 1, R. Black 1, D. Lewis 1

7-3-1992 [H] Billingshurst (L 0-1)

14-3-1992 [H] Worthing B. C. O. B (L 1-2) D. Lewis 1

21-3-1992 [H] Cowfold (L 1-2) D. Lewis 1

P24 | W5 | D3 | L16 | GF29 | GA63 | 13pts | 13th

WSL DIVISION 2, SOUTH 1992/93

5-9-1992 [A] Sidlesham Res (L 1-4) Tim Hatchard 1

12-9-1992 [A] Chichester Hospitals (L 0-3)

19-9-1992. SJC [A] Hove County (L 0-1, But we were reinstated

26-9-1992 | CCC. Capel (D 4-4) R. Black 2, T. Challen 1, A. Kynoch 1

3-10-1992. SJC [A] Steyning O. G. Res (W 2-1) R. Black 1, Tim Hatchard 1

10-10-1992 [A] South Bersted Res (L 0-3)

17-10-1992. Wittering United (L 1-7) Tim Hatchard 1

24-10-1992 [A] Petworth (D 1-1) S. Cox 1

31-10-1992 [H] Fernhurst (L 1-6) Ant Leadbeatter 1

7-11-1992. SJC [H] Rudgwick (L 0-1)

14-11-1992 [A] Maple Leaf Rangers (L 1-2) Tim Hatchard 1

21-11-1992 | CCC replay [H] Capel L 1-3) R. Black 1

28-11-1992 [A] Bracklesham (W 3-1) T. Challen 1, Tim Hatchard 1, N. Zalesny 1

12-12-1992 [H] Angmering (L 3-5) R. Black 1, Tim Hatchard 1, C. Hutton 1

19-12-1992 [A] Wittering United (L 2-3) Tim Hatchard 2

2-1-1993 [H] Rogate (L 0-5)

9-1-1993 [H] Lancing & Sompting Legion. ,Res (W 5-0) Tim Hatchard 4, T. Challen 1

6-2-1993 [H] Bracklesham (L 2-4) Tim Hatchard 2

13-2-1993 [H] Amberley (W 3-0) T. Challen 2, C. Staples 1

20-2-1993 [A] Rogate (D 1-1) N. Zalesny 1

27-2-1993 [H] Chichester Hospitals (L 0-1)

13-3-1993 [H] Maple Leaf Rangers (L 1-2) S. Cox 1

20-3-1993 [A] Fernhurst (L 0-3)

27-3-1993 [H] Petworth (D 2-2) S. Cox 1, Tim Hatchard 1

3-4-1993 [A] Sidlesham Res (W 2-0) Tim Hatchard 1, N. Spicer 1

10-4-1993 [A] Lancing & Sompting Legion Res (W 3-2) T. Challen 1, Tim Hatchard 1, Ant Leadbeatter 1

12-4-1993 [A] Amberley (W 1-0) N. Spicer 1

17-4-1993 [H] South Bersted Res (L 0-4)

19-4-1993 [A] Angmering (W 4-2) Tim Hatchard 2, N. Spicer 2

P24 | W7 | D3 | L14 | GF37 | GA61 | 17pts | 11th

WSL DIVISION 3, CENTRAL 1993/94

4-9-1993 [H] Harting (L 2-6) Tim Hatchard 1, N. Spicer 1

11-9-1993 [H] Fernhurst. Sports (L 1-3) S. Cox 1

18-9-1993 [H] Shipley Res (W 7-0) S. Cox 2, Tim Hatchard 2, N. Spicer 2, OG 1

25-9-1993. BT [A] Fittleworth (W 5-2) S. Cox 3, G. Spicer 1, N. Spicer 1

2-10-1993. SJC [A] Lancing United (L 2-8) Tim Hatchard 1, N. Spicer 1

9-10-1993. D3CC [H] Yapton (W 8-2) Tim Hatchard 5, S. Cox 1, N. Zalesny 1, ? 1

16-10-1993. BT [A] Ambassadors (W 5-0) S. Cox 3, Tim Hatchard 2

23-10-1993 [H] Stedham United Res (W 11-0) Tim Hatchard 4, D. Smith 4, S. Cox 1, A. Staples 1, N. Zalesny 1

30-10-1993 [A] Harting (D 1-1) D. Smith 1

6-11-1993 [H] Fittleworth (L 0-2)

13-11-1993 [A] Stedham United Res (W 4-1) D. Smith 2, N. Zalesny 1, OG 1

20-11-1993 [H] Milland Res (W 5-1) S. Cox 3, Tim Hatchard 1, A. Staples 1

27-11-1993 [H] Lodsworth. (L 0-1)

4-12-1993 [A] Milland Res (D 3-3) Tim Hatchard 2, S. Buss 1

29-1-1994 [H] East Dean (W 8-0) N. Zalesny 4, S. Cox 3, Tim Hatchard 1

5-2-1994. BT [H] East Dean (W 5-2) Tim Hatchard 3, S. Cox 1, N. Zalesny 1

12-2-1994. D3CC [H] Alfold Res (W 5-1) Tim Hatchard 3, S. Cox 1, N. Zalesny 1

19-2-1994. BT [A] Southbourne Sports (L 0-4)

26-2-1994 [H] Alfold Res (D 1-1) A. Petras 1.

5-3-1994 [A] Fittleworth (W 3-1) D. Downes 1, Tim Hatchard 1, N. Zalesny 1

12-3-1994 [A] Lodsworth (D 2-2) Ant Leadbeatter 1, M. Osborne 1

19-3-1994 [A] Alfold Res (L 1-2) Tim Hatchard 1

26-3-1994 [A] East Dean (W 9-0) Tim Hatchard 7, D. Downes 1, A. McGill 1

2-4-1994. D3CC [A] Sunallon 3rds (L 0-5)

4-4-1994 [H] Barns Green (W 10-0) Tim Hatchard 4, A. McGill 3, Ant Leadbeatter 2, S. Leadbeatter 1

13-4-1994 [A] Barns Green (L 2-3) Tim Hatchard 1, A. McGill 1

16-4-1994 [A] Fernhurst Sports (W 4-2) Tim Hatchard 2, A. McGill 1, N. Spicer 1

24-4-1994 [A] Shipley Res (W 4-3) Tim Hatchard 3, S. Buss 1

P20 | W10 | D4 | L6 | GF78 | GA32 | 24pts | 5th

WSL DIVISION 3, CENTRAL 1994/95

3-9-1994 [H] Milland Res (W 5-2)

10-9-1994 [A] Northchapel (W 2-1) D. Downes 1, Welsh 1

17-9-1994. SJC [A] Yapton (L 1-2)

24-9-1994. BT [H] Bilsham United. Won but no score found

31-9-1994 [H] Harting (W 7-0)

8-10-1994. D3CC [A] West Chiltington Res (L 0-2)

15-10-1994 [H] Alfold Res (W 3-2)

22-10-1994 [A] East Dean (W 5-2)

29-10-1994 [H] Upper Beeding (L 1-2) D. Smith 1

5-11-1994. BT [A] Aldingbourne (W 3-1) Tim Hatchard 1, D. Smith 1, OG 1

12-11-1994 [H] Northchapel (W 14-2) Tim Hatchard 5, Ant Leadbeatter 4, N. Zalesny 2, D. Smith 1, K. Taylor 1, OG 1

26-11-1994 [H] East Dean (W 6-1) Tim Hatchard 4, S. Buss 1, K. Taylor 1

3-12-1994. BT [H] Yapton (W 5-1) Tim Hatchard 2, N. Zalesny 2, D. Downes 1

17-12-1994 [A] Barns Green Res (W 4-1) N. Zalesny 2, Tim Hatchard 1, Ant Leadbeatter 1

31-12-1994 [H] Lodsworth (L 0-2)

7-1-1995. BT [H] Slindon (W 2-1) S. Cox 1, T. Staples 1. AET

14-1-1995 [H] Wisborough Green (L 0-1)

4-3-1995. BT. Semi-Final [H] Angmering Res (D 4-4) D. Smith 3, M. Osborne 1. AET

11-3-1995 [A] Wisborough Green (L 1-2) D. Downes 1

18-3-1995 [H] Graffham (W 9-0) D. Smith 4, D. Downes 2, Tim Hatchard 1, J. Tewsley 1, N. Zalesny 1

25-3-1995 [H] Barns Green Res (W 3-2) D. Smith 2, Tim Hatchard 1

1-4-1995. BT Replay Semi-Final [A] Angmering Res (D 1-1) Lost 4-5) on penalties after AET

8-4-1995 [H] West Chiltington Res (L 1-2)

15-4-1995 [A] Milland Res (D 0-0)

17-4-1995 [A] Graffham (W 3-1)

19-4-1995 [A] Lodsworth (W 3-1)

26-4-1995 [A] Upper Beeding (L 0-3)

29-4-1995 [A] Alfold Res (L 3-4)

2-5-1995 [A] West Chiltington Res (L 0-1)

5-5-1995 [A] Harting (W 6-1)

P22 | W13 | D1 | L8 | GF76 | GA32 | 27pts | 4th

WSL DIVISION 3, CENTRAL 1995/96

2-9-1995 [A] Barns Green Res (W 3-0)

9-9-1995 [H] Graffham (W 5-0) Tim Hatchard 2, J. Bailey 1, S. Cox 1, C. Phillips 1

16-9-1995. SJC [H] Ashington Rovers (L 2-4)

23-9-1995. BT [H] Milland Res (L 1-2) Tim Hatchard 1

30-9-1995 [A] Milland Res (L 0-1)

7-10-1995 [H] Northchapel (W 12-2) Tim Hatchard 4, D. Smith 3, J. Bailey 2, S. Cox 1, Ant Leadbeatter 1, R. Streeter 1

14-10-1995 [H] Watersfield (W 3-2) S. Cox 1, K. Taylor 1, T. Staples 1

21-10-1995 [A] Loxwood (L 1-3) K. Taylor 1

28-10-1995 [H] Lodsworth (W 5-0) J. Bailey 3, Tim Hatchard 2

4-11-1995. CC [A] Horsham Trinity (W 1-0) R. Streeter 1

11-11-1995 [H] Milland Res (W 3-1) J. Bailey 1, Tim Hatchard 1, D. Smith 1

18-11-1995 [A] Northchapel (W 11-0) Tim Hatchard 5, D. Smith 3, K. Taylor 2, D. Downes 1

25-11-1995 [H] Wisborough Green. ,,W 6-0) J. Bailey 2, Tim Hatchard 2, D. Downes 1, D. Smith 1

2-12-1995 [A] Graffham (W 2-1) Tim Hatchard 1, OG 1

9-12-1995. CC [H] East Preston 111s (D 1-1) J. Bailey 1, AET

16-12-1995 [A] Lodsworth (W 4-2) D. Smith 2, J. Bailey 1, K. Taylor 1

6-1-1996. CC Replay [A] East Preston 111s (L 1-2) D. Angell 1

13-1-1996 [H] Barns Green Res. W. ,8-1) C. Phillips 3, D. Smith 3, D. Angell 1, K. Taylor 1

20-1-1996 [A] Fernhurst Sports (W 3-0) Tim Hatchard 2, J. Bailey 1

9-2-1996 [H] West Chiltington Res (L 1-2) C. Phillips 1

16-2-1996 [A] Wisborough Green. ,W 2-0) J. Bailey 1, D. Smith 1

23-2-1996 [H] Fernhurst Sports (W 3-2) J. Bailey 1, Tim Hatchard 1, C. Phillips 1

9-3-1996 [A] West Chiltington Res (L 3-4) Tim Hatchard 1, C. Phillips 1, D. Smith 1

16-3-1996 [H] Watersfield (L 1-2) D. Smith 1

30-3-1996 [H] Loxwood (D 1-1) Tim Hatchard 1

P18 | W12 | D1 | L5 | GF53 | GA21 | 37pts | 3rd

I believe Northchapel dropped out

WSL DIVISION 3, CENTRAL 1996/97

14-9-1996 [H] Stedham United Res (L 0-2)

21-9-1996. SJC [A] Amberley (L 0-1)

28-9-1996. CC [H] Southbourne Sports (L 1-2) J. Bailey 1

5-10-1996 [A] Fernhurst Sports (W 4-1) J. Bailey 2, K. Taylor 2, P. Sweeney 1

12-10-1996 [H] Upper Beeding (W 4-1) J. Bailey 2, D. Smith 2

19-10-1996 [A] Alfold Res (W 2-0) J. Bailey 1, D. Smith 1

26-10-1996 [A] Partridge Green (W 6-1) J. Bailey 2, D. Smith 2, P. Maynard 1, K. Taylor 1

2-11-1996 [A] Lodsworth (L 2-5) S. Buss 1, L. Wadey 1

9-11-1996 [H] Alfold Res (L 2-3) D. Angell 1, P. Sweeney 1

16-11-1996 [A] Stedham United Res (L 1-3) D. Smith 1

30-11-1996 [A] Rudgwick (W 3-2) D. Smith 1, K. Taylor 1, J. Tewsley 1

7-12-1996 [H] Partridge Green (W 8-1) C. Phillips 4, J. Tewsley 3, L. Wadey 1

14-12-1996 [A] Upper Beeding (D 1-1) C. Phillips 1

18-1-1997 [H] Fernhurst Sports (D 1-1) D. Smith 1

25-1-1997 [H] Rudgwick (W 4-1) K. Taylor 2, C. Phillips 1, J. Tewsley 1

1-2-1997 [H] Wisborough Green (W 3-0) D. Smith 2, C. Phillips 1

15-2-1997 [H] Lodsworth (W 3-1) G. Blunden 1, D. Smith 1, K. Taylor 1

22-2-1997 [A] Wisborough Green (W 7-0) P. Maynard 2, A. Staples 2, C. Phillips 1, N. Zalesny 1, OG 1

P16 | W10 | D2 | L4 | GF51 | GA23 | 32pts | 1st

WSL DIVISION 2, SOUTH 1997/98

13-9-1997 [H] Yapton (D 1-1) M. Wroe 1

10-9-1997. SJC [H] Angmering (L 2-5) Tim Hatchard 1, L. Wadey 1

27-9-1997. CC [A] Wisborough Green (W 4-1) G. Blunden 1, Tim Hatchard 1, P. Maynard 1, M. Wroe 1

11-10-1997 | CCC [A] Clymping (L 1-2) Tim Hatchard 1

18-10-1997 [H] Hunston United (D 4-4) L. Wadey 2, Tim Hatchard 1, D. Smith 1

25-10-1997 [A] Slindon (L 1-4) M. Wroe 1

1-11-1997. CC. H, Ambassadors (W 4-0) Tim Hatchard 2, D. Smith 1, M. Wroe 1

8-11-1997. Oving Social Club Res (D 2-2) Tim Hatchard 1, P. Maynard 1

15-11-1997 [A] Watersfield (L 3-4) D. Smith 2, M. Wroe 1

29-11-1997 [H] Angmering (W 2-1) Tim Hatchard 1, S. Whitehead 1

6-12-1997. CC [A] Rogate (L 1-4) J. Bailey 1

13-12-1997 [A] Clymping (L 0-1)

20-12-1997 [H] Petworth (W 2-1) S. Harrison 1, M. Wroe 1

17-1-1998 [A] Yapton (L 1-3) K. Taylor 1

24-1-1998 [H] Slindon (L 0-1)

31-1-1998 [A] Hunston United (L 1-2)

14-2-1998 [H] Clymping (L 0-3)

21-2-1998 [H] South Bersted (L 1-5) OG 1

28-2-1998 [H] Oving Social Club Res (L 2-4) S. Harrison 1, OG 1

14-3-1998 [A] Angmering (L 1-2) M. Wroe 1

28-3-1998 [A] Petworth (W 1-0) J. Bailey 1

11-4-1998 [H] Watersfield (L 1-2)

15-4-1998 [A] South Bersted (L 0-2)

P18 | W3 | D3 | L12 | GF23 | GA42 | 12pts | 10th

WSL DIVISION 3, CENTRAL 1998/99

12-9-1998 [H] Fernhurst (L 0-4)

19-9-1998. SJC [H] Brinsbury (W 4-2)

26-9-1998. D3CC [H] Shipley Res (W 2-1)

3-10-1998. SJC [A] Southbourne Sports (W 2-0)

17-10-1998. CC [A] South Bersted (L 1-9)

21-11-1998 [H] Billingshurst (L 0-2)

28-11-1998 [A] Fittleworth (L 0-3)

23-1-1999 [A] Rudgwick (W 3-1)

30-1-1999 [H] Upper Beeding (W 10-2)

6-2-1999. D3CC [H] Alfold Res (W 3-2)

13-2-1999 [H] Slinfold Res (W 2-1)

20-2-1999 [H] Wisborough Green (D 1-1)

27-2-1999 [H] Shipley Res (W 5-1)

6-3-1999 [A] Lodsworth (W 2-0)

13-3-1999. D3CC [H] Fernhurst (D 2-2)

20-3-1999. D3CC Replay [A] Fernhurst (W 3-2) AET

27-3-1999. D3CC Semi-Final [H] Partridge Green (W 2-1)

3-4-1999 [A] Upper Beeding (W 8-1)

5-4-1999 [A] Fernhurst (W 3-1)

10-4-1999 [A] Shipley Res (D 0-0)

14-4-1999 [H] Alfold Res (W 7-0)

17-4-1999 [H] Fittleworth (D 2-2)

19-4-1999 [A] Wisborough Green (D 1-1)

21-4-1999 [H] Rudgwick (W 3-0)

24-4-1999 [H] Lodsworth (W 6-0)

26-4-1999 [A] Alfold Res (D 2-2)

3-5-1999 [A] Slinfold Res (W 5-0)

5-5-1999 [A] Billingshurst (L 1-3

Final of the Division 3, Charity Cup, played at Arundel. Pulborough 3, Yapton 7

P20 | W11 | D5 | L4 | GF61 | GA27 | 38pts | 3rd

WSL DIVISION 2, SOUTH 1999/2000

4-9-1999 [A] Newtown Villa (L 1-4)

11-9-1999 [H] Wittering United (L 1-2)

18-9-1999 [H] Harting (L 0-3)

25-9-1999 [A] Yapton. ,L 1-2)

2-10-1999. SJC [A] Horsham Olympic (L 1-7)

9-10-1999 [H] Bosham Res (W 2-0)

16-10-1999 [A] Slindon (W 2-0)

23-10-1999. CC [H] Worthing B. C. O. B (L 2-6)

30-10-1999 [A] Rustington Res (L 2-9)

6-11-1999 [A] Wittering United (L 2-4)

13-11-1999 | CCC [H] Broadbridge Heath 111s (L 0-2)

18-12-1999 [H] Rustington Res (L 1-2)

8-1-2000 [A] Watersfield (D 0-0)

15-1-2000 [A] Harting (L 1-4)

22-1-2000 [H] Petworth (W 4-3)

13-2-2000 [H] Newtown Villa (D 3-3)

20-2-2000 [A] Petworth (L 1-4)

27-2-2000 [A] Bosham Res (L 1-3)

4-3-2000 [H] Watersfield (L 1-2)

11-3-2000 [A] South Bersted Res (L 0-1)

1-4-2000 [H] Yapton (L 1-6)

28 October 1995

Pulborough lost Dave Smith injured but still beat Lodsworth 5-0 to consolidate their position on top of Division Three Central. Jason Bailey hit a hat-trick and Tim Hatchard scored twice with Sean Whitehead sound in goal.

26 October 1996

Pulborough are the early pacesetters in division three central as they won for the fifth time in six matches. Jason Bailey and there is Smith both scored twice in the 6-1 win over Partridge green reserves. Goalkeeper Kevin Jones saved a penalty on his debut for Pulborough.

23 November 1996
'Boro wait for verdict on walk-off

THERE were chaotic scenes at Pulborough's home game with Milland Reserves when the visitors stormed off the pitch. Pulborough led 4-2 in the Division 3 Central clash when they were given a penalty in the last five minutes.

Milland took objection to the award, a melee ensued and their side eventually decided to leave the field.

The host club are still waiting to hear whether the result stands. Pulborough press officer Gordon Blackburn described the match as 'a fiasco'.

'Milland didn't arrive until 2.20pm and we started half an hour late,' he said. 'The first half was alright, but there were a few players booked in the second. When we were given the penalty, there was a melee around the referee and the Milland linesman came over and threw his flag down. Then the Milland players all walked off.'

Second half goals from Graham Blunden, Jason Bailey, Chris Phillips and Dave Smith had given 'Boro their commanding lead.

7th December 1996

Pulborough turned in a dazzling second-half showing to keep their place firmly among Division 3 Central's leading pack. They beat Partridge Green Reserves 8-1 after having led just 1-0 at the break. Chris Phillips made the first half breakthrough and seven goals followed in the last 25 minutes. Phillips added three more, former Horsham YMCA player John Tewsley scored a hat-trick and Liam Wadey was also on target. Green pulled one back late on and were harshly treated by the scoreline for their efforts throughout the game.

27 September 1997

Pulborough thumped Wisborough Green 4-1 to ease into the next round. Matt Wroe scored for both sides but teammates Graham Blunden, Tim Hatchard and Paul Maynard eased his embarrassment.

1st November 1997 – Cup Action

two goals from Tim Hatchard eased Pulborough into the third round of the Centenary Cup as they enjoyed a comfortable 4-0 home win over Ambassadors. Hatchard scored twice in a five-minute spell in the second half, after goals from Matt Wroe and Dave Smith had put Pulborough in control.

15th of November 1997

In Division Two South Pulborough narrowly lost to Watersfield 4-3 in a hard-fought game. Dave Smith got Pulborough's first after 30 minutes with Matthew Rowe adding to the total after 68 minutes followed by Smith again six minutes from the end. Watersfield goals came from Paul Houghton and Ashley Clark with Clark getting a hat-trick, his third in a row. Watersfield will be without him due to injury.

Pulborough FC season 2001/02 Division 3 Cup Finalists

Back row from left Russ Phillips, Stuart Underwood, Martin Ralph, Steve Adsett, Jason Bailey, Liam Wadey, Chris Phillips, Russell Davy, Jason Leadbeatter, Steve Buss (manager).
Front row from left Paul Greenfield, Matt Parry, John Hunter, Bob Burse, Gary Rothwell, Dean Angell.

ROFFEY Reserves proved that they are the outstanding side in their league when they beat Pulborough to win the Division 3 Cup and complete the double on Friday night.

It was an evening to remember for Nick Ells, who scored both Roffey goals but then got sent off ten minutes from time.

In front of a good crowd at Arundel Football Club, Ells put his side in a commanding position when he scored twice before half-time. The first came when a misunderstanding between Pulborough keeper Jonathan Hunter and his defence let Ells in to finish comfortably on the half-hour. Ten minutes later, Pulborough did not close down a free-kick and were punished again by Ells.

But Pulborough pressed after the interval and scored a deserved goal after 72 minutes when a five pass move found Dean Angell, who crossed for substitute Steve Adsett to head home.

Goalscorer Ells was then sent off for his second bookable offence in the 80th minute but Roffey rode a period of pressure to seal the cup triumph, much to the delight of manager Dave Jeal.

"It was great, but I felt sorry for Nick Ells,' he said.

Roffey stormed to the Division 3 title and Jeal felt the cup was a fitting end to a sensational first campaign in charge.

"I've enjoyed every moment, it's been a tremendous season all round. We were definitely looking for promotion at the beginning of the season but once the season got underway we thought we had a chance of winning the league and getting to a cup final."

He paid tribute to his assistant Darren Durse. "I was pleased for him. Being a Palace supporter, he doesn't win much," he joked.

Opponents Pulborough. on the other hand, have had a nearly season. Pipped for promotion from Division 4 Central after a 3-2 defeat to West Chiltington on the last weekend of the season, they were hoping for some reward in the final.

"We were sitting pretty in the league but we let ourselves down badly," said Chairman John Jupp. "The cup final was a bonus but we've ended up with nothing. We knew it would be a tough game against a team in a higher division but we closed them down from the start and a I thought a draw would have been a fair result. They defended well and did not give us any clean-cut chances."

Club Secretary Cliff Cox receiving a £50 award on behalf of Pulborough FC from the West Sussex League for being one of the top teams of the month in October 2000.

The Modern Era 2000-2010

AFTER JUST ONE season the side were back to playing junior football in Division 3 Central in 2000/01. Despite now playing in a lower league, it was a poor time and the team did not find any consistency, but at least they did not go down. Probably their two best results were against Graffham – a 7-4 win with Chris Phillips 4, Dave Smith 2 and Bobby Burse 1 – and the following week Southwater Reserve were beaten 6-l – Chris 4 and Dave 2 were on the scoresheet.

At the Club's AGM on 4th June 2001, Mr C.P. Barnett (Percy), our President for the past ten years, stood down. Mr Russ Phillips was to be our new President. A couple of issues were brought up: one concerned fundraising, the committee were doing their best to raise funds for the club, but they felt they were getting little help from the players. The other was about a manager receiving abuse from some of the players during training sessions.

Back to the football, it turned out to be a very good season. The team finished 3rd in the league and reached the final of the Division 3 Charity Cup. The first 4 league matches were wins, in which the team scored 20 goals. They were also very good defensively; in 18 league matches they only let in 18 goals. Hat-tricks were scored by Russell Davy and Gary Elliot. On the way to the final, Partridge Green were beaten 4-2, Slinfold 3-1, Yapton Reserve 3-1 and in the semi-final Paymaster were defeated. In the final they came up against Roffey Reserves. During the season, in October, the Club were presented with a cheque for £50 for winning the Team of the Month award.

At the AGM on 27th May 2002 the Chairman, Mr John Jupp, commented that this season Mr C. Parsons (Charlie) would have been our Treasurer for 50 years, a great achievement. Charlie was a very nice man and always had a joke to tell (not always clean ones!).

Charlie Parsons, celebrating 50 years as Pulborough FC's Hon. Treasurer, is awarded with a Long Service Medal from the Football Association by Becky Jupp (PFC Secretary) and a good wishes cheque from Club Chairman John Jupp.

The season was a successful one with the team in second place and gaining promotion and also winning the Bareham Trophy. This was another season when only 16 matches were played in the League. In my opinion this is not enough. I can't ever remember playing less then 20 matches. Going back to the 1950s, 60s, 70s, 80s and into the early 1990s, there were years when teams played 30 league matches a season.

Enough of my reminiscing and back to the football...

In the Bareham Trophy the team were successful in beating Slindon 11-4, with goals coming from Chris Phillips 4, Abraham Greenfield 2, Craig Jupp 2, Steve Adsett 1, Paul Greenfield 1 and Liam Wadey 1. Petworth was 6-2, Rob Symonds 2, Jason Bailey 1, Chris 1, Stuart Phillips and Dave Smith 1 scoring. Next up were Fernhurst Sports 2-0, with Gary Rothwell and Stuart Underwood on the scoresheet. In the semi-final Southbourne Sports were defeated 3-2 with Rob 2 and Gary scoring. In the final PFC beat Boxgrove 4-1.

22-9-2001 vs Ockley

A Gary Elliot hat-trick was not enough to save Pulborough from a 4-3 defeat to Ockley in the Centenary Cup. In a game littered with defensive errors and late tackles, Pulborough led 1-0 at the break but eventually lost to what their contact admitted was "a superb angled drive that deserved to win any match". He added it also made sure that the remaining players were able to walk of the pitch unaided.

13-10-2001 vs Partridge Green

Three goals in the final 10 minutes saw Pulborough cruise past Partridge Green reserves 4-2 in the Bareham Trophy. Steve Adsett gave them a half time lead but a missed penalty by Jason Bailey preceded D. Jones equaliser. Extra time looked likely before Chris Hall, Adsett and Dean Angell secured victory.

29-9-2001 vs Royal & Sun Alliance 3rds

Three goals in the first 15 minutes set up Pulborough for a 5-0 win over R&SA 3rd team. Gary Elliot struck twice and Liam Wadey deflected in a header, before Dave Smith's brilliant run and pass invited Chris Hall to make it 4-0 at half time. Despite Alliance coming back into the game, Dean Angell's header completed their misery.

6-10-2001 vs Graffham

Pulborough's John Hunter turned hero in the 4-2 extra time Division 3 Cup defeat of Graffham. In the final seconds of normal time the keeper strayed too far off his line and allowed the visitors to equalise Russell Davy's 3rd minute strike. Graffham then went ahead, before Matt Parry and Davy restored Pulborough's lead and Hunter kept out a certain own goal from Stuart Underwood. Davy completed his hat-trick with the last kick of the match.

23-2-2002 vs Yapton Reserves

Pulborough beat Yapton Reserves 3-1 in the Division 3 Cup. The home side missed several chances early on and keeper John Hunter stopped them going behind with a fine fingertip save. But they took the lead when Anthony Leadbeatter slid in a cross from 6 yards. Yapton levelled when an unlucky deflection fell kindly to a forward who headed past the stranded keeper. But Pulborough's Jason Bailey bravely headed home a corner and with 10 minutes left scored his second when he cleverly guided the ball in at the far post.

26-10-2002 vs Lodsworth

Pulborough found themselves in a seventh heaven as they hammered fellow Division 3 Central side Lodsworth 7-2. Rob Symonds scored from a tight angle to put Pulborough in front early on and Jason Bailey added a second after a fine square pass from Chris Phillips. Stuart Underwood shot home after collecting the ball from a free-kick for 3-0 but Lodsworth clawed a goal back. The young visitors continued to frustrate the home side until player-manager Matt Parry's solo run finished with him slotting home. Steve Adsett came off the bench to score number five, but another defensive lapse saw the home keeper pick the ball out of his net for the second time. Phillips netted his second, as did Adsett, to wrap up the win in the last minute.

The 2003/04 season was one of the best for some time. The team finally got their act together. They had decent runs in the cup competitions, but it was the league matches in which they did best. Only 4 games were lost and the team finished as runners up. Defensively they were very sound, with Sam Grove and Liam Wadey outstanding in central defence. Offensively, we had players who could score goals. Add a hard-working midfield and you have a chance of success. Dorking Wanderers were champions that year, but we beat them home and away.

The team probably played their best football of the season in the away match when they won 6-0, with goals coming from Chris Phillips 2, Jason Bailey, Paul Cooper, Matt Parry and Rob Symonds. The home match was much tighter and resulted in a 4-3 win. There was also a good result against Horsham Athletic, a 7-1 win, with Paul Greenfield 2, Chris 2, Jason, Abraham Greenfield and Craig Jupp scoring. The side changed very little, which gave the players a chance to gain a mutual understanding.

22-2-2003 vs Lodsworth

Seven goals, four sendings off, a 22-man brawl and a penalty kept the referee busy as Pulborough cruised to a 6-1 win over Lodsworth in Division 3 Central. Three goals in fifteen minutes put Pulborough ahead. Jason Bailey's looping header opened the scoring before Gary Rothwell reacted quickest to fire the ball under the keeper's desperate dive. Rothwell's second and the team's third came from a huge punt down the slope that evaded the home defence allowing the Pulborough man to calmly lob the keeper. After the break Rothwell completed his hat-trick when he cut in from the right and fired under the keeper.

Football took a back seat for a few minutes as both teams engaged in a scrap after Paul Greenfield went in for a fifty-fifty ball with the Lodsworth keeper, prompting a nasty reaction. When things had calmed down the official dismissed two players from each side.

When the game got going Chris Phillips scored a penalty after Paul Cooper was chopped down in the box. The visitors let their concentration lapse and allowed Lodsworth to pull one back, but a great through ball from Bailey put Rob Symonds one on one with the keeper and he fired through his legs to complete the scoring.

1-3-2003 vs Southbourne Sports Reserves

Pulborough eased themselves into the final of the Bareham Trophy with a 3-2 victory over Southbourne Res, but were pushed all the way by the lower division visitors. The home side should have opened the scoring when Gary Rothwell fired over from six yards after being set up by Jason Bailey. Rothwell again should have done better when he jinked past the defence but shot wide. However, he made amends when his fine run set up Rob Symonds who netted from an almost grounded position. Southbourne always looked dangerous from set-pieces and had a header pushed onto a post.

A long clearance from stand-in keeper Stuart "Wills" Lidbetter caught out the visitors defence and Rothwell rounded the keeper to net from a tight angle to make it 2-0. After the break the heavens opened and the visitors took advantage of the slippery pitch when a fine run from midfield was finished off with a 30 yard effort that screamed in. When the home defence failed to clear, the visitors equalised with a shot that went in off the bar.

Jason Leadbeatter deflected a goal-bound effort round the post and Pulborough took advantage when Chris Phillip's fine left wing run was finished off by Rob Symonds, who cracked the ball home from the edge of the box.

25-4-2003 Bareham Trophy Cup Final vs Boxgrove

It was third time lucky for Pulborough as they beat Boxgrove 4-1 in the final of the US Airways Bareham Trophy at Arundel on Friday night. On a wet, windy evening and on a hard, greasy pitch this was not going to be a classic final but Pulborough, who were appearing in their third final in as many years, had the best of the early chances and Rob Symonds fired over when he should have scored. However, Pulborough did not have to wait long for the opener; a mix up in the Boxgrove defence allowed the ball to bounce around and eventually drop to Paul Cooper, who fired into the roof of the net.

Boxgrove should have done better when two defenders went for the same ball and it fell kindly, but it was put wide. But the miss was not too costly when Boxgrove played down the right just before the break and equalised from a cross that was not cleared on the slippery surface. The rain stopped for the second half and Pulborough nearly retook the lead when Symonds was put through one-on-one but, with the keeper rushing out, he put his shot just past the post.

Symonds was always a threat with his pace but it was Boxgrove who came nearest to going ahead when they hit the post. The close call kick-started Pulborough into action and they peppered the Boxgrove goal. Jason Bailey, who was sporting a turban-like bandage after a clash of heads, volleyed home Pulborough's second as the cheering fans blurted out a chorus of *"he's got a pineapple on his head!"*

A fine run and shot from player/manager Matt Parry was slid in at the far post by Chris Phillips, and when Symonds was again put through, he made no mistake and nestled the ball nicely in the corner, much to the delight of the Pulborough supporters, who ran on and mobbed the goalscorer.

27-9-2003 vs Angmering

Pulborough beat Angmering 6-5 in a thrilling Chichester Charity Cup clash. Angmering went 1-0 when Pulborough player-coach Liam Wadey headed the ball into his own net. But ten minutes later the Angmering keeper brought down Chris Phillips and captain Jason Bailey calmly slotted home the penalty. After the break, Angmering took the lead with a free header in the box but Pulborough fought back and Rob Symonds fired in a rebound after the Angmering keeper spilled Shaun Jupp's shot.

A few minutes later Jupp collected the ball from the halfway line and finished superbly to put Pulborough back into the game, but this was cancelled out when the Angmering striker lobbed the visitor's keeper.

Angmering went back into the lead when a cross was scuffled over the line but Pulborough did not give up and Matt Parry beat the Angmering offside trap to level the game at 4-4. Both teams tired but Pulborough took the lead when Parry's cross found Phillips who slotted it home, but Angmering came back to equalise again to make it 5-5.

With a penalty shoot-out looming, Symonds collected Sam Grove's deflected free-kick and netted to put Pulborough into the hat for the next round

The team that day was Sam Smith, Aaron Greenfield, Jason Leadbeatter, Liam Wadey, Sam Grove, Chris Phillips, Jason Bailey, Paul Greenfield, Matt Parry, Rob Symonds, Shaun Jupp.

1-11-2003 vs Lewes Bridgeview

Pulborough beat Lewes Bridgeview in the second round of the Sussex Junior Cup. Pulborough should have been two up in the first ten minutes with Paul Greenfield hitting the post and the home keeper spilling a shot onto the upright. The visitors camped in their host's half but never took the chances they created and when Lewes did counter Sam Smith made a brilliant save to keep the scores level at the break.

After the break Pulborough continued to dominate but when Chris Phillips was robbed on the halfway line, Lewes broke quickly and a fine left foot shot in off the far post gave them the lead. Pulborough were level within minutes when Paul Greenfield found Paul Cooper, who fired into the far corner. It was Greenfield who added a second when he shot through a packed goalmouth and Phillips cemented the comeback with a low drive from the edge of the box.

17-4-2004 vs Partridge Green

Two own goals helped Pulborough finish runners-up in Division 2 North after they beat Partridge Green 3-0 in their last game of the season and rivals Wisborough Green lost to Dorking Wanderers. Pulborough had the first early chance when Partridge Green conceded a corner but could not capitalise on the opportunity. The game ebbed and flowed from end to end and Sam Grove made a great clearance on the goal line to deny the home side. Sam Smith in the visitors goal pulled off a superb diving save as Partridge Green piled on the pressure in the strong wind that hindered both sides. But the visitors started to get on top and almost went ahead when the home keeper made a superb double save from Matt Parry and Jason Leadbeatter. Rob Symonds was causing the home defence problems but it was through a stroke of luck that Pulborough took the lead just after the break when a home defender deflected a Jason Leadbeatter free-kick past his own keeper. Partridge Green almost snatched the equaliser but the ball came back off the post and landed neatly in Smith's arms. It was 2-0 moments later when a Jason Bailey free-kick found Gary Rothwell, who turned and hit a ferocious shot that cannoned off the bar and rebounded in off the defender. Minutes later the home keeper's attempted clearance hit Chris Phillips, who controlled the ball and neatly volleyed home.

3-3-2004 vs Horsham Athletic

Pulborough enjoyed a fine 7-1 win over Horsham Athletic in Division 2 North. The home side totally dominated the game and would have had the game sewn up by the break if it had not been for brave goalkeeping and wayward shooting. Jason Bailey put Pulborough one up with a low drive from the edge of the box and Chris Phillips added a second when his shot from 30 yards curled past the stranded keeper. After the break the visitors had no answer to Pulborough's fast attacking football. Bailey's effort was parried by the keeper and Paul Greenfield fired home number three. Matt Parry's cross was side footed in by Aaron Greenfield as the scoring continued and Craig Jupp curled in a free-kick from outside the box before Phillips added his second. Parry's run from the halfway line was finished when his fine cross was fired home by Paul Greenfield to complete a magnificent seven. With the game in added time Athletic stabbed the ball home for a consolation goal.

In any club or organisation problems can arise on occasions and while not dwelling on it for too long I think it relevant to mention that in the 2004/05 season PFC had a problem when some players refused to play for both first and second teams, wanting to play for only one of them. It had to be brought to their attention that they had signed on for the club and not one particular side and, if selected, they were expected to play for either team. Stepping up to play intermediate football in Division 1 proved to be a step too far for the First XI. They ended up winning just 2 games, finished bottom of the table and were relegated after just one season.

At the AGM of the 2005/06 season Mr John Jupp, our Chairman, showed a large bundle of papers to the meeting. These were all the disciplinary correspondences from the WSFA during the season. John stated that the disciplinary record for the season could best be described as poor. There were 50 bookings, of which 18 were for dissent and 5 were sendings off for foul and abusive language, which resulted in a total bill of £618 in fines. It was felt that Pulborough Football Club were getting a bad name in the league and could possibly be targeted in the future due to this reputation. Also at the meeting, Mr Toby Greenfield, Mr Charles Parsons and Mrs Lil Rhoder were made Life Members of the club.

Now playing in Division 2 North, the team had a strange season, winning just 3 games but drawing 11, with 6 losses; they finished in 7th position. It was a different matter in the cup, with the team reaching the final of the Chichester Charity Cup. They had a bye in the first round , beat Alfold 2-0 in the second round, then came up against old rivals Fittleworth and won by 4 goals to 2, with Jason Bailey, Tom Knight, Shane Lamport and Stuart Underwood on the scoresheet. In the semi-final they played Lavant and went through to the final after a 3-2 win. In the final they played Newtown Villa and lost to a good side 2-0.

The 2006/07 season was a poor one, the team finishing in 10th position. During the campaign there were good wins against Horsham Olympic 5-1 and Slinfold 6-1, but it was a season to forget. In November 2006, Mr John Wadey agreed to sponsor the club for a further three years, a very generous gesture, and the club sent a letter thanking him for his support.

The next season 2007/08 was a much improved one, with the team finishing in 4th place with 39 points. The goals were shared among 14 different goal scorers. It was hoped that the side could kick on and try to gain promotion the following season. But there were still one or two problems... on 14th May 2007 our Chairman John Jupp stated that the frequent sendings off were disgraceful and our President Mr Russ Phillips commented that there was still a lack of respect for the managers from some of the players.

At the AGM of the 2008/09 season it was decided to re-enter the Sussex Junior Cup. There were changes for the team managers, who would now have a team book in which they had to name their team, including the shirt numbers they would be wearing. A copy was to be given to the opposing team manager and one to the referee before the start of any match. Apart from a very good win, 8-1 in the Centenary Cup against Slinfold, the side got off to a bad start. Their first league win did not come until they played Partridge Green in their seventh game. Things did improve but it was still a disappointing season, since the team had hoped to be challenging for promotion. They finished in 7th place, with 26 points.

At the AGM of 2009/10 it was stated that PFC's main source of income was from the Bingo Club and thanks were given to all those who were involved in

18-2-2006 v Dorking

Pulborough's best display of the season stopped promotion hopefuls Dorking Wanderers in their tracks with a 3-2 win. Tom Bradshaw opened the Boro scoring after a five man one touch passing move, before James Underwood missed a good chance to extend the lead by shooting tamely at the keeper. Dorking forced several corners and soon headed home an equaliser. After the break the visitors piled on the pressure, which told when Stuart Underwood sliced a clearance into his own net. Bradshaw then turned provider, crossing low for James Smillie to apply the finish. Paul Greenfield then dramatically smashed in the winner with the last kick of the match.

4-3-2006 v Ockley

A dominant display saw Pulborough hit Ockley for six. Jason Bailey opened the scoring when he touched home a Rob Symonds cross, before James Underwood and Paul Greenfield scored with headers. Ockley did manage a goal just before the break as their Final ball found its target for the first time all game. Underwood added another soon after the break before Craig Jupp smashed home a free-kick from 30 yards which fizzed between the keeper's fingertips and crossbar. Emile Josiah added the sixth when he profited from a goalkeeping error, although Ockley managed a second with a late penalty.

11-3-2006 v Lavant

Pulborough booked their place in the Chichester Charity Cup Final when they overcame a stubborn Lavant side away from home. After a scrappy start both sides exchanged quick goals, James Underwood fired a low shot under the Lavant keeper's dive and a defensive mix up saw Lavant level soon after. Rob Symonds restored the advantage, but only after his first shot was saved, the rebound fell to Underwood who rode three tackles before finding Symonds to score. Further goal bound efforts from Paul Greenfield and Underwood were kept out by the Lavant keeper as they just stayed in the game. Lavant found another equaliser through a near post header from a corner. Jason Bailey sealed Pulborough's safe passage through to the Final with a late penalty after Underwood was brought down in the box.

the running of it. On the field it was to be another season when the team failed to find any consistency. I did not see the team play that season, or many games in the previous two seasons, so I asked friends who saw most of the games how the team had played. They told me that there were a few good players but that they rarely played as a team, which explains why they were inconsistent.

Looking at it from the outside, I felt that maybe some new players would freshen the side up.

A couple of action shots in 2009 *(Pulborough players in red)*
Top picture from left Paul Greenfield (hidden) James Smillie (No 9).
Bottom picture from left Sam Grove, Michael Crick (keeper), Paul Greenfield (hidden), Stuart Underwood, Tom Bolton.

Pulborough FC 200½ Division Three Charity Cup Finalists
Back row from left Russ Phillips (president), Jason Bailey, Bob Burse, Matt Parry, Russell Davy,
Liam Wadey, Chris Phillips, Steve Buss (manager), Jason Leadbeatter.
Front row Martin Ralph, Paul Greenfield, Steve Adsett, Dean Angell, Gary Rothwell,
Stuart Underwood, John Hunter.

Pulborough FC season 2005/2006 Chichester charity cup finalists
Back row from left Nick Berry, James Smillie, Stuart Phillips, Stuart Underwood, Sam Grove, Mascot
(Smithy), Jason Bailey, Michael Crick, Jason Leadbeatter, Martin Ralph.
Front row Aaron Greenfield, Shaun Jupp, Tom Bradshaw, Rob Symonds, James Underwood, Paul Greenfield,
Craig Jupp, Emil Josiah, Malc Jupp (manager).

Players 2000-2010

MICHAEL CRICK is only seventeen, but has proved to be a very good goalkeeper and is still improving.

STUART UNDERWOOD, a fearless full back who loves to tackle and is good in the air.

JASON LEADBEATTER naturally left footed and plays at full back, he is making progress in that position.

SAM GROVE plays in central defence, he is quick and reads the game well and is a good header, useful at set pieces.

CRAIG JUPP a central midfield player and a good passer, he is the teams free-kick specialist.

PAUL GREENFIELD a tough tackling midfielder who loves to get forward.

EMILE JOSIAH came to live in this country in 2003 and is a popular member of the team, he likes to play in midfield.

TOM BRADSHAW another midfielder, now in his second season with the Club, has the ability to go and play at a higher level.

JAMES UNDERWOOD another good young prospect, he plays in midfield, he is the teams long throw expert.

JAMES SMILLIE a tall skilful player who is good on the ball, he likes to get forward and score goals.

SHAUN JUPP is another young man trying to establish himself in the side, he plays as a forward.

SIMON LEADBEATTER is a reserve team regular, when called on to play never lets the side down.

STUART PHILLIPS is a regular reserve team player, he can play in defence or midfield, always reliable.

TOM KNIGHT likes to play in defence and always gives everything when asked to play.

AARON GREENFIELD a regular in midfield for the reserves and used as a substitute on several occasions.

SEAN WHITEHEAD is the second team goalkeeper, who never lets the side down when called upon.

GARY ROTHWELL was a regular goal scorer until his work took him overseas for long periods, trying to get back in the team.

JASON BAILEY, MAT PARRY, LIAM WADEY (full details elsewhere in book)

Results 2000 – 2010

WSL DIVISION 3, CENTRAL 2000/01

2-9-2000 [H] **Graffham** (W 3-2) G Elliot 1, C Phillips 1, D Smith 1

9-9-2000 [A] **Loxwood Utd** (W 5-3) D Smith 2, G Elliot 1, C Hall 1, M Parry 1

16-9-2000 **CC** [A] **Slindon** (D 3-3) G Blunden 1, C Hall 1, L Wadey 1, AET won 6-5) in penalty shoot-out

23-9-2000 **BT** [A] **Eastergate** (L 0-4)

30-9-2000 **WSLD3C** [H] **Slinfold Res** (L 2-4) G Elliot 1, C Phillips 1

7-10-2000 [H] **Fernhurst Sports** (D 1-1) G Elliot 1

14-10-2000 [H] **Southwater Res** (D 1-1)

4-11-2000 [A] **Lodsworth** (W 3-2) C Phillips 2, R Burse 1

11-11-2000 [A] **Rogate Res** (L 0-4)

18-11-2000 [H] **Rogate Res** (L 0-4)

25-1-2001 [H] **Slinfold Res** (W 3-1) C Phillips 2, M Parry 1

6-2-2001 [H] **Loxwood Utd** (D 1-1) G Elliot 1

13-2-2001 [A] **Graffham** (W 7-4) C Phillips 4, D Smith 2, R Burse 1

20-2-2001 [H] **Southwater Res** (W 6-1) C Phillips 4, D Smith 2

6-3-2001 [A] **Slinfold Res** (L 0-1)

13-4-2001 [A] **Fernhurst Sports** (L 2-4) R Burse 2

20-4-2001 [A] **Fittleworth** (L 3-4) S Buss 1, K McCaig 1, C Phillips 1

27-4-2001 [A] **Wisborough Green** (D 0-0)

3 Results not found

P18 | W7 D4 | L7 | GF44 | GA37 | 25pts | 5th

WSL DIVISION 3, CENTRAL 2001/02

8-9-2001 [H] Rogate Res (W 4-0)

15-9-2001 [A] Graffham (W 6-2) C Phillips 2, R Davy 1, G Elliot 1, S Jupp 1, L Wadey 1

22-9-2001 **CC** [H] Ockley (L 3-4) G Elliot 3

29-9-2001 **SJC** [H] Royal & Sun Alliance Res (W 5-0) G Elliot 2, D Angell 1, C Hall 1, L Wadey 1

6-10-2001 **BT** [H] Graffham (W 4-2) R Davy 3, M Parry 1

13-10-2001 **WSLD3C** [A] Partridge Green (W 4-2) S Adsett 2, D Angell 1, C Hall 1

20-10-2001 [H] Upper Beeding Res (W 5-2)

27-10-2001 [H] Lodsworth (W 5-2) S Adsett 2, J Bailey 1, G Elliot 1, L Wadey 1

3-11-2001 **SJC** [A] Paymaster No Result

17-11-2001 **WSLD3C** [H] Slinfold (W 3-1) S Adsett 1, G Elliot 1, M Parry 1

31-11-2001 [H] Graffham (L 1-2) D Angell 1

7-12-2001 [A] Billinghurst (W 3-0) G Elliot 1, Parry 1, Wadey 1

15-12-2001 **BT** [A] Eastergate (L 2-6) G Rothwell 1, OG 1

22-12-2001 [H] Fernhurst Sports Res (W 5-0) C Hall 2, G Rothwell 2, J Bailey 1

12-1-2002 [H] Upper Beeding Res (D 2-2) J Bailey 1, G Rothwell 1

16-2-2002 [A] Lodsworth (D 1-1) D Angell 1

23-2-2002 **WSLD3C** [A] Yapton Res (W 3-1)

9-3-2002 [A] Slinfold (W 4-?) D Angell 1, R Burse 1, R Davy 1, M Parry 1

23-3-2002 [A] Rudgwick (D 1-1) J Bailey 1

30-3-2002 [A] Rogate Res (D 1-1) G Elliot 1

6-4-2002 **WSL D3 Cup Semi-Final** [H] Paymaster (W 3-?) G Rothwell 2, J Bailey 1

9-4-2002 [H] Billingshurst (W 1-0) S Adsett 1

13-4-2002 [H] Rudgwick (W 3-0)

15-4-2002 [H] West Chiltington (L 0-1)

20-4-2002 [H] Slinfold (D 1-1) R Symonds 1

27-4-2002 [A] West Chiltington (L 2-3)

?-5-2002 **WSL D3 Cup Final** [at Arundel] v Roffey Reserves (L 2-0)

P18 | W10 | D5 | L3 | GF45 | GA18 | 35pts | 3rd

WSL DIVISION 3, CENTRAL 2002/03

7-9-2002 [A] Rogate Res (W 3-1) R Davy 2, R Symonds 1

14-9-2002 [H] Upper Beeding Res (W 1-0) S Adsett 1

21-9-2002 **BT** [H] Slindon (W 11-4) C Phillips 4, A Greenfield 2, C Jupp 2, S Adsett 1, P Greenfield 1, L Wadey 1

12-10-2002 **CC** [A] Petworth (W 5-3) C Phillips 2, R Davies 1, C Jupp 1, S Underwood 1

19-10-2002 **WSLD3C** [H] Selsey IIIs (L 1-2) C Phillips 1

26-10-2002 [H] Lodsworth (W 7-2) S Adsett 2, J Bailey 1, M Parry 1, C Phillips 1, R Symonds 1, S Underwood 1

9-11-2002 **BT** [H] Petworth (W 6-2) R Symonds 2, J Bailey 1, C Phillips 1, S Phillips 1, D Smith 1

16-11-2002 **SJC** [A] Wealden (L 1-3) J Bailey 1

30-11-2002 **CC** [H] Midhurst & Easebourne Utd Res L 0-2)

21-12-2002 [H] Brinsbury (D 1-1) J Bailey 1

18-1-2003 [H] Wisborough Green (D 2-2) C Phillips 2

25-1-2003 **BT** [H] Fernhurst Sports Res (W 2-0) G Rothwell 1, S Underwood 1

1-2-2003 [A] Billingshurst (L 1-2) C Phillips 1

8-2-2003 [A] Fernhurst Sprts R (W 2-0) C Phillips 1, R Symonds 1

15-2-2003 [H] Billingshurst (W 3-0) J Bailey 1, G Rothwell 1, R Symonds 1

22-2-2003 [A] Lodsworth (W 6-1) G Rothwell 3, J Bailey 1, C Phillips 1, R Symonds 1

1-3-2003 **BT Semi-Final** [H] Southbourne Sports Res (W 3-2) R Symonds 2, G Rothwell 1

15-3-2003 [A] Wisborough Green (L 0-1)

22-3-2003 [H] Rogate Res (L 1-3) C Phillips 1

5-4-2003 [H] Southwater Res (D 3-3) J Bailey 2, M Parry 1

7-4-2003 [A] Brinsbury (W 4-1) R Symonds 2, S Adsett 1, Parry 1

12-4-2003 [H] Fernhurst Sports Res (W 4-0) S Adsett 1, J Bailey 1, M Parry 1, L Wadey 1

19-4-2003 [A] Upper Beeding Res (W 3-2) S Adsett 1, C Phillips 1, L Wadey 1

25-4-2003 **Bareham Trophy Final** [at Arundel] v Boxgrove (W 4-1) J Bailey 1, P Cooper 1, C Phillips 2, R Symonds 1

3-5-2003 [A] Southwater Res (D 2-2) S Adsett 1, C Phillips 1

P16 | W9 | D4 | L3 | GF43 | GA21 | 31pts | 2nd

WSL DIVISION 2, NORTH 2003/04

6-9-2003 [H] Graffham (W 6-2) J Bailey 2, S Grove 1, C Phillips 1, R Symonds 1, L Wadey 1

13-9-2003 [A] Capel (L 0-1)

20-9-2003 **CC** [A] Rose Green Utd (W 3-1) J Bailey 1, P Greenfield 1, R Symonds 1

27-9-2003 **CCC** [A] Angmering (W 6-5) R Symonds 2, J Bailey 1 S Jupp 1, M Parry 1, C Phillips 1

4-10-2003 **SJC** [A] Southwater Res (W 4-1) J Bailey 2, M Parry 1, B Smith 1

11-10-2003 [A] Graffham (L 1-2) J Bailey 1

18-11-2003 [A] Royal & Sun Alliance Res D 2-2) P Greenfield 1, M Parry 1

25-10-2003 [H] Capel (W 4-1) J Bailey 1, S Jupp 1, B Smith 1, R Symonds 1

1-11-2003 **SJC** [A] Lewes Bridgeview (W 3-1) P Cooper 1, P Greenfield 1, C Phillips 1

8-11-2003 **CCC** [A] Graffham (L 2-3) M Parry 1, B Smith 1

22-11-2003 **CC** [A] Clymping (L 0-2)

6-12-2003 **SJC** [H] St Francis Flyers (L 2-3) S Jupp 1, C Phillips 1

20-12-2003 [H] Royal & Sun Alliance Res (D 2-2) P Greenfield 1, G Rothwell 1

3-1-2004 [H] Horsham Athletic (W 7-1) P Greenfield 2, C Phillips 2, J Bailey 1, A Greenfield 1, S Jupp 1

10-1-2004 [H] Partridge Green (W 4-1) P Greenfield 2, J Bailey 1, R Symonds 1

17-1-2004 [A] Wisborough Green (L 1-2) C Phillips 1

24-1-2004 [H] Horsham Baptists (D 1-1) P Greenfield 1

31-1-2004 [A] Dorking Wanderers (W 6-0) J Bailey 1, P Cooper 1, Ab Greenfield 1, M Parry 1, C Phillips 1, R Symonds 1

14-2-2004 [H] Horsham Olympic (W 2-0) J Bailey 2

21-2-2004 [H] Dorking Wanderers (W 4-3) J Bailey 1, C Phillips 1, L Wadey 1, OG 1

28-2-2004 [A] Horsham Athletic (L 2-4) J Bailey 1, R Symonds 1

6-3-2004 [A] Horsham Olympic (D 2-2) M Parry 1, C Phillips 1

3-4-2004 [H] Wisborough Green (D 1-1) C Phillips 1

10-4-2004 [A] Horsham Bap's (W 4-0) C Phillips 3, P Greenfield 1

17-4-2004 [A] Partridge Grn (W 3-0) C Phillips 1, G Rothwell 1, OG1

P18 | W9 | D5 | L4 | GF52 | GA25 | 32pts | 2nd

WSL DIVISION 1, 2004/05

4-9-2004 [A] TD Shipley (L 0-2)

11-9-2004 **MSC** [H] Eastergate (L 1-3) C Phillips 1

18-9-2004 CC [H] Clymping (L 3-5) S Lamport 1, C Phillips 1, S Underwood 1

25-9-2004 [A] Fittleworth (W 4-3) S Lamport 2, C Phillips 1, J Underwood 1

2-10-2004 [A] Wittering Utd (L 2-3) J Bailey 1, C Phillips 1

9-10-2004 **SIC** [H] East Grinstead Res (L 1-5) C Phillips 1

16-10-2004 [H] South Bersted (L 2-5)

23-10-2004 [H] Southwater (W 3-1) C Phillips 3

6-11-2004 [H] Lower Beeding (L 1-3) C Phillips 1

13-11-2004 [A] Angmering (L 1-8) G Rothwell 1

27-11-2004 [H] TD Shipley (L 1-2) S Richardson 1

4-12-2004 [H] Fittleworth (D 1-1) S Richardson 1

11-12-2004 [A] Faygate (L 2-3) C Jupp 1, S Lamport 1

8-1-2005 [H] Wittering (L 1-6) G Rothwell 1

29-1-2005 [A] Southwater (L 1-3)

5-2-2005 [H] West Chiltington (L 1-2) J Bailey 1

12-2-2005 [A] Dorking Wand's (L 2-3) S Lamport 1, C Phillips 1

19-2-2005 [A] Lower Beeding (D 2-2) J Underwood 1, OG 1

26-2-2005 [H] Angmering (L 2-6) G Rothwell 1, J Underwood 1

5-3-2005 [H] Dorking Wanderers (L 3-5) C Phillips 1, G Rothwell 1, R Symonds 1

19-3-2005 [A] South Bersted (L 1-2) G Rothwell 1

26-3-2005 [A] West Chiltington (L 1-2)

9-4-2005 [H] Faygate (L 2-3)

P20 | W2 | D2 | L16 | GF33 | GA65 | 8pts | 11th

WSL DIVISION 2, NORTH 2005/06

3-9-2005 [A] Watersfield (D 0-0)

10-9-2005 **CC** [A] Ockley (L 2-3

17-9-2005 [H] Horsham Olympic (D 1-1) R Symonds 1

24-9-2005 [H] Ashington Rovers (L 2-3)

1-10-2005 **SJC** [A] Worth Park Rangers (W 3-1) J Bailey 1, P Greenfield 1, J Underwood 1

8-10-2005 [H] TD Shipley Res (L 0-1)

15-10-2005 **SJC** [A] Horsham Athletic (W 4-0)

22-10-2005 [A] Fittleworth (D 0-0)

29-10-2005 [H] Watersfield (L 1-2)

5-11-2005 **SJC** [H] Wisdom Sports (W 2-0)

12-11-2005 **CCC** [A] Alfold (W 2-0)

19-11-2005 [H] Billingshurst (L 2-3)

10-12-2005 **SJC** [H] Square Deal (W 3-2) G Rothwell 2, E Josiah 1

17-12-2005 [H] TD Shipley Res (D 1-1)

31-12-2005 [H] Slinfold (W 3-1)

7-1-2006 **SJC** [H] Broadfield (L 2-6) E Josiah 1, S Underwood 1

14-1-2006 [H] Fittleworth (D 2-2) T Bradshaw 1, OG 1

21-1-2006 [A] Horsham Olympic (D 2-2)

28-1-2006 [A] Alfold (D 1-1)

4-2-2006 **CCC** [H] Fittleworth (W 4-2) J Bailey 1, T Knight 1, S Lamport 1, S Underwood 1

11-2-2006 [H] Alfold (D 0-0)

18-2-2006 [H] Dorking Wanderers Res (W 3-2) T Bradshaw 1, P Greenfield 1, J Smillie 1

25-2-2006 [A] Billingshurst (D 0-0)

4-3-2006 [H] Ockley (W 6-2)

11-3-2006 **CCC Semi Final** [A] Lavant (W 3-2) J Bailey 1, R Symonds 1, J Underwood 1

25-3-2006 [A] Dorking Wanderers Res (L 0-2)

1-4-2006 [A] Ashington Rovers (D 0-0)

8-4-2006 [A] Slinfold (L 1-2)

15-4-2006 [A] Ockley (D 2-2)

1-5-2006 **CCC Final** [at Arundel] v Newtown Villa (L 2-0)

P20 | W3 | D11 | L6 | GF27 | GA27 | 20pts | 7th

WSL DIVISION 2, NORTH 2006/07

2-9-2006 [A] Ashington Rovers (L 1-2)

16-9-2006 CCC [H] Cowfold (L 4-5)

23-9-2006 CC [H] South Bersted (L 1-5) M Parry 1

30-9-2006 [A] Wisborough Green (L 1-5) S Jupp 1

14-10-2006 [A] Dorking Wanderers Res (L 2-5) L Blunden 1, Ab Greenfield 1

21-10-2006 [H] Ashington Rovers (L 0-2)

4-11-2006 [H] Horsham Olympic (W 5-1)

9-12-2006 [H] Billingshurst (L 1-3)

24-3-2007 [A] Faygate Utd (W 3-2)

31-3-2007 [H] Alfold (D 4-4)

7-4-2007 [A] Slinfold (W 3-1)

14-4-2007 [A] Alfold (D 3-3)

21-4-2007 [A] Rudgwick (L 2-3)

24-4-2007 [H] Cowfold (L 1-3)

2-5-2007 [A] Horsham Olympic (L 1-4)

5-5-2007 [A] Cowfold (L 0-2)

30-4-2007 [A] Ockley (L 4-6)

P22 | W6 | D3 | L13 | GF48 | GA55 | 21pts | 10th

WSL DIVISION 2, NORTH 2007/08

1-9-2007 [A] Horsham Olympic (D 3-3) S Adsett 1, C Jupp 1, S Underwood 1

15-9-2007 CCC [A] Stedham Utd (L 2-4)

22-9-2007 [H] Ockley (W 2-0)

29-9-2007 [A] Capel (L 3-4) S Jupp 2, G Stevens 1

6-10-2007 [A] Wisborough Green (W 3-2)

13-10-2007 [A] Faygate Utd (L 1-3)

20-10-2007 [H] Rudgwick (L 1-3)

27-10-2007 [H] Horsham Olympic (D 0-0)

3-11-2007 [H] Partridge Green (W 4-2)

10-11-2007 [H] Holbrook F C (W 2-0)

17-11-2007 [H] Faygate Utd (W 2-1)

5-1-2008 [A] Rudgwick (W 4-3

12-1-2008 [H] Wisborough Green (W 3-0) L Blunden 1, G Stevens 1, S Underwood 1

19-1-2008 [A] Partridge Green (D 4-4)

26-1-2008 [A] Holbrook F C (D 0-0)

9-2-2008 [A] Alfold (W 6-2) Si Leadbeatter 2, S Grove 1, J Smillie 1, D Steele 1, S Underwood 1

16-2-2008 [A] Ockley (W 4-2)

23-2-2008 [A] Newdigate (W 4-3) J Smillie 2, G Stevens 1 J Underwood 1

1-3-2008 [H] Ashington Rovers (D 2-2)

15-3-2008 [H] Newdigate (D 3-3) E Josiah 1, J Underwood 1, ?1

22-3-2008 [H] Capel (L 0-4)

12-4-2008 [H] Alfold (W 3-0) E Josiah 1, G Stevens 1, J Underwood 1

28-4-2008 [A] Ashington Rovers (L 1-4) T Boulton 1

P22 | W11 | D6 | L5 | GF55 | GA46 | 39pts | 4th

WSL DIVISION 2, NORTH 2008/09

6-9-2008 [A] Partridge Green (L 0-6)

13-9-2008 [A] Horsham Olympic (D 1-1)

20-9-2008 CC [H] Slinfold (W 8-1) J Underwood 3, S Grove 2, G Graham 1, P Greenfield 1, J Smillie 1

27-9-2008 CCC [A] TD Shipley Res (L 0-2)

4-10-2008 SJC [H] White Knight (L 3-4)

11-10-2008 [A] Ockley (L 0-2)

18-10-2008 [A] Horsham Trinity (L 1-3)

22-11-2008 [H] Partridge Green (W 5-1)

29-11-2008 [A] Holbrook FC (L 1-5)

6-12-2008 [H] Horsham Olympic (W 3-0)

20-12-2008 [H] Newdigate (W 5-3)

17-1-2009 [A] Watersfield (L 2-4)

24-1-2009 [H] Horsham Trinity (L 3-5)

21-2-2009 [H] Wisborough Green (W 2-1)

28-2-2009 [H] Ockley (W 6-1)

14-3-2009 [H] Faygate Utd (L 1-4)

21-3-2009 [A] Newdigate (W 3-2)

28-3-2009 [H] Watersfield (L 4-5)

4-4-2009 [A] TD Shipley Res (W 2-1)

11-4-2009 [A] Faygate Utd (L 0-2)

18-4-2009 [H] Holbrook FC (W 4-2)

P20 | W8 | D2 | L10 | GF45 | GA52 | 26pts | 7th

WSL DIVISION 2, NORTH 2009/10

12-9-2009 CC [A] Predators

19-9-2009 CCC [H] Barns Green (L 1-2)

26-9-2009 [A] Capel (L 2-5)

10-10-2009 [A] Alfold (L 2-3)

17-10-2009 [H] Fittleworth (L 1-2)

24-10-2009 [A] Horsham Olympic (D 4-4)

31-10-200 [H] Barns Green (L 1-2)

7-11-2009 [A] Newdigate (W 3-1)

21-11-2009 [A] Horsham Trinity (W 4-1)

12-12-2009 [A] Wisborough Green (W 2-1)

30-1-2010 [H] Billingshurst Res (W 5-0)

6-2-2010 [A] Fittleworth (D 3-3)

13-2-2010 [A] AFC Roffey (W 3-2)

20-2-2010 [H] Wisborough Green (D 2-2)

27-2-2010 [H] Holbrook F C L1-3)

6-3-2010 [H] Newdigate (W 2-1)

13-3-2010 [A] AFC Roffey (D 1-1)

3-4-2010 [H] Alfold (W 2-0)

5-4-2010 [H] Capel (L 0-5)

10-4-2010 [A] Barns Green (L 0-2)

13-4-2010 [A] Billingshurst Res (W 5-3)

21-4-2010 [H] Horsham Trinity (D 3-3)

Pulborough FC 1986/87 Second XI – sponsored by the Rose & Crown
Back row from left Dean Lewis, Steve Merriot, Elaine (sponsor), Malcolm Jupp,
Geoff (sponsor), Kevin Taylor, John Naldrett.
Front row Paul Haste, Tim Hatchard, Paul Goodchild, Graham Blunden,
Stephen Hurst, Trevor Blunden, John Jupp.

Pulborough FC Second XI 1989/90
Back row from left John Stewart (manager), Trevor Blunden, Tim Hatchard, Steve Merriot, Anthony
Leadbeatter, Andy Dumbrill, Glen Phur, Colin Hutton, Jim Leadbeatter (assistant manager).
Front row John Jupp, Graham Blunden, Malcolm Jupp, Bert Merriot, Peter Wilson, John Fletcher.

The Second XI

WHEN THE FIRST XI went into the County League in 1952, the second XI took their place in the West Sussex League, which still had only one division. It was thought it would give the team a better class of football and the players would be able to fill any vacancies in the first XI when they occurred. In the first game of the season, the following team was selected to play against Graylingwell on 27th September 1952, KO 3-15: R. Heather, E. Wilks, D. Heasman, G. Purnell, F. Clark, Davies, T. Cousins, R. Maybee, D. Roberts, G. Carter, J. Greenfield, A. Lewis played in place of Wilks. They lost by 7 goals to 0. It was going to be a long, hard season for the second XI lads. They were a young, inexperienced team most of whom had not played at that level before. By the end of the season they had won only 2 games and had conceded 175 goals.

Results changed very little and the team suffered more heavy defeats over the next 2 years. But it was not all bad news, as a lot of the younger players were being given the opportunity to show what they could do. In a game against Rustington on 30th October 1953, there were 6 players under the age of 18 playing, including two fifteen-year-olds. Some of the lads would go on to play for the first XI. The scorer that day was Dean Macey; at just 15 he was one of the youngest to score for the club. The 1953/54 and 1954/55 season results do not make pleasant reading, but the players were gaining experience of playing at that level.

> ### Match Report 17-1-1953
> Pulborough Reserves rather surprisingly held their visitors Petworth to a 3-3 draw. They had 3 of their regular first team players in the team, but this did not wholly account for a vast improvement in their form. At half time the score was 1-1, Petworth's goal coming from a right wing move, a Pulborough back fluffed his clearance and before he could recover, Lucias the visitor's right winger scored. Pulborough attacked with a rush after the interval and in a very short time had scored 2 more goals, giving them a 3-1 lead. But Petworth continued to peg away and from a goal-mouth scramble the ball came through to Wallace, who reduced the lead. Play continued to be even, with Petworth striving desperately to get on terms. From another goal-mouth scramble, just before the end R. E. Taylor put Petworth level.
>
> The Pulborough team that day was, R. Heather, F. Clark, D. Heasman, G. Purnell, J. Ovenell, J. Scutt, J. Parish, E. Wilks, R. Maybee, D. Roberts, T. Cousins. Scorer R. Maybee 3.

The Second XI Restart

The second team, after not having a side in 1955/56 and 1956/57, restarted in 1957/58, when they entered the Horsham & District League Division 3. They won their first 2 matches but lost the next 3. Apart from one loss – to North Holmwood in the Junior Charity Cup – from 26th Ocotber 1957 to 4th February 1958 they won 10 games in a row and in those 10 games they scored 64 goals. Unfortunately the club has no record of the goal scorers. I managed to find two reports, they were both against East End United and they did not give the team that played for us.

26-10-1957 Pulborough 7 East End United 4

In this high scoring game the defences were overwhelmed by speedy, direct forward lines. But it must be pointed out that four of the twelve goals had a certain element of luck about them. During the first half Pulborough had enough chances to have reached double figures, only Killick's goalkeeping preventing them. Of the six goals they did score, two entered the net via the woodwork and another appeared to be offside. In an East End attack Laker missed an easy chance shooting much too high. A transformation came over the visitors' re-arranged forward line in the second half. Within 15 minutes they found the net three times and almost had a fourth goal when Clark hit the bar. The first came when the keeper dropped a Baxter shot over the line. Fleming, now leading the attack ran on to a through ball to score the second and a few minutes later Peay added a third. Pulborough added another, but East End made it 7-4, with Fleming's second goal. Back came Pulborough to hit the bar and, after Pulborough's keeper had been replaced through injury, a Clark lob produced the last goal of the game. In contrast to Pulborough, who tended to hold the ball too long, East End exploited the long ball to best advantage.

7-12-1957 East End 1 Pulborough 8

Pulborough completed the double over a much-changed East End side. The visitors were a goal up within two minutes and after half-an-hour led 5-0. Pulborough had most of the play during this period, but East End came more into the game just before the interval. The nearest they came to scoring in this half was when Batchelor's shot was pushed round the post. On the resumption Killick, now in the forward line, ran through to score from the wing. East End tightened up their defence and Pulborough rarely came within shooting range. Baxter nearly reduced the arrears, but his shot hit an upright. In the last 15 minutes Pulborough added three more goals. The game was played in a friendly atmosphere and there was not one foul throughout the match.

Some of the players who would have played for the second XI that season were: G. Burleston, M. Sargent, J. Greenfield, D. Heasman,. E. Goldsmith, M. Spain, A. Chatfield, E. Lammas, P. Goodsell, T. Bishop, L. Hamilton, D. Madgett. During the season the side scored 99 goals.

Season 1958/59 was a strange one for the team. They were unbeaten in their first 5 games, 4 wins and a draw and scoring 32 goals. They then lost the next 2 league games and 2 cup matches. By the end of the season they had scored over a hundred goals and finished in fourth place. Ken Handley scored 25 goals.

The 1959/60 season was the side's last in the Horsham & District League. After having two pretty good years, the team fell apart, for what reason I was not able to find out. They lost the first 10 games and never recovered.

Back to the West Sussex League

The 1960/61 season saw the side return to play in the 4th Division of the West Sussex League, which turned out to be far tougher than was thought. The team selected for the first game was: P. Goodsell, M. Sargent, D. Heasman, R. Hayler, G. Burletson, A. Puttock, P. Wills, T. Cousins, J. Johnson, R. Thompsett, L. Hamilton, subs N. Pope, L. Hookey. At the end of the season the side had won only 2 games. Two interesting players had signed on that year, Jeffrey Johnson, who lived in Rackham and a chap called Duthie. Jeff was deaf and dumb, a nice man and a good player, although his being unable to hear the whistle caused problems with some referees until we explained why he would sometimes carry on playing after the whistle was blown. When Mr Duthie turned up we couldn't wait to see him play. He informed us that he had played for the Scotland under-21 side, so we were expecting great things from him. He was selected to play for the team but after just 2 games was left out and never played again. He was not good enough to get into our second XI, never mind playing for his country.

The following couple of seasons were very similar, with the side in the bottom half of the table. Highlights of the campaign were hat-tricks for A. Lacey and a young Glen Lewis. I was lucky enough to score 5 goals against Cocking. I think this was the only time I played at Cocking, which was an eye-opener; when we turned up, I asked where the changing rooms were and someone pointed to a very small hut. Worse was to come, once inside there was just about room for the team but nowhere to hang your clothes, so you just had to drop them onto the ground, as there was no floor.

We were entered into the Bognor Regis Junior Charity Cup in 1961/62 but I don't know why; it was the only time we were. We beat Balls Cross in the first round 4-1, then lost to South Bersted 9-1 in the 2nd round.

The next season saw Geoff Upjohn get 2 hat-tricks in consecutive games.

The 1963/64 season was pretty horrendous. In their 30 league matches, the side conceded 197 goals. In the first 17 games there was just 1 win and 15 losses; we could not raise a side in the other. Had we not won 3 out of our last 4 games "with help from the first XI players" it would have been even more embarrassing. It was not helpful that the side was being changed virtually every match. Here is one of the teams selected at random from the season: L. Etheridge, M. Leadbeatter, K. Laker, R. Jones, D. Madgett, B. Thayre, J. Stewart, T. Roberts, P. Goodsell, R. Thompsett, M. Brown, sub C. Steele-Mills.

Things could only get better, and they did. The first game of the 1964/65 campaign resulted in a win against Fishbourne, with Glen Lewis scoring 4. Four games later came a 7-0 win against Bilsham, in which I managed to get 4 goals. A few games later Mike Brown went one better when he scored 5 against Fernhurst Reserves. But we were still letting in far too many goals. In the two matches against Funtington we conceded 24 goals but the heaviest defeat came when the team played Corinthians in a cup game; the score was 19-0.

The 1965/66 season saw the number of matches drop from 30 to 22. The side finished in 6th place. One of the reasons for the improved results was that experienced players had come into the side. Peter Chapman, Ron Maybee and Tony Spain, all ex-first XI players, helped the younger lads. The best result of the season was a 14-2 win against Graffham, with 3 players scoring 4, Mike Brown, John Stewart and Geoff Upjohn. Later on, against Lavant Reserves, Mike scored 6 and Ron got 4, Peter scored a hat-trick later in the season.

From 1966 to 1971 things changed very little; the team held its own but never got close to being promoted. It was good to see some young lads come to the club and start to make their mark. Colin Carter, Richard Czarnecki, John Habgood and Trevor Wells were all making an impression, Trevor scoring 3 on his debut for the team. Scoring goals in those years was never a problem for the 2nd XI but unfortunately we always let in far too many.

Success At Last

After many years, some of them very difficult ones, the side had at last something to be happy about. The 1971/72 season saw the side promoted after finishing 2nd in their league. They also reached the final of the West Sussex League Division 5 Charity Cup.

The first game was against Wisborough Green Reserves and they lost 1-0, the team that day: M. Pattenden, J. Harrison, M. Brown, J. Jupp. M. Leadbeatter, B. Davis, R. Branch, P. Hughes, T. Jones, T. Roberts, A. Richardson. It was quite a young side but it was good to see 45-year-old Peter Chapman bring his experience to help the team. He played virtually every game in the first half of the season. Tony Spain also played one game when he was 40 years old. The team gelled well and scored over 100 goals that season. Mike Brown, Glen Fallowfield and Geoff Upjohn were the main goal scorers. Against our local rivals Fittleworth, wins of 8-0 away and 18-0 at home were highlights of the league matches. In the Division 5 Charity Cup, the team beat Watersfield 7-1, Sunallon 5-1, Fittleworth 6-3 and in the semi-final they crushed Fernhurst 9-1, with Upjohn 4, Fallowfield 3 and Alan Richardson 2 being the scorers. Keatings were the outstanding side and they only lost one game all season and that was to us.

The 1972/73 season was a very poor one. The first XI had lost a few players so the 2nd XI players had to go into their team. During the season the team used 6 different goalkeepers, including Peter Chapman. It was no surprise when they were relegated. The side was now back in Division 5 but they found their form very quickly and were playing some good football. They had some big wins – 12-0 against Loxwood, 8-1 against Harting and 8-0 and 7-0 against Lodsworth and Cocking. They reached the semi-final of the Division 5 Charity Cup but lost to Worthing United. John Burleston scored a lot of goals that season. Promoted again.

In the 1974/75 season the team was relegated.

It was 1977/78 before the side was promoted back to Division 4. There was a mixture of experience and youth and the team played some fine football, scoring plenty of goals and conceding very few. The experienced players were mainly in defence: Clive Hamilton, Terry Hatchard and Graham Hill, the young lads, Geoff Messenger, Martin Pepper, Lee Rout, Mick Ruff, Guy Smith, Colin Spain and Colin Hutton brought skill and energy to the team. Colin Hutton playing in midfield was top scorer with 22, Martin got 18 and John Norman 17 were the other main scorers. Hat-tricks were scored by Malcolm Jupp, Colin Hutton, John Norman, Lee Rout and Mick Ruff, Martin Pepper bagged 5 in one match.

The side finished 4th the next season.

I had to retire from playing in 1979 after being injured and Mick Browning, our first XI manager, asked me if I would like to manage the 2nd XI and said he would recommend me to the committee if I agreed. It was not something I had thought about but I agreed to give it a try. Selecting a side and giving your first team talk is not easy, but once done it becomes easier. Our first game was against Ockley, which we lost 1-0. The side that I selected for that game was: R. James, J. Leadbeatter, T. Leadbeatter, L. Rout, T. Hatchard, D. Rhoder, C. Hutton, P. Welch, G. Messenger, C. Spain, D. Padwick, sub K. Filkens. In Jim Leadbeatter,

1972 2nd XI Cup Final squad

MICK PATTENDEN (born 17th Nov 1949) in Rotherfield, East Sussex, went to Billingshurst Primary School and The Weald. He worked for Spiro Gills before moving to Beverley in Billingshurst and now works for British Airways in the radiography department. He made his debut for the 2nd XI against Hunston Reserves on 7th Sept 1968 and scored twice. In his first season he was a centre forward but then took up goalkeeping and made his 1st XI debut on 4th Dec 1971 against Chichester. He was tall and slim, a good keeper and played a number of games for the 1st XI. He lives in Billingshurst.

CLIVE HAMILTON, born in Fittleworth on 5th May 1945, went to the Primary School there, then St Mary's in Pulborough and on to The Weald in Billingshurst. He worked as an apprentice brazier at Spiro Gills, then moved on to APV in Crawley and stayed for 21 years, in the welding shop. He then worked for Yellow Patter in Storrington. He played his first game for the 2nd XI on 24th Sept 1960, against LEC Sports B. He played in the forward line for several games before moving to full back. He made his first XI debut 17th Feb 1973 against Stedham. Clive could play right or left back and was a reliable and assured player. He now resides in Bognor. He also played for Petworth.

MELVIN LEADBEATTER (BILL), born in Horsham on 21st Feb 1947, attended St Mary's School in Pulborough and The Weald in Billingshurst. He started work as an apprentice painter and decorator for Wadey's in Billingshurst and later became self-employed. He made his first appearance for the second XI on 30th March 1963 against Whykians. He made his 1st XI debut against Southwick on 18th March 1972. Bill played the odd game at full back but was usually a central defender. Tall and lean, he was not the quickest but played well and was a regular 2nd team man. His only club was Pulborough, where he still lives.

DAVE STENNING, born in Pulborough on 26th Feb 1954, went to St Mary's School and The Weald in Billingshurst. He worked for Paula Rosa in Storrington for many years before he became self-employed. He made his debut for the second XI against Graylingwell Reserves 21st Sept 1968. His first XI debut was against Arundel 13th April 1972. Dave started off playing either as a forward or a half back but ended up as a full back. One of the smallest players in the club, Dave was a good header of a ball and an aggressive tackler. He now lives in Littlehampton.

GRAHAM HILL (CHARLIE) was born on 4th April 1950 in Southsea. He moved to Pulborough, went to the local Primary School and The Weald in Billingshurst. On leaving he started work for Spiro Gills, first in the office and then on the factory floor. He then went to Cheal's Nursery before becoming a self-employed gardener. He lives in Midhurst. He made his debut for the 1st XI against Selsey on 4th Sept 1971. Charlie was over 6 feet tall and great in the air, a big asset to the team at set pieces and in open play. He played many games at centre half for the first XI. He also played for Fittleworth and Milland.

ALAN RICHARDSON was born in Rustington on 3rd Feb 1948. He went to St Mary's School and The Weald in Billingshurst. He worked for Topaz in Storrington for many years and for a kitchen firm in Slinfold. He joined the Club in 1967 and made his debut for the 2nd XI on 16th Sept 1967, against Wick B. His first XI debut on 18th Oct 1969 was against Chichester. Alan usually played on the wing and could play left or right; he was quite quick and able to beat his marker. He played several times for the first XI. Alan lives in Easebourne.

STAN AUSTIN came from the Manchester area, joined the Club in 1971 and made his second team debut against Plaistow on 22nd January 1972. Stan was short and stocky and played on the left wing. Sadly, he passed away at quite a young age.

BASIL DAVIS was born in Eastbourne, 15th May 1934. During the war he was evacuated to Evesham and returned to live with his grandmother in Thakeham. He went to Thakeham and Storrington Primary Schools, then Horsham Technical College. He began work for Stockers, a Storrington firm of plumbers for 4 years, then worked for Spiro Gills as a brazier. He and his wife emigrated to Australia for £10 and have lived in Perth for nearly 40 years. He found work as a spot welder in a factory. He made his first XI debut against Wittering United 8th Sept 1962. Mostly Basil played left half. Naturally left-footed and a good passer, he was a regular in the first XI during the 1960s. He later played football and cricket for Storrington and was a fine player at both.

G. UPJOHN, JOHN JUPP, GLEN FALLOWFIELD & MICHAEL BROWN also played for this side and their full details appear elsewhere in the book.

Tony Leadbeatter I had a lot of experience, although they were coming to the end of their careers, they were still very good players and the younger players respected them. It was in October that I gave a young 16-year-old his chance in the side, Dave Smith, who went on to play senior football. In Dave Saunders and Steve Browning we had two forwards who knew how to score goals. The side played some good football, finished in 3rd position and were promoted due to the league being restructured. Others who played that season were J. Gallagher, J. Pritchard, M. Ruff, G. Smith and D. Stenning.

In the following season 1980/81, the 2nd XI were without a manager as I was appointed 1st XI manager. I asked John Stewart if he would like to manage them. He was not that keen but I told him that I would be taking the training and coaching, so he just had to select his team and give the team talk on match day, so he agreed to give it a try. The side were now in Division 3 North. There were a lot of experienced players still in the side, Tony and Jim

PFC Second XI Squad 1977/8

O.B. BACKHOUSE was the goalkeeper, he was not the tallest, but he was very useful. Bob worked for Guy Harwood at his racing stables.

GUY SMITH was born 4th November 1955 in Pulborough. He went to the local St. Mary's School before going on to The Weald in Billingshurst. On leaving he went to work for Linfields and did a five year apprenticeship, at the age of twenty he became a self employed pipe welder and site installations nationwide. At the age of 32 he went into the building industry. Guy joined the Club in 197 and made his 2nd team debut against Borough United 18th September 1976. He was played mostly as a central defender, tall and well built and a tough competitor.

GEOFF MESSENGER born 25th September 1958 in Pulborough. Attended St. Mary's School in the village and then The Weald in Billingshurst. He did his apprenticeship at the local firm of Spiro Gills and stayed there for several years. He then took up garden landscaping and is self employed. He joined the Club in 1974 and made his debut against Rogate 15th March 1975, after being a substitute on 4 occasions. Geoff played in several different positions, including goalkeeper and was a good asset to the team.

JOHN JUPP, MALCOLM JUPP, COLIN SPAIN

MARTIN PEPPER was born in Pulborough 7th November 1955. He attended the local St. Mary's before going on to The Weald School in Billingshurst. Another one who did his apprenticeship at Spiro Gills, he then moved on to work for Linfields and then went back to Spiro Gills for a while. Martin then spent several years in America. On returning he worked for Sowgat. He made his debut for the 2nd XI against Borough United 18th September 1976 and scored 2 goals. His debut for the 1st XI 30th September 1978 was against Barns Green, when he came on as a sub. He played in the forward line, mainly in the centre, he had the knack of being in the right place to score some important goals for the team.

LEE ROUT 14th January 1960 was born in St. Albans. Moving to Sussex, he lived in Durrington, he went to West Park Primary School, then to West Tarring and Finally to The Weald School in Billingshurst. He left there and went to work for Spiro Gills, where he did his apprenticeship, he then went self employed, pipe welding, he now runs Plum Heating. His 2nd XI debut came on 6th September 1975 against Bosham and he scored, his 1st XI debut was against Bourne Park Rangers 5th April 1980. Lee usually played on the wing, he could play on either side and was quick and could beat his man, scored his share of goals.

JOHN NORMAN was a Schoolteacher. He made his first appearance for the second XI 13th September 1975 against Boxgrove and scored 2 goals, he made his first XI debut against Stedham 25th November 1978. John played wide on the left, he was tall with long shoulder length hair, he scored a lot of goals for the second team.

Full details of the other players in the squad: **TERRY HATCHARD (HERB), GRAHAM HILL (CHARLIE), DAVE STENNING, CLIVE HAMILTON, COLIN HUTTON** and **MICK RUFF** are to be found elsewhere in the book.

Leadbeatter, Graham Hill, John Jupp and Rowland Branch, there were also some young players like Steve Leadbeatter and Dave Scott. The side did well, Jim Gallagher was top scorer with 16.

The 1981/82 season got off to a good start when the team won 9-4 against Kirdford, with Nick Bainbridge getting 5. Things went downhill after that and the side was relegated.

The side struggled and, at the end of the 1983/84 season, they went down to Division 5 central.

In 1984/85, after a shaky start, the side settled down and played some good football. In their last 15 games they were unbeaten, scoring 73 goals and letting in only 23. It was good to see the young players come through and be a big part of the side's successful season. Peter Bird, Richard Streeter and Tim Hatchard had come up from the minors and were giving the side a boost. Tim was having a great time, he scored 38 goals in 17 matches, notching up 3 hat-tricks, a 6 and a 7. The more experienced guys, John Jupp, Trevor Blunden, Geoff Messenger, Malcolm Jupp and Paul Goodchild gave the side stability. The second XI were known as the Yo-Yo side, as they seemed to go up one year and down the next.

I thought this an interesting item, brought up at a committee meeting on 31st January 1994:

> Malcolm Jupp reported that some second team members were unhappy following a recent management decision which arose when a first team match was cancelled at very short notice and it was decided to take over the second team fixture. Although every effort was made, a few second team players could not be contacted in time to avoid a wasted journey.

The Committee agreed that in the circumstances the correct decision had been made. J. Jupp said that if any player wished to complain regarding a management or committee decision, they should be invited to attend a committee meeting or bring the matter up at the AGM.

Another item brought up at a committee meeting of 24th May 1994:

> On the matter of a possible Club fine for excessive penalty points, C. Cox has written to the League advising them of the suspension of two players, both of whom were sent off in recent matches. Penalty points do not exceed matches played and C. Cox is optimistic that no fine will be imposed.

The 1994/95 season was a very good one for the side, they finished as runners-up. Hat-tricks were scored by Jason Bailey and Graham Blunden. It was unfortunate that no team sheets were recorded at committee meetings so I am not able to say who played for the side, it was also difficult to find the goal scorers. It was good to see the 2nd XI go back to the 3rd Division. The next year the side played in Division 3 South and were poor, losing 17 games out of 22 and conceding 70 goals.

In 1996/97 the side were put into Division 3 North. It made little difference and the side ended up at the bottom of the table.

In 1997/98 they were back playing in Division 4 South. The side did not play well but at least they were not relegated.

> **27 September 1997 – Division Four Cup**
> Andy Pavey was on the mark twice for Pulborough reserves in the 4-2 win over Walberton. Mick Ralph and Mark Woodhall also netted.

Away from the playing side, at the Club's AGM on 16th June 1997 one item brought up was registration. It was decided that it would be £20.00 for seniors in full time employment (of which £10 for Sports & Social Club membership), £15.00 for juniors (under 16), students and unemployed (of which £10 for Sports & Social Club membership). Match Fees: Home £3.00 for seniors in full time employment, £1.50 for under 16, students and unemployed; Away £2.00 for seniors in full time employment, £1.00 for under 16, students and unemployed.

The 1998/99 season was one of the worst. The side won only 1 game all season and ended up in last place. At a committee meeting on 5th July 1999, Ms Charlotte Munnery and Ms Caroline Richey were elected as Club Secretary and Minutes Secretary. I believe this was the first time that two ladies had been on the committee.

There was no improvement in 1999/2000 and the side was relegated.

In the first three years of the next decade the Second XI played in Division 5 South. They only finished 5th at the end of the 2002/03 season but were put into Division 4 South. It was to be a very good season and they ended up as champions. They scored, 46 goals and conceded 29, leading scorer was Gary Rothwell with 26. The team made a terrible start, losing their first game to Lodsworth by 7 goals to 3. The team selected for the game was: S. Lidbetter, T. Blunden, M. Ralph, P. Roberts, S. Leadbeatter, C. Jupp, P. Devlin, G. Rothwell, S. Lamport, S. Adsett, Ab. Greenfield. The best result of the season was a 7-0 win against Fernhurst Reserves. They had a good run in the Division 4 Cup, beating Amberley 3-0, Coal Exchange 5-1 and Wisborough Green Reserves 4-2, they then lost to Dorking Wanderers 3-0. During the course of the campaign 5 goalkeepers were used, S. Lidbetter, S. Whitehead, S. Jupp, M. Crick, S. Smith.

In 2004/05 the side played in Division 3 South. This proved to be a step too far and they were relegated. It was 9 games in before they won a match and things did not get any better, they finished up in last place. No goal scorers were recorded.

The following season they were back playing in Division 4 South. Although now playing in a lower Division the side did not play that well and ended up in 9th position.

The next season 2006/07 saw the side back in Division 3 South. This was because the West Sussex League had a major rethink and the divisions became more localised. Considering that they should not really have been in Division 3, the side did not do to badly, they finished in 8th position. Once again no goal scorers were recorded, not sure why.

They retained their position in Division 3 South for the 2007/08 season. Unfortunately they were just not good enough and ended up at the bottom of the Division. Only 2 games were won and 85 goals were let in.

In 2008/09 they played in Division 4 North. The standard of football was more to their liking and the side finished in 4th place. There were good results against Upper Beeding, a win by 7 goals to 0, with 6 different players scoring. Ockley Reserve were beaten home and away by the same score 7-1, with Abraham Greenfield getting 4 in the home match.

The following year they were again in Division 3 North. They were knocked out of the Bareham Trophy by Watersfield Reserve, losing by 9- 2 and the following week they lost to Holbrook Reserves 8-1 in the Division 3 Charity Cup. They picked themselves up and beat Ockley 11-1 and later on thrashed Slinfold 10-0. Sadly, once again the goal scorers were not recorded. The side finished in 6th place.

7-2-2004 v Wisborough Green

Pulborough Res eased into the next round of the Division 4 Cup following an extra time win over local rivals Wisborough Green Res. In front of a large, vocal home crowd, Wisborough took the lead in the second minute. The turning point of the game came midway through the first half when the hosts went clear on goal, but Sean Whitehead did brilliantly to tip the stinging shot over the bar. Pulborough drew level when Craig Jupp fired home after a goal-mouth melee. Shane Lamport drove a shot against the post for the visitors, but in the last minute of the half, Wisborough re-took the lead with a carbon copy of their opener. Pulborough had the better of the second half and equalised when Peter Roberts fired through a crowded box. The visitors should have wrapped the game up in the first period of extra-time, but squandered numerous chances before Abraham Greenfield scored in front of the travelling spectators, who were enjoying some banter with their opposite number. Gary Rothwell secured the game after being denied on several occasions, when he turned his marker and drove in off the post.

10-4-2004 v Ambassadors Res

Pulborough Res celebrated winning Division 4 South with a hard fought 4-3 win at Ambassadors Res. Pulborough needed all three points to secure the title and after being 3-1 up let the home side back in with some sloppy defending. The visitors opened their account when Karl Shakleton put Shane Lamport through to fire home. The home side responded by pinning their visitors back and the pressure paid off when they levelled before the break. Almost from the restart Simon Leadbeatter was brought down and Gary Rothwell scored from the spot to restore Pulborough's lead. Lamport added his second and Pulborough looked to be in control, before poor defending let Ambassadors back into the game with two quick goals, Pulborough continued to push forward and when Rothwell's shot was pushed wide by the keeper, Rob Davies scored from the corner. With 15 minutes left the visitors made their supporters go through hell before being able to celebrate at the Final whistle.

3-4-2004 v Dorking

Pulborough Res were knocked out of the Division 4 Charity Cup after losing 3-0 at a strong Dorking Wanderers Res. The visitors started brightly and created a couple of good chances, but could not find the target. The game was effectively over in a ten minute spell just before the break as Pulborough lacked the height to match their counterparts at set-pieces and conceded three goals from corners. The visitors never looked like reducing the deficit.

Second 11 results 1957 – 2010

ABBREVIATIONS

HDLD3 Horsham & District League Division 3

HDLJCC Horsham & District League Junior Charity Cup

HDLFAC Horsham & District League F [A] Cup

WSLD3 West Sussex League Division 3, Cup

WSLD4C West Sussex League Division 4 Cup

WSLD5C West Sussex League Division 5 Cup

SJC Sussex Junior Cup

CC Centenary Cup

BT Bareham Trophy

BRJCC Bognor Regis Junior Charity Cup

A is Aaron and Ab is Abraham Greenfield; T is Terry and Tim is Tim Hatchard; A is Tony, Ant is Anthony, S is Steven, Si is Simon, J is Jim and Ja is Jason Leadbeatter

HDL DIVISION 3, 1957/58

21-9-1957 [H] **Broadbridge Heath** (W 3-1)

28-9-1957 [H] **Christ's Hospital** (W 5-2)

5-10-1957 [A] **North Holmwood Res** (L 1-2)

12-10-1957 [A] **Broadbridge Heath** (L 2-3)

19-10-1957 [A] **Barns Green** (L 0-3)

26-10-1957 [H] **East End Utd** (W 7-5)

2-11-1957 HDLJCC [H] **North Holmwood Res** (L 1-6)

9-11-1957 [H] **Slinfold** (W 10-0)

16-11-1957 [A] **Alfold Res** (W 6-1)

23-11-1957 [H] **Cranleigh** (W 6-1)

30-11-1957 [A] **Baynards** (W 7-1)

7-12-1957 [A] **East End Utd** (W 8-1)

11-1-1958 [A] **Littleworth** (W 3-0)

18-1-1958 [A] **Christ's Hospital** (W 6-2)

1-2-1958 [A] **Cranleigh** (W 7-1)

8-2-1958 [H] **Littleworth** (W 4-1)

15-2-1958 [A] **West Chiltington** (L 3-4)

22-2-1958 [H] **Baynards** (W 6-1)

15-3-1958 [H] **Alfold Res** (W 8-1)

22-3-1958 [H] **North Holmwood Res** (L 0-4)

12-4-1958 [H] **Barns Green** (L 1-4)

19-4-1958 [A] **Ewehurst** (L 3-4)

P24 | W14 | D0 | L10 | GF99 | GA51 | 28pts | 5th

3 results missing. The team finished top of the Sportmanship table

HDL DIVISION 3, 1958/59

13-9-1958 [A] **Baynards** (W 10-0) K Handley 5, S Kovacs 2, M Stewart 2, OG 1

20-9-1958 [H] **Broadbridge Heath** (W 8-1) M Hatchard 3, G Parker 2, D Heasman 1, S Kovacs 1, D Madgett 1

27-9-1958 [H] **Alfold Res** (W 4-0) D Madgett 3, M Stewart 1

4-10-1958 [A] **Christ's Hospital** (D 2-2) K Handley 1, G Parker 1

11-10-1958 [H] **Cranleigh** (W 8-2) G Carter 6, S Kovacs 1, M Sargent 1

18-10-1958 [H] **Ciba Res** (L 1-2) D Heasman 1

25-10-1958 [H] **East End Utd Res** (L 1-2) D Madgett 1

1-11-1958 HDLJCC [A] **Alfold Res** (L 1-2) G Carter 1

8-11-1958 HDLFAC [H] **Roffey** (L 2-5)

15-11-1958 [A] **Loxwood** (W 8-0)

22-11-1958 [A] **Slinfold** (W 8-3) M Anscombe 2, D Heasman 2, K Handley 1, S Kovacs 1, M Stewart 1

29-11-1958 [H] **Southwater** (L 2-3) G Carter 1, S Kovacs 1

6-12-1958 [A] **Ciba Res** (L 3-4) K Handley 2, R Jones 1

13-12-1958 [H] **W Chiltington** (W 4-0) G Carter 2, K Handley 2

27-12-1958 [H] **Christ's Hospital** (L 2-7) R Jones 1, 1?

3-1-1959 [A] **Ashington** (W 6-5) M Anscombe 3, K Handley 1, D Heasman 1, D Madgett 1

10-1-1959 [A] **W Chiltington** (W 2-1) D Heasman 1, D Madgett 1

24-1-1959 [A] **Southwater** (D 2-2) E Goldsmith 1, K Handley 1

31-1-1959 [H] **Baynards** (W 5-1) D Heasman 2, G Carter 1, K Handley 1, R Jones 1

7-2-1959 [H] **Ashington** (L 1-9) J Greenfield 1

14-2-1959 [A] **Broadbridge Heath** (W 4-0) K Handley 2, D Heasman 1, M Spain 1

21-2-1959 [H] **Loxwood** (W 7-2) K Handley 3, L Hamilton 2, D Heasman 1, R Jones 1

28-2-1959 [A] **Cranleigh** (L 3-6) D Heasman 3

7-3-1959 [A] **East End Utd Res** (W 2-1) K Handley 2

21-3-1959 [A] **Ewehurst** [we scratched, unable to raise a team]

4-4-1959 [H] **Slinfold** (W 5-4) K Handley 3, D Heasman 2

11-4-1959 [H] **Ewehurst** (W 5-1) M Anscombe 2, K Handley 1, D Heasman 1, G Parker 1

P26 | W16 | D2 | L8 | GF103 | GA58 | 34pts | 4th

1 result missing

HDL DIVISION 3, 1959/60

12-9-1959 [A] **Cranleigh** (W 4-3)

19-9-1959 [A] **Broadbridge Heath** (L 2-5)

26-9-1959 [H] **Alfold Res** (L 1-3)

3-10-1959 [A] **East End Utd Res** (L 2-6)

10-10-1959 HDLJCC [A] **Baynards** (L 2-9)

17-10-1959 [A] **Old Collyerians** (L 2-8)

24-10-1959 HDLFAC [A] **Horsham Trinity** (L 0-7)

31-10-1959 [H] **Baynards** (L 1-2)

7-11-1959 [A] **Baynards** (L 1-13)

14-11-1959 [H] **Old Collyerians** (L 0-10)

21-11-1959 [A] **Loxwood** (L 3-5)

28-11-1959 [A] **Henfield Res** (L 2-9)

5-12-1959 [H] **East End Utd Res** (W 5-1)

12-12-1959 [A] **Slinfold** (L 2-7)

2-1-1960 [H] **Loxwood** (L 1-4)

9-1-1960 [A] **Kirdford** (L 2-8)

23-1-1960 [A] **Forest Old Boys** (L 0-14)

30-1-1960 [A] **Ewehurst Res** (L 1-7)

6-2-1960 [H] **Cranleigh** (L 1-5)

13-2-1960 [H] **Henfield Res** (L 1-2)

27-2-1960 [A] **Plaistow** (W 6-2)

5-3-1960 [H] **Broadbridge Heath** (L 2-5)

12-3-1960 [H] **Slinfold** (L 0-3)

26-3-1960 [A] **Alfold Res** (W 6-5)

2-4-1960 [H] **Kirdford** (L 2-5)

9-4-1960 [H] **Ewehurst Res** (L 1-4)

16-4-1960 [H] **Plaistow** (W 5-2)

23-4-1960 [H] **Forest Old Boys** (L 0-2)

P26 | W5 | D0 | L21 | GF53 | GA140 | 10pts | 12th

WSL DIVISION 4 1960/61

3-9-1960 [A] **South Bersted** (L 0-10

10-9-1960 [A] **Yapton** (L 3-8)

17-9-1960 [A] **Pagham Res** (L 3-6)

24-9-1960 [A] **Lec Sports B** (L 0-11

1-10-1960 [H] **Pagham Res** (L 1-3)

15-10-1960 [H] **Wittering Utd** (D 3-3)

5-11-1960 [A] **Southbourne Res** (L 2-5)

19-11-1960 [H] **Chidham Res** (L 2-4)

3-12-1960 [A] **Bognor B** They could not raise a side

10-12-1960 [A] **Hunston & Mundham Utd** (L 0-11

17-12-1960 [H] **Littlehampton B** (W 2-1)

24-12-1960 [H] **Fittleworth** (D 6-6)

31-12-1960 [H] **Felpham Res** (L 0-1)

7-1-1961 [H] **Shippams Athletic Res**

The correct results were very difficult to decipher from now until the end of the season so I have not recorded any more of them

P24 | W2 | D4 | L18 | GF37 | GA105 | 8 pts | 12th

WSL DIVISION 5 1961/62

2-9-1961 [A] **Birdham Utd** (L 3-6) J Johnson 2, G Lewis 1

9-9-1961 [A] **Westpark Utd** (W 2-1) G Allfrey 1, R Thompsett 1

16-9-1961 [A] **Slindon** (L 0-7)

23-9-1961 [A] **Yapton** (L 2-6) R Thompsett 1

7-10-1961 [A] **Renegades** (D 3-3) G Upjohn 2, A Lacey 1

14-10-1961 [A] **Boxgrove Res** (L 3-4) A Lacey 3

21-10-1961 [A] **Aldingbourne Res** (L 2-4) C Brown 1, A Lacey 1

28-10-1961 [H] **Yapton** (L 1-3)

4-11-1961 [A] **Hago Sports** (L 0-10

11-11-1961 [H] **Birdham Utd** (L 2-6) A Lacey 1, G Lewis 1

18-11-1961 [A] **Cocking** (W 6-1) M Hatchard 5, C Brown 1

25-11-1961 [H] **Hago Sports** (L 1-3) A Lacey 1

2-12-1961 [H] **Cocking** (W 3-0)

9-12-1961 **BT** [A] **Sidlesham Res** (L 0-6)

16-12-1961 [A] **Petworth Res** (L 1-7) R Thompsett 1

20-1-1962 [H] **Petworth Res** (W 2-1) A Lacey 1, G Lewis 1

27-1-1962 **BRJCC** [A] **Balls Cross** (W 4-1) R Thompsett 2, R Jones 1, E Roberts 1

10-2-1962 [H] **Boxgrove Res** (W 3-1) A Lacey 1, G Lewis 1, R Thompsett 1

17-2-1962 **BRJCC** [A] **South Bersted** (L 1-9)

24-2-1962 [H] **Westpark Utd** (W 5-3) G Lewis 3, C Brown 1, A Lacey 1

24-3-1962 [H] **Renegades** (L 4-7) G Upjohn 2, A Leadbeatter 1, R Thompsett 1

31-3-1962 [H] **Slindon** (L 1-3) A Leadbeatter 1

18-4-1962 [H] **Aldingbourne Res** (W 4-1) L Hamilton 2, J Leadbeatter 1, G Lewis 1

P20 | W7 | D1 | L12 | GF42 | GA78 | 15pts | 7th

WSL DIVISION 5 1962/63

8-9-1962 [A] **Whykians** (W 4-3) G Upjohn 2, D Rowland 1, R Thompsett 1

15-9-1962 [A] **Birdham Utd** (L 0-9)

22-9-1962 [A] **Milland** (L 2-3) A Smith 2

29-9,1962 [A] **Arundel B** (D 2-2) L Hamilton 1, A Smith 1

6-10-1962 [A] **Lavant Res** (W 5-0) G Upjohn 3, M Brown 1, R Thompsett 1

13-10-1962 [H] **Bognor Training College** (W 6-1) G Upjohn 3, G Allfrey 1, D Madgett 1, R Thompsett 1

20-10-1962 [A] **Renegades** (L 0-5)

27-10-1962 [H] **Lavant Res** (L 0-4)

3-11-1962 [H] **Birdham Utd** (L 2-7) D Madgett 2

10-11-1962 [H] **Renegades** (W 2-0) D Holland 1, A Smith 1

17-11-1962 [A] **Northchapel** (L 2-13) G Parker 1, A Smith 1

24-11-1962 [A] **Rogate** (L 1-11) G Parker 1

1-12-1962 **BT** [H] **Birdham Utd** (L 1-2) R Jones 1

8-12-1962 [A] **Bognor Training College** (L 3-16) L Hookey 1, R Jones 1, A Smith 1

15-12-1962 [H] **Arundel B** (L 0-3)

16-3-1963 [H] **Cocking** L 1-4) M Brown 1

23-3-1963 [A] **Lodsworth** (L 1-3) G Allfrey 1

30-3-1963 [A] **Cocking** (W 1-0)

6-4-1963 [H] **Whykians** (L 4-5) B List 1, G Parker 1, 2?

15-4-1963 [H] **Lodsworth** (L 3-4) G Lewis 1, R Thompsett 1, OG 1

20-4-1963 [H] **Rogate** (L 1-5) J Leadbeatter 1

27-4-1963 [H] **Milland** (L 0-2)

4-5-1963 [H] **Northchapel** (D 4-4) N Pope 2, M Brown 1, J Stewart 1

P22 | W5 | D2 | L15 | GF44 | GA102 | 12pts | 10th

WSL DIVISION 5 1963/64

7-9-1963 [A] **Funtington Utd** (L 2-4) G Lewis 2

14-9-1963 [A] **SEB** (L 2-13) D Lake 1, J Stewart 1

21-9-1963 [A] **Corinthians** (L 0-7)

28-9-1963 [A] **Yapton B** (L 2-6) M Brown 1, J Stewart 1

5-10-1963 [A] **Wittering Res** (L 0-14)

12-10-1963 [H] **Aldingbourne Res** (W 3-2) M Brown 3

19-10-1963 [A] **Cocking** (L 1-9)

26-10-1963 [H] **Corinthians** (L 0-7)

9-11-1963 [H] **SEB** (L 1-10)

16-11-1963 [A] **Lavant Res** (L 0-10)

23-11-1963 [H] **Bognor Training College Res** (L 0-9)

30-11-1963 [A] **Aldingbourne Res** (L 3-4) J Stewart 1, B Thayre 1, R Thompsett 1

7-12-1963 [A] **Graffham** (L 0-5)

14-12-1963 [A] **Bognor Training College Res** (L 2-9) A Puttock 1, D Rowland 1

21-12-1963 [A] **Renegades** We could not raise a side

28-12-1963 [H] **Yapton B** (L 2-10)

4-1-1964 [H] **Stedham Utd Res** (L 1-4) M Brown 1

11-1-1964 [A] **Stedham Utd Res** (D 2-2) G Upjohn 2

18-1-1964 **BT** [A] **SEB** (L 1-5) M Brown 1

25-1-1964 [A] **Tillington** (D 4-4) C Thayre 2, L Hookey 1, J Stewart 1

1-2-1964 [A] **Harting** L 1-12) C Thayre 1

8-2-1964 [A] **Amberley** No Result

15-2-1964 [H] **Lavant Res** (D 3-3) G Allfrey 1, M Brown 1, L Hookey 1

22-2-1964 [H] **Graffham** (L 0-8)

29-2-1964 [H] **Tillington** (No Result)

14-3-1964 [H] **Cocking** (L 3-4) M Brown 1, R Thompsett 1, 1?

4-4-1964 [H] **Renegades** (L 1-11) J Stewart 1

11-4-1964 [H] **Harting** (L 1-12) M Brown 1

18-4-1964 [H] **Funtington Utd** (W 3-2) G Lewis 2, T Hatchard 1

25-4-1964 [H] **Amberley** (W 5-1) G Lewis 2, G Allfrey 1, M Brown 1, J Stewart 1

27-4-1964 [H] **Wittering Res** (W 3-1) T Hatchard 1, J Leadbeatter 1, G Lewis 1

P30 | W4 | D2 | L24 | GF50 | GA197 | 10pts | 16th

One of the draws may have been a loss

WSL DIVISION 5 1964/65

29-8-1964 [A] **Fishbourne** (W 4-3) G Lewis 4

12-9-1964 [A] **Lavant Res** (L 1-6) B Tullet 1

19-9-1964 [A] **Funtington Utd** (L 0-13)

26-9-1964 [A] **Felpham Utd Res** (L 1-10) M Anscombe 1

3-10-1964 [A] **Bilsham Utd** (W 7-0) M Hatchard 4, T Roberts 1, J Stewart 1, 1?

10-10-1964 [H] **Hunston Utd Res** (W 1-0) P Chapman 1

17-10-1964 [H] **Lavant Res** (W 5-2) M Hatchard 2, D Madgett 2, J Stewart 1

24-10-1964 [H] **Graylingwell Rs** (D 2-2) M Brown 1, M Hatchard 1

31-10-1964 [A] **Hunston Utd Res** (L 0-6)

7-11-1964 BT [A] **Corinthians** (L 0-19

14-11-1964 [H] **Felpham Utd** R (L 3-9) J Stewart 2, R Thompsett 1

21-11-1964 [A] **Stedham Utd** R (L 2-3) M Brown 1, Thompsett 1

28-11-1964 [A] **Fernhurst Res** (W 6-2) M Brown 5, A Puttock 1

5-12-1964 [A] **Graylingwell Res** (L 1-4) A Puttock 1

12-12-1964 [A] **Cocking** (W 3-1) M Brown 3

19-12-1964 [A] **Tillington** (L 2-4) M Anscombe 1, A Puttock 1

2-1-1965 [A] **Aldingbourne Res** (L 2-4) M Hatchard 1, J Stewart 1

9-1-1965 [H] **Fernhurst Res** (W 5-1) M Anscombe 2, M Hatchard 1, J Stewart 1, R Thompsett 1

23-1-1965 [H] **Graffham** (W 4-1) M Anscombe 2, M Brown 1, J Stewart 1

30-1-1965 [A] **Amberley** (L 1-7) J Stewart 1

6-2-1965 [H] **Funtington Utd** (L 0-11

13-2-1965 [A] **Bognor Training College Res** (L 0-3)

20-2-1965 [H] **Aldingbourne Res** (L 0-6)

27-2-1965 [H] **Fishbourne** (L 1-4) J Stewart 1

20-3-1965 [A] **Graffham** (L 1-9)

27-3-1965 [H] **Bognor TC Res** (L 2-4) M Brown 1, B Davis 1

3-4-1965 [H] **Cocking** (W 5-3) M Brown 2, G Mason 2, OG 1

10-4-1965 [H] **Tillington** (W 3-1) C Holden 1, OG 2

17-4-1965 [H] **Amberley** (L 1-3) J Stewart 1

21-4-1965 [H] **Bilsham Utd** (W 3-0) M Anscombe 1, C Holden 1, J Stewart 1

24-4-1965 [H] **Stedham Utd Res** (W 3-0) M Anscombe 1, M Brown 1, J Stewart 1

P30 | W12 | D1 | L17 | GF69 | GA122 | 25pts | 12th

WSL DIVISION 5 1965/66

4-9-1965 [A] **Boxgrove** (L 2-5) M Brown 2

11-9-1965 [A] **Tillington** (W 3-2) B Cooke 2, J Stewart 1

18-9-1965 [H] **Boxgrove** (W 2-1) M Brown 1, D Lake 1

25-9-1965 [A] **Graylingwell Rs** (L 1-2) M Brown 1

2-10-1965 [A] **Aldingbourne Rs** (D 2-2) M Brown 1, G Upjohn 1

9-10-1965 [A] **Graffham Res** (W 14-2) M Brown 4, J Stewart 4, G Upjohn 4, 2, ?

16-10-1965 [A] **Fishbourne** (L 2-5) R Thompsett 2

23-10-1965 [H] **Aldingbourne Rs** (W 3-1) M Brown 2, J Stewart 1

30-10-1965 [H] **Graylingwell Res** (W 5-4) M Brown 2, D Holland 1, J Stewart 1, OG 1

6-11-1965 [H] **Lavant Res** (L 0-1)

13-11-1965 [A] **Southbourne Res** (W 4-1) M Brown 1, T Bryan 1, M Hatchard 1, J Stewart 1

20-11-1965 [A] **Stedham Res** (W 3-0) M Brown 1, T Bryan 1, J Stewart 1

27-11-1965 [A] **Lavant Res** (W 11-3) M Brown 6, R Maybee 4, R Thompsett 1

4-12-1965 BT [A] **Hunston Rs** (L 3-7) G Hill 1, J Woolaston 1, OG 1

1-1-1966 [H] **Fishbourne** (W 4-1) P Chapman 2, B Davis 1, R Maybee 1

22-1-1966 [H] **Graffham Res** (W 6-0) P Chapman 3, D Holland 2, J Woolaston 1

5-2-1966 [H] **Southbourne Res** (L 0-2)

12-2-1966 [A] **Bognor TC Res** (L 1-8) D Holland 1

19-2-1966 [H] H **Stedham Res** (D 1-1) R Maybee 1

5-3-1966 [H] **Lodsworth** (L 1-4) R Maybee 1

12-3-1966 [H] **Bognor TC Res** (L 2-3) G Parker 1, A Spain 1

19-3-1966 [A] **Lodsworth** (L 0-1)

9-4-1966 [H] **Tillington** (W 7-2)

P22 | W11 | D2 | L9 | GF76 | GA51 | 24pts | 6th

WSL DIVISION 5 1966/67

3-9-1966 [H] **Sweetlands Res** (L 1-10) M Brown 1

10-9-1966 [H] **Gravlingwell Res** (L 3-4) D Holland 2, J Stewart 1

17-9-1966 [A] **Fishbourne** (L 3-8) M Brown 1, D Holland 1, J Stewart 1

24-9-1966 [A] **Stedham Res** (W 4-2) A Pattenden 2, J Madell 1, J Stewart 1

9-10-1966 [H] **Wick B** (L 1-2) M Brown 1

15-10-1966 [A] **Bilsham Utd** (W 5-4) M Brown 2, D Holland 1, J Madell 1, A Spain 1

22-10-1966 [A] **Wick B** (D 2-2) M Brown 1, A Spain 1

29-10-1966 [H] **Boxgrove** (W 4-3) M Brown 2, D Holland 1, J Stewart 1

5-11-1966 [A] **Sweetlands Res** (L 2-b M Brown 1, J Stewart 1

12-11-1966 [H] **Lodsworth** (D 2-2) M Brown 1, R Thompsett 1

19-11-1966 [H] **Stedham Res** 1 2-3) D Holland 1, G Mason 1

26-11-1966 E, **Lavant Res** (W 2-1) M Brown 2

3-12-1966 BT [A] **Bosham Res** (W 1-0) J Stewart 1

10-12-1965 [H] **Aldingbourne Res** (W 10-0) M Brown 5, R Phillips 4, J Stewart 1

17-12-1966 [H] **Lavant Res** (W 4-2) M Brown 2, P Chapman 1, R Phillips 1

31-12-1966 [A] **Graylingwell Res** (L 2-3) M Brown 1, P Chapman 1

7-1-1967 [H] **Fishbourne** (D 1-1) P Chapman 1

21-1-1967 [A] **Watersfield** (W 5-3) M Brown 3, J Habgood 1, J Madell 1

4-2-1967 BT [H] **Walberton** (W 1-0) R Thompsett 1

11-2-1967 [A] **Lodsworth** (L 0-4)

25-2-1967 BT [H] **Fishbourne** (L 0-4)

4-3-1967 [H] **Watersfield** (W 4-1) M Baker 3, 1, ?

18-3-1967 [A] **Aldingbourne Res** (L 1-12 D Holland 1

25-3-1967 [A] **Boxgrove** (L 0-7)

1-4-1967 [H] **Bilsham Utd** (L 0-5)

P22 | W8 | D3 | L11 | GF57 | GA85 | 19pts | 10th

WSL DIVISION 5 1967/68

2-9-1967 [A] **Lavant Res** (W 8-0) B Cooke 4, T Wells 3, R Thompsett 1

16-9-1967 [H] **Wick B** (W 6-0) B Cooke 2, J Stewart 2, T Wells 1, OG 1

23-9-1967 [A] **Stedham Res** (W 4-1) M Baker 3, J Stewart 1

30-9-1967 [H] **Boxgrove** (W 4-1) M Baker 2, M Hayler 2

7-10-1967 BT [A] **Lavant Res** (W 6-1) M Baker 2, M Brown 2, J Stewart 1, T Wells 1

14-10-1967 [H] **Compton Valley** (L 2-6) M Baker 2

21-10-1967 BT [A] **Compton Valley** (L 1-7) M Baker 1

28-10-1967 [A] **Fishbourne** (W 5-4) M Brown 3, J Stewart 2

4-11-1967 [H] **Lavant Res** (W 4-2) T Wells 2, D Phillips 1, J Stewart 1

11-11-1967 [H] **Felpham Res** (L 2-3) M Hayler 1, T Wells 1

18-11-1967 [A] **Graylingwell Res** (D 3-3) T Wells 2, D Phillips 1

25-11-1967 [H] **Angmering Res** (W 6-1) M Brown 2, D Phillips 2, G Upjohn 2

2-12-1967 [H] **Bognor TC Res** (D 1-1) M Brown 1

16-12-1967 [H] **Bilsham** (L 1-7) M Hayler 1

30-12-1967 [A] **Felpham Res** (L 0-4)

6-1-1968 [H] **Watersfield** (L 1-10) D Lake 1

20-1-1968 [H] **Fishbourne** (W 5-1) M Brown 2, M Baker 1, R Czarnecki 1, J Stewart 1

27-1-1968 [H] **Graylingwell Res** (L 1-3) M Brown 1

3-2-1968 [A] **Boxgrove** (L 1-3) B Davis 1

10-2-1968 [A] **Bilsham** (L 1-2) M Baker 1

17-2-1968 [A] **Compton Valley** (L 0-4)

2-3-1968 [H] **Stedham Res** (D 1-1) M Baker 1

9-3-1968 [A] **Bognor TC Res** (W 5-0) J Stewart 4, B Davis 1

16-3-1968 [A] **Wick B** (L 3-5) J Stewart 2, M Baker 1

23-3-1968 [A] **Angmering Res** (L 2-3) P Chapman 1, B Davis 1

13-4-1968 [A] **Watersfield** (L 1-5) A Pattenden 1

P24 | W9 | D3 | L12 | GF67 | GA70 | 21pts | 7th

WSL DIVISION 5 1968/69

7-9-1968 [H] **Hunston Res** (L 4-7) M Pattenden 2, G Clark 1, R Phillips 1

14-9-1968 [A] **Boxgrove** (D 3-3) G Clark 1, A Richardson 1, J Stewart 1

21-9-1968 [H] **Graylingwell Res** (W 3-2) A Richardson 1, J Stewart 1, G Upjohn 1

28-9-1968 [A] **Lavant Res** (W 2-1) M Pattenden 1, J Stewart 1

5-10-1968 [H] **Felpham Res** (W 2-1) D Stenning 1, J Stewart 1

19-10-1968 [H] **Bognor C** (W4-2) M Pattenden 2, G Clark 1, J Stewart 1

26-10-1968 [H] **Lavant Res** (L 1-3) D Stenning 1

2-11-1968 BT [A] **Selsey Res** (L 0-4)

9-11-1968 [A] **Bognor C** (W 3-2) P Ransom 2, M Pattenden 1

16-11-1968 [H] **Boxgrove** (L 0-4)

30-11-1968 [H] **Cocking** (W 6-1) T Wells 3, M Pattenden 1, R Phillips I J Stewart 1

7-12-1968 [A] **Amberley** (W 4-3) G Clark 1, R Phillips 1, D Stenning 1, 1?

21-12-1968 [A] **Cocking** (L 3-4) G Clark 1, M Pattenden 1, D Stenning 1

4-1-1969 [A] **East Dean** (D 3-3) R Phillips 2, M Pattenden 1

11-1-1969 [H] **Stedham Res** (W 7-2) T Wells 3, A Richardson 2, D Stenning 1, J Stewart 1

18-1-1969 [H] **Graffham** (L 2-3) D Stenning 1, 1?

1-2-1969 [H] **East Dean** (L 0-1)

15-2-1969 [H] **Angmering Res** (W 2-1) M Bailey 1, G Mason 1

22-2-1969 [A] **Stedham Res** (L 1-6) J Stewart 1

15-3-1969 [H] **Watersfield** (W 3-2) P Chapman 1, J Stewart 1, T Wells 1

22-3-1969 [A] **Watersfield** (D 3-3) M Hatchard 1, M Pattenden 1, R Phillips 1

29-3-1969 [A] **Graylingwell** (L 0-3)

5-4-1969 [A] **Graffham** (W 5-2) M Pattenden 2, M Hatchard 1, D Stenning 1, T Wells 1

7-4-1969 [H] **Wick Res** (W 1-0) A Richardson 1

12-4-1969 [H] **Amberley** (W 2-0) T Wells 2

14-4-1969 [A] **Angmering** (L 1-3) T Wells 1

19-4-1969 [A] **Felpham Res** (L 1-3) P Chapman 1

22-4-1969 [A] **Wick Res** (D 1-1) R Czarnecki 1

26-4-1969 [A] **Hunston Res** (L 0-9)

P28 | W13 | D4 | L11 | GF67 | GA75 | 30pts | 7th

WSL DIVISION 5 1969/70

6-9-1969 [A] **Boxgrove** (L 0-7)

13-9-1969 [H] **Summerley Park Rangers** (W 6-1) T Wells 3, D Stenning 2, D Phillips 1

20-9-1969 [H] **Felpham Res** (L 0-2)

27-9-1969 [A] **Sweetlands Res** (L 3-4) K Clark 1, R Czarnecki 1, T Wells 1

4-10-1969 BT [A] **Watersfield** (L 0-4)

11-10-1969 [A] **Graffham** (D 3-3) T Wells 2, R Czarnecki 1

25-10-1969 [A] **Lavant Res** (L 1-7) A Richardson 1

1-11-1969 [H] **Wick Res** (L 1-3) T Jones 1

8-11-1969 [A] **Renegades Res** (W 2-1) M Hatchard 1, P Hedger 1

15-11-1969 [H] **Sweetlands Res** they did not arrive 2pts

22-11-1969 [A] **Eastergate Res** (W 3-2) K Holland 1, T Jones 1, Lewis 1

6-12-1969 [H] **Stedham Res** (D 2-2) T Jones 1, J Stewart 1

13-12-1969 [H] **Renegades Res** (D 1-1) P Hedger 1

20-12-1969 [A] **Summerley Park Rangers** (L 0-5)

27-12-1969 [H] **Graylingwell Res** (L 0-5)

3-1-1970 [A] **Stedham Res** (L 1-3) P Welch 1

17-1-1970 [H] **Eastergate Res** (L 1-4) M Bailey 1

24-1-1970 [H] **Angmering Res** (L 2-4) P Hedger 1, OG 1

31-1-1970 [A] **Angmering Res** (D 1-1) J Stewart 1

7-2-1970 [H] **Lavant Res** (D 2-2) T Jones 1, G Lewis 1

14-2-1970 [A] **Wick Res** (L 2-4) C Carter 1, P Hedger 1

21-2-1970 [H] **Graffham** (W 4-0) P Hedger 3, G Upjohn 1

28-2-1970 [H] **Rogate** (L 2-4) P Hedger 1, G Upjohn 1

7-3-1970 [A] **Graylingwell Res** (L 0-5)

14-3-1970 [A] **Amberley** (D 1-1) OG 1

21-3-1970 [A] **Rogate** (L 1-7) M Pattenden 1

4-4-1970 [H] **Boxgrove** (L 2-8) R Czarnecki 1, P Hedger 1

16-4-1970 [H] **Amberley** (W 5-3) G Lewis 3, T Jones 1, G Upjohn 1

25-4-1970 [A] **Felpham Res** (L 0-3)

P28 | W6 | D6 | L16 | GF46 | GA92 | 18pts | 13th

WSL DIVISION 5 1970/71

5-9-1970 [A] **Cocking** (L 1-2)

12-9-1970 [H] **Lavant Res** (W 5-3)

19-9-1970 [A] **Rogate** (L 2-3)

26-9-1970 [H] **Graffham** (W 4-3)

3-10-1970 WSLD5C [A] **Tillington** (W 7-2)

10-10-1970 [H] **Cocking** (W 9-0)

17-10-1970 [A] **Harting Res** (W 5-1)

24-10-1970 [A] **Petworth 3rds** (W 9-0)

31-10-1970 [H] **Stedham Res** (L 2-4)

7-11-1970 | WSLD5C [H] **Summerley Park Rangers** (W 3-2)

14-11-1970 [A] **Slindon Res** (W 4-2) R Czarnecki 2, B Davis 1, M Leadbeatter 1

28-11-1970 [H] **Lurgashall Res** (D 1-1)

5-12-1970 [H] **Harting Res** (W 3-1) R Czarnecki 1, T Hatchard 1, G Upjohn 1

12-12-1970 [A] **Stedham Res** (L 2-7)

19-12-1970 [H] **Eurotherm Utd** (L 1-2)

2-1-1971 [A] **Graffham** (D 2-2) T Jones 1, A Leadbeatter 1

9-1-1971 [H] **Rogate** (W 4-2)

16-1-1971 WSLD5C [H] **Rogate** (L 2-3) A Richardson 1, G Upjohn 1

23-1-1971 [A] **Eurotherm Utd** (L 1-4)

6-2-1971 [H] **Fernhurst Res** (W 7-0) T Jones 5, A Richardson 1, J Stewart 1

13-2-1971 [A] **Watersfield Res** (W 7-1)

20-2-1971 [A] **Lavant Res** (D 2-2)

27-2-1971 [H] **Petworth 3rds** (L 2-5)

6-3-1971 [A] **Lurgashall Res** (D 3-3)

13-3-1971 [A] **Fittleworth** (L 3-5)

20-3-1971 [H] **Slindon Res** (W 6-0)

27-3-1971 [H] **Amberley** (L 0-1)

3-4-1971 [H] **Tillington** (W 3-0)

10-4-1971 [A] **Fernhurst Res** (L 1-3)

15-4-1971 [A] **Amberley** (L 2-3)

17-4-1971 [A] **Tillington** They could not raise a side

19-4-1971 [H] **Fittleworth** (W 3-0)

24-4-1971 [H] **Watersfield Res** (L 0-2)

P30 | W14 | D4 | L12 | GF94 | GA62 | 32pts | 8th

WSL DIVISION 5 CENTRAL 1971/72

4-9-1971 [H] **Wisborough Green** (L 0-1)

11-9-1971 [H] **Fernhurst Res** (W 4-1)

18-9-1971 [A] **Lurgashall Res** (W 2-0)

25-9-1971 [H] **Watersfield Res** (W 7-1)

2-10-1971 [A] **Fittleworth** (W 8-0)

9-10-1971 [H] **Harting Res** (W 2-0)

16-10-1971 [A] **Plaistow** (L 0-2)

23-10-1971 [A] **Billingshurst 3rds** (W 3-0)

30-10-1971 WSLD5C [H] **Watersfield Res** (W 3-0)

6-11-1971 [A] **Fernhurst Res** (W 3-1)

20-11-1971 [H] **Kirdford Sports Res** (W 7-1)

27-11-1971 [A] **Harting Res** (D 2-2)

4-12-1971 [H] **Fittleworth** (W 18-0)

11-12-1971 [A] **Watersfield Res** (W 3-0)

1-1-1972 | WSLD5C [H] **Sunallon 3rds** (W 5-1)

8-1-1972 [H] **Billingshurst 3rds** (L 2-6)

15-1-1972 [A] **Wisborough Green Res** (W 4-1)

22-1-1972 [H] **Plaistow** (D 3-3)

29-1-1972 [H] **Lurgashall Res** (W 7-0)

5-2-1972 [A] **Petworth 3rds** (W 7-3)

12-2-1972 [A] **Tillington** (W 4-3) G Upjohn 2, S Austin 1, G Fallowfield 1

19-2-1972 | WSLD5C [H] **Fittleworth** (W 6-3) G Fallowfield 3, G Upjohn 2, S Austin 1

26-2-1972 [H] **Keatings** (D 2-2) G Fallowfield 2

4-3-1972 [A] **Kirdford Res** (W 2-1)

11-3-1972 [H] **Petworth 3rds** (W 3-0) R Branch 1, M Brown 1J Jupp 1

18-3-1972 | WSLD5C Semi Final [H] **Fernhurst Res** (W 9-1) G Upjohn 4, G Fallowfield 3, A Richardson 2

1-4-1972 [A] **Keatings** (W 2-1) A Richardson 1, G Upjohn 1

8-4-1972 [H] **Tillington** (W 6-1) G Upjohn 2, S Austin 1, R Czarnecki 1, J Jupp 1, N Turner 1

19-4-1972 West Sussex League Division 5 Charity Cup Final Played at Queen Street Horsham Thomas Keating 2, Pulborough 1, AET

P24 | W18 | D3 | L3 | GF101 | GA30 | 39pts | 2nd

WSL DIVISION 4 CENTRAL 1972/73

2-9-1972 [A] **Funtington Utd** (L 1-6)

9-9-1972 [A] **Rogate** (L 2-3)

16-9-1972 [H] **Milland** (D 2-2)

30-9-1972 [A] **Lavant Res** (L 2-3)

7-10-1972 [A] **Graylingwell** Hospital Res (L 0-3)

14-10-1972 [H] **Lodsworth** (L 3-6)

21-10-1972 [H] **Keatings** (W 4-3)

18-10-1972 [A] **Milland** (L 1-5)

11-11-1972 [A] **Lodsworth** (L 0-4)

18-11-1972 WSLD4C [A] **Amberley** (L 2-5)

25-11-1972 [A] **Graffham** (L 1-9)

2-12-1972 [H] **Billingshurst Res** (L 2-9)

16-12-1972 [A] **Bosham Res** (L 0-5)

23-12-1972 [H] **Graffham** (L 0-5)

30-12-1972 [H] **Amberley** (L 1-4)

6-1-1973 [A] **Keatings** (L 1-4)

13-1-1973 [H] **Rogate** (L 1-3)

27-1-1973 [A] **Billingshurst Res** (L 2-9)

3-2-1973 [A] **Lavant Res** (D 1-1)

10-2-1973 [A] **Amberley** (L 0-3)

17-2-1973 [H] **Funtington Utd** (L 2-6)

3-3-1973 [H] **Graylingwell** Hospital Res (L 0-5)

10-3-1973 [H] **Bosham Res** (L 2-3)

P22 | W1 | D2 | L19 | GF29 | GA101 | 4pts | 12th

WSL DIVISION 5 CENTRAL 1973/74

15-9-1973 [H] **Northchapel** (W 3-1)

22-9-1973 [H] **Cocking** (W 4-3)

29-9-1973 [A] **Lodsworth** (W 4-2)

6-10-1973 [A] **Loxwood Utd** (W 4-2)

13-10-1973 [H] **Fernhurst Res** (D 2-2)

20-10-1973 [A] **Graffham Res** (D 3-3)

27-10-1973 | WSLD5C [A] **Billingshurst 3rds** (W 6-1)

3-11-1973 [H] **Petworth 3rds** (W 4-1)

10-11-1973 [H] **Loxwood Utd** (W 12-0)

17-11-1973 [A] **Billingshurst 3rds** (W 5-2)

24-11-1973 [H] **Milland** (W 5-2)

1-12-1973 | WSLD5C [H] **Milland** (L 4-5) They played illegal player

8-12-1973 [A] **Harting Res** (W 8-1)

15-12-1973 [A] **Fittleworth** (W 5-1)

5-1-1974 [A] **Kirdford Res** (W 6-0)

12-1-1974 [H] **Graffham Res** (W 8-3) J Burleston 2, R Czarnecki 2

J Jupp 2, M Brown 1, G Upjohn 1

19-1-1974 [A] **Fernhurst Res** (L 1-2)

26-1-1974 [H] **Lodsworth** (W 8-0)

23-2-1974 [H] **Harting Res** (W 4-0)

2-3-1974 WSLD5C Replay [H] **Milland** W3-2) AET

9-3-1974 WSLD5C A **Petworth 3rds** (W 5-2)

16-3-1974 [H] **Fittleworth** (W 5-1)

23-3-1974 [A] **Northchapel** (W 4-2) 30-3-1974 [A] **Cocking** (L 0-7)

6-4-1974 WSLD5C Semi-Final [H] **Worthing Utd** (L 1-5)

13-4-1974 [A] **Petworth 3rds** (W 4-0) 20-4-1974 [A] **Milland** (W 2-1)

P24 | W19 | D2 | L3 | GF100 | GA41 | 40pts | 3rd

WSL DIVISION 4 CENTRAL 1974/75

7-9-1974 [1975] [H] **Fernhurst Sports Res** (L 1-2)

14-9-1974 [A] **Sweetlands** (D 4-4)

21-9-1974 WSLD4C [A] **Rising Sun** (L 1-3)

28-9-1974 [A] **East Dean** (L 2-6)

5-10-1974 [H] **Lurgashall** (W 4-2)

19-10-1974 [H] **Graffham** (L 0-9)

26-10-1974 [A] **Rogate** (L 0-11)

2-11-1974 [H] **Cocking** (D 1-1)

9-11-1974 [A] **Southbourne Res** (L 0-7)

23-11-1974 [A] **Graffham** (L 0-5)

30-11-1974 [A] **Lurgashall** (L 0-2)

7-12-1974 [H] **Amberley** (L 1-3)

14-12-1974 [A] **Cocking** (L 1-5)

21-12-1974 [H] **East Dean** (L 1-5)

28-12-1974 [H] **Wisborough Green Res** (D 2-2)

4-1-1975 [A] **Amberley** (L 3-7)

18-1-1975 [H] **Milland Res** (D 2-2)

1-2-1975 [A] **Wisborough Green Res** (L 1-3)

8-1-1975 [A] **Milland Res** (W 4-1)

15-2-1975 [H] **Sweetlands** (W 3-1)

22-2-1975 [A] **Southbourne Res** (L 1-2)

22-3-1975 [H] **Rogate** (L 1-4)

1-4-1975 [A] **Fernhurst Sports Res** (L 3-4)

P22 | W3 | D4 | L15 | GF34 | GA86 | 10pts | 11th

WSL DIVISION 5 CENTRAL 1975/76

6-9-1975 [H] **Bosham Res** (L 1-3) L Rout 1

13-9-1975 [H] **Boxgrove Sports Res** (W 6-0) J Norman 2, D Padwick 2, G Messenger 1, G Upjohn 1

20-9-1975 [A] **Loxwood Utd Res** (W 5-1) M Browning 1, G Messenger 1, J Norman 1, D Padwick 1, L Rout 1

27-9-1975 BT [H] **Bourne Park Rangers** (L 1-3) OG 1, AET

4-10-1975 [A] **Graffham Res** (D 2-2) S Hurst 1, D Padwick 1

11-10-1975 [H] **Funtington Utd Res** (L 2-4) J Norman 2

25-10-1975 [A] **Lodsworth** (W 6-3) J Norman 2, G Upjohn 2, L Rout 1, S Stentiford 1

1-11-1975 WSLD5C [A] **Allington** (The ref was a fireman and was called away, game cancelled)

8-11-1975 [H] **Graffham Res** (W 4-2) G Upjohn 3, L Rout 1

15-11-1975 [H] **Loxwood Utd Res** (W 11-1) G Upjohn 5, J Norman 3, G Messenger 1, OG 2

22-11-1975 [A] **Funtington Utd Res** (W 3-2) A Richardson 3

29-11-1975 [H] **Milland Res** (W 10-0) G Upjohn 5, J Norman 2, G Hill 1, L Rout 1, OG 1

13-12-1975 WSLD5C [A] **Allington** (L 1-6) J Norman 1

27-12-1975 [H] **Lodsworth** (L 2-4) A Richardson 1, L Rout 1

3-1-1976 [H] **Watersfield Res** (L 2-3) J Norman 1, OG 1

10-1-1976 [A] **Milland Res** (W 4-1) J Norman 3, G Hill 1

17-1-1976 [H] **Fittleworth** (W 4-2) A Richardson 2, J Norman 1, OG 1

31-1-1976 [A] **Boxgrove Sports Res** (W 5-1) J Norman 2, G Messenger 1, A Richardson 1, G Upjohn 1

7-2-1976 [H] **Borough Utd** (L 0-5)

21-2-1976 [A] **Bosham Res** (L 0-3)

28-2-1976 [A] **Fittleworth** (D 3-3) J Norman 2, G Upjohn 1

27-3-1976 [A] **Watersfield Res** (L 2-5) J Norman 1, L Rout 1

3-4-1976 [A] **Borough Utd** (L 2-5) J Norman 1, L Rout 1

P20 | W10 | D3 | L7 | GF73 | GA46 | 23pts | 4th

WSL DIVISION 5 CENTRAL 1976/77

18-9-1976 [A] **Borough Utd** (L 2-5) M Pepper 2

25-9-1976 BT [H] **East Preston Res** (L 0-8)

2-10-1976 [A] **Loxwood Utd Res** (W 10-1) J Norman 4, M Jupp 3, M Pepper 1 M Ruff 1, S Stentiford 1

9-10-1976 WSLD5C [A] **Watersfield Res** (L 0-2)

16-10-1976 [A] **Lavant 3rds** (W 6-0) M Pepper 3, J Norman 2, M Ruff 1

23-10-1976 [H] **Graffham Res** (D 2-2) M Pepper 1, M Ruff 1

30-10-1976 [A] **Amberley Res** (D 2-2) L Rout 1, G Smith 1

13-11-1976 [A] **Lodsworth Res** (L 2-3) J Jupp 1, J Norman 1

20-11-1976 [A] **Fittleworth** (L 3-4) M Pepper 1, T Roberts 1, M Ruff 1

27-11-1976 [A] **Milland Res** (D 4-4) J Norman 2, L Rout 1, J Stewart 1

4-12-1976 [H] **Watersfield Res** (L 1-2) OG 1

11-12-1976 [A] **Watersfield Res** (L 2-4) M Brown 1, J Norman 1

18-12-1976 [H] **Milland Res** (W 3-2) J Norman 2, M Brown 1

15-1-1977 [H] **Loxwood Utd Res** (W 8-2) M Pepper 3, M Brown 2, C Hutton 1, J Norman 1

22-1-1977 [H] **Lavant 3rds** (W 3-2) C Hutton 2, J Norman 1

29-1-1977 [H] **Storrington 3rds** (W 3-1) C Hutton 2, J Norman 1

12-2-1977 [H] **Amberley Res** (W 8-0) M Pepper 3, M Jupp 2, J Norman 2, M Ruff 1

19-2-1977 [A] **Graffham Res** (W 3-2) C Hutton 2, M Pepper 1

26-2-1977 [H] **Storrington 3rds** (D 3-3) M Brown 1, M Jupp 1, J Norman 1

5-3-1977 [H] **Fittleworth** (D 0-0)

12-3-1977 [H] **Lodsworth Res** (W 5-1) M Jupp 3, J Norman 1, L Rout 1

19-3-1977 [H] **Borough Utd** (L 1-6) L Rout 1

P20 | W9 | D5 | L6 | GF71 | GA46 | 23pts | 4th

WSL DIVISION 5 CENTRAL 1977/78

10-9-1977 [H] **Stedham Res** (W 5-0) M Jupp 3, M Pepper 1, OG 1

17-9-1977 [A] **Graffham Res** (W 4-0) M Jupp 2, A Brothers 1, C Hutton 1

24-9-1977 [A] **Lodsworth Res** (W 4-2) M Jupp 2, C Hutton 1, J Norman 1

1-10-1977 WSLD5C [H] **Felpham Utd Res** (W 3-1) C Hutton I J Norman 1, L Rout 1

8-10-1977 [H] **Loxwood Utd Res** (W 11-1) C Hutton 2, M Jupp 2, A Brothers 1, S Hurst 1, M Leadbeatter 1, J Norman 1, D Rhoder 1, D Stenning 1, 1?

15-10-1977 [A] **Milland Res** (W 3-2) M Pepper 2, 1?

22-10-1977 [H] **Lavant 3rds** (W 3-1) M Jupp 1, M Pepper 1, M Ruff 1

5-11-1977 [A] **Storrington 3rds** (W 2-1) C Hutton 1, OG 1

12-11-1977 WSLD5C [H] **Sunallon** IV (W 5-1) J Norman 2, M Pepper 2, G Smith 1

19-11-1977 [H] **Fittleworth Res** (W 4-1) M Pepper 2, C Hutton 1, M Jupp 1

26-11-1977 [A] **Loxwood Utd Res** (W 9-0) C Hutton 3, J Norman 3, M Pepper 2, G Smith 1 3-12-1977 [A] **Stedham Res** (D 1-1) D Stenning 1

17-12-1977 [H] **Milland Res** (W 2-1) J Norman 1, M Ruff 1

31-12-1977 WSLD5C [H] **Milland Res** (D 2-2) C Hutton 2, J Jupp 1, AET

7-1-1978 [A] **Fittleworth Res** (W 9-0) J Norman 3, C Hutton 2, M Pepper 2, G Hill 1, M Jupp 1

25-2-1978 [H] **Lodsworth Res** (W 5-2) L Rout 3, C Hutton 1, M Pepper 1

4-3-1978 WSLD5C Replay [A] **Milland Res** (W 5-2) C Hutton 2, J Norman 2, J Jupp 1

11-3-1978 [A] **Amberley Res** (W 3-2) C Hutton 1, J Norman 1, L Rout 1

18-3-1978 [H] **Amberley Res** (W 6-0) M Ruff 3, L Rout 1, D Stenning 1, OG 1

25-3-1978 **West Chiltington** (L 0-4)

27-3-1978 [A] **Wisborough Gr Res** (W 3-1) C Hutton 1, L Rout 1

3-4-1978 WSLD5C [A] **Cocking** (W 2-0) G Hill 1, C Spain 1

8-4-1978 [H] **West Chiltington** (D 1-1) M Ruff 1

12-4-1978 [H] **Wisborough Green Res** (W 6-0) M Pepper 5, J Norman 1

15-4-1978 WSLD5C Semi Final **Wittering & Birdham Utd** (L 1-4) J Norman 1

17-4-1978 [A] **Wisborough Green Res** (W 2-1) T Hatchard 1, C Hutton 1

22-4-1978 [H] **Graffham Res** (L 0-1)

24-4-1978 [H] **Storrington 3rds** (W 4-1) C Hutton 2, J Jupp 2

29-4-1978 [A] **Lavant 3rds** (L 2-3) M Jupp 1, L Rout 1

Two matches against **Cocking** missing, also one match against **Wisborough Green** was a friendly

P24 W19 | D2 | L3 | GF94 | GA28 | 40pts | 1st

WSL DIVISION 4 NORTH 1978/79

9-9-1978 [A] **East End Utd** (D 3-3) L Rout 2, M Pepper 1

16-9-1978 [H] **Henfield Athletic Res** (W 6-0) M Pepper 4, G Messenger 1, M Ruff 1

23-9-1978 WSLD4C [H] **Plaistow** (D 3-3) J Jupp 1, L Rout 1, M Ruff 1, AET

30-9-1978 [H] **Sunallon 3rds** (W 3-1) L Rout 2, J Jupp 1

7-10-1978 BT [A] **Harting** (W 3-2) M Pepper 2, G Lewis 1, AET

14-10-1978 [H] **East End Utd** (W 1-0) L Rout 1

28-10-1978 [H] **Loxwood Utd** (W 2-1) J Jupp 1, D Stenning 1

4-11-1978 [A] **Plaistow** (W 3-2) G Lewis 2, A Leadbeatter 1

11-11-1978 **BT** [H] **Funtington Utd** (W 4-1) G Hill 1, J Norman 1, M Pepper 1, M Ruff 1

18-11-1978 **WSLD4C** Replay [A] **Plaistow** (W 6-3) J Norman 2, M Pepper 2, G Lewis 1, C Spain 1

25-11-1978 [H] **Old Collyerians Res** (W 3-1) G Messenger 2, G Lewis 1

2-12-1978 [H] **Barns Green Res** (L 2-3) G Hill 1, L Rout 1

9-12-1978 [A] **Alfold Res** (L 1-4) J Norman 1

16-12-1978 [H] **Fittleworth** (W 3-2) G Messenger 1, J Norman 1, M Ruff 1

30-12-1978 [H] **Alfold Res** (W 2-1) M Pepper 1, D Saunders 1

13-1-1979 **BT** [A] **Wittering & Birdham Utd** (L 0-5)

3-2-1979 **WSLD4C** [H] **Alfold Res** (W 2-1) D Rhoder 1, C Spain 1

10-2-1979 [H] **Plaistow** (L 1-3) J Norman 1

24-2-1979 [A] **Northchapel** (L 2-4) D Saunders 2

10-3-1979 **WSLD4C** [A] **East Dean** (L 0-5)

17-3-1979 [H] **Northchapel** (L 0-1)

31-3-1979 [H] **Ewehurst Res** (D 2-2) J Norman 2

7-4-1979 [A] **Warnham** (W 4-1) D Saunders 3, C Hutton 1

11-4-1979 [A] **Fittleworth** (L 1-2) D Saunders 1

14-4-1979 [A] **Barns Green Res** (L 1-3) C Hutton 1

16-4-1979 [A] **Loxwood Utd** (D 2-2) J Norman 1, T Roberts 1

18-4-1979 [A] **Sunallon 3rds** (W 1-0) S Browning 1

21-4-1979 [A] **Henfield Res** (W 6-1) C Hutton 3, J Norman 1, L Rout 1, G Smith 1

23-4-1979 [A] **Old Collyerians Res** (D 2-2) L Rout 1, OG 1

28-4-1979 [H] **Warnham** (W 3-1) C Hutton 1, J Leadbeatter 1, L Rout 1

5-5-1979 [A] **Ewehurst Res** (W 2-1) G Messenger 1, L Rout 1

P24 | W13 | D4 | L7 | GF56 | GA41 | 30pts | 4th

WSL DIVISION 4 NORTH 1979/80

8-9-1979 [H] **Ockley** (L 1-2) C Hutton 1

15-9-1979 **WSLD4C** [H] **Old Collyerians Res** (W 1-0) D Padwick 1

29-9-1979 [A] **Warnham Res** (W 3-2) D Saunders 2, 1?

6-10-1979 **SJC** [H] **E Preston Res** (L 2-3) J Gallagher 1, C Spain 1

13-10-1979 **BT Milland** (W 2-1) D Saunders 2, AET

20-10-1979 [A] **North Holmwood Res** (L 3-4) G Messenger 1, D Saunders 1, OG 1

3-11-1979 [A] **Old Collyerians Res** (W 3-2) J Gallagher 1, D Saunders 1, D Smith 1

10-11-1979 **WSLD4C** [H] **Lodsworth** (D 2-2) J Gallagher 1, C Spain 1, AET

24-11-1979 [H] **Wisborough Green Res** (L 1-2) D Saunders 1

1-12-1979 [A] **Barns Green Res** (W 4-3) D Saunders 2, J Gallagher 1, L Rout 1

8-12-1979 **BT** [H] **Clymping Res** (L 0-5)

15-12-1979 **WSLD4C** Replay [A] **Lodsworth** (L 0-1)

22-12-1979 [H] **North Holmwood Res** (W 3-0) S Browning 1, G Hill 1, D Saunders 1

19-1-1980 [A] **Ewehurst Res** (W 5-0) D Saunders 2, C Spain 2, J Gallagher 1

26-1-1980 [H] **Loxwood Utd** L 0-2)

2-2-1980 [A] **Wisborough Green Res** (L 2-3) D Smith 2

16-2-1980 [A] **Loxwood Utd** W 4-0) S Browning 1, J Leadbeatter 1, D Smith 1, OG 1

23-2-1980 [H] **Slinfold Res** (L 3-6) S Browning 3

1-3-1980 [A] **Ockley** (D 2-2) C Spain 2

8-3-1980 [H] **Fittleworth** (W 3-0) S Browning 2, D Smith 1

15-3-1980 [A] **Rusper** (W 3-1) S Browning 2, J Leadbeatter 1

22-3-1980 [H] **Rusper** (W 10-0) S Browning 5, D Saunders 3, J Gallagher 1, D Smith 1

29-3-1980 [H] **Old Collyerians Res** (W 6-1) D Saunders 3, C Spain 2, S Browning 1

5-4-1980 [H] **Warnham Res** S Browning 3, J Gallagher 1

7-4-1980 [A] **Fittleworth** (D 2-2) S Browning 1, C Spain 1

10-4-1980 [H] **Barns Green Res** (L 0-1)

12-4-1980 [A] **Slinfold Res** (W 6-1) S Browning 1, J Gallagher 1, D Rhoder 1, L Rout 1, D Saunders 1, D Smith 1

15-4-1980 [H] **Northchapel** (W 4-1) S Browning 1, L Rout 1, D Saunders 1, C Spain 1

19-4-1980 [A] **Ewehurst Res** (W 1-0) D Saunders 1

24-4-1980 [A] **Northchapel** (D 3-3) S Browning 1, J Gallagher 1, M Ruff 1

P24 | W14 | D3 | L7 | GF76 | GA38 | 31pts | 3rd

WSL DIVISION 3, NORTH 1980/81

6-9-1980 [A] **North Holmwood Res** (W 3-1) D Smith 2, S Leadbeatter 1

13-9-1980 [A] **Kirdford Sports** (L 2-6) R Jupp 1, S Leadbeatter 1

20-9-1980 [A] **Wisborough Green Res** (W 5-0) J Gallagher 3, L Rout 1, D Scott 1

27-9-1980 **WSLD3C** [A] **Wisborough Green Res** (L 0-1)

4-10-1980 **SJC Shoreham Utd** (W 4-2) G Edwards 1, J Jupp 1, S Leadbeatter 1, D Scott 1

11-10-1980 [H] **Barns Green Res** (D 0-0)

18-10-1980 [H] **Fernhurst Sports Res** (W 3-0) G Edwards 2, S Leadbeatter 1

25-10-1980 [A] **Horsham Olympic Res** (D 2-2) S Leadbeatter 1, D Richardson 1

1-11-1980 **SJC** [H] **Westdene Wombats** (L 0-1)

8-11-1980 [H] **Amberley** (W 1-0) D Scott 1

15-11-1980 **BT** [A] **Lurgashall** (W 3-1) S Leadbeatter 1, D Scott 1, D Stenning 1

22-11-1980 [H] **Sunallon 3rds** (L 0-4)

29-11-1980 [H] **North Holmwood Res** (W 3-2) J Gallagher 2, G Whittle 1

6-12-1980 [A] **Northchapel** (L 0-9)

13-12-1980 [A] **Rogate** (L 1-5) G Hill 1

27-12-1980 [H] **Wisborough Green Res** (W 8-3) J Gallagher 4, M Osborne 2, S Hayter 1, L Rout 1

3-1-1981 **BT** [H] **Clymping** (L 1-2) G Hill 1

17-1-1981 [H] **Rogate** (L 2-4) R Hewitt 2

24-1-1981 [H] **Horsham Olympic Res** (W 6-1) J Gallagher 3, C Hutton 1, D Scott 1, OG 1

31-1-1981 [A] **Amberley** (W 2-0) J Gallagher 1, S Leadbeatter 1

7-2-1981 [H] **Northchapel** (L 0-1)

21-2-1981 [H] **Kirdford Sports** (L 1-7) S Hayter 1

21-3-1981 [A] **Alfold Res** (W 3-2) S Hayter 1, J Gallagher 1, S Leadbeatter 1

28-3-1981 [A] **Barns Grn Res** (W 4-2) J Gallagher 2, C Hutton 2

4-4-1981 [A] **Alfold Res** (L 2-6) S Hayter 1, C Hutton 1

11-4-1981 [A] **Sunallon 3rds** (D 2-2) L Rout 2

18-4-1981 [A] **Fernhurst Res** (L 1-3) D Saunders 1

P22 | W10 | D4 | L8 | GF51 | GA60 | 24pts | 4th

WSL DIVISION 3, NORTH 1981/82

5-9-1981 [H] **Kirdford Sports** (W 9-4) N Bainbridge 5, J Gallagher 2, G Edwards 1, R Hewitt 1

12-9-1981 [A] **Alfold Res** (W 3-1) R Jupp 1, A Maynard 1, OG 1

19-9-1981 **BT** [A] **East Preston** Youth Club L-1-5) R Jupp 1

26-9-1981 **WSLD3C** [H] **Alfold Res** (W 1-0) S Hayter 1

3-10-1981 **SJC** [A] **Southbourne Sports** (L 2-7) OG 2

10-10-1981 [H] **East End Utd** (L 2-4) S Barber 1, G Messenger 1

17-10-1981 [H] **Rogate** (D 2-2) S Barber 1, S Nicholls 1

24-10-1981 [A] **Capel** (L 0-5)

31-10-1981 [H] **Barns Green Res** (D 1-1) S Gabbitt 1

7-11-1981 [H] **Alfold Res** (L 1-5) R James 1

14-11-1981 [A] **Kirdford Sports** (L 1-4) J Gallagher 1

21-11-1981 [H] **Fernhurst Sports Res** (W 3-1) D Collins 1, J Dunne 1, S Hayter 1

28-11-1981 [A] **Warnham** (L 0-5)

4-12-1981 **WSLD3C** [H] **Warnham** (L 1-3) K Blackburn 1, AET

23-1-1982 [A] **Fernhurst Sports Res** (W 3-2) S Hayter 1, S White 1, OG 1

30-1-1982 [H] **Capel** (L 1-5) D Collins 1

6-2-1982 [A] **East End Utd** (D 2-2) S Hayter 2

13-2-1982 [H] **Wisborough Green Res** (L 0-4)

20-2-1982 [A] **Rusper** (L 0-6)

27-2-1982 [H] **Amberley** (D 0-0)

6-3-1982 [A] **Barns Green Res** (W 2-1) S Hallett 2

20-3-1982 [H] **Warnham** (L 1-6) S Gabbitt 1

27-3-1982 [H] **Rusper** (L 0-6

3-4-1982 [A] **Rogate** (L 0-5)

7-4-1982 [A] **Wisborough Green Res** (L 1-6) S Hayter 1

10-4-1982 [A] **Amberley** (L 0-2)

P22 | W5 | D4 | L13 | GF32 | GA78 | 14pts | 11ᵗʰ

WSL DIVISION 4 CENTRAL 1982/83

4-9-1982 [H] **Lurgashall** (L 2-5) C Hallett 1, B Heasman 1

11-9-1982 **BT** [H] **Angmering** (L 1-8) Tim Hatchard 1

18-9-1982 [H] **Storrington 3rds** (L 4-7) C Hallett 1, Tim Hatchard 1, M Osborne 1, L Rout 1

25-9-1982 | **WSLD4C** [A] **Yapton Res** (W 4-3) M Osborne 3, L Rout 1

2-10-1982 **SJC** [H] **Horsham Baptists** (L 1-5) L Rout 1

9-10-1982 [A] **Lodsworth** (W 3-1) C Hallett 3

16-10-1982 [H] **Petworth Res** (L 2-7) C Hallett 1, D Smith 1

23-10-1982 [A] **Stedham Utd Res** (L 3-9) Tim Hatchard 2, D Smith 1

30-10-1982 [A] **Steyning Old Grammarians** (L 1-3) G Blunden 1

6-11-1982 | **WSLD4C** [A] **Southwater 3rds** (D 1-1) D Smith 1, AET

13-11-1982 [A] **Milland Res** (L 3-4) D Smith 2, OG 1

4-12-1982 | **WSLD4C** Replay [H] **Southwater 3rds** (W 2-0) D Smith 1, OG 1

11-12-1982 | **WSLD4C** [A] **Billingshurst Res** (L 0-4)

18-12-1982 [A] **West Chiltington** (L 1-2) G Messenger 1

3-1-1983 [H] **Fittleworth** (L 2-9) G Blunden 1, G Messenger 1

8-1-1983 [A] **Fittleworth** (L 0-8)

22-1-1983 H **Lodsworth** (L 0-3)

5-2-1983 [H] **Plaistow** (L 2-3) G Blunden 1, G Messenger 1

26-2-1983 [H] **Steyning Old Grams** (L 2-4) L Rout 1, D Scott 1

5-3-1983 [A] **Petworth Res** (L 3-10) G Blunden 1, M Osborne 1, D Scott 1

12-3-1983 [H] **Loxwood Utd** (D 3-3) G Blunden 1, B Heasman 1, L Rout 1

19-3-1983 [A] **Stedham Utd Res** (L 1-4) G Blunden 1

26-3-1983 [A] **Plaistow** (L 0-3)

2-4-1983 [A] **Loxwood Utd** (D 1-1) S Hurst 1

16-4-1983 [H] **W Chiltington** (W 2-0) B Heasman 1, K Wilby 1

23-4-1983 [A] **Storrington 3rds** (L 2-5) G Blunden 1, P Mose 1

30-4-1983 [H] **Milland Res** (W 6-2) D Fry 2, P Scott 1, B Heasman 1, M Spicer 1

P22 | W4 | D2 | L16 | GF41 | GA88 | 10pts | 10ᵗʰ

WSL DIVISION 4 CENTRAL 1983/84

3-9-1983 [H] **Lurgashall** (L 0-5)

10-9-1983 [A] **Loxwood Utd** (L 1-5) G Blunden 1

17-9-1983 **BT** [A] **Chichester 3rds** (L 0-7)

24-9-1983 | **WSLD4C** [A] **West Chiltington** (L 0-2)

1-10-1983 **SJC** [A] **Cowfold** (L 3-4) S Hill 2, M Jupp 1

8-10-1983 [H] **Harting** (L 1-5)

22-10-1983 [A] **Wisborough Green Res** (L 2-4) G Blunden 2

29-10-1983 [H] **Lavant 3rds** (W 7-3) G Blunden 2, P Bird 2, R Streeter 2, R Dawson 1

5-11-1983 [A] **Lodsworth** (L 1-8) R Streeter 1

12-11-1983 [A] **Lurgashall** (L 1-11) P Bird 1

19-11-1983 [A] **West Chiltington** (L 0-2)

26-11-1983 [A] **Stedham Utd Res** (L 1-4) P Goodchild 1

3-12-1983 [A] **Lavant 3rds** (L 3-5) P Bird 1, B Heasman 1, R Streeter 1

10-12-1983 [H] **Steyning Old Grams** (L 3-5) P Bird 1, B Heasman 1, R Streeter 1

17-12-1983 [H] **Milland Res** (D 2-2) S Hill 1, M Jupp 1

31-12-1983 [H] **Wisborough Green Res** (L 0-5)

7-1-1984 [A] **Plaistow** (L 4-6) K Filkens 2, R Dawson 1, R Jupp 1

21-1-1984 [H] **Stedham Utd Res** (L No score found

28-1-1984 [A] **Harting** (L No score found

4-2-1984 [H] **Plaistow** (L No score found

11-2-1984 [A] **Milland Res** (L 2-4) W Cobbett 1, R Streeter 1

18-2-1984 [H] **Lodsworth** (L 2-4)

25-2-1984 [A] **Steyning Old Grams** (L 0-9)

10-3-1984 [H] **West Chiltington** (W 4-2) W Cobbett 2, P Bird 1, R Streeter 1

17-3-1984 [H] **Loxwood Utd** (L 0-5)

P22 | W2 | D1 | L19 | GF37 | GA106 | 5pts | 11ᵗʰ

WSL DIVISION 5 CENTRAL 1984/85

1-9-1984 [H] **Boxgrove Res** (L 0-2)

8-9-1984 **BT** [H] **Chichester** Hospital Res (L 1-5) P Bird 1

29-9-1984 [A] **Lodsworth Res** (L 0-2)

6-10-1984 [H] **Billingshurst 3rds** (D 0-0)

13-10-1984 [H] **West Chiltington Res** (W 6-1) Tim Hatchard 3, P Bird 2, G Messenger 1

20-10-1984 | **WSLD5C** [A] **Petworth 3rds** (L 2-4) P Bird 1, Tim Hatchard 1

27-10-1984 [A] **Amberley Res** (D 1-1) R Jupp 1

10-11-1984 [H] **Lavant 3rds** (W 14-0) Tim Hatchard 7, G Blunden 2, T Blunden 2, R Jupp 2, M Jupp 1

17-11-1984 [H] **Loxwood Utd Res** (W 6-1) Tim Hatchard 3, G Blunden 1, J Jupp 1, R Jupp 1

24-11-1984 [A] **Petworth 3rds** (D 4-4) J Jupp 2, M Cordingley 1, J Geddes 1

1-12-1984 [H] **Loxwood Utd Res** (W 7-1) Tim Hatchard 6, T Blunden 1

8-12-1984 [A] **West Chiltington Res** (W 3-2) Tim Hatchard 2, G Blunden 1

15-12-1984 [H] **Amberley Res** (W 4-2) R Jupp 2, G Blunden 1, D Scott 1

22-12-1984 [A] **Boxgrove Res** (W 2-1) Tim Hatchard 1, R Jupp 1

29-12-1984 [H] **Barns Green Res** (W 3-1) P Goring 1, R Jupp 1, R Streeter 1

6-2-1985 [H] **Graffham Res** (W 7-1) Tim Hatchard 7

13-2-1985 [H] **Petworth 3rds** (W 3-1) T Hatchard 2, G Blunden 1

9-3-1985 [A] **Barns Green Res** (W 2-1) G Blunden 1, R Jupp 1

16-3-1985 [A] **Graffham Res** (D 2-2) T Hatchard 1, R Streeter 1

23-3-1985 [A] **Billingshurst 3rds** (W 10-3) P Bird 3, T Hatchard 3, F Rhoder 3, R Streeter 1

6-4-1985 [H] **Lodsworth Res** (W 5-2) Tim Hatchard 2, P Bird 1, G Blunden 1, F Rhoder 1

The 1984-85 season was a strange one. Up to 8-12-84 the results and goalscorers are correct but I believe at least one or maybe two teams may have dropped out.

P18 | W12 | D4 | L2 | GF65 | GA28 | 28pts | 2ⁿᵈ

WSL DIVISION 4 CENTRAL 1985/86

31-8-1985 [A] **Stedham Res** (D 2-2) P Bird 2

7-9-1985 [A] **East Dean** (L 0-3)

14-9-1985 [A] **Cocking** (W 4-0) G Blunden 2, G Messenger 1, R Streeter 1

28-9-1985 **WSLD4C** [A] New Park (D 3-3) R Jupp 1, D Leadbeatter 1, K Taylor 1

5-10-1985 [A] **Lurgashall** (L 3-4) G Blunden 1, R Jupp 1, K Taylor 1

12-10-1985 [H] **Milland Res** (W 6-2) K Taylor 2, T Blunden 1, J Jupp 1, D Lewis 1, R Streeter 1

19-10-1985 **WSLD4C** Replay [H] New Park (L 0-1)

26-10-1985 [H] **Loxwood Utd Res** (W 4-2) K Taylor 2, G Blunden 1, A Vincent 1

2-11-1985 [H] **Plaistow** (W 4-2) R Streeter 2, T Blunden 1, D Gilby 1

9-11-1985 [H] **Cocking** (W 11-0) G Blunden 3, D Leadbeatter 3, R Streeter 2, K Taylor 2, P Goodchild 1

16-11-1985 **BT** Yapton (L 1-5)

23-11-1985 [H] **East Dean** (D 3-3) R James 1, R Streeter 1, K Taylor 1

30-11-1985 [A] **Lodsworth** (W 5-1) R James 3, D Leadbeatter 1, K Taylor 1

7-12-1985 [H] **Wisborough Green Res** (W 5-1) D Gilby 2, T Blunden 1, R Streeter 1, K Taylor 1

14-12-1985 [A] **Loxwood Utd Res** (D 2-2) R James 1, K Taylor 1

21-12-1985 [H] **Lurgashall** (L 2-4) G Blunden 1, D Gilby 1

11-1-1986 [A] **Wisborough Green Res** (L 2-4) T Blunden 1, M Harrison 1

25-1-1986 [A] **Milland Res** (W 2-0) R Streeter 1, K Taylor 1

8-3-1986 [H] **Stedham Res** (L 1-2) R James 1

22-3-1986 [H] **Lodsworth** (W 3-1) D Lewis 2, G Blunden 1

12-4-1986 [A] **Fernhurst Sports Res** (W 6-3) K Taylor 3, G Blunden 1, D Lewis 1, R Streeter 1

19-4-1986 [H] **Fernhurst Sports Res** (W 1-0) D Lewis 1

P20 | W11 | D3 | L 6 | GF67 | GA38 | 25pts | 3rd

WSL DIVISION 3, CENTRAL 1986/87

6-9-1986 [H] **Billingshurst Res** (L 0-2)

13-9-1986 [A] **Lodsworth** (L 3-4) P Goodchild 1, S Hurst 1, K Taylor 1

20-9-1986 **BT** [H] **Felpham Utd Res** (L 1-2) R Streeter 1

27-9-1986 [A] **Amberley** (L 1-3) K Taylor 1

4-10-1986 **SJC** [A] **Broadwater Saints** (L 0-4)

11-10-1986 **WSLD3C** [A] **Horsham Baptists** (L 1-2) G Blunden 1

18-10-1986 [A] **Rogate** (W 6-4) Tim Hatchard 2, G Blunden 1, P Goodchild 1, S Merriot 1, R Streeter 1

25-10-1986 [H] **Harting** (D 1-1) Tim Hatchard 1

1-11-1986 [H] **West Chiltington Res** (L 0-6)

15-11-1986 [H] **Petworth Res** (L 1-3) Tim Hatchard 1

22-11-1986 [H] **Fittleworth** (W 3-2) P Goodchild 1, Tim Hatchard 1, K Taylor 1

29-11-1986 [H] **Lodsworth** (L 1-7) S Cox 1

6-12-1986 [A] **Lurgashall** (W 2-1) S Cox 1, K Taylor 1

20-12-1986 [H] **Funtington Utd** (D 1-1) F Bushby 1

27-12-1986 [A] **Petworth Res** (W 1-0) F Bushby 1

3-1-1987 [H] **Amberley** (W 1-0) Tim Hatchard 1

31-1-1987 [H] **Graffham** (W 4-1) S Cox 2, G Blunden 1, F Bushby 1

7-2-1987 [A] **Graffham** (W 2-1) S Cox 1, K Taylor 1

14-2-1987 [A] **Rogate** (W 6-0) S Cox 2, K Taylor 2, P Goodchild 1, S Hurst 1

21-2-1987 [A] **Funtington Utd** (L 2-8) G Blunden 1, S Cox 1

28-2-1987 [A] **Harting** (L 0-5)

7-3-1987 [A] **Billingshurst Res** (L 0-2)

14-3-1987 [H] **Lurgashall** (W 2-1)

21-3-1987 [A] **West Chiltington Res** (L 0-1)

28-3-1987 [H] **Fittleworth** (W 4-1) Tim Hatchard 2, 2?

P22 | W10 | D2 | L10 | GF41 | GA53 | 22pts | 4th

WSL DIVISION 3 CENTRAL 1987/88

5-9-1987 [H] **Chichester** City **3rds** (D 1-1)

12-9-1987 [A] **Boxgrove Sports** (D 1-1)

19-9-1987 [A] **Loxwood Utd** (L 0-3)

26-9-1987 [H] **Petworth Res** (D 1-1)

3-10-1987 [A] **Lodsworth** (D 1-1) Tim Hatchard 1

31-10-1987 [H] **Billingshurst Res** (L 0-3)

7-11-1987 **BT** [H] **Aldingbourne** (L 1-2) S Cox 1

14-11-1987 [A] **Rogate** (L 2-4) Ant Leadbeatter 1, G Macari 1

21-11-1987 **WSLD3C** [H] **Loxwood Utd** (L 2-3) Tim Hatchard 1, S Merriot 1

28-11-1987 [A] **Amberley** (L 0-4)

5-12-1987 [H] **Stedham Utd Res** (W 4-2) G Blunden 2, Tim Hatchard 2

12-12-1987 [A] **Petworth Res** (D 1-1) C Staples 1

19-12-1987 [H] **Lodsworth** (L 0-4)

9-1-1988 [A] **Chichester** City **3rds** (L 1-6) Tim Hatchard 1

16-1-1988 [A] **Fittleworth** (L 2-6) G Blunden 1, Tim Hatchard 1

23-1-1988 [H] **Amberley** (L 0-4)

20-2-1988 [H] **Fittleworth** (W 4-2) Tim Hatchard 2, N Bainbridge 1, S Merriot 1

5-3-1988 [A] **Stedham Utd Res** (L 0-3)

19-3-1988 [A] **Billingshurst Res** (W 3-2) S Cox 1, Tim Hatchard 1, S Merriot 1

2-4-1988 [H] **Boxgrove Sports** (L 0-1)

6-4-1988 [H] **Loxwood Utd** (D 4-4) G Blunden 1, M Harrison 1, Tim Hatchard 1, K Taylor 1

P20 | W4 | D6 | L10 | GF25 | GA53 | 14pts | 10th

WSL DIVISION 4 CENTRAL 1988/89

3-9-1988 [A] **Milland Res** (L 3-4) D Lewis 3

10-9-1988 [H] **Lurgashall** (L 0-1)

17-9-1988 **SJC** [H] **Supreme Heating** (W 2-0) G Blunden 1, R Jupp 1

24-9-1988 [A] **Northchapel** (W 2-0) Tim Hatchard 1, F Rhoder 1

1-10-1988 **SJC** [A] **Angmering** (W 3-1) Tim Hatchard 1, R Jupp 1, S Merriot 1

8-10-1988 **BT** [H] **Ford Utd** (L 1-5) R Jupp 1

15-10-1988 **WSLD4C** [A] **Horsham Trinity** (L 1-4) Tim Hatchard 1

29-10-1988 [H] **Harting** (D 2-2) R Jupp 2

5-11-1988 **SJC** [A] **Partridge Green** (L 1-3) Tim Hatchard 1

12-11-1988 [A] **Alfold Res** (W 7-3) Tim Hatchard 4, S Merriot 2, A Dumbrill 1

19-11-1988 [H] **Cocking** (W 4-1) Ant Leadbeatter 2, Tim Hatchard 1, C Hutton 1

26-11-1988 [A] **Shipley Res** (W 2-1) G Blunden 1, C Hutton 1

3-12-1988 [H] **Graffham** (L 1-2)

10-12-1988 [A] **Barns Green Res** (W 7-3) Tim Hatchard 3, G Phur 2, C Hutton 1, S Merriot 1

17-12-1988 [H] **Billingshurst Res** (L 1-2) G Phur 1

31-12-1988 [A] **Cocking** (W 4-1) Tim Hatchard 1, Ant Leadbeatter 1, A Petras 1, G Phur 1

7-1-1989 [A] **Lurgashall** (L 1-4) Tim Hatchard 1

14-1-1989 [H] **Milland Res** (W 7-2) Tim Hatchard 3, Ant Leadbeatter 2, G Blunden 1, S Merriot 1

28-1-1989 [H] **Alfold Res** W 7-0) Tim Hatchard 4, S Merriot 2, Ant Leadbeatter 1

11-2-1989 [H] **Steyning Old Grams Rs** (W 2-1) G Blunden 2

4-3-1989 [A] **Graffham** (W 4-2) K Taylor 2, P Wilson 2

11-3-1989 [H] **Northchapel** (W 12-0) Tim Hatchard 6, P Wilson 3, G Blunden 1, Ant Leadbeatter 1, K Taylor 1

18-3-1989 [A] **Harting** (W 2-0) G Blunden 1, J Jupp 1

25-3-1989 [H] **Barns Green Res** (D 1-1) P Wilson 1

1-4-1989 [A] **Billingshurst Res** (W 4-2) T Hatchard 2, J Fletcher 1

8-4-1989 [H] **Shipley Res** (W 7-1) Tim Hatchard 4, C Hutton 2, P Wilson 1

17-4-1989 [A] **Steyning Old Grams Rs** (W 2-1) Tim Hatchard 1, P Wilson 1

P22 | W15 | D2 | L5 | GF83 | GA35 | 32pts | 2nd

WSL DIVISION 3, CENTRAL 1989-1990

9-9-1989 [A] **Liss Athletic Res** (L 0-2)

16-9-1989 BT [A] **Elmer Beach** (W 3-1) G Blunden 2, F Rhoder 1

23-9-1989 [A] **Stedham Utd Res** (W 3-1) S Whitehead 2, R Streeter 1

14-10-1989 WSLD3C [A] **Roffey Res** (W 4-3) G Blunden 2, C Merriot 1

21-10-1989 [H] **Boxgrove** (W 3-2) C Adsett 1G Blunden 1, C Merriot 1

28-10-1989 WSLD3C [H] **Horsham Olympic Res** (L 1-4) G Blunden 1

4-11-1989 [A] **Stedham Utd Res** (L 0-3)

11-11-1989 BT [A] **Oving Social Club Res** (L 1-2) S Whitehead 1

18-11-1989 [H] **Fernhurst Sports** (D 2-2) A Dumbrill 1, K Taylor 1

25-11-1989 [A] **West Chiltington Res** (W 3-0) Tim Hatchard 2, M Osborne 1

2-12-1989 [A] **Petworth Res** (W 4-2) K Taylor 3, Tim Hatchard 1

9-12-1989 [A] **Ashington** Rovers ,W 4-3) R Streeter 2, Tim Hatchard 1, G Phur 1

16-12-1989 [H] **Ashington** Rovers (W 3-2) Tim Hatchard 2, S Whitehead 1

30-12-1989 [H] **Stedham Utd** Rs (D 2-2) Tim Hatchard 1, K Knaggs 1

6-1-1990 [H] **West Chiltington Res** (W 8-2) Tim Hatchard 3, R Streeter 3, J Jupp 1, 1?

13-1-1990 [A] **Boxgrove** (W 5-1) Tim Hatchard 3, J Jupp 1, Ant Leadbeatter 1

20-1-1990 [H] **East Dean** (W 7-0) G Blunden 3, K Taylor 3, Tim Hatchard 1

27-1-1990 [A] **Lurgashall** (L 1-2) R Streeter 1

24-2-1990 [A] **Milland Res** (D 1-1) G Blunden 1

3-3-1990 [H] **Lodsworth** (W 2-1) G Blunden 2

10-3-1990 [A] **Lodsworth** (L 0-3)

17-3-1990 [H] **Liss Athletic Res** (L 2-3) G Blunden 1, C Merriot 1

24-3-1990 [A] **Fernhurst Sports** (L 0-2)

31-3-1990 [H] **Petworth** R (W 3-2) S Cox 1, C Merriot 1, G Phur 1

7-4-1990 [H] **Lurgashall** L 0-1)

30-4-1990 [H] **Milland Res** (L 0-2)

P22 | W11 | D3 | L8 | GF53 | GA36 25pts | 4th

WSL DIVISION 3, CENTRAL 1990/91

1-9-1990 [H] **Liss Athletic Res** (W 4-1) S Whitehead 2, C Hutton 1, Ant Leadbeatter 1

8-9-1990 [A] **Lodsworth** (D 1-1) C Hutton 1

15-9-1990 BT [A] **Angmering** (L 0-4)

22-9-1990 SJC [A] **Plaistow & Kirdford** (W 4-2) Tim Hatchard 1, R Jupp 1, C Merriot 1, OG 1

29-9-1990 | WSLD3C [A] **Ashington** Rovers (W 2-0) Tim Hatchard 1, S Whitehead 1

6-10-1990 SJC [H] **Haywards Heath Utd Services** (L 4-5) Tim Hatchard 3, N Zalesny 1

13-10-1990 [H] **Fernhurst Sports** (D 0-0)

20-10-1990 [H] **Fittleworth** (L 2-5) J Jupp 1, A McGill 1

27-10-1990 [H] **Harting** (W 6-4) S Whitehead 2, G Blunden 1, S Cox 1, J Jupp 1, R Streeter 1

3-11-1990 [H] **Petworth** R (L 2-7) R Streeter 1, S Whitehead 1

10-11-1990 [H] **East Dean** (L 1-3) N Monahan 1

17-11-1990 [A] **Fernhurst Sports** (L 2-4) S Cox 1, J Fletcher 1

24-11-1990 [H] **Lodsworth** (L 2-5) J Jupp 1, S Whitehead 1

1-12-1990 [A] **Steyning Old Grammarians Res** (L 0-7)

8-12-1990 [H] **Ashington** Rovers (L 0-6)

15-12-1990 [A] **Northchapel** (D 6-6) Ant Leadbeatter 2, R Streeter 2, I Dumbrill 1, N Spicer 1

22-12-1990 [A] **East Dean** (W 5-1) Tim Hatchard 2, N Monahan 2, Ant Leadbeatter 1

19-1-1991 [A] **Liss Athletic** Rs (L 3-4) Tim Hatchard 2, S Whitehead 1

26-1-1991 [A] **Fittleworth** (L 2-5) Tim Hatchard 2

2-2-1991 WSLD3C [H] **Fittleworth** (W 3-2) Tim Hatchard 2, G Blunden 1

16-2-1991 [H] **Steyning Old Grammarians Res** (D 1-1)

23-2-1991 [A] **Petworth Res** (D 0-0)

2-3-1991 [H] **Stedham Utd Res** (L 2-3) Ant Leadbeatter 1, C Merriot 1

9-3-1991 [A] **Ashington** Rovers (W 3-2) Tim Hatchard 1, D Rhoder 1, N Zalesny 1

16-3-1991 [H] **Northchapel** (L 3-7) Tim Hatchard 3

23-3-1991 [A] **Stedham Utd Res** (L 1-2) S Whitehead 1

30-3-1991 [A] **Harting** (W 6-1) T Hatchard 4, G Blunden 1, OG 1

6-4-1991 WSLD3C [H] **Sidlesham** R (L 3-4) Streeter 2, Zalesny 1

P22 | W5 | D5 | L12 | GF52 | GA76 | 15pts | 9th

WSL DIVISION 3, CENTRAL 1991/92

7-9-1991 [H] **Graffham** (W 4-1) Phur 2, Dumbrill 1, Hutton 1

21-9-1991 SJC [A] **Aldingbourne** (W 4-0) C Hutton 2, I Dumbrill 1, J Fletcher 1

28-9-1991 WSLD3C [H] **Bognor Motors** (L 2-3) J Fletcher 1, N Monahan 1

5-10-1991 SJC [A] **Brighton Electric** (L 0-1)

12-10-1991 BT [A] **Manor Athletic** (L 1-2) C Hutton 1

26-10-1991 [H] **Liss Athletic Res** (L 0-9)

2-11-1991 [A] **East Dean** (D 0-0)

9-11-1991 [H] **Milland Res** (L 1-2) A McGill 1

23-11-1991 [A] **Stedham Utd Res** (L 0-1)

30-11-1991 [H] **Watersfield** (W 3-0) N Baker 1, C Hutton 1, S Whitehead 1

7-12-1991 [H] **Fittleworth** (L 1-6) OG 1

28-12-1991 [H] **Ashington** Rovers (L 1-3) A McGill 1

4-1-1992 [H] **Lodsworth** (L 2-3) A McGill 2

11-1-1992 [A] **Billingshurst Res** (L 1-2) S Cox 1

18-1-1992 [A] **Watersfield** (W 1-0) S Cox 1

1-2-1992 [A] **Lodsworth** (D 0-0)

8-2-1992 [H] **Stedham Res** (L 2-4) D King 1, A Petras 1

15-2-1992 [H] **East Dean** (D 2-2) Tim Hatchard 1, S Whitehead 1

22-2-1992 [A] **Milland Res** (L 0-1)

29-2-1992 [A] **Fittleworth** (L 2-5) S Cox 2

7-3-1992 [A] **Graffham** (W 3-2) S Cox 1, M Wroe 1, OG 1

14-3-1992 [A] **Liss Athletic Res** (L 3-6) I Dumbrill 1, J Fletcher 1, Tim Hatchard 1

21-3-1992 [A] **Wisborough Green** (L 1-8) D King 1

28-3-1992 [H] **Billingshurst Res** (W 9-0) S Cox 3, Tim Hatchard 2, Ant Leadbeatter 2, J Fletcher 1, N Spicer 1

4-4-1992 [H] **Wisborough Green** (L 0-1)

11-4-1992 [A] **Ashington** Rovers (L 2-7) T Hatchard 1, N Spicer 1

P22 | W5 | D3 | L14 | GF38 | GA63 | 13pts | 10th

WSL DIVISION 3, CENTRAL 1992/93

12-9-1992 [H] **Lodsworth** (L 2-5) Tim Hatchard 1, C Merriot 1

26-9-1992 BT [H] **Liss Athletic Res** (L 1-6) R Streeter 1

3-10-1992 [H] **Shipley Res** (D 3-3) A McGill 3

10-10-1992 | WSLD3C [H] **Oving Social Club Res** (W 1-0) R Streeter 1

17-10-1992 [A] **Liss Athletic Res** (L 1-4) M Peacock 1

24-10-1992 [H] **Watersfield** (W 2-1) J Fletcher 1, M Jupp 1

1-10-1992 [A] **Lodsworth** (W 2-1) A McGill 1, N Monahan 1

14-11-1992 | WSLD3C [H] **Cranleigh** (L 3-4) G Blunden 1, N Monahan 1, D Streeter 1

5-12-1992 [H] **Liss Athletic Res** (L 1-2) C Hutton 1

2-12-1992 [A] **Watersfield** (L 1-2) R Jupp 1

2-1-1993 [A] **Fittleworth** (L 0-7)

16-1-1993 [H] **Stedham Utd Res** (W 3-2) N Monahan 2, G Blunden 1

6-2-1993 [A] **Northchapel** (L 2-6) N Monahan 2

13-2-1993 [A] **Milland Res** (L 1-4) G Blunden 1

20-2-1993 [H] **Northchapel** (L 1-4) C Hutton 1

27-2-1993 [A] **East Dean** (L 1-8) N Monahan 1

5-3-1993 [H] **Fittleworth** (W 2-0) S Cox 1, A McGill 1

13-3-1993 [A] **Stedham Utd Res** (L 0-7)

20-3-1993 [H] **Milland Res** (L 0-2)

27-3-1993 [H] **East Dean** (L 1-4) Ant Leadbeatter 1

3-4-1993 [H] **Barns Green Res** (L 2-3) G Blunden 1, J Fletcher 1

10-4-1993 [A] **Shipley Res** [A] D 0-0)

24-4-1993 [A] **Barns Green Res** N Spicer 1

P20 | W4 | D2 | L14 | GF26 | GA68 | 10pts | 10th

WSL DIVISION 4 CENTRAL 1993/94

4-9-1993 [A] **Plaistow** [H] **Lodsworth Res** (W 5-1) P Whatford 2, D Downes 1, D Peacock 1, M Peacock 1

11-9-1993 [H] **Fernhurst Sports Res** (W 5-2) A McGill 2, R Jupp 1, S Leadbeatter 1, P Whatford

1 18-9-1993 [H] **Fittleworth Res** (L 1-5) A McGill 1

2-10-1993 [H] **Lodsworth Res** (D 2-2) G Blunden 1, A McGill 1

16-10-1993 [H] **Loxwood** (D 0-0)

23-10-1993 [A] **Upper Beeding** (L 2-5) D Downes 1, A McGill 1

30-10-1993 [H] **Billingshurst Res** (D 2-2) G Blunden 2

6-11-1993 | WSLD4C [A] **Plaistow** (W 4-1) N Monahan 2, D Peacock 1, A Staples 1

13-11-1993 [H] **Watersfield Res** (L 2-3) G Blunden 2

27-11-1993 [A] **Lodsworth Res** (W 2-1) N Monahan 2

4-12-1993 [H] **Plaistow** (W 6-1) A McGill 3, G Blunden 1, N Monahan 1, D Peacock 1

11-12-1993 [H] **Graffham** (W 3-1) G Blunden 2, N Monahan 1

18-12-1993 [A] **Fittleworth Res** (L 3-6) D Angell 1, G Blunden 1, D Smith 1

15-1-1994 [H] **Rudgwick Res** (L 0-1)

22-1-1994 [H] **Upper Beeding** (W 2-1) Tim Hatchard 1, OG 1

29-1-1994 [A] **Fernhurst Sports Res** (D 5-5) D Peacock 2, D Angell 1, M Croft 1, A McGill 1

12-2-1994 [A] **Watersfield Res** (W 5-1) Downes 1, Hutton 1, 3?

19-2-1994 [A] **Graffham** (L 0-3)

5-3-1994 [H] **West Chiltington Res** (L 0-3)

12-3-1994 | WSLD4C [A] **Billingshurst Res** (W 3-2) N Monahan 1, D Peacock 1, P Whatford 1

19-3-1994 [A] **Loxwood** (L 0-4)

26-3-1994 [A] **W Chiltington Res** (L 2-10) C Adsett 1, D Angell 1

2-4-1994 | WSLD4C [A] **Henfield Res** (L 1-4) D Peacock 1, AET

4-4-1994 [A] **Billingshurst Res** (D 1-1) D Downes 1

16-4-1994 [A] **Rudgwick Res** (L 0-3)

P22 | W7 | D5 | L10 | GF48 | GA61 | 19pts | 8th

WSL DIVISION 4 CENTRAL 1994/95

3-9-1994 [H] **Broadbridge Heath 3rds** (W 4-1)

10-9-1994 [H] **Stedham Utd Res** (W 3-2)

17-9-1994 [H] **Rudgwick Res** (W 2-1)

24-9-1994 [H] **Lodsworth Res** (L 1-3)

31-9-1994 [A] **Alfold Res** (D 2-2)

8-10-1994 [H] **Loxwood** (W 5-1,

15-10-1994 [A] **Billingshurst Res** (W 4-1) D Angell 1, J Bailey 1, G Blunden 1, J Fletcher 1

22-10-1994 [H] **Rogate Res** (D 0-0)

29-10-1994 [A] **Shipley Res** (D 3-3) G Blunden 2, S Cox 1

5-11-1994 [H] **Billingshurst Res** (W 3-1) J Bailey 1, J Fletcher 1, A Henderson 1

12-11-1994 | WSLD4C [A] **Broadbridge Heath 3rds** (L 2-9) G Blunden 2

19-11-1994 [H] **Fittleworth Res** (W 4-2) G Blunden 3, J Bailey 1

3-12-1994 [A] **Stedham Utd Res** (L 0-1)

17-12-1994 [H] **Cocking** (D 0-0)

31-12-1994 [A] **Rogate Res** (W 2-0) D Angell 1, J Bailey 1

7-1-1995 [A] **Rudgwick Res** R 5-0) G Blunden 2, D Angell 1, G Messenger 1, M Osborne 1

14-1-1995 [A] **Fittleworth Res** (L 0-2)

4-3-1995 [A] **Loxwood** (W 2-1) J Bailey 1, G Messenger 1

11-3-1995 [H] **Lurgashall** (W 5-1) D Angell 2, J Bailey 1, G Blunden 1, Knight 1

18-3-1995 [A] **Cocking** (L 2-3) G Blunden 2

25-3-1995 [A] **Lurgashall** (W 3-1) N Zalesny 2, D Angell 1

1-4-1995 [H] **Shipley Res** (W 5-1) J Bailey 3, A Henderson 2

8-4-1995 [A] **Broadbridge Heath 3rds** (L 0-4)

22-4-1995 [H] **Alfold Res** (W 4-0)

P24 | W14 | D5 | L5 | GF61 | GA33 33pts | 2nd

WSL DIVISION 3, SOUTH 1995/96

2-9-1995 [H] **Bilsham Utd** (L 1-3) ,

9-9-1995 [A] **Hunston Utd** (L 1-4) G Messenger 1

16-9-1995 [A] **Angmering Res** (L 1-4)

23-9-1995 [H] **Lancing Utd Res** (W 3-2) G Blunden 1, K Furlonger 1, K Taylor 1

30-9-1995 [H] **Rustington Res** (W 6-1) D Reilly 2, G Blunden 1, P Maynard 1, A McGill 1

7-10-1995 [A] **Ferring Res** (L 3-4) G Blunden 2, C Phillips 1

14-10-1995 WSLD3C [A] **Lancing** UnitedRes (L 2-5) C Phillips 1, N Zalesny 1

21-10-1995 [H] **Chichester** Hospital Res (L 0-3)

28-10-1995 [A] **Lavant** (L 1-5) C Jupp 1

4-11-1995 [H] **Angmering Res** (L 3-5) Tim Hatchard 2, D Smith 1

18-11-1995 [H] **East Preston 3rds** (L 1-3) K Furlonger 1

25-11-1995 [A] **Slindon** (L 1-7)

9-12-1995 [H] **Hunston Utd** (L 1-3) G Messenger 1

6-1-1996 [H] **Ferring Res** (L 1-2) OG 1

13-1-1996 [A] **Lancing Utd Res** (L 0-2)

20-1-1996 [H] **Lavant** (W 2-1) G Blunden 1, R Jupp 1

2-2-1996 [A] **Bilsham Utd** (W 4-0) G Blunden 1, S Cox 1, A Henderson 1, R Streeter 1

9-2-1996 [A] **East Preston 3rds** (L 0-2)

23-2-1996 [A] **Chichester** Hospital Res (W 3-2) R Streeter 2, A Green 1

2-3-1996 [A] **Eastergate Utd** (L 3-4) D Angell 2, C Phillips 1

9-3-1996 [H] **Eastergate** (L 0-4)

16-3-1996 [A] **Rustington Res** (L 0-4)

30-3-1996 [H] **Slindon** (L 1-5)

P22 | W5 | D0 | L17 | GF36 | GA70 | 15pts | 9th

WSL DIVISION 3, NORTH 1996/97

7-9-1996 [H] **Faygate Utd** (L 2-5)

14-9-1996 [A] **Friends Provident** (W 6-1) P Benham 2, G Blunden 2 M Ralph 1, M Wardell 1

21-9-1996 **BT** [H] **Milland** (W 7-2) P Benham 3, G Blunden 1, R Jupp 1, G Messenger 1, M Ralph 1

28-9-1996 [A] **Ockley** (L 0-5)

5-10-1996 [H] **Southwater Res** (L 0-2)

12-10-1996 WSLD3C [A] **Chichester** Hospital **Res** (L 0-7)

19-10-1996 **BT** [H] **Stedham Utd Res** (L 1-4)

9-11-1996 [A] **Capel** (L 0-4)

16-11-1996 [H] **Sun Alliance 3rds** (L 0-2)

23-11-1996 [A] **Southwater Res** (L 2-3) S Cox 1, P Maynard 1

30-11-1996 [H] **Lower Beeding** (W 1-0) M Ralph 1

7-12-1996 [H] **Horsham Trinity** (D 3-3) D Angell 1, P Benham 1, N Ralph 1

14-12-1996 [H] **Newdigate** (L 2-4) D Angell 1, N Ralph 1

24-1-1997 [A] **Faygate Utd** (D 2-2)

31-1-1997 [A] **Newdigate** (D 3-3) J Bailey 2, M Wardell 1

7-2-1997 [H] **Friends Provident** (L 3-4) N Ralph 1, D Smith 1, L Wadey 1

14-2-1997 [A] **Lower Beeding** (L 1-5)

21-2-1997 [H] **Capel** (L 3-4) J Bailey 2, S York 1

1-3-1997 [H] **Ockley** (L 0-1)

Horsham Trinity & Sun Alliance scores missing but both were lost

P18 | W2 | D3 | L13 | GF32 | GA55 | 9pts | 9th

WSL DIVISION 4 SOUTH 1997/98

13-9-1997 [A] **Oving Social Club Res** (D 2-2)

20-9-1997 [A] **Watersfield Res** (W 7-1) A Pavey 3, S Adsett 1, Si Leadbeatter 1, S Whitehead 1, S York 1

27-9-1997 WSLD4C [H] **Walberton** Village (W 4-1) A Pavey 2, M Ralph 1, M Wardell 1

4-10-1997 **BT** [A] **Petworth Res** (D 1-1) M Wardell 1

11-10-1997 [H] **Boxgrove** (L 1-5) D Angell 1

18-10-1997 [A] **Rustington Res** (D 3-3) A Pavey 1, R Jupp 1, S Whitehead 1

25-10-1997 [H] **Angmering Res** (L 2-4)

1-11-1997 [A] **Walberton** Village (D 4-4) A Pavey 2, D Clegg 1, S York 1

8-11-1997 [H] **Emsworth Res** (L 1-3) S Adsett 1

15-11-1997 **BT** Replay [H] **Petworth Res** (L 3-5) D Clegg 1, M Ralph 1, S Whitehead 1

29-11-1997 [A] **Boxgrove** (L 0-4)

6-12-1997 [H] **Broadwater Saints** (L 2-3) T Hutchings 1, 1?

24-1-1998 [A] **Amberley** (L 0-1)

31-1-1998 [H] **Oving Social Club Res** (L 1-2)

7-2-1998 WSLD4C [H] **Lurgashall** (W 4-2) N Ralph 2, S Adsett 1, D Angell 1

14-2-1998 [A] **Angmering Res** (L 1-3)

21-2-1998 [A] **Emsworth Res** (L 1-4)

7-3-1998 [H] **Rustington Res** (W 4-0) N Ralph 2, S Whitehead 2

14-3-1998 WSLD4C Semi-Final [H] **North Holmwood** (D 2-2) N Ralph 2

28-3-1998 [H] **Amberley** (W 2-0) A Pavey 2

11-4-1998 [A] **Broadwater Saints** (W 3-2)

15-4-1998 [H] **Watersfield Res** (W 2-1) A Pavey 1

Walberton score not found but Pulborough won

In the semi-final we played an ineligible player, so no replay

P18 | W6 | D3 | L9 | GF36 | GA47 | 21pts | 7th

WSL DIVISION 4 SOUTH 1998/99

12-9-1998 [A] **Oving Social Club 3rds** (L 2-5) Blunden 1, Smillie 1

26-9-1998 [A] **Rustington 3rds** (L 1-3)

3-10-1998 [H] **East Dean** (L 0-4)

10-10-1998 WSLD4C [H] **Newdigate** (L 1-3)

17-10-1998 [H] **Clymping Res** (L 3-8)

24-10-1998 [A] **Amberley** (W 3-1)

7-11-1998 [A] **GCRI** (L 2-5)

21-11-1998 [H] **Broadwater Saints** (L 2-8)

28-11-1998 [H] **Oving Social Club 3rds** (L 1-5)

12-12-1998 [A] **Clymping Res** 1, 4-7)

9-1-1999 [H] **Rustington 3rds** (L 1-5)

16-1-1999 [A] **Broadwater Saints** (L 3-7)

30-1-1999 [A] **Ferring Res** (L 2-3)

20-2-1999 [A] **East Dean** (L 1-4)

6-3-1999 [H] **Amberley** (L 1-7)

27-3-1999 [A] **Ambassadors** (L 1-8)

3-4-1999 [H] **GCRI** (L 3-8) 12-4-1999 [H] **Ambassadors** (D 0-0)

16-4-1999 [H] **Ferring Res** (L 2-4)

P18 | W1 | D1 | L16 | GF32 | GA92 | 4pts | 10th

WSL DIVISION 4 SOUTH 1999/2000

4-9-1999 [H] **Yapton Res** (L 1-6)

11-9-1999 [A] **Chichester** Hospital **Res** (L 0-6)

18-9-1999 [H] **Newtown Villa Res** (L 2-6)

25-9-1999 **BT** [H] **Slindon** (W 2-0)

2-10-1999 WSLD4C [A] **Ockley** (W 2-1)

9-10-1999 [A] **The Lamb** (L 3-8)

16-10-1999 [H] **Ferring Res** (L 0-3)

23-10-1999 [A] **GCRI** (L 0-2) 30-10-1999 [H] **Lancing Utd** (L 1-2)

6-11-1999 **BT** [A] **Boxgrove** (W 3-1)

20-11-1999 WSLD4C [H] **Southwater Res** (W 3-1)

4-12-1999 **BT** [A] **Oving Social Club Res** (L 0-3)

11-12-1999 [A] **Amberley** (L 1-2)

18-12-1999 [A] **Ambassadors** (L 1-4)

8-1-2000 [H] **GCRI** (L 1-5)

15-1-2000 WSLD4C [A] **G C R I** (L 1-4)

22-1-2000 [H] **Storrington 3rds** (W 3-2)

29-1-2000 [A] **Ferring Res** (L 0-9)

5-2-2000 [H] **The Lamb** (W 3-2)

12-2-2000 [A] **Lancing Utd** (L 0-1)

26-2-2000 [H] **Ambassadors** (L 1-7)

12-3-2000 [H] **Amberley** (L 3-6)

19-3-2000 [A] **Newtown Villa Res** (D 1-1)

26-3-2000 [H] **Storrington 3rds** (W 3-0)

2-4-2000 [A] **Yapton Res** (L 2-5)

9-4-2000 [H] **Chichester** Hospital **Res** (D 2-2)

P20 | W3 | D2 | L15 | GF28 | GA79 | 11pts | 10th

WSL DIVISION 5 SOUTH 2000/01

2-9-2000 [A] **Red Star Rife** (W 2-1) C Jupp 1, S Whitehead 1

9-9-2000 [H] **Lavant** (L 0-4)

23-9-2000 [H] **Ambassadors Res** (L 0-4)

30-9-2000 [H] **Wittering Res** (L 2-3) S Jupp 1, Si Leadbeatter 1

7-10-2000 | WSLD5C [H] **Henfield 3rds** (L 2-3) A Pavey 2

14-10-2000 [A] **Cocking** (L 2-4) A Pavey 1, S Whitehead 1

21-10-2000 [A] **Newtown Villa 3rds** (L 2-10)

28-10-2000 [H] **Storrington 3rds** (W 2-1) S Jupp 2

18-11-2000 [H] **Boxgrove Res** (W 5-4) P Greenfield 1, S Jupp 1, A Parker 1, A Pavey 1

13-1-2001 [A] **Wittering Res** (L 2-9) A Pavey 2

27-1-2001 [H] **Newtown Villa 3rds** (L 1-7)

3-2-2001 [H] **Cocking** (L 5-6) J Bailey 2, C Jupp 2, S Jupp 1

24-2-2001 [A] **Storrington 3rds** (L 1-4) S Jupp 1

3-3-2001 [H] **Red Star Rife** (D 0-0)

10-3-2001 [A] **Graffham Res** (D 3-3)

17-3-2001 [H] **Fittleworth Res** (W 2-1) L Blunden 1, S Dancey 1

7-4-2001 [H] **Graffham Res** (L 0-8)

18-4-2001 [A] **Watersfield Res** (D 1-1)

21-4-2001 [A] **Fittleworth Res** (L 0-1)

The paper seems to have got some results wrong

P18 | W3 | D3 | L12 | GF28 | GA72 | 9pts | 11ᵗʰ

WSL DIVISION 5 SOUTH 2001/02

8-9-tool [H] **Clymping Res** (L 2-7)

22-9-2001 [A] **Amberley** (L 2-5) R Symonds 2

29-9-2001 [A] **Predators Res** (L 0-10

6-10-2001 [A] **Graffham Res** (D 1-1) R Symonds 1

13-10-2001 WSLD5C [H] **Lodsworth** (L 2-4) R Symonds 2

20-10-2001 [H] **Chichester** Hospital **3rds** (D 3-3)

27-10-2001 [A] **Ambassadors Res** (W 3-2) Rothwell 2, C Jupp 1

3-11-2001 [H] **Fittleworth Res** (L 1-4)

10-11-2001 WSLD5C Reinstated [A] **Horsham Baptists Res** (W 5-4) P Greenfield 2, R Symonds 2, G Rothwell 1

24-11-2001 [A] **Clymping Res** (L 0-3)

31-11-2001 [A] **Chichester** Hospital **3rds** (L 2-3) S Phillips 1, R Symonds 1

7-12-2001 [H] **Ambassadors Res** (W 4-1) Rothwell 3, C Jupp 1

14-12-2001 [H] **Storrington 3rds** (W 4-3) P Devlin 1, A Parker 1, N Ralph 1, R Symonds 1

2-2-2002 | WSLD5C [H] **Henfield 3rds** (L 1-4)

9-2-2002 [H] **Amberley** (D 3-3) C Jupp 2, S Dancey 1

16-2-2002 [A] **Storrington 3rds** (L 3-5)

9-3-2002 [H] **Graffham Res** (L 1-2) A Parker 1

30-3-2002 [A] **Fittleworth Res** (D 1-1)

P16 | W4 | D4 | L8 | GF31 | GA52 | 16pts | 8ᵗʰ

WSL DIVISION 5 SOUTH 2002/03

7-9-2002 [H] **Coal Exchange** (L 0-4)

14-9-2002 [H] **Petworth 3rds** (D 4-4) S Jupp 2, P Devlin 1, A Parker 1

21-9-2002 [A] **Coal Exchange** (L 2-4) R Davies 1, D Richards 1

28-9-2002 | WSLD5C [H] **Amberley** (L 0-1)

5-10-2002 [A] **Ashington** Rovers **Res** (L 2-5) G Rothwell 2

12-10-2002 [H] **Ambassadors Res** (L 2-4) K Shakelton 1, G Rothwell 1

19-10-2002 [A] **W Chiltington** R (D 2-2) A Parker 1, G Rothwell 1

26-10-2002 [A] **Amberley** (W 6-1) G Rothwell 4, P Devlin 1, D Richards 1

9-11-2002 [A] **Ambassadors Res** (L 0-3)

16-11-2002 [A] **Petworth 3rds** (W 3-1) C Jupp 2, S Jupp 1

7-12-2002 [H] **Rose Green** (W 2-0) C Jupp 1, P Roberts 1

14-12-2002 [H] **West Chiltington Res** (W 7-1) G Rothwell 4, C Jupp 1, S Jupp 1, Si Leadbeatter 1

28-12-2002 [A] **Fittleworth Res** (L 2-6) G Rothwell 1, OG 1

11-1-2003 [A] **Rose Green** (W 1-0) S Underwood 1

25-1-2003 [H] **Fittleworth Res** (W 2-0) C Jupp 1, K Shacketon 1

8-2-2003 [H] **Amberley** (D 0-0)

22-2-2003 [A] **Ashington** Rovers **Res** (W 4-1) M Ives 2, A Greenfield 1, C Jupp 1

P16 | W7 | D3 | L6 | GF39 | GA36 | 24pts | 5ᵗʰ

WSL DIVISION 4 SOUTH 2003/04

6-9-2003 [A] **Lodsworth** (L 3-7) C Jupp 2, Ab Greenfield 1

27-9-2003 | WSLD4C [H] **Amberley** (W 3-0) C Jupp 2, Rothwell 1

4-10-2003 [H] **Graffham Res** (W 5-4) Ab Greenfield 3, S Lamport 1, G Rothwell 1

11-10-2003 BT [A] **Predators** (L 1-8) G Rothwell 1

18-10-2003 [A] **Ambassadors Res** (W 3-1) S Lamport 3

25-10-2003 [A] **Newtown Villa Res** (W 1-0) K Shackelton 1

1-11-2003 [A] **Amberley** (W 1-0) G Rothwell 1

8-11-2003 | WSLD4C [H] **Coal Exchange** (W 5-1) G Rothwell 4, Si Leadbeatter 1

15-11-2003 [H] **Amberley** (W 3-0) G Rothwell 3, OG 1

29-11-2003 [H] **Fernhurst Res** (W 7-0) R Davies 2, Si Leadbeatter 2, Ab Greenfield 1, P Roberts 1, G Rothwell 1

6-12-2003 [A] **A&B Rovers R** (D 2-2) Ab Greenfield 1, Rothwell 1

17-1-2004 [H] **Newtown Villa Res** (W 5-3) Ab Greenfield 2, G Rothwell 2, R Davies 1

24-1-2004 [A] **Lodsworth** (L 2-6) P Roberts 1, K Shackelton 1

7-2-2004 WSLD4C [A] **Wisborough Green Res** (W 4-2) Ab Greenfield 1, C Jupp 1, P Roberts 1, G Rothwell 1

14-2-2004 [A] **Fernhurst Res** (W 3-1) G Rothwell 2, OG 1

28-2-2004 [H] **Graffham Res** Received points

6-3-2004 [H] **Coal Exchange** (D 0-0)

13-3-2004 [A] **A&B Rovers R** (W 5-0) G Rothwell 4, Shackelton 1

27-3-2004 [A] **Coal Exchange** (D 2-2) S Lamport 1, G Rothwell 1

3-4-2004 | WSLD4C Semi-Final [A] **Dorking Wanderers Res** (L 0-3)

16-4-2004 [A] **Ambassadors Res** (W 4-3) S Lamport 2, R Davies 1, G Rothwell 1

P16 | W11 | D3 | L2 | GF46 | GA29 | 36pts | 1ˢᵗ

WSL DIVISION 3, SOUTH 2004/05

4-9-2004 [A] **Chichester** Hospital **3rds** (L 0-7)

11-9-2004 [H] **Rustington Res** (L 2-4) K Shackelton 2

18-9-2004 SJC [A] **Harbour View** (L 1-4) Si Leadbeatter 1

25-9-2004 | WSLD3C [H] **Lancing Utd Res** (L No score

2-10-2004 [A] **Ambassadors** (L 0-3)

9-10-2004 BT [A] **Angmering Res** (L 0-3)

16-10-2004 [A] **Yapton Res** (L 0-4)

6-11-2004 [A] **Fernhurst** (W 2-1)

13-11-2004 [H] **Lodsworth** (D 1-1)

11-12-2004 [H] **Chichester** Hospital **3rds** (L 0-3)

15-1-2005 [H] **Yapton Res** (L 2-3)

22-1-2005 [H] **Ambassadors** (L 4-5)

29-1-2005 [H] **Angmering Res** (L 2-4)

5-2-2005 [A] **Petworth Res** (W 6-4)

12-2-2005 [H] **Graffham** (L 1-3)

19-2-2005 [H] **Lancing Utd Res** No Result

26-2-2005 [A] **Lodsworth** (L 1-5)

12-3-2005 [H] **Petworth Res** (W 4-1)

19-3-2005 [A] **Lancing Utd Res** (L 0-1)

26-3-2005 [A] **Graffham** (L 1-6)

20-4-2005 [H] **Fernhurst** (D 3-3)

27-4-2005 [A] **Rustington Res** (L 0-8)

30-4-2005 [A] **Angmering Res** (L 1-7)

P20 | W3 | D2 | L15 | GF30 | GA73 | 11pts | 10ᵗʰ

WSL DIVISION 3, SOUTH 2005/06

10-9-2005 [A] **Newtown Villa Res** (L 0-5)

17-9-2005 BT [H] **Eastergate Utd Res** (L ?-7)

24-9-2005 WSLD4C [A] **Coal Exchange** (W 1-0)

1-10-2005 [H] **Graffham Res** (W 10-0)

8-10-2005 [A] **Coal Exchange** (W 2-0)

15-10-2005 [H] **West Chiltington Res** (L 0-2)

29-10-2005 [A] **Amberley** (W 7-2)

12-11-2005 [A] **Boxgrove** ,L 1-5)

19-11-2005 [A] **Milland** (L 1-2)

26-11-2005 [H] **Coal Exchange** (L 0-3)

17-12-2005 [H] **Petworth Res** (W 3-2)

14-1-2006 [A] **Square Deal** (L 0-3)

21-1-2006 **WSLD4C** [A] **Boxgrove** (L 1-5) J Smillie 1

28-1-2006 [A] **West Chiltington Res** (L 0-3)

4-2-2006 [A] **Graffham Res** (W 8-0)

11-2-2006 [H] **Petworth Res** (L 3-4)

25-2-2006 [H] **Newtown Villa Res** (W 4-1)

11-3-2006 [H] **Milland** (W 3-0)

18-3-2006 [H] **Square Deal** (L 1-2)

1-4-2006 [H] **Amberley** (W 5-1)

8-4-2006 [H] **Boxgrove** (L 1-2)

18-4-2006 [H] **Middleton on Sea** (L 2-5)

29-4-2006 [A] **Middleton on Sea** (L 1-2)

P20 | W7 | D0 | L13 | GF50 | GA46 | 21pts | 9th

WSL DIVISION 3, SOUTH 2006/07

2-9-2006 [A] **Milland** (D 2-2)

9-9-2006 [H] **Petworth Res** (W 3-2)

16-9-2006 **WSLD3C** [A] **Horsham Baptists** (L 1-2)

23-9-2006 [A] **Angmering Res** (D 1-1)

30-9-2006 [H] **Yapton Res** (W 2-0) T Boulton 1, Ab Greenfield 1

7-10-2006 [H] **Ambassadors** (L 0-5)

14-10-2006 **BT** [H] **Hunston** (L 2-6)

21-10-2006 [A] **Boxgrove** (L 0-3)

28-10-2006 [H] **Milland** (L 2-5)

4-11-2006 [A] **Petworth Res** (W 3-1)

11-11-2006 [H] **Angmering Res** (W 4-2)

18-11-2006 [A] **Newtown Villa Res** (L 0-7)

2-12-2006 [A] **Hunston** (W 3-2)

16-12-2006 [A] **Middleton on Sea** (L 1-4)

23-12-2006 [A] **Yapton Res** (D 1-1)

13-1-2007 [H] **Middleton on Sea** (L 1-5)

3-3-2007 [H] **Hunston** (L 0-3)

24-3-2007 [H] **Newtown Villa Res** (L 3-6)

31-3-2007 [A] **Square Deal** (L 0-2)

7-4-2007 [H] **Square Deal** (D 1-1) Two results not found

P20 | W6 | D4 | L10 | GF27 | GA52 | 22pts | 8th

WSL DIVISION 3, SOUTH 2007/08

1-9-2007 [A] **Barnham Res** (L 0-12

8-9-2007 [A] **Petworth Res** (L 1-2)

22-9-2007 [A] **Lodsworth** (L 0-6)

29-9-2007 [H] **Petworth Res** (W 2-1)

6-10-2007 [H] **General Henry** (L 1-13

13-10-2007 [A] **Predators Res** (L 0-3)

27-10-2007 **BT** [A] **Fernhurst** (L 0-8)

3-11-2007 **WSLD3C** [A] **Faygate Utd Res** (W 4-0) Ab Greenfield 3, D Farrell 1

10-11-2007 [A] **Selsey Town** (L 2-9) Ab Greenfield 1, A Pavey 1

24-11-2007 [A] **Angmering Res** (L 1-4) Si Leadbeatter 1

1-12-2007 [A] **Square Deal** (L 2-3) Ab Greenfield 1, C Jupp 1

15-12-2007 [H] **Ambassadors** (W 4-2) Ab Greenfield 2, C Jupp 2

29-12-2007 [H] **Lodsworth** (L 1-2) C Jupp 1

5-1-2008 [H] **Predators Res** (L 0-4)

26-1-2008 [H] **Angmering Res** (L 3-8) Ab Greenfield 2, T Boulton 1

9-2-2008 **WSLD3C** [H] **Barnham Res** (L 2-11) L Blunden 1, S Parker 1

16-2-2008 [A] **Ambassadors** (L 2-5) T Boulton 1, Ab Greenfield 1

5-4-2008 [H] **Selsey Town** (L 2-4) Ab Greenfield 1, S Phillips 1

11-4-2008 [H] **Square Deal** (L 1-2)

15-4-2008 [A] **Newtown Villa Res** (L 0-1)

19-4-2008 [H] **Barnham Res** (D 1-1)

22-4-2008 [H] **Newtown Villa Res** (D 1-1) T Boulton 1

6-5-2008 [A] **General Henry** (L 0-3)

P20 | W2 | D2 | L16 | GF24 | GA85 | 8pts | 11th

WSL DIVISION 4 NORTH 2008/09

6-9-2008 [A] **Cowfold Res** (L 0-7)

13-9-2008 [H] **Ashington** Rovers **Res** (L 0-3)

20-9-2008 [A] **Upper Beeding Res** (W 3-2) Ab Greenfield 1, A Pavey 1, T Pepper 1

27-9-2008 **BT** [A] **The Wheatsheaf** (L 0-2)

4-10-2008 [A] **Rudgwick Res** (L 1-2)

11-10-2008 [H] **Faygate Utd Res** (W 4-1) Ab Greenfield 2, T Pepper 1

18-10-2008 [H] **Upper Beeding Res** (W 7-0) Ab Greenfield 2, Si Leadbeatter 1, A Parker 1, M Parry 1, A Pavey 1, T Pepper 1

25-10-2008 **WSLD4C** [A] **Newtown Villa 3rds** (L 1-2) Ab Greenfield 1

1-11-2008 [H] **West Chiltington Res** (W 7-4) A Parker 2, M Parry 2, A Pavey 2, Ab Greenfield 1

8-11-2008 [A] **Ockley Res** (W 7-1) Ab Greenfield 2, M Parry 2, A Pavey 2, Si Leadbeatter 1

15-11-2008 [H] **Wisborough Green Res** (W 5-0) Ab Greenfield 1, M Parryl A Pavey 1, 2?

22-11-2008 [A] **Ashington** Rovers **Res** (W 2-1)

29-11-2008 [H] **Cowfold Res** (L 0-3)

20-12-2008 [A] **Faygate Utd Res** (D 1-1)

3-1-2009 [H] **Rudgwick Res** (D 0-0)

21-2-2009 [A] **Horsham Trinity Res** (L 1-2) S Phillips 1

28-2-2009 [A] **Henfield Res** (L 0-3)

7-3-2009 [H] **Henfield Res** (L 1-5) T Blunden 1

14-3-2009 [A] **Wisborough Green Res** (D 1-1) M Parry 1

21-3-2009 [H] **Ockley Res** (W 7-1) Ab Greenfield 4, M Parry 1, T Pepper 1, S Skilton 1

11-4-2009 [A] **West Chiltington Res** (W 4-0) D Farrell 1, Ab Greenfield 1, S Jupp 1, S Parker 1

25-4-2009 [H] **Horsham Trinity Res** (D 1-1)

P20 | W9 | D4 | L7 | GF52 | GA37 | 31pts | 4th

WSL DIVISION 3, NORTH 2009-2010

5-9-2009 [A] **TD Shipley Res** (L 0-2)

12-9-2009 [H] **Henfield Res** (W 2-1)

19-9-2009 [A] **Ockley** (W 2-1)

26-9-2009 [H] **Holbrook FC Res** (W 4-2)

3-10-2009 [H] **TD Shipley Res** (L 3-4)

24-10-2009 [H] **Horsham Baptists** (D 0-0)

31-10-2009 [A] **Southwater Res** (L 0-6)

7-11-2009 [H] **Ockley** (W 11-1)

14-11-2009 [A] **Slinfold** (L 1-3)

21-11-2009 [A] **Ashington** Rovers **Res** (L 2-4)

12-12-2009 [H] **Slinfold** (W 10-0)

23-1-2010 [H] **Cowfold Res** (L 2-6)

6-2-2010 [H] **Southwater Res** (L 2-6)

20-2-2010 [A] **Ashington** Rovers **Res** (L 2-4)

27-2-2010 [A] **Holbrook FC Res** (D 4-4)

13-3-2010 [A] **Cowfold Res** No score found

20-3-2010 [H] **Rudgwick** (L 2-3)

27-3-2010 [A] **Horsham Baptists** (W 4-1)

5-4-2010 [A] **Henfield Res** (W 3-0)

21-4-2010 [A] **Rudgwick** (D 0-0)

P20 | W7 | D2 | L11 | GF54 | GA48 | 23pts | 7th

Codmore Hill FC 1936/7 – Horsham & District Division 3 Champions
Back row l to r Ben Clark, Les Smith, Colin Pellett, Boozy Pellett, Percy Barnett, Unknown
Midlle row Unknown, Unknown, Len Edwards
Front row Unknown, Unknown, Unknown, Dick Geening, Arthur Barnett

Codmore Hill Football Club

I'VE SPOKEN TO many people around the village and the majority of them did not know that in the 1930s the village had two teams, Pulborough FC and Codmore Hill FC.

The Club was formed in the 1934-35 season and only played up to the 1938-39 season. They did not reform after the war of 1939-45. There is an industrial site at the bottom of Codmore Hill, just off the A29 where from the 1920s into the 1940s there was a brickworks and it was here that the Codmore Club was founded. I don't know how many of the players actually worked there; I am guessing that people who lived to the north of the village probably played for the Codmore club rather than coming into the village to play for Pulborough FC. On the opposite side of the A29 is Blackgate Lane and in the second field behind St Richard's Cottages in the lane is where the Codmore Hill Club had its ground.

The Codmore team played in yellow shirts and blue shorts. They played in the Horsham & District League, starting off in Division 3B. For a new club they did quite well for a couple of seasons, but in 1936-37 they won the title to gain promotion to Division Two. They did so by winning every league game. They won eighteen consecutive league games, scoring 93 goals and conceding only eleven, a remarkable feat for any team.

In Division Two they continued to do well, finishing in second place in the 1938-39 season.

The Club officials were:

President Captain J. Henderson

Secretary Mr A. H. Edwards

Vice-President Mr A. Pellett

Officials Mr B. Clark, Mr L. Smith.

Some of the players from 1934-1939 were:

Mr C.P. Barnett, Mr A. Barnett, Mr C. Pellett, Mr H. Pellett, Mr T Hampshire, Mr R Davey, Mr L. Edwards, Mr W. Short, Mr W. Float, Mr G. Hampshire, Mr R. Greening, Mr J. Stear.

Owing to wartime commitments the Codmore Hill club could not raise a side for the 1939/40 season so Mr A. Barnett, Mr C.P. Barnett, Mr H. Pellett and Mr R. Greening came to play for

1937 – Codmore Hill vs Southwater

Mister Richardson said he refereed the match between Southwater and Codmore Hill on the former's ground on October 23. It was a first round replay in Horsham Intermediate Charity Cup competition and it resulted in a victory for Codmore Hill by 4 goals to 2.

However, during the game he had to order Cockhead of Southwater and Short of Codmore Hill off the field for violent conduct. He alleged that Cockhead struck Short, who hit back, and he added that it had been reported to him that as Cockhead was leaving the field he also struck another Codmore Hill player, Barnett.

Both Cockhead and Short admitted the offences, the Southwater player alleging that he hit first because he had been deliberately tripped by Short. The latter said he acted on the spur of the moment when he retaliated.

Codmore Hill FC – Results 1934-39

1934/35 DIVISION 3B
15-09-1934 [H] Southwater (L 0-8)
22-09-1934 [A] Slinfold (L1-5)
06-10-1934 [H] Coolham United (L0-8)
13-10-1934 [A] West Chiltington (L0-10)
20-10-1934 H Loxwood (L1-2)
03-11-1934 [A] Kirdford (L1-4)
17-11-1934 [H] Balls Cross & Ebernoe (L0-6)
24-11-1934 H&DJCC [A] Rusper (L0-10)
31-11-1934 [H] Watersfield (W5-4)
29-12-1934 [A] Watersfield (W3-1)
19-01-1935 [H] Kirdford (W2-1)
26-01-1935 [A] Balls Cross & Ebernoe (L1-4)
09-02-1935 [A] Coolham United (L2-3)
16-02-1935 [H] West Chiltington (L0-4)
23-02-1935 [A] Ashurst (L2-6)
02-03-1935 [H] Slinfold (W6-0)
16-03-1935 [A] Loxwood (L1-4)
23-03-1935 [H] Ashurst (D1-1)
30-03-1935 [A] Southwater (L0-10)
P18 | W4 |D1 | L13 | GF26 | GA97 | 9pts |7th

1935/36 DIVISION 3B
14-09-1935 [A] Ashurst (L3-5)
21-09-1935 [H] Kirdford (W4-1)
28-09-1935 [H] Loxwood (D1-1)
12-10-1935 [A] Nuthurst (L2-3)
19-10-1935 [H] West Chiltington (L0-3)
H&DJCC 26-10-1935 [H] Loxwood (D1-1)
02-11-1935 [H] Slinfold (L0-4)
09-11-1935 H&DJCC [A] Loxwood (L1-2)
16-11-1935 [A] Balls Cross & Ebernoe (W7-0)
14-12-1935 [A] Coolham United (L1-3)
28-12-1935 [A] Loxwood (L1-4)
11-01-1936 [A] Slinfold (W6-0)
18-01-1936 [H] Davis Estates (W9-2)
25-01-1936 [A] West Chiltington (L1-5)
01-02-1936 [A] Davis Estates (W5-0)
08-02-1936 [A] Kirdford (W2-0)
15-02-1936 [H] Balls Cross & Ebernoe (W4-1)
22-02-1936 [A] Coolham United (W19-0)
29-02-1936 [H] Nuthurst (W5-0)
02-03-1936 [H] Ashurst (W5-1)
P18 | W11 | D1 | L6 | GF76 | GA30 | 23pts |5th

1936/37 DIVISION 3B
18-09-1936 [H] Ockley (W6-1)
25-09-1936 [A] Rudgwick (W4-1) A Barnett 1, R Davey 1, OG 2
03-10-1936 [H] Plaistow Juniors (W5-0)
10-10-1936 [A] Slinfold (W2-1)
17-10-1936 [H] Loxwood (W2-0)
31-10-1936 [A] Balls Cross & Ebernoe (W3-2)
07-11-1936 [H] Pulborough (W6-1)
14-11-1939 [H] Broadbridge Heath II (W4-2)
21-11-1936 [A] Ashurst (W4-0)
28-11-1936 H&DJCC [H] Kays (L1-2)
05-12-1936 [A] Loxwood (W3-2)

19-12-1936 [H] Balls Cross & Ebernoe (W4-0)
16-01-1937 [A] Broadbridge Heath II (W5-0)
23-01-1937 [H] Slinfold (W8-1)
30-01-1937 [A] Pulborough (W7-0)
06-02-1937 [A] Plaistow Juniors (W10-0)
13-02-1937 [H] Rudgwick (W8-0)
20-02-1937 [H] Ashurst (W10-0)
03-04-1937 [A] Ockley II (W4-0)
P18 W18 D0 L0 GF93 GA11 36pts Champions

1937/38 DIVISION 2
02-10-1937 [H] Partridge Green (L2-4)
09-10-1937 [A] Barns Green (W8-0)
16-10-1937 H&DJICC [H] Southwater (D0-0)
23-10-1937 H&DICCR [A] Southwater (W4-2)
30-10-1937 [H] Kays (L0-2)
06-11-1937 [H] Forest Rangers (W7-3)
13-11-1937 [A] Southwater (L1-3)
20-11-1937 H&DICC [H] West Chiltington (D1-1)
04-12-1937 H&DICCR [A] West Chiltington (W1-0)
08-01-1938 [A] Warnham (D2-2)
15-01-1938 [A] West Chiltington (D0-0)
29-01-1938 [H] Southwater (D2-2)
19-02-1938 [H] Barns Green (W4-2)
26-02-1938 [A] Kays (D2-2)
05-03-1938 [H] Warnham (W3-0)
12-03-1938 [A] Forest Rangers (W5-0)
19-03-1938 [A] Partridge Green (L3-5)
26-03-1938 [H] West Chiltington (W2-0)
02-04-1938 [H] Sussex Bricks (W3-2)
09-04-1938 H&DICC SF N Kays (L3-4)
23-04-1938 [A] Sussex Bricks (W2-1)
P16 W8 D4 L4 GF46 GA28 20pts

*A good first season in Division 2, reaching the Semi-Final of the Intermediate Cup, losing out to **Kays** by 3-4 (played at **Loxwood**)*

1938/39 DIVISION 2
17-09-1938 [H] Sussex Bricks (D1-1)
01-10-1938 [H] Nuthurst (W2-1)
15-10-1938 H&DICC [A] 4th Royal Sussex Regiment (L0-5)
22-10-1938 [A] Slinfold (L0-9)
05-11-1938 [A] West Chiltington (W3-0)
12-11-1938 [H] Staplefield (W5-0)
19-11-1938 [A] Pulborough (W1-0)
03-12-1938 [H] West Chiltington (W3-0)
10-12-1938 [A] Balls Cross & Ebernoe (W6-1)
31-12-1938 [H] Warnham (W4-1)
07-01-1939 [H] Pulborough (L1-2)
14-01-1939 [A] Sussex Bricks (L1-5)
28-01-1939 [A] Loxwood (W6-0)
04-02-1939 [H] 4th Royal Sussex Regiment (W5-3)
18-02-1939 [A] Staplefield (W6-2)
25-02-1939 [A] Nuthurst (D2-2)
11-03-1939 [H] Loxwood (W4-3)
25-03-1939 [H] Slinfold (W2-0)
01-04-1939 [A] Warnham (D0-0)
P22 W15 D3 L4 GF54 GA36 33pts 2nd

Trial Match for Horsham & District League XI 1938

Kick-off is at 3:15 pm when the sides will line up as follows:

- R. Steel (Five Oaks), W. Short (Codmore Hill), R. Castle (Lower Beeding), S. Lamb (Loxwood), G. Winton (West Chiltington), H. Packham (Twineham), H.A. Frogley (Pulborough), R. Weeks (Ashington), K. Roberts (Ashington), J. Hampshire (West Chiltington), A. Martin (Twineham).

- R. Jepson (Horsham), H. Parsons (Henfield), A. Davies (Five Oaks), D. Kennard (Loxwood), F. Burdfield (Partridge Green), R. Hart (Ockley), J. Locke (Partridge Green), T. Hampshire (Codmore Hill), G. Voice (Five Oaks), W. Coles (Crawley), J. Merrit (Ashington).

Mister A.E. Richardson will referee.

October 1936 – Rudgwick 1 Codmore Hill 4

For their home match against Codmore Hill in Division 3B on Saturday, Rudgwick had to field a weakened side, and as a result were convincingly defeated. They were on the defensive from the start and, after a melee in front of their goal, a defender miskicked into the net.

Rudgwick retaliated and the equaliser came from a well combined effort between their left half, centre forward and outside right, the latter scoring. But five minutes before half-time Codmore Hill regained the lead through Davey.

In the second half Rudgwick fell away and for the second time one of their defenders put the ball into his own goal. They were continually hard-pressed after this and, although the Rudgwick goalkeeper brought off many fine saves, he was unable to prevent Barnett from getting number four.

Codmore Hill FC dinner-Successful First Season Celebration

Codmore Hill, who entered Division III B of Horsham and District League this season, held a successful dinner at The Five Bells Inn, Pulborough on Friday, when there was in attendance of about 30.

This was the first event of its kind organised by the club, who have had quite a successful playing and financial season, and the members hope to hold a dinner every year. They have a loyal band of officials, players and supporters, and believe in a spirit of good fellowship off, as well as on, the field.

At the dinner, however, a matter which caused deep regret was the absence through illness of Captain J Henderson, the president, but his place was admirably filled by Mr B. Clarke, who presided. The latter proposed the toast of the club, whose colours were used in decorations for the dining hall and tables.

Mr Clarke expressed the members thanks to the Hon Secretary Mr H. Edwards, the other offices and committee, for the work they had done during this, their first season.

Mr Edwards in reply thanked Mrs Smith, Mrs B Edwards, Mrs Oldbury, Mrs Atfield, Mrs Carby, Mrs J.E. Edwards, Miss K. Wallace, Miss G. Edwards and Mrs Leeson for their help in making the evening such a success. He was sure, he said, that every member joined with him in thanking Mrs Smith for providing refreshments for the team at every match.

Mr Edwards pointed out that it was their chairman who had advanced a loan to start the club and he was glad to say that this had now been paid off and that there was a good balance to hand.

Before wishing the club every success, Mr A Pellett, vice president, said he was glad that such a club had been started at Codmore Hill. It was a good thing for the men's social activities and for their minds and bodies, and he hoped they would always pull together as they had done during their first season.

A delightful concert was sustained by a party from Horsham, including Mr H. Rowland and Mr H. Bedford.

Horsham and District Mini Minor League 1979/80
Under 13's champions, six aside winners and cup finalists
back row left to right Mick Hatchard (manager), Nigel Turner, Richard Streeter, Brian Heasman, David Hill,
Mark Street, John Herbert, Tim Hatchard, Joe Dyer, Colin Spain (assistant manager)
front row Steve Hill, Simon Sweet, Kevin Munday, John Medway, Peter Bird, Matt Chapman.

Pulborough Under-15 XI – Chichester & Bognor Minor League 1980/81
displaying their 1980 season trophies for winning the league and six-a-side competition
back row left to right Joe Dyer, Peter Bird, John Herbert, Matt Chapman,
Steve Marsh, Chris Shine, Richard Streeter.
Front row Brian Heasman, Steve Hill, John Medway, Jason Sammons, Tim Hatchard, Kevin Monday.

The Pulborough Minors

I N 1977 I was asked if I could arrange a few friendly matches for the young boys of the village. They played some matches, the first, I recall, was played on the pitch at St. Mary's School.

The boys were very keen and wanted to join a League, so that they could play every week. I explained to them that it was not that simple, you had to have people to run the club and be affiliated to a league. A meeting was held and David Herbert was appointed as our Treasurer and Peter Chapman our Secretary, I was to manage the team and Colin Spain was to be my assistant. He refereed some games and also ran the line. We then had to ask Pulborough Parish Council to provide a pitch, which they did, and we played on the bottom end of the recreation ground. I then got permission from Pulborough Football Club to use their lights for training; they were very helpful.

We were then entered into the Under-13 section of the Horsham Mini Minor League in the 1978/79 season. The team played in blue shirts, white shorts and blue and white socks.

It was now time to start coaching the lads. When they were just playing friendly matches I had wanted them to enjoy playing football and to go out and express themselves. The boys were all local and the youngest team in the Division.

The team did OK, although they had some heavy defeats, but they were learning how to play as a unit. The following season 1979/80 we were put into the reserve section of the Under-13s. The whole squad were still young enough to play in that Division.

The season was to be a great one for the team. We had some really good individual players but were now working as a team and playing some very fine football. The team finished as league champions, won the six-a-side tournament and reached the Cup Final.

The final was played at Goring's Mead in Horsham against Loxwood. There was nothing to choose between the sides and the match was drawn. The replay was an evening game played at Queen Street, Horsham's ground.

Throughout the year the team had built a reputation for playing good football and there was always a good crowd to watch the home matches. We decided to make the evening a special one and hired a coach to take the team and supporters to the game. Playing on a ground like Queen Street was exciting for the boys, they had only been used to playing on small pitches on local recreation grounds or even school pitches.

The game was very much like the first one, with neither side able to create many chances. Loxwood took the lead from a slight lapse in concentration on our part but there was plenty of time left in the game and we were confident we could score. Credit to Loxwood, they man marked our two most dangerous players, Tim and Brian, and despite all our pressure we found it hard to get into goal scoring positions.

Then, with almost the last kick of the game, our chance came… A cross came in and, with their goalkeeper stranded, all our player had to do was nod the ball into an empty net. He somehow missed the goal. A minute later, the referee blew the whistle for the end of the game.

The boys were obviously disappointed, but once we got back to the dressing room, I reminded them of what they had achieved that season and they were a little happier.

The squad of players we had were: J. Herbert, M. Chapman, J. Medway, K. Munday, S. Hill, N. Turner, R. Streeter, S. Sweet, P. Bird, T. Hatchard, B. Heasman, J. Dyer, M. Sweet and D. Hill.

Six of the players went on to play for Pulborough FC but unfortunately four others left the area. S. March, J. Salmon and C. Shine were also part of the squad over the next three years. The results were difficult to find but those shown here are the ones I did manage to locate.

We would like to have stayed in the Horsham & District Mini Minor League, but unfortunately there was not a Division for an under-14 side. We then entered the Chichester & Bognor District Minor League, which did have a Division for the under fourteens. This was a tougher League and although the boys were meant to be in the same age group, we came across some very big lads in some of the sides. I was not able to find the results of all the matches we played, but I have recorded the ones I did find.

It was a difficult season for the boys, but they never gave up and gained valuable experience. The best result of the season was a win by 3 goals to 2 against Selsey, who had previously beaten us in the Cup 16-2.

SCORES 1979/80 – HORSHAM & DISTRICT MINI MINOR LEAGUE

[A] Loxwood (D 1-1)
[H] Tigers (W 13-1) T Hatchard 9, B Heasman 3
Roffey Robins Cup [A] Tigers (W 5-1)
[A] Henfield (W 5-3)
[H] Roffey Robins United (W 3-1)
[H] Cranleigh (D 2-2)
[A] Rovers (W 6-1)
[H] Lower Beeding (L 2-3)
[H] Roffey Wanderers (W 6-2)
Roffey Robins Cup [A] Rovers (W 7-2)
[A] Tigers (W 5-0)
[H] Sparrows (W 7-0)
[H] Henfield (W 4-2)
[A] Cranleigh (W 3-2)
[H] Rovers (W 13-4)
Roffey Robins Cup, Semi-Final [A] Lower Beeding (W2-0)
[H] Roffey Robins United (W6-1)

SCORES 1980/81 – CHICHESTER & BOGNOR DISTRICT MINOR LEAGUE

21-9-1980 [H] Tangmere Spitfires (L 2-13)
18-9-1980 [A] Felpham Colts (W 5-3)
12-10-1980 [H] Whyke Colts (L 2-13)
19-10-1980 [H] Bognor Martlets (L 5-10)
26-10-1980 [A] Selsey (L 2-16) (Challenge Cup)
2-11-1980 [A] Bosham Cygnets (L 3-10)
9-11-1980 [A] Petworth Panthers (L 3-10)
23-11-1980 [A] Tangmere Spitfires (L 4-6)
30-11-1980 [H] Selsey (W 3-2)
14-12-1980 [A] Chichester (W 4-3)
21-12-1980 [H] Yapton & Ford United (L 0-13)
4-1-1981 [H] Westmeads (L 2-13)
25-1-1981 [H] Felpham Colts (W 6-2)
15-2-1981 [A] Bognor Martlets (L 1-7)
1-3-1981 *Invitation Cup Semi-Final* [A] Chichester (L 1-6)
15-3-1981 [H] Bognor Cygnets (W 3-2)
29-3-1981 [A] Selsey (L 1-10)

PFC Minors – Players 1980/81

JOHN HERBERT was our goalkeeper. He was quite tall and a very good keeper, not afraid to come out and go down at players' feet. He was safe and reliable. He played for Billingshurst and Broadbridge Heath when moving on to play in the men's game. He lives in Hampshire.

MATTHEW CHAPMAN was our right-side defender. A strong player, he was known as "Chopper Chapman" – no need to say any more! He lives in Pulborough.

JOHN MEDWAY played in central defence and was captain. He was probably our best player. He had the ability to read the game, was skilful and never panicked when the team was under pressure. He lives in Hove.

KEVIN MUNDAY was a central defender. He was very quick and full of energy, never gave up and was a hard tackler. His pace was a good asset for the team. He lives in Pulborough.

STEVE HILL was our left-side defender. He was not that tall but was good in the air and a very aggressive tackler. He was another one who never knew when he was beaten. He went on to play for Pulborough FC and still lives in the village.

PETER BIRD usually played right midfield. He was a strong player who liked to get up-field to support the forwards and scored his share of goals, but still did his defensive work well. He went on to play for Pulborough FC, Storrington, Ashington and East Preston.

RICHARD STREETER played centre midfield. He was tall and strong, not the quickest of players but very skilful and able to beat opponents and set his forwards up. Richard went on to play for Pulborough FC. He lives in Surrey.

JOE DYER played up front on the right. He was never that fast and not the most athletic, but he always worked hard for the team and did not let anyone down. He lives in Petersfield.

TIM HATCHARD was our centre forward. From an early age he knew where the goal was and became a prolific goal scorer for the team. He also worked hard and had the knack of being in the right place at the right time. He went on to play for Pulborough FC. He lives in Rustington.

NIGEL TURNER played left midfield. He was slight of build but still got stuck in and won tackles. Skilful, with a natural left foot, he always worked his socks off. He moved to live in the Eastbourne area.

BRIAN HEASMAN played wide left up front. Naturally left footed, he was the fastest player in the squad, went past defenders with ease to get crosses in and scored a lot of goals. He had a great partnership with Tim Hatchard and went on to play for Pulborough FC. Lives in Pulborough.

MARK SWEET played in midfield. Another very quick player, although not a big lad he was not afraid to get stuck in and never let the side down.

SIMON SWEET, like his brother, played in midfield and always played well when in the side.

PULBOROUGH Benevolent Cup 1924

The Pulborough FC team who won the Pulborough Benevolent Cup in 1924
The only players I have been able to identify are, in the back row the goalkeeper, W. Woods, in the middle row, on the left, W. Harwood, in the front row holding the cup, W. Bevan, next to him, V. Corden. The Johnson brothers are possibly, in the middle row, centre and in the front row, second from the left.
(Photo by kind permission of Joyce Woods)

6th April 1924
Well done Pulborough and Storrington!

On Saturday between 500 and 600 people were present at the final for the Benevolent Cup. Both teams played their hardest but, as the referee stated, it was a good and very clean game. In fact, the official in charge said it was the best game between villages he had ever taken. The Robins won the toss and kicked against the wind. R. Kirby soon scored a fine goal from a clever centre by A. Sully. In the latter part of the second half, Jessie Johnson scored from a pass by W. Bevan. No further goals were netted. In defence, the Robins lived up to their name by preserving their goal intact. They have only yielded one goal during the cup competition and W. Woods is to be praised for his fine work as goalie, for Storrington made many a good attempt. All the players did well.

When the match was over the captain was carried shoulder high by his team to where the cup was presented by Mrs Neston Diggle, who said she wished the team every success and congratulated them on their well-deserved efforts.

Cup Matches

The Pulborough Benevolent Cup

The Pulborough Benevolent Cup was donated to the Club by Captain Neston Diggle, RN, CMG, the Club's President. It was to be a knock-out competition between local clubs by invitation only, to be run by Pulborough Football Club. All matches were to be played on the Club's home ground at Soper's Meadow.

I believe the first competition was held during the 1923/24 season. I could find nothing after the 1938/39 season, when war broke out. It was a difficult task trying to find the results of the matches played, but I did manage to locate most of the games played by the Pulborough sides. During the years the competition was played, the teams invited to participate were: Billingshurst, West Chiltington, Fittleworth, Storrington, Dial Post, Ashington, Washington, Bury & West Burton United, Marley Sports, Thakeham Tiles, Petworth, Wisborough Green, Rudgwick, Sutton & Bignor, Codmore Hill, Pulborough 1st and Pulborough 2nd.

The inaugural game of the competition saw 'The Robins' play against Washington, on 6th October 1923, which resulted in a win for Pulborough, but I was unable to find the score. The 2nd XI played on 1st December 1923 and lost their match against Bury & West Burton United. The first Semi-Final took place on 16th February 1924, when Storrington defeated Billingshurst to reach the final. In the other Semi-Final, played on 15th March 1924, Pulborough played Petworth and won by 2 goals to 1. So the Final was to be Storrington versus their old enemy, Pulborough.

The Final was held on 6th April 1924, at Soper's Meadow.

The 1924/25 season saw 'The Robins' play Fittleworth in the first round, which resulted in a convincing win by 9 goals to 1. The match was played on 30th November 1924, the goal scorers were J. Johnson 3, H.

Match Report 25-4-1925
AN EXCITING CUP FINAL

The Final of the Pulborough Benevolent Cup was played at Sopers on Saturday before a record crowd and the home supporters had the satisfaction of seeing their favourites retain the trophy. Pulborough winning the toss, faced the breeze and the game started at a fast pace, both sides attacking in turn.

Petworth were a little superior at the start, but Pulborough soon settled down, it was unfortunate that a visiting player badly hurt his leg in a tackle after fifteen minutes play, which necessitated his absence for the rest of the game, but hard knocks were taken and given in the best spirit.

The forwards kept the game open and the defences had to watch every move, Brockhurst ran out to clear and later punched away in good style. A free kick, taken by Kenward narrowly missed, but shortly before the interval, Wadey trapped the ball from a similar kick and Bevan promptly netted, this being the only goal scored at half time. The home team pressed on the resumption, but Petworth broke away and an appeal for a penalty for hands, which the referee ignored, a regrettable incident then occurred, for as a result of a remark by a Petworth player, the referee ordered him off the pitch. Petworth resorted to the one back game in an effort to keep their charge intact, but a feature of the match was a 20 yard drive by the outside left, which Brockhurst tipped over for a fruitless corner.

After the match, the Cup and medals were presented to the winners by Mrs Neston Diggle, who congratulated them on winning the trophy in successive seasons. Receiving the cup, the captain W. Hampshire remarked that it was a pity that both sides could not win, cheers for the losers and for Captain and Mrs Diggle were heartily responded to.

The winning team was composed of as follows: N. Brockhurst, R. Kenward and E. Johnson, W. Harwood, W. Hampshire and A. Pink, J. Johnson, R. West, W. Bevan, W. Wadey and H. Cosens. As a result of the match, the sum of £7 was raised.

Cosens (Tim) 2, W. Bevan 1, D. Kirby 1, W. Harwood 1, R. Habbin 1. In the second round on 21st March 1925 they were up against Wisborough Green and came out on top by 3 goals to nil; W. Harwood, W. Wadey and R. West were the scorers. The final was played on 25th April 1925 when Pulborough defeated Petworth 1-0. W. Bevan scoring the only goal of the game. 'The Robins' had retained the cup.

The following year, 1925/26 was a very eventful one, with the last game of the season being the final of the Benevolent Cup, which turned out to be a farce. In the 1st round the 1st XI beat Dial Post 3-0 on 12th December 1925. On 2nd January 1926 the second XI defeated Bury & West Burton United 2-1, with A. Cheesman scoring both goals. The only other match I could find was the semi-final between Fittleworth and Billingshurst, with Fittleworth going through to the final to play Pulborough. The Final was on 1st May 1926, with Fittleworth winning 10-1. The match was a farce because 'The Robins' had already played five games that week, including a game on Friday evening and a Cup Final on Saturday afternoon, then had to dash back to Pulborough to play in their own competition. The players were exhausted before the game started but, to their credit, they finished the game. A win in their own competition would have been the icing on the cake for the team, in what had otherwise been a very successful season.

The 1926/27 season saw the Cup return to Pulborough, with the team winning through to the Final. In the Semi-Final they played Bury & West Burton on 16th April 1927 and had a comfortable 6-1 win. In the other Semi-Final, it was Storrington who made it through to play Pulborough in the Final, but I could not find out who they played.

For the first time since the competition originated in 1923/24, the team failed to reach the Final in 1927/28. In the first round they lost to Storrington by 4 goals to 0, although this was no surprise, as they could only raise 9 players. I could not discover why they could not muster a full team. In the two Semi-Finals, Storrington defeated Dial Post and Storrington lost to Ashington. The Final 4th April 1928, proved to be a rather one-sided contest, with Petworth demolishing Ashington by 10 goals to 1.

The following season 1928/29, we again failed to reach the final. The first semi-final on 20th April 1928 saw Storrington defeat Wisborough Green 5-2. The second one saw Pulborough take on Petworth, with the latter coming out on top by 2 goals to 0. The final between Storrington and Petworth was played on 5th May 1929, the result I was unable to find.

1925/6 – Discreditable Incidents

The Littlehampton and District Benevolent Cup has been the chief topic of interest among local footballers. Wick and Pulborough, having drawn the semi-final game at Pulborough, replayed at Wick on Wednesday last. Wick led by the only goal till just on time, when Pulborough equalised; extra time was played without further score and arrangements were made for the game to be replayed at Arundel on the Friday.

A large crowd assembled for this match at 6:30. It was a severe test for a young and experienced referee to take charge of the game in which everyone knew a good deal of feeling was likely to be shown. It was a discreditable affair, to both teams, to the respective captains and, most of all, to the partisan spectators. Three men were sent off the field. Pulborough won. The play was not worth describing.

For the final at Wick on Saturday between Pulborough and Arundel, Strudwick (the Arundel captain) won the toss for the right to play in his club's own colours (both clubs being red) and consented to the game being 40 minutes each way, as Pulborough had to play another final tie against Fittleworth the same evening. A large crowd was present and a clean, interesting game resulted.

Quite early a penalty was awarded to Pulborough and this opened the scoring. Strudwick made the score level but Pulborough and again took the lead and at halftime led by 3-1. With the wind behind them in the second half Arundel had all the play and did everything but score until awarded a penalty, from which Ayling netted.

Many fine saves were made by the Pulborough goalkeeper and Pulborough won the cup by 3-2. The only misbehaviour was on the part of a section of spectators, one of whom received a lesson on his jaw from an Arundel lad that he is not likely to forget.

After missing out in the two previous years, Pulborough got back on track for the 1929/30 season. In the first of the semi-finals, Dial Post were opposed by West Chiltington, with Dial Post going through to the final. The second semi-final, played on 13th April 1930, saw Pulborough play Petworth, with 'The Robins' winning by 5 goals to 1. Goal scorers for Pulborough were R. Crowther 2, W. Harwood 1, J. Johnson 1, R. West 1.

In the 1930 final at Soper's Pulborough beat Dial Post 6-4.

The Pulborough Benevolent Cup winning team 1930
Not sure who is who in the photo but the team was:
S. Picton, W Woods,
F Cousens F Newman,
E heasman, T Beaven,
J Johnson, R West,
W harwood, R Crowther
and R Goodsell.

23.04.1930 v Petworth

Rain fell continually throughout the match at Sopers on Wednesday evening between Pulborough and Petworth in the Semi-Final of the Pulborough Benevolent Cup, but in spite of the weather over two hundred people were in attendance. Pulborough won by five goals to one ad will meet Dial Post in the Final. Crowther was the first to score for Pulborough, Harwood added the second, two nil at half-time. In the second half Petworth made several attacks, but were unable to score. J. Johnson scored the third and Crowther and West added two more. Standing scored for Petworth just before time.

Petworth: S. Adsett, H. J. Wells, A. Adsett, W. B. Scott, J. Stillwell, H. Head, H. Townsend, A. Taylor, R. Vincent, N. L. Knight, J. Standing.

Pulborough: S. Picton, H. Johnson, W. Woods, F. Newman, E. Heasman, J. Beacher, C. Goodsell, R. Crowther, W. Harwood, R. West, J. Johnson.

May 1930 – Cup Final

In the seventh final of the Pulborough and District Benevolent Cup, which was played at Sopers Meadow on Saturday between Pulborough and Dial Post, the former, after a hard struggle, won the cup by 6 goals to 4, though the visitors were leading at half time.

The cup and medals were presented to the winners by Mrs Neston Diggle, who was accompanied by Captain Neston Diggle, the Club President, and her son, Sir Walter Barttelot.

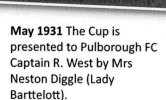

May 1931 The Cup is presented to Pulborough FC Captain R. West by Mrs Neston Diggle (Lady Barttelott).

The cup-winning team 1931: *back row second from left* W. Woods, S. Picton, E. Heasman; *middle row centre* F. Cousins, then W. Harwood; *front row 2nd from left* R. West, *4th from left* T. Bevan, then R. Crowther.

In the 1930/31 season Pulborough were again successful and won the competition for the fifth time. The semi-final, on 21st February 1931, was against our near neighbours West Chiltington, who were comprehensively beaten 6-0. Goals scored by E. Johnson 2, J. Johnson 2, T. Bevan 1 and G. Oakley 1.

The other semi-final was between Dial Post and Storrington, with Dial Post being victorious, this meant a repeat, of the 1929/30 Final.

Pulborough failed to retain the cup during the 1931/32 season. We were drawn to play Ashington in the first round and this game was drawn, the match was played on 30th January 1932. The replay on 12th March 1932, resulted in a

1st May 1931 – Cup Held Fast by Pulborough

On Saturday Pulborough retained possession of Pulborough and District Benevolent Cup by beating Dial Post. On play, the latter should have won but their forwards failed in straight and quick shooting. They had a penalty given against them, from which Pulborough scored their first goal through H Johnson; this was the only goal of the first half. In the second, Dial Post equalised through D Johnson but in the last minute, by a clever goal, J Johnson won the cup for Pulborough. In the absence of the President (Captain W Neston Diggle), who is abroad, Mrs Diggle, who was accompanied by her son, Sir Walter Barttelot, presented the cup and medals and the teams were entertained to tea at the Five Bells Inn.

win by 3 goals to 1. The semi-final was against Petworth on 4th May 1932 and 'The Robins' lost 0-2. The team that day was, S. Picton, E. Johnson, E. Heasman, J. Sopp, J. Beacher, W. Woods, J. Johnson, F. Mathews, W. Harwood, D. Adamson, R. Goodsell.

The winners of the cup that year were Petworth, who beat Storrington 3-1. In the 1932/33 and 1933/34 seasons Pulborough did not have a football club; I think the reason for this was that we had no ground to play on. The Benevolent Cup competition was continued, with matches being played on the Watersfield ground. The next two years 1932/33 and 1933/34, Billingshurst were the winners. On 6th May 1933 they beat West Chiltington 2-1 and the following season they beat Storrington 2-0. Both games were played on the Watersfield ground.

The 1934/35 season saw the Cup go to Marley Sports, who beat Pulborough by 2 goals to nil. In 1935/36 the competition was played on the Pulborough ground and I think this was the same place as our present ground. The winners were Wisborough Green, who beat the holders Marley Sports 2-1.

I was unable to find the winners of the 1936/37 competition. The 1937/38 final was contested by Washington and Ashington and finished as a draw 3-3. The replay took place during the the following season but I was not able to find the result.

The 1938/39 competition saw Codmore Hill play Washington in the Semi-Final. This was a good game, with Washington Finally winning 5-4. The other Semi-Final was won by West Chiltington. The Final was played on 12th April 1939 and again I could find no result. Whichever team won the cup, they must still be in possession of it, as Pulborough FC do not have it!

The Pulborough Benevolent Cup for Junior Sides

During the 1927/28 season, a new competition was formed. A trophy had been donated by our President Captain Neston Diggle, for boys teams from the area. It was called the Diggle Challenge Cup. I was able to find some of the winners of the cup, but not all of them. The first holders of the Cup were Wisborough Green. The 1928/29 winners were Easebourne, who beat Wisborough Green 8-1. Easebourne won again in 1931. In 1932 the Finalists were Billingshurst and West Chiltington, with Billingshurst coming out on top by 3 goals to 1. The following year 1933, Billingshurst retained the Cup by beating Ashington 4-2 in the Final. In 1934, it was Ashington who came out on top, when they beat Billingshurst 7-1. The Storrington boys won the Cup in 1935, 1937 and 1939. There were several years when Pulborough failed to enter a team. My thanks to Peter Harrison, who played for the Storrington boys in those Finals, for allowing me to photograph his medals from those competitions.

The Marley Cup

This was a competition organised by Storrington FC, to be played for by local Clubs, all games to be played on the Storrington ground. The first year of the competition was 1984 and the Clubs taking part were Amberley, Ashington, Pulborough, Storrington, Storrington Priory, Fittleworth, Watersfield and West Chiltington.

I was not able to find the results of every match we played in, nor could I find the goal scorers, or the teams that played in the finals. The results of the 1984 competition were:

28-04-1984 Storrington 0 Pulborough 2
02-05-1984 Ashington 0 Pulborough 0
05-05-1984 Storrington Priory 1 Pulborough 1 (M Jupp)
09-05-1984 West Chiltington 0 Pulborough 1 (D King)
12-05-1984 **The Final** Storrington Priory 1 Pulborough 3 (D Fry, D King, D Scott)

In the 1985 Final we lost to Storrington:

29-04-1985 Storrington 0 Pulborough 0
08-05-1985 West Chiltington 0 Pulborough 1 (C Hutton)
14-05-1985- Storrington Priory 1 Pulborough 8
(D Scott 3, M Harrison 2, P Bird, P Goring, D King)
15-05-1985 Ashington 0 Pulborough 1 (S Leadbeatter)
17-05-1985 The Final Pulborough 0 Storrington 1 AET

In 1986 we were winners again, in the 3 years of the competition we had the Final on each occasion, winning twice.

17-05-1986 Amberley 0 Pulborough 2 (D Leadbeatter, M Ruff)
21-05-1986 Watersfield 1 Pulborough 4 (N Bainbridge, P Bird, K Furlonger, D Lewis)
23-05-1986 **The Final** Storrington 1 Pulborough 1 AET

Pulborough won 5-3 in a penalty shoot out. Scorers were P. Bird, K. Furlonger, C. Hutton, D. Lewis and C. Spain. The final gave me the opportunity to give a young 15-year-old his debut in the first XI. Dean Lewis played very well and had the nerve to step up and take a penalty, which he scored, to help us win.

We played poorly in the 1987 competition and went out in the 1st round:

06-05-1987 Ashington 0 Pulborough 0
12-05-1987 Ashington 1 Pulborough 1 AET (we lost 2-3 in penalty shootout)

In 1998 we reached the Final for the fourth time:

25-04-1988 Amberley 0 Pulborough 1 (T. Hatchard)
12-05-1988 Storrington Priory 2 Pulborough 3 (K. Furlonger, C. Hutton, S. Leadbeatter)
18-05-1988 The Final Storrington 4 Pulborough 1 (M. Harrison 1)
The team was M. Jupp, M. Osborne, D. Rhoder, K. Furlonger, C. Spain, S. Leadbeatter, C. Hutton, D. King, M. Harrison, T. Hatchard, K. Taylor, Subs N. Bainbridge, C. Staples.

The 1989 season saw the side in the Final once again:

11-05-1989 Fittleworth 0 Pulborough 2 (D. Lewis, D. Smith)
16-05-1989 Storrington Priory 0 Pulborough 5 (C. Hutton 2, T. Hatchard, D. Lewis, D. Smith)
22-05-1989 The Final West Chiltington 2 Pulborough 1 (D. Smith)

We were very unlucky in the final. We played well and did not deserve to lose. We lost to a fluke goal from one of our former players.

The Football Club has no records of us playing in the 1990 competition, so I have no idea if we participated. Over the next 3 years, 1991, 1992, 1993 I have found some results, but there are no records to say if the side reached any finals:

11-04-1991 West Chiltington 4 Pulborough 2 (S. Cox, D. Lewis)
30-04-1991 Pulborough 5 Amberley 2
07-05-1991 Storrington Veterans 0 Pulborough 2 (R. Streeter 2)
07-04-1992 West Chiltington 4 Pulborough 1 (D. Lewis)
11-04-1992 Watersfield 2 Pulborough 2 (I. Dumbrill, M. Wroe)
21-04-1992 Amberley 0 Pulborough 3 (D. Lewis 2, S. Cox 1)
02-05-1992 Storrington 2 Pulborough 1 (N. Spicer)
23-04-1993 Storrington Veterans 2 Pulborough 2 (L 4-6 on penalties)

All matches were played on the Storrington ground.

Pulborough FC Marley Cup winners 1983/84 Season
back row l to r Toby Greenfield (chairman), Trevor Blunden, Mick Osborne, Peter Bird, Dave King, Mick Ruff, Colin Spain, Paul Gibson, Mick Hatchard (manager).
Front row John Jupp, Terry Roberts, Dave Fry, John Geddes, Colin Hutton, Malc Jupp, Stephen Hurst.

The Steyning Traders Floodlight Cup

This competition was run by Steyning Football Club, for invited clubs, the games played on the 'Shooting Field', Steyning's home ground, under lights. The first competition was held during the 1986/87 season. It was a good experience for those who had never played under floodlights before. Once again, not all the results were in the Club's archives.

20-10-1986 Durrington 0 Pulborough 1 (S Leadbeatter)
??-02-1987 Semi-Final – Steyning Old Grammarians 0 Pulborough 1
30-03-1987 The Final – Billingshurst 0 Pulborough 0 AET
13-04-1987 The Final replay – Billingshurst 1 Pulborough 0 AET

In both games there was nothing to chose between the two teams, Billingshurst, from the Premier Division were favourites, but we more than matched in the two games. Both matches went into extra-time and either team could have won. The fact that the Billingshurst goalkeeper was made 'Man of the Match' shows that we could easily have won.

On 9 November 1987 the result was Slinfold 3 Pulborough 5
(M Harrison 3, N Bainbridge, K Taylor).

On 29 February 1988 it was Billingshurst 1 Pulborough 0.
Billingshurst were becoming our bogey team; we lost out again in extra-time.

On 7 September 1988 Watersfield and Pulborough drew, after extra-time and we lost on penalties. We played very poorly and did not deserve to win.

On 23 October 1989 the score was Watersfield 2 Pulborough 1 (N. Bainbridge)

In 1990 the competition was renamed **The Chalcroft Floodlight Cup**

12-11-1990 Ashington 1 Pulborough 5 (D Lewis 2, G Blunden, C Hutton, OG)

08-04-1991 Steyning Old Grammarians 6 Pulborough 0

The Squad for the two matches against Billingshurst in 1986 was:

P. Gibson, D. Leadbeatter, C. Spain, D. Rhoder, K. Furlonger, D. King, C. Hutton, S. Leadbeatter, M. Harrison, P. Bird, N. Bainbridge, T. Hatchard, A. Henderson, S. Hurst, M. Osborne, Manager M. Hatchard.

The Dickie Taylor Memorial Cup

I believe this cup was donated by Mr Dick Taylor, a former Petworth player. It was run by the Petworth Football Club and was for sides from the junior Divisions. The first competition we entered was in 1990.

16-12-1990 [A] Petworth 4 Pulborough 2 (G Blunden, S Whitehead)

24-01-1993 Fittleworth 11 Pulborough 0

06-03-1994 Fittleworth 4 Pulborough 2

20-04-1997 The Final Pulborough lost to Petworth

Pulborough also appeared in the final in 2002

Pulborough FC Team – Dickie Taylor Trophy Season 2001/02
Back row from left Matt Parry, Steve Adsett, mascot (Mickey), Stuart Lidbetter, Sam Groves, Peter Roberts, Stuart Phillips, Trevor Blunden, Malcolm Jupp (manager).
Front row from left Shaun Jupp, Rob Symonds, Craig Jupp, Aaron Greenfield, Jason Leadbeatter, Anthony Parker, Chris Phillips.

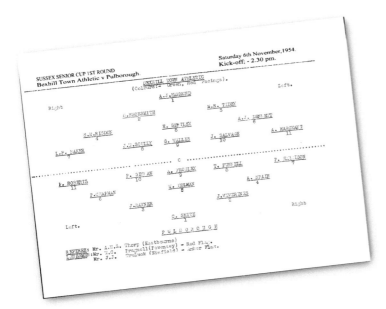

Pulborough Football Club ~ 195

Friendly Matches 1946-2010

14-9-1946 [A] West Chiltington (L 1-3)

11-1-1947 [H] Billingshurst (L 2-3) played with 10 men

11-9-1947 [A] Fittleworth (W 4-0)

13-9-1947 [H] Billingshurst (W 3-1)

17-9-1947 [H] Fittleworth (W 5-1)

15-11-1947 [H] Worthing Police (W 8-4)

22-11-1947 [H] Storrington (W 9-0)

27-11-1947 [A] Storrington (L 3-5)

14-4-1948 [A] Horsham A (L 1-4)

11-9-1948 [H] West Chiltington (W 3-1)

15-9-1948 [A] Horsham A (L 1-2)

8-1-1949 [A] Storrington (D 0-0)

2-4-1949 [H] Arundel (L 2-4)

29-8-1949 [H] Sussex Bricks (W 5-2)

3-9-1949 [H] Bury (L 1-3)

10-9-1949 [A] Fittleworth (D 2-2)

17-9-1949 [H] Fittleworth (D 1-1)

18-2-1950 [A] Denmead (W 2-1)

5-4-1950 [H] Barclays Bank (W 2-1)

14-4-1950 [H] Old Portshmouthians (D 2-2)

16-4-1950 [H] Denmead (D 2-2)

1950 Champions vs Rest of West Sussex League [at Arundel] (L 1-3)

26-8-1950 [H] Danson Sports Club (L 3-6) P. Roberts 3

2-9-1950 [H] Billingshurst (W 2-0) P. Harrison 2

6-9-1950 [A] Billingshurst (W 5-0) P. Roberts 5

30-9-1950 [A] Barclays Bank (W 2-1) P. Harrison 1 P. Roberts 1

2-4-1951 [H] Streatham (W 4-2) P. Harrison 2 B. Wells 2

1951 [H] West Sussex Police (L 4-5)

1951 [H] Storrington (W 5-4)

10-11-1951 [A] Hove (W 12-1) P. Roberts 6 P. Harrison 2 B. Wells 2, J. Ovenell 1, D. Roberts 1

26-12-1951 [A] Horsham Reserves (L 1-7) A. Frogley 1

17-9-1952 [H] Midhurst (L 2-6) B. Wells 2

25-10-1952 [H] Turners Hill (W 5-4) A. Smith 2, B. Wells 2, D. Roberts 1

Between 1952 and 1979 there were a number of matches played but no results were recorded

26-8-1979 [H] Youth Team (W 7-0) J. Jupp 3, N. Bainbridge 1, R. Chandler 1, C. Spain 1, D. Stenning 1

4-9-1979 [A] Plaistow (D 3-3) C. Hutton 1, R. Jupp 1, N. Marshman 1

21-10-1979 [H] Youth Team (W 9-2) J. Pritchard 4, N. Turner 2, R. Jupp 1, C. Spain 1, S. White 1

12-8-1980 [A] Southwater (L 0-5)

16-8-1980 [A] Alfold (L 2-5) R. Hewitt 1, C. Hutton 1

30-8-1980 [A] Watersfield (W 3-1) D. Smith 2, N. Bainbridge 1

10-10-1981 [A] Wittering & Birdham United (L 1-2) OG 1

18-8-1982 [H] Shipley (L 2-3) J. Gallagher 1, S. Leadbeatter 1

24-8-1982 [H] Tabernacle (L 0-1)

28-8-1982 [H] Billingshurst (W 7-?) C. Hutton 2, S. Leadbeatter 2, J. Gallagher 1, A. Kynoch 1, C. Spain 1

4-8-1983 [H] Horsham Olympic (W 3-2) D. Smith 2 R. Hewitt 1

13-8-1983 [A] Loxwood (W 1-4) R. Hewitt 2, P. Mose 1, M. Ruff 1

16-8-1983 [H] Slinfold (W 2-1) D. King 2

17-8-1983 [H] Slinfold (W 6-0) R. Hewitt 2, D. Fry 1, L. Rout 1, OG 1, 1?

21-8-1983 [A] West Chiltington (D 1-1) P. Bird 1

23-8-1983 [H] Petworth (W 4-0) S. Leadbeatter 2, C. Hutton 1, D. King 1

25-8-1983 [H] Amberley (L 2-6) P. Bird 1, H. Agourram 1

28-8-1983 [H] Wisborough Green (D 3-3) P. Mose 1, A. Petras 1, OG 1

30-8-1983 [A] Sunallon (L 1-3) S. Freegard 1

30-8-1983 [H] Watersfield (W 4-3)

14-8-1984 [H] Barns Green (L 1-3) C. Spain 1

21-8-1984 [A] Watersfield (L 0-3)

23-8-1984 [A] Chichester Hospital (D 4-4) D. Fry 1, M. Harrison 1, D. King 1, C. Spain 1

28-8-1984 [H] Petworth (L 0-2)

14-8-1984 [A] Steyning OG (L 1-4) D. Lewis 1

18-8-1986 [H] Wick Res (W 4-2) M. Harrison 2, P. Bird 1, C. Spain 1

20-8-1986 [A] Midhurst Res (W 2-0) N. Bainbridge 1, OG 1

23-8-1986 [A] Lancing & Sompting Legion (L 1-2) M. Harrison 1

26-8-1986 [H] Durrington (L 0-2)

1-8-1987 [A] Broadbridge Heath (W 2-0) M. Harrison 1, D. Lewis 1

11-8-1987 [H] Wisborough Green (D 0-0)

15-8-1987 [H] Haywards Heath Reserves (W 4-2) N. Bainbridge 2, S. Leadbeatter 1, K. Taylor 1

18-8-1987 [A] Chichester Reserves (W 5-2) K. Taylor 2, N. Bainbridge 1, Tim Hatchard 1, C. Hutton 1

1-9-1987 [H] British Airtours (W 2-1) K. Furlonger 2

9-8-1988 [H] Worthing BCOB (L 2-3) D. Lewis 1, K. Taylor 1

13-8-1988 [H] Worthing Civic (W 9-0) N. Bainbridge 2, G. Blunden 2, D. Leadbeatter 1, S. Leadbeatter 1, C. Spain 1, D. Smith 1, OG 1

17-8-1988 [A] Portfield Reserves (W 2-0) D. Lewis 1, K. Taylor 1

17-8-1981 [H] Wisborough Green (L 1-3) Tim Hatchard 1

19-8-1985 [H] Grenediers (W 3-2) D. Rhoder 1, K. Taylor 1, P. Wilson 1

23-8-1989 [A] Portfield Reserves (W 5-2) K. Furlonger 1, G. Phur 1, C. Spain 1, N. Spicer 1, P. Wilson 1

Other matches were played but not recorded.

Pulborough FC Presidents

CAPTAIN NESTON WILLIAM DIGGLE, CMG, RN (7 Jan 1881–17 Dec 1963) was the second husband of Lady Gladys Barttelot (nee Gladys St Aubyn Angove). They married in April 1920 and lived at Stopham House. Lady Gladys's first husband, Lt-Col Sir Walter Balfour Barttelot, was killed in action in Iran in 1918. Their son, Sir Walter Barttelot inherited his title. Captain Diggle served on the ship the Grafton and saw action in Gallipoli during the First World War, he retired in 1926. He was a friend of Sir Winston Churchill and was at one time Naval Attaché in Rome. He left Stopham in 1938. He was President of Pulborough FC from 1922 until 1938. Neston was a lover of all sports, he donated trophies to the Bowling Club, the Cricket Club, the Snooker Club, the Tennis Club and to the Football Club, some of these trophies are still played for today. The Pulborough Benevolent Cup and the Pulborough Boys Cup were trophies played for by the Football Club. On more than one occasion Neston helped the Club out of financial problems. He was Chairman of the local British Legion. He was a great patron to the parish and a huge loss when he moved away in 1938 to reside in Wiltshire.

MR G.R. NEWBURY was President from 1938 to 1940.

MR W. J. HARWOOD (WALLACE) was born in Worthing in 1906 and sadly passed away 16th February 1965, while on holiday abroad. He was the son of Mr Tom Harwood, the local policeman. Wallace went to the local St. Mary's School. On leaving School I was told that he went to work for Rice Brothers, but I cannot confirm this. In the early 1930s he and Mr Evershed started a garage business in London Road in Pulborough, Wallace carried on when Mr Evershed left the business. He also set up a factory behind Sopers Cottages which made munitions for the war period. These ventures were a great success and after the war he opened a new factory in London Road called Spiro Gills; the gilled tubes the firm made were exported worldwide. At one time the firm employed over 200 people and was very successful. The company was eventually sold to APV, a Crawley company. Wallace was well known in the county and people recognised his car with its personalized number plate. In his younger days he was a keen sportsman, playing snooker and tennis; he loved horse racing and was often seen at Goodwood. He joined the Club in the 1921/22 season as a junior and played until 1935, when he retired. He was at one time captain of the team. He played in several different positions and was a good player. He was a committee member and in 1949 was elected as President, a position he held until 1955. As a player, committee member and then as President, Wallace was a very important and valued member of the Club.

MR ELLIS ROBERTS was born in Trawsfynydd, North Wales on 17th June 1906. He went to the local School in Trawsfynydd and then onto Blaenau Ffestiniog, where he passed his exams to go to university. Unfortunately, because he had 5 siblings, this was not financially possible. In 1923, at the age of 17, he moved to London, despite not knowing anybody. He managed to find work as an agent with the Prudential Insurance Company. He was then moved to Pulborough, just before war commenced. Ellis joined the RAF and was later mentioned in dispatches. After leaving the forces he worked as a Civil Servant until he was medically retired just before his 60th birthday. He died in Worthing Hospital on 29th September 1980. Ellis joined the Club in 1947, was a committee member and in 1950 became Chairman until 1955, when he was elected as President of the Club. He resigned from this position in 1963 having been a very fine member of the Club.

MR W. J. HARWOOD, was again elected as President in 1963 until his untimely death in 1965.

MR VICTOR CORDEN (1903-1987) was born above the chemist's shop at Swan Corner at the bottom of Church Hill, son of Mr L.N. Corden, the local pharmacist. Victor went to St Mary's School and Midhurst Grammar. Victor spent some time in Highcliffe, which in those days was in Hampshire, this was work related, but while he was there he played sport for them. He worked as an optician before becoming a pharmacist, he took over from his father and worked in the shop at Swan Corner until he retired. Victor was a very active man, he was in the Observer Corps and was a very keen member of the bell ringers at St Mary's Church. He was a very good all round sportsman, winning trophies for snooker and tennis, he was also secretary of the Mens' Club. Victor joined 'The Robins' in 1920 when the Club restarted after the war, he was captain of the side from 1928 to 1931, when he had to retire from playing because of knee problems. He played in several positions, full back, half back and in attack, he was a versatile and very good player. He was elected President in 1965 and remained until 1987, our longest serving President.

JEFF ?. There is no record of his surname, was President in 1988-1989 and 1989-1990. He was Landlord of the Rose and Crown.

MR CHARLES P. BARNETT (PERCY) was born in Wisborough Green on the 22nd of September 1914. He went to School in Petworth and then to St Mary's School in Pulborough. He was brought up by his grandmother. On leaving School he went to work for Allfrey's as a plumber. He did his two years National Service in the Royal Engineers, he was recalled in 1945 for a clean up campaign and spent time in Belgium. On leaving the forces he went to work at Spiro Gills, staying there until he retired. During the 1930s he played for Codmore Hill FC. Percy joined Pulborough FC in the 1939/40 season. After the war the Club resumed in 1946 and Percy started playing again, finishing his career in 1949, but on the odd occasion, if short of players he would turn out for the Club, at the end of the 1952-1953 season he played in the County League for us at the age of 39. He made 52 appearances for the Club. He was a tough tackling defender who gave his opponents a hard time. He became Club Secretary in 1949 and stayed until 1958. In 1958 he was elected onto The Council of the Sussex County Football Association, he was also on the selection committee for the West Sussex League Intermediate side. He was later made a Life Member of the West Sussex League. At one time Percy was our groundsman and he also ran the line. He was made President in 1991 and stood down in 2001. He umpired for the local cricket team and played bar billiards for the Arun Hotel. Percy was a great servant to Pulborough FC and to the County. He passed away in 2004.

MR RUSS PHILLIPS joined the Club in 1966 and left in 1970. He was a Physical Training Instructor with the Army. He went to play for other Clubs and then into coaching and managing different Clubs. Russ became manager of Pulborough FC in 1993 and left this position at the end of the 1994/95 season. He became President of the Club in 2001 and is still our President today. I am sorry not to have more information.

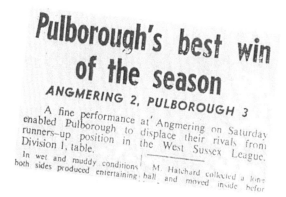

Pulborough's best win of the season

ANGMERING 2, PULBOROUGH 3

A fine performance at Angmering on Saturday enabled Pulborough to displace their rivals from runners-up position in the West Sussex League. Division 1, table.

In wet and muddy conditions both sides produced entertaining ball and moved inside befor M. Hatchard collected a long

Pulborough FC Chairmen

I can find no information of the Club's chairmen before 1928, but they obviously had one and also a committee who ran the Club. Mr A. Brockhurst was the chairman at the start of the 1928/29 season and continued until the 1931/32 season, when the Club for some reason did not have a side. Mr Brockhurst was the owner of New Place Manor, a vast estate which stretched from the Manor House, south as far as Rectory Lane, east as far as Broomers Hill Lane, to the north down to the railway line and west to the A29.

CAPTAIN CLARK was made Chairman 28th September 1934 until 8th October 1934.

MR W. BARTLETT was Chairman from 8th October 1934 until the end of the season, he was thought to be a clerk at NatWest Bank in Station Road.

CAPTAIN CLARK was re-elected as Chairman 25th July 1935 until the end of the season.

MR R. GOODSELL (REG) was made Chairman at the start of the 1936/37 season and resigned from this post in 1948. He was a former player and lived in Mare Hill.

MR W.A. BAILEY (WALLY), was elected chairman 11th August 1948 and stood down at the end of the 1949/50 season. He lived in Rectory Close. On leaving the forces he went to work in the office at Spiro Gills, he was also clerk for the local parish council. Wally was a well respected man in the community, he was the father of Malcolm, who went on to become well known in football circles.

MR E. ROBERTS, see Presidents.

MR S. POORE (STAN) was made chairman in 1957 until the end of the 1958/59 season. See players from 1946/52.

MR L. GREENFIELD (TOBY), was born in Pulborough 26th June 1931. He went to the local St. Mary's School. On leaving School at fourteen years of age, he started work at New Place Manor as a waiter. He did his National Service in the army, with the Royal Engineers. On leaving the forces in 1952 he started work at Spiro Gills in the gilling shop, he stayed there until 1993, he retired from working in 1999. Toby was a committee member in 1957 and in 1959 he became chairman until the end of the 1972/73 season. He was not player, but he was a linesman for the Club for many years, Finally calling it a day in 1985.

BASIL THAYRE was born in Upperton, near Petworth, 16th June 1933. He went to School in Sutton, then Duncton and then onto Midhurst Grammar School. His first job was working as a welder in Grimsby. Coming back to Sussex, he started to work for W.G. Keyte, an engineering firm in Billingshurst. He did his National Service in the army with REME. On leaving the army he joined the Police Force, then spent time in the Merchant Navy, then became a driver, working for Watts. Basil then started his own business. He was appointed chairman at the start of the 1973/74 season. He resigned at the end of the 1974/75 season. He played for the Club and also for Tillington. He lives in Petworth.

MR L. GREENFIELD (TOBY) was re-elected 27th May 1975 and at the end of the 1977/78 season Toby did Finally retire, he was a huge loss to the Club, after giving to many years service to the Club. He still lives in the village.

MR M. RALPH (MICK), was born in Haslemere on 30th October 1943. At five years of age he was put into an orphanage for four years. When he was nine he came to live in Pulborough and was brought up by the Edwards family, who lived at the bottom of Codmore Hill in a bungalow called 'The Oaks'. He attended North Heath School and then went to Rydon County Secondary School, where he stayed on for an extra year and left when he was sixteen. In 1959 he went to work for Spiro Gills and would spend the next 35 years there. He then went to work for Trans Cool Ltd and then onto Trans Cool Systems. He took over as temporary chairman 7th July 1978, for about six months. He played for the Club and he also played for Fittleworth, usually as a full back. Mick is a very fine bowls player, he has played for Pulborough and also Fittleworth, he has also represented the County. Mick still lives in the village.

MR A. PAYNE (ALBERT) was born in Shoreham 15th June 1930. He came from a Fittleworth family and he grew up there, going to the local School. Albert left School at fourteen years of age and started work at Mr Gadd's farm in Fittleworth. In 1955 he set up his own fencing company, he still works part time, with his son Terry now taking the major role. He was made chairman during the 1978/79 season and retired at the end of the 1987/88 season. He did not play, but he was linesman for many years. Albert was a loss to the Club, having supported the Club as chairman, linesman and as a spectator. He now lives in West Chiltington.

MR S.A. PETRAS (TONY) was born in Dorking 1st July 1957. He went to Billingshurst junior School and then to Collyer's School in Horsham. On leaving there he started to work at Sun Alliance, he also worked as a lifeguard, at a leisure centre, a sales rep for Carringdales and Gray and Rowsell. He was appointed chairman at the start of the 1989/90 season and resigned at the end of the 1990/91 season. Tony played football and cricket for Pulborough and Billingshurst and was very good at both sports. He now lives in Storrington.

MISS C. RICHARDS (COLLEEN) was born in Rustington 25th July 1964. She went to the local St. Mary's School and then to The Weald in Billingshurst. After leaving school she went work for Sun Alliance in Horsham and went on to British Caledonian Airways; she now works at Lodge Hill. On 24th June 1991 Colleen was elected as the Club's first chairwoman, a post she held for one year. She was also secretary of the Club at one time. At the start of the 1989/90 season the Club decided to run a Sunday side and Colleen was appointed joint manager of the team, a job she carried out until the start of the 1990/91 season. Colleen lives in the village.

MR J. JUPP (JOHN) was born in Pulborough 25th December 1950. He attended the local St Mary's School and then The Weald in Billingshurst. On leaving he went to work in Storrington for Ross Chickens, then went to Spiro Gills in 1971 and stayed there until 1993. In 1994 he went to work for the Post Office and is still there today. He joined the Club in 1969 and made his second team debut against Summerley Park Rangers on 13th September 1969. His first team debut was against Inland Revenue 8th December 1973. He was Captain of the second team in the 1975/76 season. He played in several different positions, but mainly in midfield, he always tried to play the right way by trying to pass the ball and not using the long ball. At the start of the 1983/84 season he became the manager of the second XI for a year. John was elected as Chairman of the Club on 22 June 1992 and resigned in 2010. During his time as Chairman he worked very hard for the Club, often attending meetings when other members of the Committee were not able to. With him in charge the Club was always run very well with the off the field activities. He was a big loss to the Club when he retired. He still lives in the village.

MR J. DAVY (JEFF) was born in Shoreham 26th April 1953. He went to Storrington Primary School and then to Rydon County Secondary in Thakeham. On leaving school he started work as an apprentice plumber with Stockers of Storrington, leaving there he continued with the trade and now works for himself. Jeff was elected as chairman in 2010. In his playing days Jeff played for Amberley, Fittleworth and Storrington. Jeff lives in the village.

Pulborough FC Managers

MALCOLM BAILEY. Although Malcolm was not our manager, I want to mention him, because he was the first person to come and help with training and coaching during the 1970/71 season. He was born in 1951 in Pulborough and attended St Mary's School before going on to Collyer's in Horsham. At Collyer's he played for North West Sussex Schools XI at under 15, Sussex County Schools XIs at U15 and U18.

Whilst at School he qualified as a preliminary FA coach. He was in the Sussex FA youth XI that reached the FA County Youth Cup Final in 1969. He played for FA Youth and Colts XIs in his final year at school. Malcolm made his senior debut for Lewes in the Athenian League and in the 1970/71 season won a winners' medal in the Sussex Senior Cup. In the same year he represented the Sussex Senior XI. He then went to Cambridge University and in 1970 as a freshman he gained his Blue, played four times at Wembley undefeated and was captain of the side in 1973.

In 1970/71 he was selected for FA XIs. He continued to play senior football, eventually signing for Horsham and playing in the Isthmian League, winning the Sussex Senior Cup with them. In 1974 he began teaching at Charterhouse, in the geography department, and in 1980 he took over the School's 1st XI. He coached in soccer camps in the USA for three summers. Malcolm also spent a year in New Zealand teaching and coaching.

Other clubs he played for were Sutton United, where he played in the 1st round of the FA Cup against Bournemouth in 1975, Camberley Town, Woking, Malden Vale and Godalming Town. He was awarded his FA Full Licence (UEFA) and was later a Level 1 Educator. He was awarded FA Regional Coach of the Year for services to OCFC and School football. Malcolm was unable to play many games for Pulborough FC, as he was playing senior football, but whenever possible he would play for us, it never bothered him in which team he played, first or second XIs, he was always happy to help the Club. He was without doubt one of the finest players ever to play for the Club and one of the nicest men you could ever wish to meet.

MICK BROWNING (1975-80). Mick was born on 17th June 1940, in Horsham. He attended School in Clarence Road, then Denne Road, before going on to Collyer's School. On leaving, he went to work for British Rail for about a year, then started work as a sales rep and eventually became a buyer for a company based in London. He spent about ten years there, before moving on to Lucas Batteries in Hove, close to the old Goldstone Ground. Mick's long involvement with football began at the age of 12, when he ran the line for Horsham YMCA. Two years later he was playing for the club.

At the age of sixteen he was playing for Horsham, where he stayed for two years. Around this time Mick was attracting the attention of professional clubs and was offered trials with 20 of them, including, Nottingham Forest, Manchester City and Tottenham. He had about 6 months playing at Reading and the following season played for Addlestone. He then returned to play for Horsham for a couple of years. At the age of 20 Mick was probably playing the best football of his life and spent the next 4 years playing for one of the top amateur clubs in the country, Tooting & Mitcham. He then returned to his home club, Horsham, where he took over as manager for the next 2 years. He spent the next year managing APV Athletic. He was then asked to go back to be the manager of Horsham YMCA, which he did for 3 years. Now in his early thirties he played for Lewes, Maidstone, Worthing and finished his playing career at Petworth.

At the start of the 1975/76 season Mick took over as manager of Pulborough FC and stayed for 5 years. He then moved on to manage Sun Alliance, again staying for 5 years. He then took on the role of Manager/Chairman at Horsham Olympic. Now into his fifties, he became Horsham Reserve team manager. At the age of 53 Mick was made Chairman of Horsham FC and stayed for 7 years before taking a year off and a well-earned rest. He was then persuaded to come back to Horsham as Director of Football.

Now in his mid-sixties, he became Chairman of Horsham YMCA, a post he still holds today. Mick's Honours: Sussex Youth Representative, 2 England Amateur Caps v Scotland, scored the winning goal v New Zealand, scored again. Won 49 caps for Sussex, Sussex Sunday Rep games, played for British Railways against French Railways, represented the Isthmian League and the Athenian League, played in FA Games, was called up for Great Britain XI. Mick was awarded a medal for 50 years service to football, an honour given to very few people. Another very nice man.

My thanks to both Malcolm and Mick for their information.

MICK HATCHARD (1980-1990) See Author's notes.

ANDY KYNOCH (1990-1992). Andy became Player/Manager of the club at the beginning of the 1990 season. He found it difficult after being a player to become a player/manager. He became frustrated because of poor results and in October of 1992 he resigned, feeling that he could no longer motivate the players. This was a great shame, as nobody gave more to the club than Andy. He introduced a "Goal of the Month" award to try and motivate the players and brought new sponsors into the club. The committee reluctantly accepted his resignation, thanked him for his dedication and expressed the wish that he remain with the club on the committee and concentrate on playing.

KEVIN TAYLOR/COLIN SPAIN (1992-1993). The committee asked Kevin Taylor if he would take over as first team Manager, with the assistance of Colin Spain. They both agreed. Taking over in difficult circumstances, they worked hard for the club. At the end of the season they both stated that they wanted to resign their positions, as it was not easy to combine playing and managing and they both wanted to play in the coming year.

RUSS PHILLIPS (1993-1996). Unfortunately, I have not been able to obtain all the information that I required. Russ, I believe, was born in the Nottingham area. In his early years he was in the forces and was based at Thorney Island, where he was a PT instructor. He first played for the club in 1967. His first XI debut was against Ferring Reserves 14th September 1968. He left the Club in 1969. He played for Billingshurst, Petworth and, I think, other clubs. Russ took over as manager of Pulborough in 1993. The team came close to getting promotion on a couple of occasions, but just missed out. He left in 1996. He coached or was manager at Billingshurst and Horsham. He was made President of the club in 2001 and is still our President today.

MICK HATCHARD/KEITH CLARK (1996-1998). When I was asked to take over as manager again, in 1996, I had Keith as my assistant. He was born in Rustington 9th February 1954. He attended Coldwaltham Primary School and went on to Herbert Shiner in Petworth. After leaving school he went to work for Mr Allfrey in Lower Street, Pulborough and spent 4 years there as an apprentice builder, before becoming self-employed. Keith joined the club at the start of the 1969/70 season and played his first game on 15ᵗʰ September 1969 for the second XI against Felpham. He made his first XI debut 19ᵗʰ February 1972 against Littlehampton and left at the end of that season. He was a forward and a very fine player, as he proved when he went on to play County League football.

Despite a horrendous motorcycle accident when he was about 19 and lost the use of one eye, Keith came back to play at senior level. He was a forward and scored a lot of goals, he had the ability to hold the ball up and bring other players into the game. He played for Watersfield, Littlehampton, Arundel and Billingshurst. He represented the West Sussex League side. Towards the end of his career he was Player/Manager of Watersfield. Keith was also a very good cricketer. He now lives in Shoreham.

DAVID SMITH (1998-1999). Dave was born in Pulborough 13ᵗʰ May 1963. He went to St Mary's School, then attended The Weald School in Billingshurst. On leaving The Weald he did a hotel management course at Chichester College, then spent time working for Spiro Gills, before moving on to work for Lorlin Electronics in Billingshurst. Dave was self-employed for a while and then went to work for Royal Mail, where he is still employed. He made his debut for the club on 20ᵗʰ October 1979 against North Holmwood for the second XI and played his first game for the first XI on 13ᵗʰ September 1980 against Lavant. He left the club just before our first League match in 1983. He returned to play for the club at the start of the 1998/99 season.

He could play in any position up front, but was usually on the wing. He was very quick and for someone not that tall he was superb in the air, scored a lot of goals and made many others for his team, using his great pace. It was a big loss to the team when he moved on in 1983. Dave played senior football for Horsham and Horsham YMCA, and was very successful. He played for the Sussex County League side and was also selected for the Sussex XI. He took over as manager of 'The Robins' in 1998 and resigned in December 1999. Dave was very committed as a player and as a manager and I think he felt he was not getting the same commitment from some of the players. It was sad to see him leave. He now lives in Billingshurst.

STEVE BUSS (1999-2002). Once again I have not been able to obtain all the information I required. Steve, I believe, joined the club at the beginning of the 1993/94 season and I think his first game was against Harting 0 4ᵗʰ September 1993. The club has no archives to tell me when he left the club as a playing member. He played for Amberley and I think he played for Fittleworth and Watersfield. As a player for us he was fully committed and a very strong tackler, a good defender, who was usually on the left side of the defence. Steve was asked if he would take over as manager in December 1999. It is never easy at the best of times, taking over in mid-season was going to be even harder. I know he had some problems with some of the players, but he did his best for the club. He finally resigned in 2002.

MATT PARRY/LIAM WADEY (2002-2004). At the AGM of 2002-2003, there were no nominations for the position of first team manager, so it was decided that Matt Parry and Liam Wadey would take on the running of the team. Matt was born in Carshalton in 1977. He went to Merrow School and then Cranleigh, before going to Godalming College. On leaving there he went to work for Friends Provident. I believe he joined the club in 1998. He played in several different positions, but was usually found in the forward line. He was a very good club man, as a player and committee member and did a fine job of managing the team. Matt also played for Bramley and Ewhurst. He resigned in 2004, so he could concentrate on playing. He lives in Billingshurst.

LIAM WADEY was born in Chichester on 5th June 1976. He attended St Mary's School, the Weald School in Billingshurst, then studied at Chichester College for two years. Liam started work for Pattinson Pressings as a toolmaker, before moving on to Welch Machining, just outside West Chiltington. He joined the Club in 1996 and soon became a regular first team player. He was a central defender, very good in the air and a very fine man marker. When going forward for set pieces, he scored a few goals. He stepped in when the club was not able to find a manager for the first team. He and Matt did a fine job for the club in difficult circumstances. Liam played for Loxwood before coming to us. He lives in Partridge Green.

ADAM MASTERS (2004-2005). Adam became manager at the start of the 2004-2005 season. The only information I have is that he played for Lancing and Sompting Legion. It was a short and unhappy period for him. For some reason the players and supporters did not take to him and he left at the end of the season.

MALCOLM JUPP (2005-2011) was born in Pulborough on 5th April 1957. He went to St Mary's School before going on to The Weald School in Billingshurst. On leaving he went to work for Linfields in Thakeham, then left and worked for Spiro Gills. When the firm closed he joined a Billingshurst company, where he still works. He signed on for the club at the start of the 1973/74 season and played his first game for the second XI against Northchapel on 11th September 1973. He made his first XI debut 22nd December 1973 against Lavant. He had a rather mixed playing career; he began as a goalkeeper, then after a few years started playing as a forward, then reverted back to being a goalkeeper.

When playing in the forward line he scored his share of goals. As a goalkeeper he was a good shot stopper, with quick reflexes. Malc, I believe, stopped playing in 1994. He took over as manager in 2005. This was a difficult decision for the committee because he had no experience in taking training or coaching. To his credit, he realised that he needed some assistance and John Jupp, Dave Smith and I helped out as much as possible during his first year. Going through the Club's archives, it mentions that he was looking for some help with the team, but it does not say if assistance was given. It was not until 2009 that that he was given an assistant.

MARTYN RALPH (2009-2011). Martyn was born in Chichester on 30th January 1971. He attended St Mary's School in Pulborough before going on to The Weald School in Billingshurst. His first year in work was at World Map Ltd, he then went to Spiro Gills for the next six years and has been at Duncan Reeds Ltd for the last 18 years. He played for Graffham FC for 5 years before joining us in 1994. I could find no team sheets that told me when he played his first games for the club. Martyn was a versatile player, he played in every position in defence and also turned out in midfield. He was a very committed man, strong in the tackle and tried to use the ball well, someone you wanted on your side. In 2009 he was appointed to assist the first team. He did a fine job and was of great assistance to Malcolm. Martyn and Malcolm both left in 2011.

Second Team Managers

MICK HATCHARD (1979-1980).

JOHN STEWART (1980-1983). John was born on 26th October 1946 in Pulborough. He attended St Mary's School and then Worthing Technical College. On leaving, he started work for Willmer's as an apprentice electrician, then moved on to Allfrey's, where he stayed for many years, until leaving to become a self-employed electrician. He joined the club at the beginning of the 1962/63 season and made his debut for the second XI on 23rd March 1963, against Cocking. John never played for the first XI, a great shame; he said that he wanted to play, even just one game, but he never got his wish. Due to his size and the fact that he wore spectacles, he always played on the wing. He was very quick and could beat defenders and scored quite a few goals. Although he had no experience of coaching or managing, he was persuaded to give it a go. As second XI manager his task was to select the team and be with them when they played. He did not have to take training sessions, but he often came along and wanted to learn. He had the respect of the players and proved to be a good manager. John was a great club man, was vice-captain of the second XI one year and team secretary in 1966. He was the club's representative on the Sports and Social Club Committee for many years. Sadly, John passed away on 2nd October 2010, after a massive heart attack. He was a nice guy, liked by everyone.

JOHN JUPP (1983-1984).

JOHN STEWART/JIM LEADBEATTER (1989-1991).

COLIN SPAIN (1991-1992).

KEVIN TAYLOR (1992-1992).

KEITH KNAGGS (1992-1993). Keith joined the Club in 1986 and made his debut 31st January 1987 against Graffham and his first XI debut against Southwater 22nd April 1987. He took over as manager in December 1992 and resigned at the end of the season.

MALCOLM JUPP (1993-1996).

MALCOLM JUPP/COLIN MARTIN (1996-1999).

COLIN MARTIN (1999-2000). Colin was born in Colliers Wood, South London 30th August 1950. He attended Orange Park School. On leaving there he started work as an apprentice electrician for Girdler, he also spent time at AD Reeves. He worked at Gatwick Airport as an electrician, before he became Project Manager. His first club as an adult was playing for Swan Athletic, he then went on to Tooting and Mitcham. In 1996 he was assistant manager with Malcolm. In 1999 he took over as manager and left at the end of the season. Colin was also on the committee and put in a lot of hard work, organised raffles and prizes and was a very valued member of the club. He left at the end of the season. He was involved in the management of T.D. Shipley. Colin lives in Crawley.

MALCOLM JUPP/MARK WARDELL (2000-2002). Mark was born in Chichester 23rd May 1964. He went to Petworth Primary School before going on to Midhurst Grammar School. On leaving he started work for Elliott, Henley and Wardell as an apprentice electrician. He then went self employed in the building trade. He played for Watersfield, Graffham and then came to Pulborough. I believe he joined us in the mid-1990s and stopped playing in 2003. Mark played as a defender, usually at centre half. A big man, over six feet tall and well built, he was a good old-fashioned, no-nonsense defender. He was assistant manager from 2000 to 2002. He also served on the committee. Mark lives in the village.

MALCOLM JUPP/MARTYN RALPH (2002-2005).

NICK BERRY/MARTYN RALPH (2005-2010). Nick was born on 22nd February 1970 in Dorking. He went to St Mary's School in Pulborough and The Weald in Billingshurst. On leaving he worked for double glazing firm Sussex Aluminium, then for Stewart electronics and is now at ELP. He played for Graffham for a number of years before joining Pulborough. He played in midfield in his early days, then settled down to play as a full back.

Pulborough FC supporters on the way to watch their team play at Arundel on 17th September 1921.

Author's Notes

I was born at 9 Elm Grove, Horsham on 9th February 1943. My family moved to live in Stane Street Close Pulborough just after the war. I attended St Mary's School then Rydon County Secondary in Thakeham. Many other families had just moved into Stane Street Close and there were a lot of youngsters about my age, boys and girls. On the green, in the middle of the estate, many hours were spent playing football or cricket and sometimes rounders, but mainly football and nearly everyone would join in. As November 5th got close, lots of us would go out to the local woods and meadows to collect anything that would burn for our bonfire, which was held on the green. There was always a huge bonfire and everybody from the estate would come out to watch. I was fortunate to grow up with some good young people and I am pleased to say that I am still friends with them today.

I loved sport from an early age and when I went to Rydon School I had the opportunity to participate in athletics, cricket and football. I was not that great at cricket, not a very good batsman, but I opened the bowling for the School team, enjoyed the fielding and had quite a good arm. The athletic season was an enjoyable one. In the 4 years that I was at school I was unbeaten over 100 yards and 220 yards, but was no good over anything longer. I represented the school in the Sussex Schools Championships, where I came second in the 100 yards. Something I forgot, while at St Mary's I represented the area in the West Sussex Rural Schools Sports Association Athletic Championships, held on 19th June 1954, when I finished in second place again.

Back to Rydon School, the football season was the one I enjoyed the most. In my first year I played for my house side (Weald) and then for the School XI and stayed there until I left. At the age of thirteen I was playing for the West Sussex Schools teams at under-fourteen and under-fifteen level. I was lucky enough to score a hat-trick on my debut for the U-15 side.

Just after my fifteenth birthday I was seen by a Portsmouth FC scout, while playing for my school team and was asked to go for a trial with them. On 22nd of April I went for the trial at Fratton Park, where a team of trial players played against their under-19 side, which was their youth team. Playing against lads 3 or 4 years older than me was tough. I did not play well and my chance was gone. The only good experience of the day was playing at Fratton Park. On the way in to the ground I was stopped by Derek Dougan, who asked if I was going to play in the trial match and wished me the best of luck. In 1959 I was selected for the Sussex Boys Club side, who were playing in the National Association of Boys Clubs Championships.

I left school in 1958 and started work for W.G. Keyte and Son, an engineering firm in Billingshurst and attended Crawley College once a week. I stayed there for 28 years and finished my working life with Royal Mail, retiring in 2008 when I reached 65.

My football career started in 1957, when I was fourteen years old. A friend who lived in West Chiltington persuaded me to sign on for them; they played in the old Horsham & District League. I would cycle to Thakeham to play for the school team in the morning, then cycle to

West Chiltington to have lunch and play for them in the afternoon, then cycle back to Pulborough in the evening. My memory is not the best, but my first recollection of being asked to play for Pulborough was on the school bus. I was on the bus when Shirley Barnett got on and handed me an envelope. When I opened it, it was from Mr Percy Barnett, Secretary of Pulborough FC. Inside was a note, saying that I had been selected to play for the first XI against Bognor Town Reserves on 29th March 1958 and that if I wanted to play would I sign the enclosed form and return it to him as soon as possible.

I had a short spell at Horsham at the start of the season and, after playing in a first XI against a second XI, and playing reasonably well, I spoke with the coach about my chances of getting games with the first XI. He was honest with me and told me that I would not get into the first XI, but he said I should stay and try to improve my game, as I had potential. Not long after I left and as I had friends in the Horsham area, they persuaded me to go and play for Forest Old Boys. In my first game I was lucky enough to score a hat-trick. Towards the end of the season I played in the only Cup Final of my career, but sadly the team lost.

After my two years away I came back to Pulborough and played the rest of my football with them. My playing days finished in 1979, when I sustained a broken leg and ligament damage. At 36 it was time to give up. Mick Browning, who was the first XI manager, asked me if I was interested in taking over as second XI manager the next season, 1979/80, so I agreed to give it a try. The following year Mick left and I took over as first team manager – and for the next ten years as well. I really needed a break from football, but I had a call from the chairman of Watersfield FC, who asked me if I was able to take over as manager of their club for the 1990/91 season, so I went to Watersfield.

I then thought I was going to get my rest away from the game but in July 1991 I took a phone call from a committee member of Loxwood FC, inviting me to a meeting with their committee with a view to taking over as their manager. The meeting went well and I agreed to take over. Things went very well and by January we were one of the favourites for promotion. But there were problems off the field; one committee member left and someone was brought in to replace him. It was not long before I was being told that I could not select certain players, but that I should pick others. No manager worth his salt is going to be told who to select, so I decided I would see out the season, but would resign at the end of it.

It looked as if I was going to get my rest from the game at last, but I was mistaken. I was informed by a friend that Billingshurst FC were going to offer me the position as manager of their club and in 1992 I became their manager. I had two very enjoyable seasons there and we were good enough to win the League in our first season together. I had a very good squad of players and off the field a fine committee who allowed me to get on with the job of managing the club. I would have liked to stay on, but I was unable to give the club my full commitment, so had to leave. My reasons for leaving were that Trish, my wife, had just come out of hospital after a serious operation and we had recently moved house. I needed to have time at home. Although it was a busy time at home, it was good to have a break from football.

At the start of the 1996/97 season, I was appointed manager of Pulborough FC once again and brought in Keith Clark as my assistant. We had a good first season and the team finished as champions. I had one more season, but was finding it hard to give enough time to do the job that I wanted to do. I had a word with Keith and told him of my decision to give up, but that if he wanted to carry on as manager, I would help him as much as I could. He decided he would not continue without me.

Back in the 1960s I was asked if I could arrange a few friendly matches for some of the young lads in the village, this I was able to do, it was good to see so many of them go on to play for

Pulborough Youth Team (exact date unknown)
back row left to right Mick Hatchard (manager), Nick Hoffman, Mick Ruff, Rowland Branch, John Jupp, Trevor Johns, Roy Collins, Ian Anderson, Dave Clare (assistant manager)
front row Malcolm Jupp, Bob Chandler, Martin Pepper, Ron Warner, Guy Smith, Dave Beer.

Pulborough. I think it was 1976 or 1977 that I helped set up a boys team and they were entered into the Horsham Mini Minor League, I was manager and Colin Spain was my assistant, once again several of the lads went on to play for Pulborough.

My time in football was an enjoyable one, I was fortunate to play with some very fine players and in a very good standard of football. As a manager you are always under pressure, but you know this when you take the job. There were good times when you registered in time to play on Saturday. That was how I came to play for 'The Robins'.

As a young lad of eight or nine I would go and watch the team in their red shirts in front of hundreds of supporters and hope that one day I would be good enough to play for them. To be in the same team with some of the players who had been so successful in the early 1950s was something special for me.

There are good times, when your club is successful and I was lucky that I had seasons when the team I was with won league titles, or reached cup finals. On the downside, I was not a very good loser, although I would usually blame myself, rather than the team, but there were occasions when I did blow up. You need a thick skin to be a manager. There are always spectators who love to criticise and make comments about players or the team. I would usually ignore them, but sometimes I would think, "If you think you're so good, why don't you have a go at being the boss?" There was never any chance of that, of course. It's easy to criticise, but how many would have the courage to step up, put their name forward and actually become a coach or manager?

I live in the village and at the time of the book being published my wife Trish and I have been married for 51 years. We had 3 children, Allison, Tim and Martin. Sadly, on 13th November 1973, the worst day of our lives, we lost Martin, who had a rare type of leukaemia. Allison lives in the village and Tim lives in Rustington.

News clippings

In the course of my research in the archives of the local newspapers, looking for information about PFC, I stumbled upon a variety of general news items about Pulborough and its inhabitants, a selection of which I include here for the benefit of anyone who finds them as interesting as I did...

CRICKET CLUB HAS 100 PER CENT. SUPPORT

The retirements of Mr. H. E Cosens, Chairman for five years, and Maj. C. T. Hennings, Secretary for three years, were announced at the annual meeting of Pulborough Cricket Club at the Arun hotel on Friday. Tributes were paid to them for their work, and it was decided to make Mr Cosens an honorary life member. Mr Cosens, who first played for the club in 1914, and has held a number of offices, including that of Captain and Vice-Captain, said he would be pleased to accept. Mr. Cosens, reminding members that the club was revived a few years ago when there was practically no support, said he now regarded it as one of the organisations of the village which had 100 per cent. co-operation. Members were asked to assist with the work in extending the table. It was announced that a dance would be held at the Village Hall on Whit Monday. Officers elected: President, Comdr. M. Thornton; Chairman, Mr F. B. Kay; Secretary, Miss V. Spain; Treasurer, Mr. W. H. Fowler; Team Secretary, Mr. C. P. Barnett; Captain, Mr. P. E. Chapman; Vice-Captain, Mr T Cousins. The rest of the club's annual business was completed at a meeting last October.

WEDDING OF MISS R. H. AYSH

Miss Rosalie Helen Aysh, second daughter of Mr. and Mrs. J. D. Aysh, of Hardham Priory, Pulborough, was married at Pulborough Parish Church on Saturday to Mr. Ian Fraser Garloch, only son of Mr. Fraser Garloch, of London, and Mrs. Batholomew, of Lairg, Sutherland. Miss Aysh, a member of a well-known farming family, is also a well-known show jumper, and Mr. Garloch has ridden at point-to-point races. Given away by her father, the bride wore a gown of white lace, with a net veil held in place by an orange blossom headdress, and carried a bouquet of lilies and mixed white flowers. She was attended by her four sisters, the Misses Diana, Veronica, Loraine and Sonia Aysh, who were dressed in white nylon, with headdresses of pink roses and lilies-of-the-valley, and carried matching bouquets. Mr. Derek Twogood was best man. The Rev. W. R. Lloyd, Rector of Hardham, officiated, assisted by the Rev. G. H. W. Royle, Rector of Pulborough. After the service about 150 guests attended a reception at the bride's home.

PULBOROUGH

The death occurred on Sunday of Mrs. Maria May Greenfield, wife of Mr. Cecil Greenfield, who has a grocery business at Marehill. Mrs. Greenfield, who died in hospital at Hove, was the daughter of the late Mr. and Mrs. Raymond Goatcher, formerly of Gentle Harry's Farm, West Chiltington, and the funeral is to be this (Thursday) morning at West Chiltington Church. In addition to her husband she leaves a grown-up son.

His rubber boot slipping on the clutch of his car was blamed by Martin Broderick, of Blackgate-lane, Pulborough, at Petworth Court on Friday, for a collision with a lorry at Toat cross-roads. Pleading guilty to careless driving, he was fined £5, with £1 11s. costs. Supt. Doney said the lorry driver, who was on the Pulborough-London road, thought defendant, who was stopped at the junction, would let him pass. Suddenly he shot out of the lane and there was a collision.

PULBOROUGH

An ambulance driver of the first world war, Mrs. Constance Woodeson Burnford, of Upper Nash, Nutbourne, Pulborough, who told the police she had driven for years all over the world with a clean record, was fined £3 at Petworth on Friday for careless driving. She pleaded guilty. Supt. Doney said two constables on traffic patrol duty at Harborough-hill, West Chiltington, saw defendant drive a car across the junction from Monkmead-lane without stopping at the halt sign. Her speed was 20-25 m.p.h. Defendant told them she had used the road for years and never noticed the sign.

DOG WORRIED SHEEP

Trevor Blunden, of Little Brinsbury Farm, Pulborough, was fined £5, with £2 0s. 8d. costs, at Petworth on Friday for being the owner of a dog which worried sheep belonging to Mr. D. W. Marten, a neighbouring farmer. Supt. Doney said that Mrs. Marten went to a field near her home at Gennets Farm to check the flock of 61 sheep. She found a sheep running with its wool hanging and two others lying down. She also saw defendant's alsatian, which was later found to have blood on its chest. Mr. Marten said two ewes were slaughtered and a third died on the following day.

PULBOROUGH

The sale of work recently held by members of the Congregational Church, opened by Mrs. B. A. Townend, of Worthing, raised £112 for the Extension Fund.

Col. A. C. Wilkinson spoke about the British Commonwealth, with particular reference to Australia and New Zealand, when a meeting of the Women's Section of the Pulborough Conservative Association was held at the Red Lion Tea Room last Wednesday. There were nearly 50 members and friends present, and the Chairman, Mrs. V. Clare, presided.

A meeting of representatives of Pulborough's Football, Cricket, Bowling and Stoolball Clubs decided at the Five Bells last Wednesday to discuss the holding of a joint fête on June 21. Various suggestions were made and the people present were asked to report to their committees to bring further ideas to the next meeting on January 14. Officers elected: Chairman and Treasurer, Mr. E. Roberts; Secretary, Mrs. L. Greenfield.

REVISED POSTAL SERVICES

Changes in the postal services on Saturdays are to be introduced throughout the country to effect economies. In Pulborough from Saturday, December 14, there will be only one delivery on Saturdays, and a morning collection made in conjunction with the delivery. Letter boxes which at present do not receive a collection on Sundays will, from December 15, be cleared on Sundays, and there will be some slight alterations in the present times of collections on Sundays from other boxes. The new times of collections will be shown on the letter boxes from December 9.

The grand piano which has been in use at Pulborough Village Hall since the building was opened in 1932, is worn out and needs replacing. The Hall Committee would be pleased to hear from anybody who has a piano which could be lent or given.

Pulborough and District Photographic Society met at their new headquarters in the Church Room, last Wednesday, when over 30 members were shown a colour film on wild life in Kenya, taken and shown by the Competition Secretary, Mr. H. O. Thomas. Mr. Thomas was thanked by the Chairman Mr. A. G. M. Moss.

PAYING FOR THE PAVILION

The limit on grants from the County Council, which was set by Chanctonbury R.D.C. last week, has affected Pulborough Parish Council's £2,800 scheme for providing a pavilion to replace the old building at the Playing Field. The Council was told on Thursday that at least one-quarter of the cost of any scheme must be raised by local effort. The position is to be explained at the annual Parish meeting on March 23 to test the feeling of residents. A £160 estimate for providing nine additional lamps at London-rd. was shelved until the road widening is finished. It was felt that there was no urgent need for the extra lighting before the winter. To meet next year's expenditure the Council is to precept for a 4d. rate for lighting and a 4d. rate, which includes 3½d. for the Playing Field, for general expenses. The rates are unchanged. A letter was received from the County Surveyor stating that the traffic island at the foot of Church-hill was to be lighted.

CRICKET CLUB MEETING

At the annual meeting of Pulborough Cricket Club, held at the Arun hotel on Friday, the Captain, Mr. P. E. Chapman, said that the club had had a very successful season last year. Out of the 31 matches arranged, 16 were won, eight lost, five drawn, and two cancelled through bad weather. The best batting averages were P. Harrison (19.18) and G. Mason (18.5). He mentioned the outstanding feat of K. Blackman in taking 124 wickets for an average of 6.467 runs. The ball with which he took his 100th wicket is being mounted and is to be presented to him. The skipper expressed the thanks of the club to Mrs. Spain and her helpers for the excellent teas provided through the season. The Treasurer reported quite a good financial position. The annual dance this year will be on Whit-Monday. Election of officers: President, Comdr. M. Thornton; Chairman, Mr. F. B. Kay; Treasurer, Mr. W. H. Fowler; Secretary, Miss V. E. Spain; Team Secretary, Mr. A. P. Spain; Captain, Mr. P. E. Chapman; Vice-Captain, Mr. T. Cousins; Committee, Messrs. K. Blackman, R. Maybee and R. Cooper and Mrs. Spain; Groundsman, Mr. C. P. Barnett; Umpire, Mr. S. Poore.

FIFTY YEARS A SADDLER

Mr. Walter Langham (67), who has completed nearly half-a-century at the saddler's shop at Church-hill, Pulborough, retired on Monday. "I did not want to stop," he told the "W.S.G." "I have found that increasing overhead costs have beaten me." The saddler's in the village was established in 1766 by George Albery, a member of a well-known Horsham family of Quakers and saddlers. At the moment, however, the future of the business is in doubt because there appears to be nobody to continue. Mr. Langham, who was born at Findon, started his craft as an apprentice at the age of 13 and then completed seven years as a racing saddler specialist there before moving to Pulborough as a journeyman in 1911. He took over the business 17 years ago. Although there used to be six hands at the shop, Mr. Langham has found in recent years that there is only enough work for himself. "The trouble has been caused by mechanisation, which has taken horses away. At one time there were between 60 and 80 cart-horses alone to provide work." He added that he had undertaken all sorts of work in leather, such as bag repairs and travel goods, but years ago a saddler would not have done it. Mr. Langham will continue to live at Rivermead, Pulborough, and looks forward to more time for gardening.

DEATH OF MR. J. P. HENLY

The death occurred on Sunday, after a short illness, of Mr. John Peckham Henly (84). He was the youngest son of Mr. George Henly, farmer, barge owner, and owner and first licensee of the Dog and Duck, at Bury, where he was born. He was a steam engineer and went to the South African War as a transport driver (steam engines). Later he worked for the Table Bay Harbour Board before going to Australia as engineer on a tug. He spent 11 years around the coast of South Africa, and three years around the coast of Australia. When he returned to England he took to driving steam engines, after spending some time working for the Thames Conservancy. He married Miss Ethel Jennings, daughter of Mr. W. F. Jennings, proprietor of the Swan hotel, Pulborough. He is survived by a son, Mr. Jack Henly, and daughter, Mrs. Mary Henly Wood. Mr. Henly was a member of the Loyal Castle Lodge of Oddfellows for many years.

PARISH COUNCIL AND PLAYING FIELD UPKEEP

Pulborough Parish Council is planning for the future maintenance of the Playing Field when the present contract of Messrs. J. Cheal and Sons ends in March. Much of Thursday's meeting was again devoted to the question of liability for the maintenance of the bowling green under the terms of conveyance when the old club conveyed the land to the Council to be used as a supplement to the Playing Field. The Bowling Club wrote a letter stating that, without prejudice to any right which they or their successors might have under the agreement of 1947, they were prepared to maintain the playing area of the Council's green. The letter included a condition that it was generally understood that the green cost far in excess of any other playing area to maintain, and in consideration of the Council's obligation to the donors of the ground, the club asked the Council to assist towards the maintenance with a grant from parish funds. It was decided by seven votes to three to give the club one-third of the product of a 1d. rate, about £50, and review the matter annually. This proposal will be submitted for the club's observations. An amendment to give £25 was lost by seven votes to three. The Council also decided to purchase the necessary materials to destroy the weeds on the cricket table at the Playing Field. Mr. H. E. Cosens said the head groundsman of the Sussex County Cricket Club had recommended that the weeds would have to be removed to produce good cricket. A quotation for £110 5s. from Messrs. Cheal for the upkeep of the outfield at the Playing Field, excluding the area of the cricket table, will be considered by the Playing Field Committee. The contract would cover the period from May to October inclusive. The Clerk, Mr. W. A. Bailey, reported that after deducting for various grants towards the cost of the new bus shelter at the bottom of Marehill, the Council would pay about £11 of the total cost of £46. It was felt that the Council should look into the possibility of insuring the shelter and also the seats in the parish. Mr. Bailey said the County Architect was obtaining tenders for work on the dangerous wall at Pulborough School playing ground.

PULBOROUGH

The recent collection for the National Cancer Relief Fund in Pulborough and district amounted to £61 11s. Mrs. A. E. Knight wishes, through the "W.S.G.", to thank all who helped to collect and those who gave so generously.

The funeral service took place at Pulborough Parish Church on Friday of Mr. Daniel Muggeridge (89), who died at his hime, 23, Sopers, Pulborough, on April 29. Mr Muggeridge, who lived alone, was found dead by a rent collector. He was born at Loxwood and had been a farm worker until a few years ago. He is survived by a son and three daughters.

Two boys, aged 16 and 14, pleaded guilty at Petworth Juvenile Court on Friday to stealing a metal vice worth £5 from Messrs. Cheal's Nurseries at Pulborough. They were conditionally discharged on payment of 15s. costs. Insp. Ellis said the boys were interviewed by the police after they had been seen entering a shed at New Place Farm from which the vice was missing. Mrs. Phillips was looking out of her kitchen window when she saw them with a "black object."

ST. JOHN AMBULANCE INSPECTIONS

The annual inspection of the Pulborough Ambulance-Nursing Division of the St. John Ambulance Brigade and the Ambulance Cadet Division was held on April 30 at the Five Bells hall. The inspecting officers were the Area Commissioner, Mr. W. F. Jupp, the Area Superintendent, Miss M. E. Young, and the Area Cadet Officer, Mr. R. Morris. The divisions paraded under Supt. L. Atfield and with the Nursing Officer, Mrs. P. Granger, and Cadet Officer J. Henly the members gave a good display of their training. The Area Commissioner said he was pleased with the work the Division was doing and with the hut at the Swan bridges. He looked forward to the completion of the headquarters hut in the Village Hall field. The Area Commissioner presented Cadet Tony Wilson with his certificate upon promotion to corporal and also Cadet Michel Matthews with his second

Index